REINVENTING MAIMONIDES IN
CONTEMPORARY JEWISH THOUGHT

THE LITTMAN LIBRARY OF
JEWISH CIVILIZATION

Life Patron
COLETTE LITTMAN

Dedicated to the memory of
LOUIS THOMAS SIDNEY LITTMAN
*who founded the Littman Library for the love of God
and as an act of charity in memory of his father*
JOSEPH AARON LITTMAN
and to the memory of
ROBERT JOSEPH LITTMAN
who continued what his father Louis had begun

יהא זכרם ברוך

'Get wisdom, get understanding:
Forsake her not and she shall preserve thee'

PROV. 4:5

*The Littman Library of Jewish Civilization is a registered UK charity
Registered charity no. 1000784*

Reinventing Maimonides in Contemporary Jewish Thought

❖

JAMES A. DIAMOND
AND
MENACHEM KELLNER

London
The Littman Library of Jewish Civilization
in association with Liverpool University Press

The Littman Library of Jewish Civilization
Registered office: 14th floor, 33 Cavendish Square, London w1G 0PW

in association with Liverpool University Press
4 Cambridge Street, Liverpool L69 7ZU, UK
www.liverpooluniversitypress.co.uk/littman

Managing Editor: Connie Webber

Distributed in North America by Longleaf Services
116 S Boundary St, Chapel Hill, NC 27514, USA

© James A. Diamond and Menachem Kellner 2019

All rights reserved.
No part of this publication may be reproduced,
stored in a retrieval system, or transmitted, in any form or by
any means, without the prior permission in writing of
the Littman Library of Jewish Civilization

This book is sold subject to the condition that it shall not, by way
of trade or otherwise, be lent, re-sold, hired out or otherwise circulated
without the publisher's prior consent in any form of binding or cover
other than that in which it is published and without a similar condition
including this condition being imposed on the subsequent purchaser

Catalogue records for this book are available from the
British Library and the Library of Congress

ISBN 978–1–835539–95–8

Publishing co-ordinator: Janet Moth
Copy-editing: Lindsey Taylor-Guthartz and Norm Guthartz
Proof-reading: Philippa Claiden
Index: Meg Davies
Designed and typeset by Pete Russell, Faringdon, Oxon.

To our friendship

◆

טובים השנים מן האחד

Acknowledgements

♦

THE TALMUD cites a prominent rabbi who acknowledges those mentors instrumental to his own erudition as follows: 'I have learned much from my teachers, and even more have I learned from my friends, yet what I have learned from my students exceeds both.' We, the co-authors of this book, have the rare privilege of being both academic colleagues specializing in the same fields and sharing together a deep ongoing friendship. In addition, over the past few decades we have intellectually enriched one another to the point of blurring the lines between teacher and student. All the dimensions of that rabbinic adage therefore apply to our own study and knowledge of the Jewish intellectual tradition. Moses Maimonides, the crux of this book, considers 'the friendship of a student for a teacher and a teacher for a student' emblematic of its ideal rabbinically prescribed form, where 'each desires to assist the other in order to achieve a mutual good'. Thus, in the spirit of this book, our friendship itself is an existential reinvention of Maimonides in the twentieth century which we hope will last well into the twenty-first. We therefore dedicate this book to the reciprocal relationship of teacher, friend, and student that threads through all its chapters.

We each also owe special thanks as follows.

JAMES DIAMOND: I would like to express my gratitude to Cambridge University Press for permission to reprint a revised version of chapter 9 of my book *Maimonides and the Shaping of the Jewish Canon* (New York: Cambridge University Press, 2014), 'R. Naftali Zevi Yehudah Berlin: Loving God Strictly Rabbinically', and parts of chapter 10, 'R. Abraham Isaac Kook; A Kabbalistic Reinvention of Maimonides' Legal Code'. Parts of Chapter 3 of the present book appeared previously in my 'R. Abraham Isaac Kook and Maimonides: A Contemporary Mystic's Embrace of a Medieval Rationalist', in James A. Diamond and Aaron Hughes (eds.), *Encountering the Medieval in Modern Jewish Thought* (Leiden: Brill), 101–28, and I thank Brill for permission to reprint here.

MENACHEM KELLNER: I would like to thank Batya Stein for her exemplary translations of my chapters in this book, and to the publishers of the original Hebrew articles for permission to publish them here in English. 'Rabbi Joseph B. Soloveitchik and Maimonides' appeared originally in D. Schwartz and E. Kanarfogel (eds.), *Manhigut ruḥanit bedor tahapukhot: demuto uketavav shel harav yosef halevi soloveits'ik* (Jerusalem: Urim, 2018), 97–113. 'Rabbi Elhanan Wasserman on Maimonides, and Maimonides on "Reb Elhanan"' appeared originally as two articles: 'Rabbi Elḥanan Wasserman on Maimonides and Maimonides on Reb Elḥanan' (Heb.), in Yedidya Stern et al. (eds.), *Al da'at hakahal: dat upolitikah behagut yehudit: sefer yovel likhvod avi'ezer ravitski*, vol. ii (Jerusalem: Israel Democracy Institute and Merkaz Zalman Shazar, 2012), 595–629, and 'Between the Torah of Moses and the Torah of Elhanan' (Heb.), in Daniel Lasker (ed.), *Maḥshevet yisra'el ve'emunat yisra'el* (Beersheva: Ben-Gurion University Press, 2012), 249–68. 'Each Generation and Its Maimonides: The Maimonides of Rabbi Aharon Kotler' appeared originally as 'Each Generation and Its Maimonides: Rabbi Aharon Kotler's Maimonides' (Heb.), in Uri Ehrlich et al. (eds.), *Al pi habe'er: meḥkarim mugashim leya'akov blidstin* (Beersheva: Ben-Gurion University Press, 2008), 463–86. 'What, Not Who, Is a Jew: Halevi–Maimonides in Those Days, Rabbi Aviner and Rabbi Kafih in Our Days' appeared under the same title in Hebrew in *Mesorah leyosef*, 9 (2016), 99–120.

Finally, thanks to Lindsey Taylor-Guthartz and Seth Kadish for their expert editorial skills, to Seth for his fine afterword, and to the whole team at the Littman Library for their professionalism in shepherding the manuscript to its final publication.

Contents

Note on Transliteration		x
Introduction		1
JAMES A. DIAMOND AND MENACHEM KELLNER		
1. Rabbi Naftali Tsevi Yehudah Berlin: The Love of Israel versus the Love of the Mind		9
JAMES A. DIAMOND		
2. Rabbi Joseph B. Soloveitchik and Maimonides		39
MENACHEM KELLNER		
3. Rabbi Abraham Isaac Kook and the Mystification of Maimonidean Rationalism		59
JAMES A. DIAMOND		
4. Maimonides and Rabbi Kalonymus Kalman Shapira: Abandoning Reason in the Warsaw Ghetto		87
JAMES A. DIAMOND		
5. Rabbi Elhanan Wasserman on Maimonides, and Maimonides on 'Reb Elhanan'		107
MENACHEM KELLNER		
6. Each Generation and Its Maimonides: The Maimonides of Rabbi Aharon Kotler		149
MENACHEM KELLNER		
7. What, Not Who, Is a Jew: Halevi–Maimonides in Those Days, Rabbi Aviner and Rabbi Kafih in Our Day		175
MENACHEM KELLNER		
Afterword		195
SETH AVI KADISH		
Bibliography		203
Index		227

Note on Transliteration

◆

THE TRANSLITERATION of Hebrew in this book reflects consideration of the type of book it is, in terms of its content, purpose, and readership. The system adopted therefore reflects a broad approach to transcription, rather than the narrower approaches found in the *Encyclopaedia Judaica* or other systems developed for text-based or linguistic studies. The aim has been to reflect the pronunciation prescribed for modern Hebrew, rather than the spelling or Hebrew word structure, and to do so using conventions that are generally familiar to the English-speaking reader.

In accordance with this approach, no attempt is made to indicate the distinctions between *alef* and *ayin*, *tet* and *taf*, *kaf* and *kuf*, *sin* and *samekh*, since these are not relevant to pronunciation; likewise, the *dagesh* is not indicated except where it affects pronunciation. Following the principle of using conventions familiar to the majority of readers, however, transcriptions that are well established have been retained even when they are not fully consistent with the transliteration system adopted. On similar grounds, the *tsadi* is rendered by 'tz' in such familiar words as barmitzvah. Likewise, the distinction between *ḥet* and *khaf* has been retained, using *ḥ* for the former and *kh* for the latter; the associated forms are generally familiar to readers, even if the distinction is not actually borne out in pronunciation, and for the same reason the final *heh* is indicated too. As in Hebrew, no capital letters are used, except that an initial capital has been retained in transliterating titles of published works (for example, *Shulḥan arukh*).

Since no distinction is made between *alef* and *ayin*, they are indicated by an apostrophe only in intervocalic positions where a failure to do so could lead an English-speaking reader to pronounce the vowel-cluster as a diphthong—as, for example, in *ha'ir*—or otherwise mispronounce the word. An apostrophe is also used, for the same reason, to disambiguate the pronunciation of other English vowel clusters, as for example in *mizbe'aḥ*.

The *sheva na* is indicated by an *e*—*perikat ol*, *reshut*—except, again, when established convention dictates otherwise.

The *yod* is represented by *i* when it occurs as a vowel (*bereshit*), by *y* when it occurs as a consonant (*yesodot*), and by *yi* when it occurs as both (*yisra'el*).

Introduction

JAMES A. DIAMOND AND MENACHEM KELLNER

MOSES MAIMONIDES was the most eminent authority of rabbinic law and Jewish thought in the medieval Jewish world, proficient in all its canonical sources up to his time. In a broader sense, he was also a master of the scientific/philosophical corpus of his day, as demonstrated not only by his writings, but by his rise to a position of official physician at Saladin's royal court in Egypt. As a result, what he had to say on matters crucial to Jewish existence and the practice of Judaism has seminally influenced the evolution of Jewish thought, worship, and observance ever since. Without this potent combination of both rabbinic expertise and philosophical acumen, Maimonides could easily have been ignored by devotees of either school, and thus would not loom as large over the development of Jewish thought as he does, or indeed even be the subject of the present book. Maimonides was the quintessential Jewish sage, at home in all rabbinic disciplines. He perfectly fits the rabbinic model of the *talmid ḥakham* (scholar) who is 'proficient in Bible, Mishnah, Talmud, *halakhot*, and *agadot*'.[1]

He augmented—or, as Menachem Kellner describes it, encumbered[2]— Judaism with the Thirteen Principles of faith, a pioneering fundamental credo which quickly became sacrosanct. Despite a long history of scepticism towards its authoritativeness by the elites of rabbinic law, it is still safe to characterize it as having achieved canonical status in Judaism.[3] He also compiled the first comprehensive code of Jewish law in the history of Judaism. Though Joseph Karo's *Shulḥan arukh* superseded its practical authority from the sixteenth century on, Maimonides' *Mishneh torah* nevertheless became the third prong of the rabbinic academic canon, alongside the Hebrew Bible and the Talmud. Joseph Karo indeed thought of himself as a successor to Maimonides, whom he considered the most central and authoritative figure in halakhah even centuries after his death.[4]

[1] See *Shir hashirim rabah* 5: 13.
[2] Kellner depicted aspects of the Maimonidean legacy as encumbering Judaism in *Must a Jew Believe Anything?*
[3] Shapiro, *Limits of Orthodox Theology*. Shapiro's work developed in response to a spirited assertion of the Principles' canonical status by Yehuda Parnes in 'Torah u-Madda'.
[4] As Mor Altshuler states, Karo 'aspired to become Maimonides' successor and the mediator

The Rambam of the *Mishneh torah* was canonized almost immediately. His slightly older contemporary, Rabad (Rabbi Abraham ben David of Posquières, c.1125–1198), wrote a series of caustic glosses on the work during Maimonides' lifetime. While people often focus on the criticisms in the glosses, the fact that an authority of Rabad's stature saw fit to write them shows clearly how important he thought the book was.[5] Whether examined in critical academic or devotional rabbinic settings, it is arguably the most microscopically studied text in all the halls of Jewish learning to this day. A renowned contemporary scholar of Jewish history and jurisprudence, who also happens to be the son of one of the central figures examined in this book, assessed the *Mishneh torah* as 'the rarest of things—a book of law, a work of sequitur, discursive reasoning that is, at the same time, a work of art'.[6]

Maimonides' philosophical magnum opus, the *Guide of the Perplexed*, remains the most important and influential synthesis of science and the Jewish tradition. No serious attempt to broach this issue can do so without some dialogue with that work, even today when both sides of the science–faith equation have been radically revamped or, worse, debunked. It is difficult to find such 'serious' attempts in current times, considering the abysmal deterioration in the level of discussion in certain Orthodox rabbinic circles. Maimonides explicitly acknowledges that the interpretation of the Torah must coincide with demonstrated scientific truths since 'the gates of figurative interpretation' are always available for that purpose.[7] If vigorous debates can persist in modern times over whether the age of the universe is short of six thousand years, then we suspect Maimonides would be quite happy to have his name omitted from the conversation.[8]

While the *Mishneh torah* soon achieved canonical status, the fate of the *Guide of the Perplexed* was very different. Indeed, to a great extent, students of the *Mishneh torah* often were ignorant of the *Guide of the Perplexed*, while students of the latter were rarely expert in the former. Yet even his most fervent opponents could not shunt him aside. The raging debate over Maimonidean thought that ensued for centuries after his death, and indeed until the present day, would never have transpired had Maimonides only authored the *Guide of the Perplexed*.[9]

between the medieval *Mishneh torah* and his own times'. See Altshuler, 'Rabbi Joseph Karo', and Twersky, 'The *Shulhan 'Aruk*'.

[5] On Maimonides' 'heroic' stature, see Twersky, 'Some Reflections'.
[6] Soloveitchik, '*Mishneh Torah*'. Compare Gillis, *Reading Maimonides*, 12–20.
[7] See *Guide* ii. 25 (pp. 327–8); page numbers in parentheses refer to Pines' translation.
[8] See for example R. Dr Natan Slifkin's 'Rationalist Judaism' blog that deals with this issue (as well as others in the conflict between what is often thought to be Jewish dogma and science), at <www.rationalistjudaism.com>.
[9] As Silver notes in his account of the medieval Maimonidean controversy, 'It was not

This schizophrenia over Maimonides' legacy reaches its climax in statements emerging out of the heart of the rabbinic world and of the scholarly world that are mirror images of each other. On one hand, a leading eighteenth-century rabbinic authority, Rabbi Jacob Emden, suggested that the *Guide* was a forgery and could not possibly have been penned by the author of the *Mishneh torah*.[10] On the other hand, one of the most renowned twentieth-century scholars of Jewish thought, and in particular of Maimonides, could demote the *Mishneh torah* to simply an avocation, or a minor distraction from Maimonides' philosophical project.[11]

Thus, every path in Jewish thought and law from the twelfth century onwards bears some imprint of Maimonides. So formidable was his intellectual legacy that even the particular crystallization of kabbalah, a trend in Jewish theology absolutely inimical to the general thrust of his rationalism,[12] would have been unimaginable without his work.[13] A quick glance through the index of virtually any current scholarly or rabbinic study, be it on a modern, Renaissance, or medieval topic in Jewish studies, is certain to reveal multiple entries under his name. His thought evoked adoption, opposition, revision, or reinvention, but never indifference.

In light of this overwhelming Maimonidean shadow, cast over Jewish thought since the twelfth century, it is worthwhile to consider the following thought experiment: what would Judaism look like today had Maimonides not lived?

- Had Maimonides not created the first systematic and comprehensive code of Jewish law (*Mishneh torah*), would his successors in that project, Rabbi Jacob ben Asher, author of the *Arba'ah turim*, and Rabbi Joseph Karo, author of the *Shulḥan arukh*, have had the vision and courage to

---

Maimonides' theological ingenuity, but his rabbinic omnicompetence and genius which made his philosophic work a *cause célèbre*.' Silver, *Maimonidean Criticism*, 20.

[10] See J. Schacter, 'Rabbi Jacob Emden's "Iggeret Purim"'. See further Davidson, *Moses Maimonides*, 421–2.

[11] In his doctoral dissertation Aviezer Ravitzky explained that, after Maimonides' death, his legacy was debated by two kinds of Maimonideans: those who emphasized the *Guide* at the expense of the *Mishneh torah* and the reverse. See Ravitzky, 'The Thought of R. Zerahiah'. The late Professor Shlomo Pines is an example of a 'philosophic' Maimonidean. On p. xxvii of his magisterial introduction to his translation of the *Guide* he calls Maimonides' halakhic work an 'avocation'.

[12] For a full-length study of this opposition, see Kellner's *Maimonides' Confrontation*.

[13] See e.g. Wolfson, 'Beneath the Wings', which states categorically that the entire spiritual–intellectual landscape of the 'masters of Jewish esoteric lore [was] incubated in the shadows of the great eagle' (p. 210). Compare Idel, *Kabbalah: New Perspectives*, 253, and Kellner, *Maimonides' Confrontation*, 7–9.

embark on what would have been, if not for Maimonides, a revolutionary innovation? Might Judaism still be a religion of law without a legal code?

- Had Maimonides not defined Judaism as a belief system (with his Thirteen Principles), would it be possible to speak of Jewish *orthodoxy* (*orthos* + *doxos* = 'straight beliefs') in any technical sense? Would Judaism today be a religion without defined and obligatory beliefs, a religion of orthopraxy?

- Had Maimonides not thrown the massive weight of his considerable authority behind the project of integrating science and Judaism (in *Guide of the Perplexed*), how much room would the Jewish world have made for rationally oriented Jews in the Middle Ages and today? Would we have had a 'modern orthodoxy', or an institution of higher learning like Yeshiva University which integrates Torah with the advances of the modern age?

- Would the Zohar, the kabbalistic tradition, and ultimately ḥasidut have been possible without the provocation of Maimonides' rationalism?

- What would modern messianic theologies and aspirations have looked like without Maimonides' vision of the messianic era? Maimonides sought to lower messianic fervour by treating messianism in the most naturalistic way possible, as a process which takes place in *this* world, without overt divine intervention, and with no violations of natural law. Ironically it is this approach to the messiah that makes possible both the mystical religious Zionism of the followers of Rabbi Abraham Isaac Kook and the this-worldly hasidic messianism of Habad-Lubavitch—for good or for ill, depending on your perspective.

- Finally, had Maimonides not enunciated a universalist vision of Judaism, would almost all Jews today be even more particularist than they are?

This thought experiment allows us to understand why James Diamond has argued that 'at virtually every critical turn in Jewish thought, one confronts Maimonidean formulations in one way or another'. In *Maimonides and the Shaping of the Jewish Canon* Diamond set out to prove that the collected works of Maimonides, alongside the Bible, Talmud, and Zohar, 'comprise the core spiritual and intellectual canon of Judaism'.[14] This view received unexpected support when, within weeks of each other, two very different people commented in the popular press about the Jewish canon. In a joint interview with

---

[14] Diamond, *Shaping of the Jewish Canon*, 266.

the Israeli *Makor rishon* newspaper in January 2017, the sons of Rabbi Adin Even-Yisrael Steinsaltz, one of the most outstanding Jewish educators and talmudists of our time, were asked which books their father hoped to finish expounding. They answered: the standard Jewish canon—Bible, Mishnah, Talmud, Rambam. In the *Jewish Press* a few weeks later (24 February 2017), Rabbi Marc Angel was asked what was the best book on Judaism he had ever read; he answered: 'The primary sources are best: Tanach [Bible], Talmud, Rambam.'

The Steinsaltz brothers come from a world infused with Habad hasidism, and Rabbi Angel from the world of Sephardi spirituality. Both, when asked to define the Jewish canon, included 'Rambam'. Now the Steinsaltz brothers meant Rambam of the *Mishneh torah* (which their 'family firm' is indeed publishing with a commentary), not the Maimonides of the *Guide of the Perplexed*. Rabbi Angel, on the other hand, certainly alluded to both figures: Rambam/ *Mishneh torah* and Maimonides/*Guide of the Perplexed*. The very fact that two distinctly different expositors of Maimonides in the latter half of the twentieth century, Rabbi Menachem Mendel Schneerson, the Lubavitcher Rebbe (1902–94), and Professor Yeshayahu Leibowitz (1903–94, facetiously called the 'Leibowitzer Rebbe'), could each present himself as *the* authoritative spokesperson of Maimonides in our world speaks volumes about his 'canonical' status.

The essays in this book cumulatively demonstrate that Maimonides' legacy remains vibrantly alive and well into the twenty-first century. They appear in the following order. We start with the work of Rabbi Naftali Tsevi Yehudah Berlin (1816–93), the well-known 'Netsiv of Volozhin'. He is the only one of our figures not to have actually lived in the twentieth century, but in many ways he is as much a figure of the twentieth century as of the nineteenth. He remained the dean of the renowned Ets Hayim yeshiva in the Lithuanian town of Volozhin, the Harvard equivalent of all eastern European rabbinic academies, for forty years until its closure in 1892. The list of those enrolled in his yeshiva during his tenure includes some of the most central Jewish figures in the early part of the twentieth century. He also influenced almost all the other figures with whom we deal; indeed, several of the other figures treated in this book were tied to him directly or indirectly.

Netsiv is followed by his great-great-grandson, Rabbi Joseph B. Soloveitchik of Russia, Berlin, Boston, and New York (1903–93). Rabbi Soloveitchik carried on the family tradition of deep engagement with Maimonides (in his case, primarily the Maimonides of the *Mishneh torah*, but, unlike his forebears, also the Maimonides of the *Guide of the Perplexed*). Netsiv was an Old World yeshiva head, and his descendant an Old World-trained head of a yeshiva in the New World. Rabbi Soloveitchik was deeply influenced by the book *Nefesh haḥayim*, written by another ancestor of his and teacher of Netsiv, Rabbi Hayim Volozhiner (1749–1821). Rabbi Abraham Isaac Kook (1865–1935), whom we treat next, was himself a student of Netsiv. He is reported to have said, after his one meeting with Rabbi Soloveitchik, that the experience of speaking with the young Rabbi Soloveitchik reminded him of his earliest years when he was a student attending the lectures of Reb Hayim Brisker (Rabbi Soloveitchik's grandfather) at the Volozhin yeshiva, and that 'the power of genius of the grandfather now resides with the grandson'.[15] Rabbis Kook and Soloveitchik are further related by their connections to Orthodox Zionism. Rabbi Kook was the first chief rabbi of Mandatory Palestine, whose theological legacy towers over modern religious Zionist thought. Rabbi Soloveitchik became an active exponent of religious Zionism, which he viewed as a stage in Jewish history that ended the divine hiddenness (*hester panim*) characteristic of the long period of Jewish exilic existence. While Rabbi Kook brought the traditions of eastern Europe to what became the modern State of Israel, Rabbi Soloveitchik, rabbinically shaped by eastern and central Europe, brought both traditions to the United States.

We then turn to rabbis Kalonymus Kalman Shapira (1889–1943) and Elhanan Wasserman (1874–1941), who eminently represent the last testament of east European hasidic and mitnagdic intellectual traditions and who never left their homeland. Their murders reflect the total annihilation of eastern European Jewry and all its cultural, social, and intellectual institutions. However, the murderers failed to annihilate Rabbi Shapira's and Rabbi Wasserman's own intellectual legacies. Their voices still resonate loudly in the contemporary halls of Jewish learning through the written work they left behind.

Fleeing the Nazis, Rabbi Aharon Kotler (1891–1962), one of the exceptions to the rule of genocide that dominated the years between 1939 and 1945, escaped and brought those same traditions to the United States. Preserving the Old World in the New, he sought to re-create the yeshivas of eastern Europe on the soil of the *goldeneh medinah* of America (which he saw as anything but golden). In addition to many interconnections between them, Rabbis Wasserman and Kotler both appear to have been unable to read Maimonides as anything other than an east European yeshiva head. Rabbi Shapira, a hasidic *rebbe*, was similarly constrained to read Maimonides in line with his own kabbalistically infused tradition.

Finally, we close with the other new world, that of modern Israel, of

[15] Saks, 'Rabbi Soloveitchik Meets Rav Kook'.

rebirth, of Zionism, completing the connective thread spun by Netsiv and the Hovevei Tsiyon movement, of which he was a leader. In Israel we deal with the Maimonides of Rabbi Joseph Kafih (1917–2000) and of Rabbi Shlomo Aviner (born 1943). Rabbi Kafih was born in Yemen and Rabbi Aviner in France. Both were close to Rabbi Tsevi Yehudah Kook (1891–1982), son of Rabbi Abraham Isaac Kook, but ended up in very different places vis-à-vis Maimonides. Rabbi Kafih became one of the twentieth century's foremost scholars of Maimonides, translating his works from the Arabic, and annotating almost all of them. Rabbi Aviner's devotion to Rabbi Kook, and through him to Judah Halevi, led him to adopt a restrained appreciation for Maimonides. Conversely, Rabbi Kafih's Maimonidean temperament led him to say many caustic things about Halevi.

When writing the chapters of this book we certainly were not trying to ignore non-Orthodox thinkers, nor did we intend to scant the work of academic scholars of Maimonides. We followed our interests independently and were surprised to discover, after the fact, how well they intersected with each other. What has resulted from this confluence is a study of how Orthodox rabbis read Rambam over the course of the twentieth century. One of the greatest twentieth-century philosophers famously asserted that the entire European philosophical tradition 'consists of a series of footnotes to Plato'.[16] The studies in this book combine to reinforce an equally apt characterization of all of Jewish thought since the Middle Ages as a series of footnotes to Maimonides.

[16] Whitehead, *Process and Reality*, 39.

ONE

Rabbi Naftali Tsevi Yehudah Berlin: The Love of Israel versus the Love of the Mind

JAMES A. DIAMOND

Introduction: A Love of Community

The distances in time and place between twelfth-century Egypt and nineteenth-century imperial Russia make it hard to compare intellectual discourse from two such diverse domains. However, the figure of Moses Maimonides tends to bridge gaps or even chasms in Jewish intellectual history. Though the two environments could not be more dissimilar politically, culturally, spiritually, juridically, or philosophically, in modern times Jewish theologians, exegetes, halakhists, and philosophers continue to engage with and reinterpret their medieval precursor Maimonides at every turn. While Maimonidean thought is not immune to the evolutionary currents inevitably propelled by historical change and scientific progress, it nevertheless hovers over these currents' Jewish dimension. Maimonides always lurks in the background, waiting to be enlisted, challenged, or adapted and reread into new modes of thought.

Such is the case with Rabbi Naftali Tsevi Yehudah Berlin, known by his acronym Netsiv (1816–93), one of the most prominent Jewish figures of the nineteenth century. He powerfully influenced the direction taken by twentieth-century rabbinic thought, and influenced all the personalities that will be studied in this book. At the age of 36 he became dean of the renowned Ets Hayim yeshiva in the Lithuanian town of Volozhin, the Harvard equivalent among eastern European rabbinic academies. He remained at its helm for forty years until its final closure, a year before his death, in 1892. The list of those enrolled in the yeshiva during his tenure includes many of the most central Jewish figures in the nineteenth and early twentieth centuries, both within the narrow confines of the rabbinic world and in the broader sphere of secular Jewish politics, literature, and thought.[1] At one end of the spectrum

---

[1] For fascinating accounts by former students reminiscing about their time at the Volozhin yeshiva, see Etkes and Tikochinski (eds.), *Memoirs of the Lithuanian Yeshiva*, 218–59.

stand the revered deans of two other 'Ivy League' rabbinic academies in Slobodka and Telz, Moshe Mordekhai Epstein (d. 1933) and Shimon Shkop (d. 1939). At the other end are Mikhah Yosef Berdyczewski (d. 1921) and Hayim Nahman Bialik (d. 1934), two of the most celebrated secular Hebrew poets and pioneers of the renaissance of modern Hebrew letters.[2] Many factors account for such a diverse student body during a vibrantly complex and revolutionary period in Jewish thought and politics; among them would certainly be Netsiv's relatively welcoming personality and ideology.[3]

Caution dictates reticence when applying such terms as 'tolerance' and 'pluralism', which have so many contemporary connotations under the colloquial umbrella of 'live and let live'. Such notions do not pertain to the unswerving orthodoxy of Netsiv. However, in a more limited sense, Netsiv advocated a certain tolerance, perhaps pragmatic and yet still uncharacteristic of his rabbinic background, that he best expressed in an observation concerning secular Jews in his commentary on the Song of Songs.[4] In an excursus on Songs 4: 13, 'Your limbs are an orchard of pomegranates', Netsiv plays on *shelaḥayikh*, the word here translated as 'limbs', which contains the Hebrew root for the word 'send'; he interprets this as a metaphor for those who have been sent away from the community of believers, but still remain ethically virtuous. They have abandoned orthodoxy and 'do not accept the yoke of Torah and commandments', yet are still naturally good, kind, and charitable human beings, 'saturated with charity [*tsedakah*] and generosity [*gemilut ḥesed*] like a pomegranate'.[5] They are empty of divine commandments, but replete with natural humanistic ethics. Their associations, even with reprobates (*letsim*), will thus benefit the world, 'since their joining together will lead to acts of kindness if circumstances that call for compassion and mercy arise, resulting in mutual assistance'.[6] Netsiv's 'tolerance' of secular Jews does not in any way

---

[2] For a list of students enrolled in the yeshiva, and short descriptions of the more prominent ones during Netsiv's tenure, see Agranovsky and Leiman, 'Three Lists'.

[3] See J. Schacter's discussion of Haskalah influences and Netsiv's relative and limited openness to it in his 'Haskalah', esp. 91–103.

[4] Most famously emblematic of this tolerance are his comments on the Tower of Babel story in his commentary *Ha'amek davar*. He considers the sameness of thought (*devarim aḥadim*) and ideology as intrinsically bad. On Netsiv's tolerance, see Joseph, 'As Swords Thrust', and Ravitzky, 'The Question of Tolerance'.

[5] *Metiv shir*, in *Rinah shel torah*, 57 (citing BT *Ber*. 57a as his rabbinic source). See also BT *San.* 37a. The original source links this idea to S. of S. 4: 3 and 6: 7. All citations of Netsiv's commentary on S. of S. are from this edition, which includes short and long versions, plus an essay on antisemitism entitled *She'er yisra'el*. The commentary was first published in 1886; a second, posthumous edition appeared in 1894. For a bibliographical survey of Netsiv's corpus see Malachi, 'Literary Work' (Heb.), esp. 238. According to Meir Bar-Ilan, *Metiv shir* was originally published long after it was actually written; Bar-Ilan, *Rabbi of Israel* (Heb.), 24. All translations of *Metiv shir* are my own.   [6] *Metiv shir*, 57.

imply condoning what he was convinced was errant behaviour, but rather stemmed from what has been characterized as his 'deep-seated aversion to communal strife'.[7]

What immediately confronts us here is an important divergence from Maimonides' thought: Netsiv's sentiment is in direct opposition to Maimonides' view that any gathering of *letsim* must lead to mockery of the Jewish canon, making light of its revered sages, and ultimately end in heresy.[8] In other words, Maimonides did not suffer fools gladly. Netsiv's relative tolerance, and his emphasis on embracing community in all its diversity, is not a tangential curiosity.[9] As we shall see, it is central to his view of the love of God, and expresses one of a number of critical theological departures from individualistic medieval approaches that Maimonides strongly advocated.

In this chapter, therefore, I focus on Netsiv's engagement with Maimonides in his commentary on the Song of Songs, that quintessential biblical book of love. In it he voices many of the theological positions that he expresses elsewhere in his corpus, and it thus offers a convenient compendium of his thought. In particular, the Song presents an exegetical opportunity to present God and Israel as the protagonists in a romantic ode to love. This interpretation is in marked distinction from what might be considered the intellectual narcissism of his medieval rationalist predecessors. Indeed, Netsiv explicitly approves of Abraham Ibn Ezra's disparagement of that trend among the 'critical scholars' (*anshei meḥkar*) of his era, who treated the Song as an allegory of 'attachment between the supernal soul and the body', rather than one revolving around the 'assembly of Israel' (*keneset yisra'el*).[10] The tenor of Netsiv's commentary thus mirrors the empathetic character of his life. Rabbi Abraham Isaac Kook, the first Ashkenazi chief rabbi of twentieth-century Palestine

---

[7] See Gil Perl and his sobering analysis in 'No Two Minds Are Alike', 81.

[8] See Maimonides' articulation of the dangers in a 'gathering of reprobates' (*yeshivat letsim*) at the very end of *MT* 'Laws of Leprosy Defilement', and my analysis of this non-halakhic passage in ch. 2 of Diamond, *Converts, Heretics, and Lepers*, 33–53. For Maimonides, this group's intellectual and moral fibre inevitably deteriorates to the point of undermining the fundamental tenets of monotheism.

[9] Netsiv's advocacy of communal leadership might in theory be somewhat at odds with the often tense relationship between his yeshiva and the local community in Volozhin. See Etkes, 'A Shtetl with a Yeshiva', esp. 46, where Netsiv's sensitivity to this issue is evident in his defence of the community's less than enthusiastic attitude towards his yeshiva.

[10] *Metiv shir*, 2. Halkin asserts that Maimonides was 'the spiritual father of the group of commentators who substituted the individual for the nation as the theme of the allegory' of S. of S.; see 'Ibn Aknin's Commentary', 396. According to Kellner, Maimonides was the first to veer from the rabbinic paradigm of a relationship between God and Israel, which avoided the individual slant for fear of its vulnerability to misinterpretation and the danger of extolling the physical or erotic dimensions over the spiritual/communal one; see his comment in Levi ben Gershom, *Commentary on Song of Songs*, trans. Kellner, 31.

and another of Netsiv's illustrious students, who will be the focus of a later chapter in this volume, recalled how Netsiv 'exerted great effort to inculcate in the hearts of his students love of the nation and devotion to the assembly of Israel'.[11]

Consistent with his concern for the corporate integrity of his coreligionists, Netsiv methodically restores the Song's allegory from the private sphere to its original rabbinic place in the public realm, symbolizing the relationship between the nation and God. This factor, more than any other, shapes Netsiv's position on love, in sharp relief to Maimonides' highly intellectualized model. We shall use the term 'allegory' as one that best captures Netsiv's exegetical methodology for a modern critical audience.[12] But Netsiv himself, perpetuating a prominent tradition of commentary on the Song, would have considered that allegory to be the 'plain sense' of the book. As Rabbi Kook described it in his memoir of Netsiv, the commentary is 'in the manner of the plain sense' (*baderekh hapeshat*), which rules out any possibility of reading the Song according to its patent sense of romantic human love.[13] Netsiv's great-great-grandson, Rabbi Joseph B. Soloveitchik, the rabbinic authority of twentieth-century Modern Orthodoxy and the subject of another chapter in this book, still adheres religiously to that approach in his own engagement with the Song.[14]

In this context it is worth noting a striking phenomenon in contemporary translations of the Song for Orthodox Jewish audiences. ArtScroll, the most popular and broadly distributed of such translations, published a paternalistic translation of the Song, which offers allegory as the 'literal' translation. A non-Hebrew speaker is simply deceived into thinking that the allegorical layer is what the Hebrew actually reflects. For example, that reader would be misled into believing that Songs 1: 13, 'My beloved is to me a pouch of myrrh which lies all night between my breasts', actually reads in its original Hebrew as something like this: 'But my Beloved responded with a bundle of myrrh—the fragrant atonement of erecting a Tabernacle where His Presence would dwell amid the Holy Ark's staves.' When ArtScroll 'protects' non-Hebrew-speakers from the Song's patent eroticism, does it assume that a Hebrew-speaking audience, like the one to whom it was originally addressed, can be trusted with the text? ArtScroll claims that 'a literal translation would be misleading—even false—because it would not convey the meaning intended by King

[11] Kook, *Ma'amarei hare'iyah*, 123–6 (esp. 126).
[12] There are a number of full-length works in Hebrew on Netsiv's exegetical methodology. See Elyakim, *Netsiv's Ha'amek davar* (Heb.); Kats, *Netsiv's Thought* (Heb.); Neugroschel, *Netsiv's Thought* (Heb.). For a concise survey of his methodology see Davidowitz, 'Characteristic Aspects' (Heb.).   [13] Kook, *Ma'amarei hare'iyah*, 126.
[14] Joseph B. Soloveitchik, 'And From There You Shall Seek' (Heb.).

Solomon the composer'.[15] But should not Solomon, traditionally credited with the Song's authorship, have known better than to write a misleading and false book in the native language of his readership? As for Netsiv's commentary on the Song of Songs, a tendentiously Orthodox English translation of it follows suit when it claims, in its preface, that Netsiv's commentary is not allegory but rather the plain sense.[16]

Awakening the Heart of Leadership

Even though Maimonides lived a life of practical dedication to the public, his theoretical orientation was far more individualistic and internalized, especially about love. This is the tenor of the final chapter of his *Book of Knowledge* in the *Mishneh torah* ('Laws of Repentance', chapter 10), where the Song becomes his biblical vehicle for the philosophical conception of love of God. Abraham is the biblical paragon of a lover of God who 'worships out of love, occupies himself with the Law and the commandments, and walks in the path of wisdom moved neither by the fear of the bad, nor to merit the good, but does what is true simply because it is true and ultimately benefit ensues'. Rather than a public, socially responsible Abraham whose love translates outwardly into communal responsibility, Abraham's love in 'Laws of Repentance' is private and self-contained, with no evident communal application.[17]

This is best expressed by Maimonides' radically intellectualized interpretation of a central Song verse: 'I sleep but my heart awakes; it is the voice of my beloved that knocks' (5: 2). For Maimonides, this verse captures the very apex of human perfection, which borders on a functional solipsism. Maimonides expresses the same idea in the *Guide*, where the 'intellect is wholly turned toward Him, may He be exalted, so that in his heart he is always in His presence, while outwardly he is with people'.[18] It is no coincidence that Maimonides frames the book entitled 'Knowledge' (*mada*) with two commandments whose fulfilment involves knowledge: it opens with the commandment 'to know that there is a prime existence' and closes with the commandment to love intellectually, 'with the knowledge that one knows of Him'.

[15] Scherman and Zlotowitz (eds. and trans.), *Siddur Eitz Chaim*, 328.
[16] *The Commentary of Rav Naftali Tzvi Yehuda*, trans. Landesman.
[17] Abraham assumes many other guises in the Maimonidean corpus: as a prophet exemplifying the highest levels of prophecy short of Moses (*Guide* ii. 45 (pp. 401–2)); as a philosopher arriving independently at universal truths and teaching them universally (*MT* 'Laws of Idolatry', 1: 3; *Guide* ii. 38 (pp. 376–8); *Epistle to Yemen*, 147); as an ethical model of the golden mean (*MT* 'Laws of Ethical Qualities', 1: 7); as a personality who acts beyond the Law (*MT* 'Laws of Mourning', 14: 2); and the 'father of all nations' and therefore of all converts (*MT* 'Laws of First Fruits', 4: 3). For a survey of all these Maimonidean variations of Abraham, see Turner, 'The Patriarch Abraham' (Heb.).   [18] *Guide* iii. 51 (p. 623).

This interpretative overlay threatens an excessive emphasis on contemplative individual perfection at the expense of community involvement. It is in opposition to it, therefore, that Netsiv prefaces his commentary on the same verse with a long excursus on the responsibility that a leader or sage bears to the community. Love's menacing enemy, hinted at in the verse, is for Netsiv a kind of spiritual pessimism on the part of the leadership, as opposed to intellectual shortcomings. What follows in the Song, beginning with this verse, is rooted in anguish over an anticipated time 'when the great ones are not attuned to the needs of the community, and the divine indwelling [shekhinah] suffers over this, as it were, for her love for the assembly of Israel'.[19] Consistently, Netsiv's theological angst is an extension of his halakhic posture; for instance, he discourages litigation by strict law in favour of compromise, out of concern for the cohesion of the community. He expresses an emotional rationale behind this halakhic preference, for 'whenever my eyes observe a dispute among the Jewish communities a fire burns within me; accordingly I cannot be silent until I have spoken on the subject'.[20] Netsiv thus shifts the metaphor outwards from its Maimonidean privileging of the inner world of the mind. He cannot tolerate a religious life so detached from its external facade that it robotically manifests civic-mindedness almost as an afterthought. Even the very term 'thought' would exaggerate the intentionality of Maimonides' perfected intellect with respect to social commitment.

For Netsiv, 'sleep' signifies a pervasive spiritual malaise that can only be remedied by a 'waking heart'. The leader, the 'heart' of the people, who is alert to their desperate condition, provokes the 'sound of the beloved', or God, 'to focus and attend to correcting what is flawed'.[21] At the heart of Netsiv's theoretical concern for community is what his son, Meir Bar-Ilan, lovingly described as a magnanimous spirit whose interests went far beyond the walls of his rabbinic academy: 'There was, so it appears, an internal need to be close to whatever transpired in the broader world. His nature was not alien to the world, to everything that occurs, as long as it was not antithetical to the love of Torah.'[22] The operative component of Netsiv's broadness is this last proviso, which also implies that, subject to certain constraints, public life not only complements the religious moment of love but is integral to it. Netsiv's

---

[19] *Metiv shir*, 60.

[20] See *Meshiv davar* 3: 10. See the discussion of this responsum as an ideal ruling for a turbulent and divisive time, one that required a 'synthesis of law and justice', in Elon, 'The Values of a Jewish and Democratic State', 224–6. [21] *Metiv shir*, 62–3.

[22] Bar-Ilan, *From Volozhin to Jerusalem* (Heb.), 1: 138. Though this was written in regard to Netsiv's reading of newspapers, it reflects his overall *Weltanschauung*. Once again, one needs to temper any modern notions of worldliness when it comes to Netsiv; the operative condition here is 'as long as it was not antithetical to the love of Torah'. As Stampfer puts it in *Lithuanian*

involvement in the Zionist Hibat Tsiyon movement is one manifestation of his commitment to communal leadership. There is a letter in which Netsiv paraphrases this very expression from the Song in order to indicate his commitment to both the Zionist enterprise and his own local community, 'for though my heart is awake, I am not asleep'. In the same letter he adopts another of the Song's locutions to express his passion for settlement of the Land of Israel, 'for the voice of our beloved God knocks on our hearts to see to the good of our Holy Land'.[23] Maimonides' lover is an obsessive philosopher committed to thought, while Netsiv's is an obsessive community leader committed to Zionism.

The Lover as Priest

Netsiv immediately charts a course for the Song that steers its direction along an entirely different route than that which Maimonides set for it. First, he emphasizes its special appeal as lying in its particularistic character, addressed to Israel. It thus stands in stark contrast to the more universalistic message of Ecclesiastes, which, as he understands it, was communicated to an integrated audience of Jews and non-Jews. Since Ecclesiastes reached out to all, Solomon resorted in it to the universal language of 'ethical enquiry'. Second, he notes the Song's devaluation of philosophy in favour of Torah study and practice as the instruments of love and fear of God, 'for one who has accessed the reasoning of the Torah no longer needs philosophical investigation to achieve fear of God'.[24] Third, he finds that the Song is not just an allegory of love, but itself inspires that love, 'for Solomon conveyed the Song of Songs to arouse the love of God in the heart of Israel'. Finally, and most pointedly aimed at the Maimonidean conception of love, which *conditions* it on a trans-normative intellectual experience, for Netsiv the Song actually *limits* love to the normative practice and study of Torah.

Netsiv charts an evolution of Jewish spirituality that vaguely parallels Maimonides' view of the gradual restriction of the options available for religious worship. He suggests that once certain unbounded manifestations of love for God, such as private altars, were outlawed, Solomon instituted another spiritual outlet in its place by composing the Song. It takes the desperate need to voice that love and channels it through the power of the Torah: 'For Solomon was particularly motivated to do this at the time of constructing the

Yeshivas, Netsiv 'was not opposed to the Haskalah per se but to *bitul torah*, the waste of time that could be used for Torah study' (p. 163).

[23] See Landau, 'The Netsiv of Volozhin' (Heb.), 276. For an extensive bibliography of Netsiv's active participation in the early Zionist enterprise see J. Schacter, 'Haskalah', 12 n. 121.

[24] *Metiv shir*, 1.

Temple, which entailed banning private altars through which the righteous ones of the generation were accustomed to acquiring and expressing love of God.'[25] Thus Netsiv, even in his preface, sharply distinguishes himself from the Maimonidean approach, which views the sacrificial cult as a concession to ancient habitual polytheistic behaviour that is to be gradually modified. If, for Maimonides, sacrifice is a pagan ritual from which the monotheist must be incrementally weaned,[26] for Netsiv it is a sign of spiritual virtue that is to be regulated, but perpetuated all the same in the normative cultic framework of the Torah. Solomon's passionate love of God, which was expressed through private altars, actually caused him to ignore his civic duties and procrastinate in constructing the Temple, 'for this was the shame of Solomon, that he was so steeped in love to the point of neglecting the building of the Temple, so that he could continue with the worship of private altars'.[27]

The Song's message substitutes for the spirit of sacrifice, but at the same time reinforces it. It is a 'fundamental' (*ikar*) means of love along with Torah study.[28] For Maimonides, in contrast, the Song teaches a method of love that is driven by thought, one which usurps and abolishes sacrifice and the religious proclivity for it. Here again Netsiv resorts to cultic terminology that switches the ideal personality from philosopher to communal activist. The qualification of a particular tribe as priests in the Maimonidean scheme is but one component in the overall strategy of limiting the sacrificial impulse on the road to its total abrogation. Netsiv, however, resurrects the priestly class in the contemporary sage, who becomes a modern-day intercessor, but by way of prayer instead of animal sacrifice: 'And just as the priests and the Levites were obligated to bring the Israelite sacrifices to draw down the aura [*hashpa'ah*] . . . so the sages of our time are obligated to pray on behalf of Israel.'[29] Netsiv does classify two types of leaders, one religious, who is charged with 'halakhic guidance and expanding Torah and fear of God', and the other political, who 'deals with the needs of the community'.[30] But the role of the learned sage is still communal in the sense of catering to the spiritual needs of the community.

Reasoned Commandments versus Commandments that Transcend Reason

Netsiv's view of Jewish law and national identity as transcending, respectively, reason and nature, permeates his view of love in the Song and forcefully mili-

---

[25] *Metiv shir*, 1. Netsiv returns to this theme later in the commentary, when he expounds upon the dangers posed by obsessive love to religious observance. [26] *Guide* iii. 32 (pp. 526–7).
[27] *Metiv shir*, 85. [28] Ibid. 2. [29] Ibid. 15. [30] Ibid.

tates against Maimonidean theology. Maimonides understands every commandment teleologically, as aimed towards inculcating correct 'opinions, moral qualities, and political civic actions'.[31] He diagnoses those who ennoble divine law precisely because of its mysteriousness, considering 'it a grievous thing that causes should be given for any law', and who are most satisfied if 'the intellect would not find a meaning for the commandments and prohibitions', as having succumbed to 'a sickness that they find in their souls'.[32] If God teaches something in the Torah, then, as Kenneth Seeskin succinctly puts it, 'The proper way to pay homage to God's superiority is not to set aside one's intellectual faculties, but to recognize that as a perfect being, God must also be a perfect educator.'[33] One might have thought that more than enough time had passed, some eight centuries after Maimonides wrote these words, for this 'sickness' to have been cured, eradicated, or at least quarantined. Yet in a blatant challenge to Maimonidean rationality, Netsiv conditions love of God on exposing oneself to this very 'sickness'. He subverts Maimonides' collapse of any distinction between non-rational (ḥukim) and rational (mishpatim) commandments into a single overarching rational classification, collapsing them instead into a uniform scheme of non-rationality. Thus even that dimension of the law which reason would seemingly dictate as necessary for the normal functioning of any civil society he infuses with meta-legal mystery, for 'even those commandments which apparently even human reason would engender, were not decreed by the Torah from the aspect of human reason, but rather from the aspect of the non-rational (ḥuki) dimension of the Torah'.[34]

The implications of this transcendent view of Jewishness and Jewish law fundamentally challenge the Maimonidean programme for becoming a God-lover. Maimonides' normative formulation of the command to love God is purely in terms of the natural: 'From the point at which one contemplates [yitbonen] His great and wondrous works and creatures, and from them obtains a glimpse of His wisdom [ḥokhmato], which is incomparable and infinite, he immediately loves, praises, and glorifies Him and longs with an exceeding longing to know [leida] His great Name.'[35] Though divine wisdom is ultimately unattainable, whatever it is we can know of it is available only

---

[31] *Guide* iii. 31 (p. 524).
[32] Ibid. (p. 523).
[33] Seeskin, *Maimonides: A Guide for Today's Perplexed*, 94.
[34] *Metiv shir*, 6. For a discussion of this and a list of sources in Netsiv's writings advocating such a 'non-rational' perspective on law, see Perl, *The Pillar of Volozhin*, 232–3. The boldest such assertion is articulated in his comment on Lev. 19: 37 in *Ha'amek davar*. His aversion to historical rationalization of commandments, however, does not prevent him from providing his own historicization of biblical law at times. See Elyakim, 'Netsiv's Autonomy' (Heb.), esp. 103–13.
[35] *MT* 'Laws of the Foundations of the Torah', 2: 2.

through God's creation or nature. Nature is the sole object of contemplation for acquiring knowledge of God, and, since love directly corresponds to knowledge, love can only emerge precisely from a constant engagement with nature. For Netsiv, since there is a transcendent dimension to everything Jewish, love of God must be anchored in transcendence. Nature and the world surrounding us are insufficient to consummate that love.

Yet Netsiv goes even further in repelling any kind of naturalism within this spiritual realm, not only protesting its inadequacy, but actually calling it an impediment to Jewish realization of a passion for God. In the Song, the lover's shame at being 'blackened' by the sun (1: 6), which Netsiv takes as representing nature, highlights Israel's supranatural existence, since 'Israel is beyond nature, and their world is maintained by divine providence, which is contingent on Torah, worship, and good deeds; consequently when Israel pursues nature, and turns away from divine governance, they are not as successful as non-Jews.'[36] Every component of this position is anathema to the entire Maimonidean oeuvre—the ontological distinction between Jews and non-Jews,[37] the devaluation of nature and its study, and the direct link between divine providence and the commandments, rather than the intellect.

Loving God constitutes a commandment that is anchored in a transcendent realm. Thus, by Netsiv's logic, it can only be properly fulfilled by abandoning science, by diverting attention from nature, and by distancing oneself from the body of human knowledge that has developed independently of the Torah. Consequently, in a mirror image of Maimonides' formulation for attaining a love of God, Netsiv states the following: 'The love of nature that rages within me prevents me from diverting attention away from worldly necessities towards taking pleasure in solitude and the realization of love of God, even though I am fully aware that it comprises the supreme pleasure for the soul that overwhelms all material ones. Thus it is our obligation and is appropriate for us to immerse our minds in the love of God.'[38] To 'immerse' one's mind in the love of God entails precisely the abandonment of nature, what Maimonides views as the object of the mind that leads to love of God. Nature, for Netsiv, alienates us from God, rather than shepherding us towards him.

Lover as Scholar/Practitioner

Netsiv demands the suppression of that very passionate obsession with creation that Maimonides considers the operative ingredient of love for God,

[36] *Metiv shir*, 11.
[37] See Kellner's book-length study on Maimonides' universalism, *Maimonides on Judaism*.
[38] *Metiv shir*, 22.

since it mires one in the here and now and thus bars access to the transcendent realm where the ontological bond between God and Israel can be forged. Paradoxically but consistently, Netsiv senses a danger in *any* obsession, whether it is with the here and now or with the transcendent. His powerful sense of communal responsibility and loyalty to rabbinic law force him to pose a further challenge to the intensity of Maimonides' isolated God-lover, whose mind is fixated abstractly on God, that most obscure of all objects of desire.[39] In a cautious retreat from unbounded passion divorced from practicality, Netsiv reminds the reader of ancient Israel's inability to tolerate direct contact with the divine for fear of physical demise.[40] According to Netsiv, they demanded a cessation of such immediacy in favour of 'a love of God by way of the light of the Torah—they requested the light of the Oral Torah [*torah shebe'al peh*] so that they could tolerate it'.[41]

For Netsiv the more proximate love gained through the Written Torah needs to be filtered through the Oral Law, a dilution that is necessary for a sustainable relationship. This is consistent with Netsiv's general approach throughout his writings in reading rabbinic law back to Sinai and beyond.[42] Abraham provides a striking example of Netsiv's approach: the knowledge and study of rabbinic law and its derivational logic is extended not just into the pre-rabbinic period, but all the way back to the pre-Sinaitic patriarch.[43] Abraham, for Netsiv, pioneered yeshiva-style Torah study and dedicated himself to it tirelessly.[44] For our purposes, this is another blow to the Maimonidean construct of spiritual romance. Whereas Maimonides' lover ascends from the practical intellect to the theoretical intellect, rising in the Jewish hierarchy from the 'small thing' of halakhah and Oral Law to the 'great thing' of physics and metaphysics, Netsiv reverses the direction.[45]

---

[39] As Brill notes, 'Neżiv, unlike Maimonides, finds fault in an isolationist spirituality that lacks social involvement'; see his, 'Dwelling With Kabbalah', 137.

[40] Exod. 20: 16: 'If we hear the voice of the Lord our God any longer we shall die.'

[41] *Metiv shir*, 5.

[42] Two extreme exegetical illustrations of this that pervade his entire rabbinic project are the following: (1) The simple biblical verb for 'command', *tsav*, refers to the Oral Law, which overlays the Written Law. See *Emek hanetsiv*, ii. 233. (2) The simple biblical term for laws or statutes, *ḥukim*, refers throughout the Bible to the principles of rabbinic hermeneutics. For a discussion and copious references that appear throughout Netsiv's corpus see Perl, *The Pillar of Volozhin*, 180–2 and 190–1. However, it would be wrong to characterize Netsiv as ruling out any independent human contributions to the development of rabbinic law. See the discussion of this in Harris, *How Do We Know This?*, 239–44; Harris maintains that, although the 'exegetical means to create halakha' are Moses' legacy to the Jews, 'the hermeneutical principles that expanded the range of halakha were the product of deep and rational reflection on the oral traditions entrusted to Moses and their connection to Scripture' (p. 242).   [43] See *Ha'amek davar* on Gen. 26: 5.

[44] See Netsiv's comment in *Ha'amek davar* on Gen. 12: 17.

[45] As Warren Zev Harvey notes, 'Maimonides' identification of metaphysics with "a great

Solomon's bed is described in the Song as 'surrounded by sixty warriors of the warriors of Israel' (3: 7). Netsiv reads this verse according to the 'plain sense' (*peshat*), as the place Solomon reserved for loving God 'through the power of the Torah by surrounding himself with sixty Torah experts'. On the metaphorical plane (*derash*), Solomon signifies God himself, who 'designates a place to cohabit with Israel in love, that is the four cubits of halakhah'.[46] The true lover for Netsiv, on both the exoteric and esoteric levels of meaning, inhabits the realm of law as both scholar and practitioner.

Compare this to Maimonides' lover, who is transported beyond the normative realm to that of pure thought. No image evokes the extent of this abstraction as a religious ideal like that of the bed. When speaking of prayer, Maimonides describes how it might be surpassed by a far more advanced form of silent meditation, 'limiting oneself to the apprehensions of the intellects'.[47] His biblical prooftext for this assertion presents the bed as a metaphor for the most private space conducive to such meditation: 'Commune with your heart upon your bed and be still' (Ps. 4: 5). Prayer is the most pervasive and dominant commandment in the Jewish ritual system. A Jew's daily cycle is measured in terms of prayer intervals and blessing opportunities. An observant Jew's calendar is governed by prayer frequency and appointed times. The sages considered prayer to be 'worship of the heart' that replaced the most prominent feature of ancient Judaism, the Temple sacrificial cult.[48] Praise, supplication, entreaty, appreciation, contemplation—virtually every facet of one's relationship with God—are articulated through prayer.[49] In its demand for a quorum (*minyan*) as its ideal forum, it is also essentially a communal ritual which continuously draws the individual into the group to commune with God. For Maimonides, then, the privacy of one's bed is the image that best captures an ideal of love that is wholly divorced from halakhah and society.[50]

---

thing" and the 608 non-metaphysical commandments with "a small thing" establish the supremacy of the *vita contemplativa* over the *vita activa*.' See his 'Aggadah in Maimonides', 201.

[46] *Metiv shir*, 41. Though the figure of Solomon is at times associated with ethics, by and large his name is associated with intellectual apprehension, the proper way to achieve it, and the limits on teaching subjects that lead to its ultimate attainment. For a very different construct of Solomon from Netsiv's, see Klein-Braslavy's chapter on 'Solomon and Metaphysical Esotericism' in *King Solomon* (Heb.), ch. 3.   [47] *Guide* i. 59 (p. 140).

[48] See BT *Ta'an*. 2*a*; BT *Ber*. 26*b*; *MT* 'Laws of Prayer', 2: 5; *Sifrei devarim*, 'Ekev' 41.

[49] *MT* 'Laws of Prayer', 1: 2.

[50] For a valiant attempt to integrate Maimonides' philosophical and halakhic notions of prayer and its efficacy, see Benor, *Worship of the Heart*. Benor considers Maimonides' conception of prayer 'to be an attempt to attain an awareness of being before the presence of God'. This notion has both a cognitive and emotive structure that caters to both the contemplative intellectual and the common man (p. 129).

In vivid contrast, Netsiv's exegesis of the bed imagery takes an image that is seemingly representative of privacy, a place of isolation and an interval free of behavioural activity, and brings that image into the public sphere of halakhah and Torah study. It is thus a total subversion of Maimonides' use of the image to signify consummate spiritual internalization, where the only human faculty exercised is thought. According to Netsiv, the time 'most conducive to receiving the Holy Spirit in accordance with the desire of God and those who yearn for it' is precisely during the central prayers of the Jewish liturgy.[51]

At one point Netsiv resorts to an extreme formulation inverting the means and ends of study and love, when he considers how the rabbinic blessing that asks for comprehension of Torah begins with a declaration of the love between God and Israel. For Netsiv, only one beloved of God is privy to the secrets of Torah, and that is why love prefaces the supplication for understanding, 'since the purpose of prayer is to enlighten us with understanding His holy Torah'.[52] Netsiv thus once again reverses the route of human perfection mapped out by Maimonides, for whom philosophical perfection rises from normative content (external conduct such as prayer) to thought (internalization of prayer to meditation) and ultimately to love (philosophical investigation).[53] But Netsiv's Torah scholar begins with love as the basis for Torah study.

The Spatial Co-ordinates of Love

Netsiv's anti-natural stance on love directs one back to the role of the Temple and the sacrificial cult within Judaism. If one must transcend creation in order to reach love, then God provides a much-needed place that is conducive to the activity which brings about love, a spatial retreat from the natural world. That space is the Temple, which, according to a rabbinic tradition, was suffused by perpetually occurring miracles.[54] Thus, for Netsiv, it provides the optimum environment for aspiring to a non-natural state, 'for there is nothing better than to stand in a place where nature and the sun are not that dominant'.[55] It is an environment defined by the miraculous and wholly insulated from the natural.

[51] *Metiv shir*, 101.   [52] Ibid. 81.
[53] Maimonides pares down any association with others to the barest minimum necessary for sustaining physical subsistence: 'If the perfect man who lives in solitude thinks of them at all' it is either to prevent harm or gain advantage; *Guide* ii. 36 (p. 372). For a concise summary of the extensive debate on whether political activity or individual intellectual perfection is the final end of man for Maimonides, between scholars such as Lawrence Berman and Shlomo Pines in favour of the former and Miriam Galston and Warren Zev Harvey supporting the latter, see S. Harvey, 'Maimonides in the Sultan's Palace'.   [54] Mishnah *Avot* 5: 8.   [55] *Metiv shir*, 24.

For Maimonides the Temple was something vividly different: like the priests and sacrifices, it is a spatial restriction on pagan modes of worship. Maimonides' interpretation of Jeremiah's problematic assertion that there were no commandments regarding sacrifices at the time of the exodus from Egypt (Jer. 7: 22–3), clearly belying the pentateuchal accounts, substantiates this view:

> For he says that the first intention consists only in your apprehending Me and not worshipping someone other than Me. . . . Those laws concerning sacrifices and repairing to the Temple were given only for the sake of the realization of this fundamental principle. It is for the sake of that principle that I transferred these modes of worship to My name so that the trace of idolatry be effaced and the fundamental principle of My unity be established. You, however, came and abolished this end, while holding fast to what has been done for its sake.[56]

The very mishnaic source Netsiv refers to that corroborates the Temple's association with miracles is itself embedded among other miraculous lists, but Maimonides explains them all away as ultimately natural themselves. 'Miracles' like the splitting of the Reed Sea can all ultimately be considered 'natural' in the sense that they were pre-programmed into nature at Creation.[57] Maimonides' explanation of some of the 'miracles' endemic to the Temple sanctum reflects their naturalism as well. For example, the smoke from the sacrifices was never swept away 'because the air was calm'. And no one ever complained about being cramped, or left the Temple precinct for more spacious quarters, since 'during the prostration there was no pushing and shoving out of the abundance of awe there was for this place'.[58] Netsiv dismantles the entire Maimonidean edifice of natural spirituality grounded in a profound understanding of the creation, and replaces it with a realm higher than nature, inhabited exclusively by the nation of Israel.

Halakhic Lover versus Scientific Lover

Songs 3: 1–2 states, 'Upon my couch at night, I sought the one I love—I sought but found him not. I must rise and roam the town through the streets and squares. I must seek the one I love. I sought but found him not.' These verses provide Netsiv with the exegetical ground for an open challenge to Maimonides' formulation of the commandment to love God (as explained in chapter 2 of 'Laws of the Foundations of the Torah', the first section of his *Mishneh torah*). Netsiv finds the Song's pessimistic sentiment, expressing the

[56] *Guide* iii. 32 (p. 530).   [57] Ibid. ii. 29 (pp. 345–6); *Commentary on the Mishnah, Avot* 5: 5.
[58] *Commentary on the Mishnah, Avot* 5: 5.

elusiveness of love and the frustrated quest for it, to be especially apt for a direct attack on Maimonides' rationalist means of attaining it. His argument is that the exasperated lover in this verse is precisely the one who complies with Maimonides' recipe for spiritual love, which inevitably leads to failure. Netsiv takes further issue with what he considers to be Maimonides' 'misquotation' of a halakhic midrash that conditions love of God on a scientific understanding of nature and the creation, since 'out of this you will come to recognize He who spoke and the world came to be'.[59] For Netsiv, the referent of 'out of this' points to a phrase in the verse that follows the commandment to love God, namely 'Take to heart these instructions which I command you this day' (Deut. 6: 6). This forms an inextricable link between the 'heart' which dedicates itself to commandments of this verse, and the 'heart' in the previous verse which is committed to the love of God.[60]

Netsiv's 'heart' is a very different one from that of Maimonides, who views its referent as 'denoting the intellect'.[61] The halakhic midrash according to Netsiv is therefore opposed to Maimonides' programme for love, 'since scientific knowledge is not assimilated into the heart of the scientist in order to love God since he remains distant from it, that is from things that are holy. However, when he immerses his heart and soul in divine laws which lead to holiness, then he "will recognize He who spoke and the world came to be".'[62] Torah and its normative content become the instruments of love for Netsiv, rather than merely what Maimonides considers them to be: the pragmatic framework within which one can best cultivate science and philosophy as the only true instruments of love.[63] Netsiv promotes a 'heart' of subordination rather than a 'heart' of intellect.

---

[59] *Sifrei devarim*, 'Va'ethanan' 33: 6.

[60] Others, of course, sensed this glaring omission in Maimonides' formulation of the love commandment in *MT* 'Laws of the Foundations of the Torah', ch. 2, which conditions love of God solely on knowledge, without reference to the Torah and its contents. For one prominent forerunner to Netsiv's opposition on this point, which acknowledges science as a means to love but only as a preliminary which must be supplemented by the Torah and commandments, see the discussion of Maharal in Elkouby, 'The Love of God', 47–9. Netsiv sides with his rabbinic predecessor and many others in rejecting 'Maimonides' essential intellectualism'.

[61] See *Guide* i. 39 (p. 89), which also appropriately ends by defining 'heart' in Deut. 6: 5 as 'all the forces of the body, for the principle of all of them derives from the heart'. This deepens the role of the intellect, since it subordinates all human activity to intellectual endeavour, reading Deut. 6: 5 as an obligation to 'make His apprehension the end of all your actions'.

[62] *Metiv shir*, 38.

[63] See for example *MT* 'Laws of the Foundations of the Torah', 4: 13, for one of his clearest statements on the purely utilitarian function of commandments as mere preliminaries to the higher purpose of science and philosophy. There is no intrinsic value to commandments other than their functionality.

God and Human Beings: Reciprocal versus Unilateral Love

Netsiv extends his opposition to rationalistic Maimonidean love even further, however, in a total subversion of Maimonides' overarching view of Torah, science, and love of God. For Maimonides there is a direct correlation between knowledge and love, best expressed in his halakhic work by the assertion that 'it is evident that love of God cannot be ingrained . . . except by way of the knowledge one knows of Him; as the knowledge so the love—if little then little and if much then much'.[64] There is corresponding clarity on this issue in his philosophical work, which cross-references itself to his formulation in the *Mishneh torah*. The all-consuming love demanded by Deuteronomy 6: 5 'becomes valid only through the apprehension of the whole of being as it is and through the consideration of His wisdom as it is manifested in it'.[65] But here Netsiv adds a further ingredient needed for the attainment of the love which is a corollary of the Torah's transcendence, beyond performance of the commandments. Since love is not anchored in the natural, a Jew can do what love requires by fulfilling the commandments but still be frustrated in his quest, 'for the love of God requires heavenly assistance that is only extended to those who merit it, and this does not mean to one involved in scientific investigation that concerns nature and human reason'.[66] For its ultimate achievement, love requires divine grace. Netsiv correctly understood the danger of Maimonides' elimination of any active divine involvement in the elemental religious impulse and goal (consistent with the overall thrust of his religious philosophy). Supplementing human endeavour with divine grace further undermines Maimonidean intellectualism.

In a direct challenge to Maimonides' *Mishneh torah* formulations, Netsiv begins his commentary with this very notion, namely that 'it is not wholly dependent on us, rather it requires heavenly assistance'.[67] Here he further evaluates Maimonides' rationalist account of love and undermines the very core of Maimonides' role for God and divine law within the process of human perfection. After acknowledging the utility and necessity of Maimonides' intellectual route towards love, he also points out its limitations as a mere preliminary to the journey towards the realm of the transcendent:

for all this advice [Maimonides' requirement at the end of 'Laws of Repentance' that man must dedicate himself to understanding and becoming proficient in the sciences] only serves to bring man towards love of God, but does not bring closer

---

[64] *MT* 'Laws of Repentance', 10: 6. [65] *Guide* iii. 28 (pp. 512–13). See also iii. 52 (p. 630).
[66] *Metiv shir*, 38. [67] Ibid. 4.

the supernal Mind to reach man and pour on him the holy spirit . . . for love is consummated only when the beloved becomes intimate enough to pour out the spirit of its love to the one who yearns for its proximity.[68]

Netsiv thus dismantles the Maimonidean hierarchy in which human intellect is the only actor, the sole conduit through which a passive, supreme Intellect can be accessed. He demotes intellect to a preparatory role, one which qualifies man to be a *recipient* of divine grace. Netsiv replaces Maimonides' one-sided love of a passive divine beloved with a kind that more closely approximates the mutually embracing feelings of human love. His addition of divine intervention as an essential component of the human–divine relationship adds a sorely lacking ingredient to Maimonides' theology of 'radical human responsibility', which places spiritual fulfilment solely in the hands of the human actor.[69] On this issue Netsiv's position is somewhat analogous to the notion of grace in Christianity, which also entails a component of giving from God that human action on its own cannot obtain.[70]

Here Netsiv draws us away from the secluded intimacy of Maimonidean love and back into the sage's role in the public sphere. His prayers are needed to assist in attracting divine grace. For Maimonides, while love is directly proportional to the grasp one has of the workings of nature, or all those disciplines falling within the rubric of science, it is also accompanied by an overwhelming sense of inadequacy and self-acknowledged limitations, 'standing with meagre and deficient knowledge before absolute proficiency in all knowledge'.[71] Thus, paradoxically, mastery of the mechanics of creation is at the same time counteracted by realization of the limits of human intellection, and by its ultimate failure compared to the infinite knowledge possessed only by God.

Netsiv's idea of dependence on divine grace therefore hones in on another verse which is central to Maimonides' Song hermeneutic: 'Let him kiss me with the kisses of his mouth' (S. of S. 1: 2). For Maimonides this verse signifies the very apex of human perfection, achieved with any certainty by only three people in Israel's prophetic history, all members of Judaism's founding

[68] Ibid.

[69] Jerome Gellman states, 'Armed with a sense of self responsibility, the reader is freed from the motive of seeking self-aid, in order to pursue the goal of love of God—a relationship based on disinterested worship. . . . A sense of radical freedom and competence in cognition makes possible a relationship to God not grounded in one's needs for oneself.' See his 'Radical Responsibility in Maimonides', 263.

[70] The subject of grace in Christianity is a vast one. For just one illustrative statement that parallels Netsiv's notion, McKenny states that God's grace in Christian moral theology 'as pure gift is unconditioned by human action, and thus radically disrupts human moral striving, yet also demands confirmation in human conduct'; McKenny, *Analogy of Grace*, 25.

[71] *MT* 'Laws of the Foundations of the Torah', 2: 2.

family—Moses, Aaron, and Miriam. They share in a unique type of death described as a divine 'kiss', indicating a life that ends saturated, as far as is humanly possible, in knowledge of universal truths. It is a state where the intellect is empowered to such an extent that the physical body can no longer tolerate it: 'The intellect rejoices in what it apprehends . . . this apprehension increases very powerfully, joy over this apprehension and a great love for the object of apprehension become stronger, until the soul is separated from the body at that moment in this state of apprehension.'[72] Maimonides identifies this intellectualized kiss of death with Songs 1: 2, as the logical culmination of a life of courting God in pursuit of knowledge. In other words, every effort in life must be exerted towards reaching a goal where there is a fusion of the knower—through all the knowing he has accumulated—and the known, to whatever degree the divine can be known.

Everything about this process and goal is autonomous. In a vivid image presented by Jacob's famous dream of the ladder that Maimonides favours, the seeker ascends the ladder of knowledge in order to apprehend 'He who is stably and permanently at the top of the ladder'.[73] It is only the seeker who moves at all on the ladder, which is anchored between God at its summit and the earth below. What is sought is simply there forever, immutably anticipating the seeker's arrival.

But Netsiv cannot tolerate a love of God that lacks the mutuality which informs all true human love, and thus transforms this verse into a petition that conditions human love for God on God's own response. In his comment on Songs 1: 2 he explicitly inveighs against Maimonidean one-sidedness, for 'this first song is a prayer for achieving the love of God, a pleasure which supersedes all others for a Jewish soul'. He then forcefully attacks Maimonides' view as cited above: 'Despite the fact that this is dependent on human will, and it consists of a formal positive commandment to love God as stated in the Shema, and as we clarify further on regarding Maimonides' law in "Laws of the Foundations of the Torah", still the matter is not wholly dependent on us, but we require heavenly assistance to grace the passion of one who aspires to it, if it is merited.'[74]

Because of his emphasis on the active dimension rather than the contemplative, Netsiv resists the supremely humbling moment to which Maimonides' love aspires. Such a love is prone to encourage a quietistic existence. He therefore adopts a more empowering model of man in partnership with God, a notion with deep kabbalistic roots. Netsiv distinguishes between two synonyms for 'lover' in verse 16, the 'beloved' (*dod*) and the 'darling' (*re'a*). The two terms pose a contrast between an inferior and a superior kind of

---

[72] *Guide* iii. 51 (p. 627). [73] Ibid. i. 15 (p. 41). [74] *Metiv shir*, 4.

love: 'The *dod* is the term for a lover who cleaves through thought, while the *re'a* combines thought (or counsel) with action. The Torah sages are classified as *re'im* because they participate in the creation [*ma'aseh bereshit*] . . . and by virtue of the fact that they transform the words of the Torah into the truth of the Torah, they become partners with God in the creation.'[75] Netsiv thus completes his subversion of Maimonides. He transforms the term for creation, *ma'aseh bereshit*, which for Maimonides is a subject of the intellectual examination that serves as the basis for love, into an object that the lover constructs. The former entails a subservience of the lover to the knowledge inherent in creation, while in the latter the lover imposes his mind upon the creation, effecting change in it. Maimonides' lover of God is affected by his knowledge of the creation, while Netsiv's lover affects the creation.

Anthropocentric versus Theocentric Lovers

Much of what drives Netsiv's antipathy (to put it mildly) to Maimonides' theology of love lies in his rejection of Maimonides' anti-teleological view of the cosmos. According to Maimonides one cannot determine a causal hierarchy in creation, in the sense of ascribing one part of existence as ancillary to another. All that one can conclude is that every part of creation 'conformed to His intention and purpose' and nothing more.[76] God created all things 'for their own sakes and not for the sake of something else'. Any investigation into the final aim of any component of existence is doomed to failure, and the 'quest for the final end of all the species of beings collapses'.[77] The corollary of this teleological scepticism, which irked many of Maimonides' theological antagonists, is the devaluation of humanity in the scheme of the universe, for 'it should not be believed that all the beings exist for the sake of the existence of man'.[78]

Netsiv is among those whose religious sensibility does not allow for antiteleology and anti-anthropocentrism. In a pointed attack on the latter, he asserts that, despite what appears to be the material world's lowliness, 'all of existence was created for the sake of the saint [*tsadik*] and his actions in this world'.[79] In biblical support of this anthropocentrism he cites and explains a

---

[75] Ibid. 79. [76] *Guide* iii. 13 (p. 453).
[77] Ibid. (p. 452). Warren Zev Harvey considers Maimonides' position quite radical in that 'its strong anti-anthropocentric and anti-teleological views had (as far as I am aware) no parallel in medieval philosophical literature'; see his 'Portrait of Spinoza as a Maimonidean', 164. Parens has challenged this view, claiming that Maimonides did in fact endorse a limited Aristotelian-like teleology which could account for some things existing 'for the sake of others' in his *Maimonides and Spinoza*, 153–61.   [78] *Guide* iii. 13 (p. 452).   [79] *Metiv shir*, 78.

phrase, one which for Maimonides signifies the opposite of Netsiv's explanation: '"Nevertheless as I live and as the Lord's Glory fills the earth" [Num. 14: 21], that is the purpose of the creation and its maintenance in order that the earth shall be filled with God's glory, thus He[80] is the foundation and pillar of the world.'[81] Netsiv consciously adopts this to invert Maimonides' shifts in focus from human beings to God, from anthropocentrism to theocentrism. The nearly identical phrase in Isaiah, 'The whole earth is full of His glory' (6: 3), signifies for Maimonides 'that the whole earth bears witness to His perfection',[82] diverting attention away from the world as the pinnacle of creation and towards its role as evidence of divine existence.

Netsiv's anthropocentrism shores up the value of human action in the world, in another direct challenge to Maimonides' minimization of action in favour of thought. Maimonides' analysis of the term 'glory' measures it solely in terms of thought: the earth is filled with God's glory in the sense that either human beings contemplate him or the material world provides the basis for human meditation on his existence. Here it is important to cite Maimonides' perspective on precisely how the earth is filled with his glory, because it is a striking antithesis to Netsiv's appropriation of the very same phrase:

For the true way of honouring Him consists in *apprehending* His greatness. Thus everybody who *apprehends* His greatness and perfection, honours Him according to the extent of his *apprehension*. Man in particular honours Him by speech so that he indicates thereby that which he has *apprehended by his intellect and communicates it to others*. Those beings that have no apprehension, as for instance the minerals, also as it were honour God through the fact that by their very nature they are indicative of the power and wisdom of Him who brought them into existence. For this induces him who considers them to honour God either by means of articulate utterance or without it if speech is not permitted to him. . . . Accordingly it is said of that which is devoid of apprehension that it praises God. . . . It is in view of this notion being named glory that it is said 'The whole earth is full of His glory'.[83]

No clearer statement could be formulated to convey the thoroughly contemplative and philosophically oriented theocentrism to which Maimonides subscribed. The only human activity outside the mind that the verse allows for is

---

[80] Since Netsiv begins this thought with the idea that all of creation exists on account of the saint in this world, it seems probable that this pronoun completes that principle: since the saint is instrumental in manifesting the divine presence, he is thus the sustainer of the world.

[81] *Metiv shir*, 78.   [82] *Guide* i. 19 (p. 46).

[83] Ibid. 64 (p. 157, my emphasis). Isa. 6: 3 appears once again in *Guide* iii. 52 (p. 630), in a context that is also bracketed by intellect, establishing it at the beginning as 'the bond between us and Him', and concluding with the notion that love of God is purely a function of intellect, for love is achieved 'through the opinions taught by the Law, which include the apprehension of His being as He, may He be exalted, is in truth'.

teaching what has been apprehended by the mind to others. All this is captured by the very same biblical idiom that Netsiv adopts to endorse human beings and the material world as the telos of all creation.

A corollary of Netsiv's anthropocentric view is that the earth itself is the telos of all creation, a proposition vindicated by another biblical prooftext that can only be fully appreciated in its Maimonidean role. By way of imperial imagery, Isaiah extols a divine expansiveness in God's proclamation that 'the heaven is My throne and the earth is My footstool' (66: 1). Netsiv explains that a king sits on his throne not for the sake of the throne, but for the purpose of governing his kingdom outside the palace: 'So are the heavens God's throne, but the earth is His footstool, that is the aim of all His thoughts and the goal is the earth.'[84] Again, on the crucial issue of teleology, Netsiv subverts Maimonides' exegesis to render its converse. In Maimonides' lexicography, the term 'heavens' conveys superiority or 'My existence, grandeur, and power', while the term 'throne' signifies 'the greatness of the individual who is considered worthy of it'.[85] Rather than minimizing the effect of the throne metaphor, and diverting attention elsewhere than the location of the throne, as Netsiv proposes, Maimonides focuses on it as an accentuation of the grandeur of its occupant and emphasizes the separateness of its locale. Another chapter in the *Guide* elaborates further on the terms 'throne' and 'feet' as they are biblically attributable to God, viewing them as a hierarchy of being with the throne at the summit and the earth below the feet. The conclusion towards which this exegesis of throne and feet develops is a hierarchy of creation composed of two distinct realms, a superior heaven that consists of a 'sublimity of that matter and its nearness to Him' and an inferior 'defectiveness' of earth.[86]

When the term 'feet' absorbs its philosophical nuance from the Maimonidean lexicon, Netsiv's own appropriation of it as *elevating* the status of the earth vis-à-vis the creation in its entirety comes into even sharper distinction. A Sinaitic hierophany envisions a 'work of the whiteness of sapphire stone under His feet' (Exod. 24: 10), presenting a grossly anthropomorphic depiction demanding a different sense that alleviates such philosophical distortion of the nature of God. The last phrase, 'under His feet', indicates a notion of causality, in this case the sense of 'He being the cause and because of Him'.[87] Once the term 'feet' is understood as a metaphor for causality, one is directed to Maimonides' conception of God's place in the chain of causation that ends in the earth. He instructs us to read each and every biblical ascription of an event to divine will as a metaphor for the natural causation that God initiated at Creation, 'who has made the natural things pursue their course'.[88] Thus

[84] *Metiv shir*, 78. [85] *Guide* i. 9 (p. 35). [86] Ibid. ii. 26 (pp. 331–2).
[87] Ibid. i. 28 (p. 61). [88] Ibid. ii. 48 (p. 410).

every narrative that conveys direct divine intervention in a literal reading really refers to any one of those natural proximate causes behind which 'God, considered as efficient cause, is then the remotest one'.[89] For Maimonides, while the image of the earth as a footstool philosophically captures the remoteness of God, since that is a correct understanding of nature and God, it paradoxically brings one closer to God. The intensity of love is directly proportional to that understanding. But Netsiv appropriates that very same prooftext to draw God back into the kind of relational immediacy with the world, which is the only way to ground love properly.

No theological belief offends Maimonides' view of natural causation more than the existence of angels, which proliferate in primitive religious consciousness. Maimonides appropriates that very belief in the service of his own world-view, transforming angels from divine delegates incessantly realizing God's will in the world into the quintessential metaphor for natural causation. The term 'angels' signifies every single causal force in the world, 'for all forces are angels'. This comprehensiveness drains the term of any of its traditional ontological connotations, rendering it virtually meaningless. It thoroughly overhauls a superstition into an emblem of science.[90] But Netsiv repatriates the angelic role to its mythical origins, to complete the reversal of Maimonidean naturalism and restore a divine presence in every aspect of the world. The capacity for love is possible only with a Being who is ever-present and cognizable, one who is 'manifest in every agent of His entourage, for there is nothing that is done without His knowledge and will, and that is the meaning of "He is pre-eminent among ten thousands" (S. of S. 5: 10): He is evident in the thousands of forces in the world'.[91] Populated by a myriad of supernatural beings carrying out divine orders at every turn, the world becomes a far more opportune place to achieve love of God.

Does the Lover Need To Be Cured?

The discussion leads us now to the central verse for Maimonides' allegorical understanding of the Song, namely 'for I am sick with love' (2: 5). The lover of God is 'constantly focused on God, as if he were a lovesick person whose attention is not distracted from that woman on whom he is constantly focused [*shogeh*], whether sitting, standing, eating, or drinking . . . All of the Song of Songs is a metaphor for this matter.'[92] For Maimonides, ideal spiritual love is

---

[89] *Guide* i. 69 (p. 168).   [90] Ibid. ii. 6 (pp. 261–5).   [91] *Metiv shir*, 73.
[92] Warren Zev Harvey translates the term *shogeh* as 'ravished' and concludes on the basis of this and other treatments of sex in *Mishneh torah* that there is room for erotic love within Maimonidean thought when it is performed for the sake of knowing God. As such the sexual act

what the Song calls a 'sickness' because it defies the norm signified by a healthy life. The daily routine of a 'healthy' existence involves engagement in civic, familial, ritual, and commercial activity. It thus entails a mind occupied by many different things, and therefore the norm is also a life of distractions. If 'sickness' connotes the irregular, then in this case it indicates an obsessiveness that does not allow for any distractions. It is rather the 'healthiness' of a mundane existence that must be cured by the 'sickness' of a philosophical life that transcends the mundane. Because this is the central peg in Maimonides' construction of the Song's message, Netsiv directly challenges Maimonides' reading of the verse and transforms it from a description of love's ideal state to a plea for its attainment.

Netsiv understands 'sickness' in its ordinary sense as a deficiency or abnormality. The verse therefore means that 'I lack love of God . . . thus the Song reverts to prayer and supplication to attain love of God by way of Torah.'[93] This reading is a corollary of his anti-naturalist stance, since it posits human dependency on God in all of one's endeavours. No activity can be conducted nor any goal achieved independent of divine will, not even love of God. No matter how much the lover exerts himself, the relationship is only fully realized by the grace of the divine beloved. In a final blow to the Maimonidean edifice of religious love, Netsiv not only rules out the study of creation as a means to love, but even brands it an obstacle, 'for the primary difficulty in attaining love of God, even when the soul aspires passionately to it, is the love of nature . . . and this love displaces love of God'.[94] Netsiv then offers the *coup de grâce* to the Maimonidean model of autonomous achievement. Angels, whose popular conception is anathema to Maimonidean naturalism, become an intrinsic element of the love process, for one must 'prostrate oneself in song to the angels for assistance to attain this pleasure'.[95] Once again, much of Netsiv's antagonism is motivated by Maimonides' strong current of independence and solitude and the danger that it poses for the role of a Jew as an integral part of the community or nation. Here Netsiv teaches that one cannot entirely rely on one's own efforts in the metaphysical realm, and this serves as a model for *imitatio Dei* by promoting the positive religious value of interdependence in the physical realm.

Unlike Maimonides' ideal of sickness, Netsiv understands it in its patent sense: rather than an emblem of a perfected state that must be attained, it represents a malaise that must be remedied. Netsiv rejects the Maimonidean

is elevated from a purely clinical act performed as part of a healthy regimen, like daily exercise, to an aspect of the 'ravishing' love for God; W. Z. Harvey, 'Sex and Health in Maimonides', 38–9. I do not see any such place for erotic love, but rather a demand to channel eros away from sexual relations and towards an intellectually erotic attachment to God.

[93] *Metiv shir*, 28.   [94] Ibid.   [95] Ibid.

sense of illness along with the intense heterosexual relationship Maimonides diagnoses as its aetiology—neither is an appropriate metaphor for the love of God. The latter leads Netsiv to reject the spousal relationship altogether as the ideal model for spiritual love! Songs 8: 1 provides him with a textual opportunity for advancing an alternative human model for spiritual love, when the lover laments the need to be modest with her love: 'If only it could be as with a brother, as if you had nursed at my mother's breast: then I could kiss you when I met you on the street and no one would despise me.' Netsiv finds the yearning for a free, public expression of love appealing, even though the lover in the verse is presently barred from it. Prophets, he says, are appropriately compared to women in their relationship with God, since 'it is not customary for a woman to offer her love to her husband except when it is favourable him'.[96] Netsiv thus characterizes any rabbinic advocacy of solitude and privacy as an inferior mode for cultivating spiritual love, one which correlates to the analogous spousal mode where intimacy is restricted by 'modesty and shame'. However, in a startlingly explicit formulation, he endorses the sibling model of love as an ideal, because it is not limited by the sexual mores which confine sexuality to the bedroom and it can be publicly flaunted. It is temporally and spatially unrestricted.

The sense of the lover's plea here, according to Netsiv, is to free her love from the restraints normally associated with lovers and elevate it to a sibling-like love where 'a sister kisses her brother and it is no disgrace to shower on him the full strength of her love, to embrace him, and to kiss him whenever the love for him overwhelms her, even in the marketplace'.[97] Netsiv here articulates his boldest challenge to the Maimonidean model of spiritual love, whose earthly model best captures its austerely internal, isolated, and near-ascetic quality. Maimonides was willing to set aside his disdain for the erotic and the sexual for the sake of communicating the ultimate fulfilment of a supreme religious mandate. Netsiv, likewise, was willing to resort to an incestuously charged image precisely in order to dispel the Maimonidean ideal of love. By replacing it with a publicly oriented one, Netsiv repatriates the God-lover back to the community and the public sphere where he belongs.

Netsiv further tempers the Maimonidean notion of obsessive love of God by introducing into the conversation the peculiar idea of God 'hiding his face' (*hester panim*). The infatuated lover is not the correct model, because the

---

[96] *Metiv shir*, 103.

[97] Ibid. That the explicit language used by Netsiv here is particularly jarring to the religiously Orthodox ear is evidenced by Landesman's tempered translation: 'If the relationship is like that of brother and sister, then a public display of affection would not be considered brazen or improper' (p. 258). The replacement of 'kissing', 'embracing', and 'overwhelming love' (or literally 'when her love for him burns in her heart') with 'affection' is telling.

intense singular focus it connotes is detrimental to the pursuit of the active life and the performance of commandments. The analogy of human love captures not the ideal but the danger of obsessive love, 'since it is evident that it is impossible to attend to many worldly matters while steeped in love and intimacy'.[98] As a corrective to such blinding love, which leaves no room to attend to the beloved's practical needs, the beloved ignores the lover until she craves the resumption of the beloved's attention. At that point the beloved advises the lover of his reliance on her for household upkeep, which has been neglected by her obsessive love. Therefore, 'it is better not to focus your love for me constantly'.[99] Jewish history mirrors the course of this unhealthy relationship when spirituality overwhelms the normative dimension of Judaism and requires a 'hiding of the face' to recalibrate the proper balance of spirituality and performance. Accordingly, Netsiv reads the Song's words 'Turn your eyes away from me' (6: 5) as a warning 'not to immerse your minds in me more than necessary', 'for they overwhelm me', since they believe that 'I am satisfied simply with love; but this is not true since fulfilment of the commandments is a "need on high", therefore I will hide my face from you.'[100]

With this exegesis Netsiv turns the Maimonidean model of the obsessed lover on its head. What leads to God's concealment from the people is precisely the kind of all-absorbing love Maimonides advocates as ideal! Its consequence is not spiritual bliss and proximity to God but rather the opposite: a total rupture in the human–divine relationship. For Maimonides, 'hiding the face' is precisely the consequence of an interregnum in the God-lover's obsessiveness. Worldly affairs detract from the intellectual focus that keeps him within God's protective gaze if his thought 'is free from distraction, if he apprehends Him, and rejoices in what he apprehends'.[101] It is only when the lover lapses from his engulfing desire that alienation from God occurs. This is what the Bible means when it has God threaten, 'And I will hide my face from them and they will be devoured' (Deut. 31: 17).

But even here the debate between medieval Jewish rationalism and a nineteenth-century Lithuanian yeshiva head runs deeper. For Netsiv, it is a human condition that causes 'hiding of the face' only in the sense of inviting a divine response, one which consciously acts to correct that condition. Netsiv's stance has Maimonides clearly in its sights here as well, since Maimonides' God is immutable and immune to affectation. Maimonides emphasizes this in his short excursus on the 'hiding of the face' phenomenon: 'It is clear that we are the cause of this "hiding of the face", and we are the agents who produce this separation.'[102] There are two very distinct components to this proposition. If Maimonides had only written that humans are the cause of 'hiding of the

[98] *Metiv shir*, 87.   [99] Ibid.   [100] Ibid.   [101] *Guide* iii. 51 (p. 625).   [102] Ibid. (p. 626).

face', then he and Netsiv might have had a meeting of minds. But he further emphasized that humans are the sole 'agents' who produce the separation, denying any divine agency. For Maimonides, any encounter with God (if one can legitimately use this distinctly modern term that smacks of the relational for Maimonides) involves an active lover who moves towards his beloved. The latter remains firmly and immovably ensconced in its own space, waiting for the lover's approach through knowledge. Any negative or positive impact on this relationship stems from the lover below. He either fails in his venture, and thus attracts the metaphor of a 'hiding' God, or succeeds in his intellectual endeavours and metaphorically 'sees' God. To see is surely a powerful element of proximity between two human lovers, and it always connotes 'the mind's turning and directing itself to the contemplation of a thing' on the metaphysical plane.[103]

From Eden to Sinai: Netsiv versus Maimonides

It is instructive to conclude this chapter about a nineteenth-century model of Judaism that was constructed in opposition to its twelfth-century Maimonidean antecedent with how they collide in terms of two pivotal biblical moments that they both perceive as exemplars of the love of God. The first is the brief moment of Adam and Eve in the Garden of Eden before sin. The second is Israel at Sinai (which Maimonides conceives of as a momentary return to the intellectual footing of utopian Eden). According to Maimonides, much like the sleepwalking state achieved by Moses on the way to the final 'kiss of death' as described previously through the Song's imagery, Adam, before his sin, found himself in a state where his focused mind was divorced from his body as far as humanly possible. He then operated at the very highest human level of intellection, as 'he had no faculty that was engaged in any way in the consideration of generally accepted things, and he did not apprehend them'.[104] All matters within the realm of morality and politics, which are considered 'good' or 'bad' as opposed to the 'true' or 'false' of objective science, were not in Adam's purview. He was thus impervious to the 'badness' of his nakedness, since he had no operational capacity to evaluate it as such.

It seems likely that Netsiv formulated his analysis of Adam's obliviousness to his nakedness in direct opposition to Maimonides' philosophical psychoanalysis. In his commentaries on Genesis and on the Song of Songs, Netsiv cross-referenced his analysis of Adam's shamelessness and his preference for sibling over spousal love and explicitly connected the two. They both reveal the same concern over the highly abstruse and socially disengaged love con-

[103] *Guide* i. 4 (p. 28).   [104] Ibid. 2 (p. 25).

sidered ideal by Maimonides. 'Nakedness' for Netsiv is a metaphor of the prophetic state, which requires the stripping away of one's physicality so that there can be a total union with the divine. At the same time, Adam's lack of shame over his carnal exposure represents precisely the ability to maintain one's humanity and involvement with human affairs simultaneously.[105] In his commentary on Genesis, Netsiv echoes the perspective he voices in the Song, which advocates sibling romance as a better model for transcendent love, since it can be conducted in public. As Netsiv puts it, 'That is what the poet longs for, that love of God should be commonplace to the extent that there is no shame in conjoining with the supernal mind "while in the marketplace".'[106] I lay emphasis on the final words because they so strikingly stake out a position in contrast to Maimonides' thoroughly detached portrait of Adam, whose love for God is an extreme intellectual asceticism entirely oblivious to worldly affairs.

The 'opening' of Adam's and Eve's eyes as a result of the sin (Gen. 3: 7) is for Maimonides not a cessation of blindness but a metaphor for a transition in consciousness, for 'there had been no membrane over the eye that was now removed, but rather he entered upon another state in which he considered as bad things he had not seen in that light before'.[107] Netsiv, on the other hand, reads the phrase literally, as a sensual enhancement of vision.[108] He then attends to the resultant cognition of nakedness, which signals a lapse into a state where human wisdom, both practical and theoretical, becomes disengaged from cleaving to God. Thus Adam 'deteriorated from the level of wisdom by way of the Holy Spirit and remained with the wisdom of science and human cognition'.[109] Scientific wisdom is what exclusively consumed Adam's mind. Netsiv therefore reverses the direction of the Maimonidean decline of the human condition. His Adam begins with a coupling of spiritual intimacy together with reasoned involvement in human affairs, to which all the intellectual faculties are dedicated. Human degeneration amounts to a decoupling of the two. Maimonides' pristine Adam begins his earthly existence with an intellectual focus that is spiritual love. Adam subsequently becomes distracted from what Maimonides considered the only legitimate subject— philosophy—to an inferior one that is outside philosophy's purview.

The second biblical moment in which Netsiv distinguishes himself from a Maimonidean conceptualization is the revelation at Sinai, the foundational event at which Judaism and the Jewish nation were forged. Here the discus-

[105] *Ha'amek davar* on Gen. 3: 1, 24: 'For this [the prophetic detachment from worldly affairs] was not the case with pre-sin Adam, who was naked but without a separation from human concerns.'   [106] *Ha'amek davar* on Gen. 2: 25.   [107] *Guide* i. 2 (p. 25).
[108] *Ha'amek davar* on Gen. 3: 7, 27.   [109] Ibid.

sion moves from the universalist circumstance of the Adam narrative, which is about humanity, to the particularistic situation of Israel and its unique encounter on a national scale with the divine. Maimonides' vision of Sinai is complex and requires intricate unravelling, but it is sufficient for our purpose here to stress its highly intellectualized grounding. The two cardinal principles of monotheism, namely the existence of God and his unity, are normatively articulated by the first two 'commandments': 'I am the Lord your God' and 'Thou shall have no other gods'. Maimonides then distinguishes between these first two commandments and the remaining eight along precisely the same lines as his description of pre-sin and post-sin Adam's contemplative focus. The first two beliefs are philosophically available to all thinking human beings, and can be established through rigorous logical argument. They comprise universal truths that 'are knowable by human speculation alone'. The latter eight commandments 'belong to the class of generally accepted opinions and those adopted in virtue of tradition, not to the class of the intellect'.[110] In other words, the Sinaitic epiphany replicates the intellectual transition of pre- to post-sin Adam. It shifts from the subject matter of the first two commandments, or that belonging to the world of truth and falsehood, to that of the next eight, which pertain to subjective judgements of good and bad. Maimonides grounds Sinai, and *ipso facto* Judaism as a religion, in a mass experience of philosophical enlightenment.

Netsiv, consistent with his view of human relationships and communal interests as integral aspects of spiritual love, empties Sinai of its Maimonidean intellectualism. Rather than anchor Judaism in a thoroughly intellectual experience, he roots it in community and ethics. He first states that Moses, who is the Maimonidean beacon of intellectual perfection, was privileged to govern Israel precisely because of his impeccable moral constitution (not his intellect), 'for what inspired God to endow Moses with the Holy Spirit was his good deeds'. Then Netsiv directs his attention to that quality of Israel which warranted the Holy Spirit at Sinai, namely ethics, but in particular an ethic that is expressed nationally (as opposed to the personal ethic of Moses in his 'good deeds'). The national ethic identified by Netsiv is a communal spirit, the sense of togetherness and unity with which Israel stood at the foot of Mount Sinai: 'And similarly when all of Israel approached Sinai it was privy to the Holy Spirit even before possessed of any Torah "because they were encamped in peace".'[111] Thus, if Sinai is Judaism's foundational event, then the religion and the people emerge from an exquisitely public instant of a relationally integrated collective, as opposed to Maimonides' individually thinking minds.

[110] *Guide* ii. 33 (p. 364).   [111] *Metiv shir*, 106.

Our overview of Netsiv's engagement with and opposition to Maimonides can help us better understand the sentiments expressed by two of Netsiv's most prominent disciples, men who ultimately turned their back on the yeshiva world and the kind of theology typified by Netsiv. Mikhah Yosef Berdyczewski penned a brief review of Netsiv's commentary on the Song, which was published together with Netsiv's essay on antisemitism. He praised the latter work as a model for the rabbinic world, 'leaving the talmudic focus to attend to issues relevant to the nation as well'.[112] However, Netsiv's commentary did not receive as favourable a review from Berdyczewski, who wrote that one 'who is encumbered by a mountain of laws and regulations is bound often to distort its plain sense'. Berdyczewski's critique is best appreciated in contrast to Maimonides' explication of the Song. Although Maimonides also did not follow the plain sense in his exegesis, he could not be accused of reading 'a mountain of laws and regulations' into it. On the contrary, for him the Song endorses a life of thought over action, the pursuit of philosophy and science over observance.

A line of poetry composed by Hayim Nahman Bialik, another of Netsiv's wayward students, becomes more nuanced when read in light of Netsiv's opposition to Maimonides. One of his reminiscences about the yeshiva in Volozhin concerns those who were expelled for various malfeasances. Among those ejected from the yeshiva for such religious violations as smoking on the sabbath, socializing with girls, and gambling is also 'the one who hid himself with the *Guide of the Perplexed*'.[113] All of the thinkers we examine in this book likewise 'hide themselves', discreetly or overtly, with Maimonides' legacy. They all struggle to hold on to the Great Eagle's influence, which has hovered over all Jewish thought for the last eight centuries, or to liberate themselves from it. But they never ignore him.

[112] Berdyczewski, 'Netsiv's Song of Songs' (Heb.), 2.
[113] Bialik, 'The Yeshiva Student (HaMatmid)'.

TWO

Rabbi Joseph B. Soloveitchik and Maimonides

MENACHEM KELLNER

THE CENTRAL ROLE of Maimonides in the life and thought of Rabbi Joseph B. Soloveitchik is unquestionable,[1] as a moving autobiographical passage in his *And from There You Shall Seek* dramatically attests:

I remember myself as a child, a lonely, forlorn boy. I was afraid of the world. It seemed cold and alien. I felt as if everyone were mocking me. But I had one friend, and he was—please don't laugh at me—Maimonides, the Rambam. How did we become friends? We simply met!

The Rambam was a regular guest in our house. Those were the days when my father, my mentor, was still living in the home of my grandfather, the great and pious Rabbi Elijah Feinstein of Prushna.[2] Father sat and studied Torah day and night. A rather small group of outstanding young Torah scholars gathered around him and imbibed his words thirstily.

Father's lectures were given in my grandfather's living room, where my bed was placed. I used to sit up in bed and listen to my father talk. My father always spoke about the Rambam. This is how he would proceed. He would open a volume of the Talmud and read a passage. Then he would say, 'This is the interpretation of Rabbi Isaac and the [other] Tosafists; now let us see how the Rambam interpreted the passage.' Father would always find that the Rambam had offered a different interpretation and had deviated from the simple way. My father would say, almost as a complaint against the Rambam, 'We don't understand our Master's reasoning or the way he explains the passage.' It was as if he were complaining to the Rambam directly, 'Rabbenu Mosheh, why did you do this?'

My father would then say that, prima facie, the criticisms and objections of the Rabad are actually correct. The members of the group would jump up and each of them would suggest an idea. Father would listen and rebut their ideas, and then repeat, 'Our Master's words are as hard to crack as iron.' But he would not despair;

---

[1] For a comprehensive bibliography of R. Soloveitchik's writings and studies, see Turkel, 'Partial Bibliography'. Dov Schwartz deals at length with the ties of R. Soloveitchik's thought to Maimonides in *The Philosophy of Rabbi Joseph B. Soloveitchik*. See also Rynhold, *Two Models of Jewish Philosophy*.   [2] The uncle of R. Moshe Feinstein (1895–1986).

he would rest his head on his fist and sink into deep thought. The group was quiet and did not disturb his reflections. After a long while he would lift his head very slowly and begin, 'Rabbotai, let's see . . .', and then he would start to talk. Sometimes he would say a great deal, other times only a little. I would strain my ears and listen to what he was saying.

I did not understand anything at all about the issue under discussion, but two impressions were formed in my young, innocent mind: (1) the Rambam was surrounded by opponents and 'enemies' who want to harm him; and (2) his only defender was my father. If not for my father, who knew what would happen to the Rambam? I felt that the Rambam himself was present in the living room, listening to what my father was saying. The Rambam was sitting with me on my bed. What did he look like? I didn't know exactly, but his countenance resembled my father's good and beautiful face. He had the same name as my father—Moses. Father would speak; the students, their eyes fixed on him, would listen intently to what he was saying. Slowly, slowly, the tension ebbed; Father strode boldly and bravely. New arguments emerged; halakhic rules were formulated and defined with wondrous precision. A new light shone. The difficulties were resolved, the passage was explained. The Rambam emerged the winner. Father's face shone with joy. He had defended his 'friend', Rabbenu Mosheh the son of Maimon. A smile of satisfaction appeared on the Rambam's lips. I too participated in this joy. I was happy and excited. I would jump out of bed and run to my mother's room to tell her the joyful news, 'Mother, Mother, the Rambam is right, he defeated the Rabad. Father came to his aid. How wonderful Father is!'

But occasionally the Rambam's luck did not hold—his 'enemies' attacked him on all sides; the difficulties were as hard as iron. Father was unable to follow the logic of his position. He tried with all his might to defend him, but he was unsuccessful. Father would sink into musings with his head leaning on his fist. The students and I, and even the Rambam himself, would tensely wait for Father's answer. But Father would pick up his head and say sadly, 'The answer will have to wait for the prophet Elijah; what the Rambam says is extremely difficult. There is no expert who can explain it. The issue remains in need of clarification.' The whole group, my father included, were sad to the point of tears.[3] A silent agony expressed itself on each face. Tears came from my eyes, too. I would even see bright teardrops in the Rambam's eyes.

Slowly I would go to Mother and tell her with a broken heart, 'Mother, Father can't resolve the Rambam—what should we do?'

'Don't be sad', Mother would answer, 'Father will find a solution for the Rambam. And if he doesn't find one, then maybe when you grow up you'll resolve his words. The main thing is to learn Torah with joy and excitement.'[4]

---

[3] See Mishnah *Yoma* 1: 5.   [4] Soloveitchik, *And From There You Shall Seek*, 143–5.

These touching words are powerful evidence of Maimonides' significance to Rabbi Soloveitchik. As an independent thinker who had been deeply involved in European intellectual life before the Second World War, however, he did not blindly adopt Maimonides' philosophical positions: (1) At times, he agrees with Maimonides but presents his thought in a way that his audience can easily accept, as an illuminating example below will show. (2) At times, he agrees with Maimonides and presents his thought in rather sharp terms, which might evoke resistance among his more traditional readers. (3) At times, he tries to bring Maimonides closer to his own views through recourse to interpretation. (4) At times, Rabbi Soloveitchik adopts positions opposed to those of Maimonides without saying so. In order to spell out the dispute that I detect between Rabbi Soloveitchik and Maimonides on certain topics, I will refer to Maimonides' interpretation by Professor Isadore Twersky (1930–97), Rabbi Soloveitchik's son-in-law, who, in my view, often understood Maimonides better than his father-in-law.[5]

Individual Providence

I begin with a text in which Rabbi Soloveitchik presents Maimonides correctly, but in a language acceptable to contemporary traditional Jews. For Maimonides, as is widely known, the key to individual providence is intellectual perfection.[6] One who attains it is subject to divine providence, and one who does not is not subject to divine providence. One who attains greater intellectual perfection has greater providence than one whose intellectual attainments are more limited. There is no difference between Jew and non-Jew in this matter. This approach already evoked fierce opposition in Maimonides' times,[7] and still does so today. I remember a conversation with a rabbi and *dayan* (rabbinic judge) in Haifa, whose wife had attended my course on Maimonides and was exposed to his theory of providence. The poor rabbi tried in all ways possible to avoid admitting that Maimonides had indeed meant what he wrote in the *Guide of the Perplexed* iii. 17.

---

[5] In this chapter, I cite only selected examples of the disputes between R. Soloveitchik and Maimonides. Lawrence J. Kaplan's *Maimonides between Philosophy and Halakhah* appeared after this chapter had been completed. Among other surprising readings there, R. Soloveitchik appears to turn Maimonides into a pantheist; see pp. 144–9 in the text and pp. 32–7 in Kaplan's introduction.

[6] This perfection is contingent on ethical perfection. The best and proven (but not the only) way to reach ethical perfection is to observe the commandments. See Kellner, *Maimonides' Confrontation*, 34–5, 59–66, and id., *They Too Are Called Human* (Heb.).

[7] Samuel Ibn Tibbon and his son Moses were already divided on this question in the 13th century. See Diesendruck, 'Samuel and Moses ibn Tibbon', and Ravitzky, 'Samuel Ibn Tibbon'.

How does Rabbi Soloveitchik present Maimonides' stance? Consider the following:

> The gist of Maimonides' view is that man occupies a unique position in the kingdom of existence and differs in his ontological nature from all other creatures. With reference to all other creatures, only the universal, not the particular, has a true, continuous existence; with respect to man, however, it is an everlasting principle that his individual existence also attains the heights of true, eternal being. Indeed, the primary mode of man's existence is the particular existence of the individual, who is both liable and responsible for his acts. Therefore, it is the individual who is worthy of divine providence and eternal life. Man, in one respect, is a mere random example of the biological species—species man—an image of the universal, a shadow of true existence. In another respect he is a man of God, possessor of an individual existence. The difference between a man who is a mere random example of the biological species and a man of God is that the former is characterized by passivity, the latter by activity and creation. The man who belongs solely to the realm of the universal is passive to an extreme—he creates nothing. The man who has a particular existence of his own is not merely a passive, receptive creature but acts and creates. Action and creation are the true distinguishing marks of authentic existence.[8]

So far, this is a text that the rabbi I mentioned above would not oppose in any way. But he would surely fail to notice that the subject is humanity in general, not Jews. He would emphasize the words 'it is the individual who is worthy of divine providence and eternal life' and would think that the issue at stake here is the accepted view that grants every Jew individual providence.

Such a person might proceed to the next paragraph and attempt to read it in light of the previous one, although that might prove hard:

> However, this ontological privilege, which is the peculiar possession of the man who has a particular existence of his own, a privilege that distinguishes him from all other creatures and endows him with individual immortality, is dependent upon man himself. The choice is his. He may, like the individual of all the other species, exist in the realm of the images and shadows, or he may exist as an individual who is not a part of the universal and who proves worthy of a fixed, established existence in the world of the 'forms' and 'intellects separate from matter' [*MT* 'Laws of the Foundations of the Torah', 4: 9]. Species man or man of God, this is the alternative which the Almighty placed before man. If he proves worthy, then he becomes a man of God in all the splendor of his individual existence that cleaves to absolute infinity and the glorious 'divine overflow'. If he proves unworthy, then he ends up as one more random example of the biological species, a turbid and blurred image of universal existence.

[8] Soloveitchik, *Halakhic Man*, 124–5.

Not every human being (or even every Jew), then, is worthy of providence and, consequently, of a share in the world to come. One who chooses to cleave to the divine overflow, meaning one who perfects his or her intellect sufficiently, is watched over and attains eternal life. One who does not perfect his or her intellect is not watched over and does not attain eternal life: he or she is merely a turbid and blurred image of general reality.

My formulation of this view is sharp and blatant. Rabbi Soloveitchik, following Maimonides, wrote it so that a non-philosophical Jew (such as the Haifa rabbi) would not understand it and would think that Maimonides speaks like a 'normal' rabbi of today.[9] Rabbi Soloveitchik then cites at length from the *Guide of the Perplexed* iii. 18, and sums up:

Man, at times, exists solely by virtue of the species, by virtue of the fact that he was born a member of that species, and its general form is engraved upon him. He exists solely on account of his participation in the idea of the universal. He is just a member of the species 'man', an image of the universal. He is just one more example of the species image in its ongoing morphological process (in the Aristotelian sense of the term). He himself, however, has never done anything that could serve to legitimate his existence as an individual. His soul, his spirit, his entire being, all are grounded in the realm of the universal. His roots lie deep in the soil of faceless mediocrity; his growth takes place solely within the public domain. He has no stature of his own, no original, individual, personal profile. He has never created anything, never brought into being anything new, never accomplished anything. He is receptive, passive, a spiritual parasite. He is wholly under the influence of other people and their views. Never has he sought to render an accounting, either of himself or of the world; never has he examined himself, his relationship to God and his fellow man.[10]

Powerful words, but they pale by comparison to what follows:

He lives unnoticed and dies unmourned[!].[11] Like a fleeting cloud, a shadow, he passes through life and is gone. He bequeaths nothing to future generations, but dies without leaving a trace of his having lived.[12] Empty-handed he goes to the grave, bereft of *mitzvah* performances, good deeds, and meritorious acts, for while living he lacked any sense of historical responsibility and was totally wanting in any ethical passion. He was born involuntarily, and it is for this reason and this reason alone that he, involuntarily, lives out his life (a life which, paradoxically, he has

---

[9] On the 'art of writing' in Maimonides, see Kellner, 'Literary Character'.
[10] Soloveitchik, *Halakhic Man*, 126–7.   [11] A notion that contradicts halakhic rulings.
[12] In a posthumous book, *The Emergence of Halakhic Man*, Rabbi Soloveitchik emphasized that the immortality of the soul is essentially the impression that is left from people's lives after their death (p. 169). The text of this book was found in Rabbi Soloveitchik's estate and was prepared for publication by his disciples, with the consent of his family.

'chosen'!) until he dies involuntarily. This is man as the random example of the biological species.

The man of the biological species is one who has not perfected his intellect, even slightly,[13] and therefore has no providence. Relying on these statements, it appears we can say that the Holy One, blessed be he, views the man of the species only as a man of the species rather than as a separate personality.

By contrast, other people rise above the category of 'man of the species':

But there is another man, one who does not require the assistance of others, who does not need the support of the species to legitimate his existence. Such a man is no longer a prisoner of time but is his own master. He exists not by virtue of the species, but solely on account of his own individual worth. His life is replete with creation and renewal, cognition and profound understanding. He lives not on account of his having been born but for the sake of life itself and so that he may merit thereby the life in the world to come. He recognizes the destiny that is his, his obligation and task in life. He understands full well the dualism running through his being and that choice which has been entrusted to him. He knows that there are two paths before him and that whichever he shall choose, there must he go. He is not passive but active. His personality is not characterized by receptivity but by spontaneity. He does not simply abandon himself to the rule of the species but blazes his own individual trail. Moreover, he, as an individual, influences the many. His whole existence, like some enchanted stream, rushes ever onward to distant magical regions. He is dynamic, not static, does not remain at rest but moves forward in an ever-ascending climb. For, indeed, it is the living God for whom he pines and longs. This is the man of God.

The fundamental of providence is here transformed into a concrete commandment, an obligation incumbent upon man. Man is obliged to broaden the scope and strengthen the intensity of the individual providence that watches over him. Everything is dependent on him; it is all in his hands. When a person creates himself, ceases to be a mere species man, and becomes a man of God, then he has fulfilled that commandment which is implicit in the principle of providence.[14]

We can hardly visualize a situation wherein Maimonides would write with an enthusiasm similar to that of Rabbi Soloveitchik, placing such strong emphasis on human creativity and in a style so clearly influenced by twentieth-century religious existentialism. Yet it is not hard to see true Maimonidean teachings behind these words either.

This combination of Maimonides and Rabbi Soloveitchik results in an interesting stance: the commandment is to attain providence (R. Soloveit-

---

[13] Carlos Fraenkel has persuaded me that, according to Maimonides, 'popular' knowledge can, to some extent, be considered knowledge. See Fraenkel, 'Theocracy and Autonomy', 355.

[14] Soloveitchik, *Halakhic Man*, 127–8.

chik); observing this commandment requires a person to perfect his or her intellect (Maimonides). In my understanding, Maimonides would have formulated the first point slightly differently: there is a commandment of *imitatio Dei*;[15] this commandment is fulfilled by perfecting the intellect as far as possible. This in turn demands a high level of moral perfection, for which the proven course, though not the only one, is observing the commandments. It is those who observe the commandment of *imitatio Dei* who have providence. Rabbi Soloveitchik, in my view, writes about providence in what is clearly a Maimonidean 'spirit' and, in principle, he clearly understood Maimonides' intention.[16]

The Holiness of Israel

There is another issue where Rabbi Soloveitchik adopts a distinctly Maimonidean position, but without mentioning Maimonides:

Why God could not enter into an intimate relationship with Abraham in Mesopotamia and had to guide him into a new land is an old problem. Judah Halevi, in his *Kuzari*, explains it with the uniqueness of the Land of Israel as an ideal land for the meeting of God by man. He attributes metaphysical qualities to the land and endows it with a spiritual climate: *hayyei neshamot avir artzekh* ('the air of your land is the breath of life for our souls'; Judah Halevi, *Tziyon ha-lo tishali, kinnot letishah be-Av*). Of course, the old myth of the temperate climate which is ideal for the development of man was exploited by Halevi.[17] Nahmanides, in his commentary to Lev. 18: 25, followed in Halevi's footsteps, as did the mystics. For them, the attribute of *kedushah*, holiness, ascribed to the Land of Israel is an objective metaphysical quality inherent in the land.

With all my respect for the Rishonim [earlier authorities], I must disagree with such an opinion. I do not believe that it is halakhically cogent. *Kedushah*, under a halakhic aspect, is man-made; more accurately, it is a historical category. A soil is sanctified by historical deeds performed by a sacred people, never by any primordial superiority. The halakhic term *kedushat ha-aretz*, the sanctity of the land, denotes the consequence of a human act, either conquest (heroic deeds) or the mere presence of the people in that land (intimacy of man and nature). *Kedushah* is

[15] This is clearly a Maimonidean innovation. See the *Book of Divine Commandments*, positive commandment 8, and *MT* 'Laws of Ethical Qualities', 1: 1. See also Kellner, *Maimonides on Human Perfection*, 41–5.

[16] As Daniel Rynhold mentioned to me, we should not forget that R. Soloveitchik's Maimonides is the Maimonides of Hermann Cohen. For a discussion of this important point, see Ravitzky, 'Rabbi J. B. Soloveitchik on Human Knowledge'. See also Ch. 3 in this volume.

[17] On the theory of climates in medieval Jewish thought, see Melamed, *On the Shoulders of Giants* (Heb.), 42–3, 229–34.

identical with man's association with Mother Earth. Nothing should be attributed a priori to dead matter. Objective *kedushah* smacks of fetishism.[18]

The question is: why did Abraham need to wander away from his native land and go to Canaan in order to create an intimate relationship with God? According to Judah Halevi and Nahmanides, the answer is clear: the Land of Israel has unique attributes. Rabbi Soloveitchik simply rejects this answer and does not even pin this rejection on Maimonides, although he could have done so.[19] No, he simply says that he disagrees with Judah Halevi and Nahmanides on this issue. Their stance is simply not cogent in halakhic terms and, as shown below, Rabbi Soloveitchik holds that the only possible Jewish perspective is the halakhic one. Rabbi Soloveitchik's ability to challenge, on such a central philosophical question, two *rishonim* of Judah Halevi's and Nahmanides' stature (not to mention, as he notes, all the kabbalists who followed them[20]) is truly surprising. His reasons are surprising too: holiness is not at all a metaphysical category, essential to the object, the place, the time,[21] or the person. Holiness is the result of a human act, a historical category. The holiness of the Land of Israel follows from acts of a holy people (I return below to the essence of the Jewish people's holiness). To ascribe 'objective' holiness (meaning a holiness that is essential and not history-bound) to an object is actually a kind of fetishism. This extreme statement is surprising—it fits well with Maimonides' approach but is far removed from the world in which Rabbi Soloveitchik was brought up, and also from the approach taken in Rabbi Hayim of Volozhin's *Nefesh haḥayim*, which greatly influenced Rabbi Soloveitchik and which he often mentions. His stance is also distant from that endorsed by most of his disciples who, as far as I can judge, are persuaded of the essential, 'objective' holiness of the Land of Israel in general and of Jerusalem in particular, far beyond their historical/halakhic importance.

A similar view is stated in Rabbi Soloveitchik's *Halakhic Man*:

Holiness does not wink at us from 'beyond' like some mysterious star that sparkles in the distant heavens, but appears in our actual, very real lives. 'And one called to another and said: Holy, holy, holy is the Lord of hosts; the whole earth is full of His glory. They received one from another and said: Holy in the highest heavens, His divine abode; holy upon the earth, the work of His might; holy forever and to all

---

[18] See Soloveitchik, *The Emergence of Halakhic Man*, 149–50.

[19] I hope that I have by now demonstrated that, in Maimonides' view, there is no immanent holiness; see Kellner, *Maimonides' Confrontation*, ch. 3. Another potential source for R. Soloveitchik's view on this matter is Meir Simhah Cohen of Dvinsk, *Meshekh ḥokhmah*, on Exod. 19: 13 and 32: 19.

[20] Possibly hinting that R. Soloveitchik denied the tannaitic source of the Zohar.

[21] On the holiness of time, see Soloveitchik, *The Halakhic Mind*, 47.

eternity' (Isa. 6: 3 and Targum [Yonatan] ad loc.). The beginnings of holiness are rooted in the highest heavens, and its end is embedded in the eschatological vision of 'the end of days'—holy forever and to all eternity. But the link that joins together these two perspectives is the halakhic conception of holiness: holy upon the earth, the work of His might—the holiness of the concrete . . . Holiness consists of a life ordered and fixed in accordance with Halakhah and finds its fulfillment in the observance of the laws regulating human biological existence, such as the laws concerning forbidden sexual relations, forbidden foods, and similar precepts. And it was not for naught that Maimonides included these prohibitions in his *Book of Holiness*.

Holiness is created by man, by flesh and blood. Through the power of our mouths, through verbal sanctification alone, we can create holy offerings for the Temple treasury and holy offerings for the altar. The land of Israel became holy through conquest, Jerusalem, and the Temple courts—through bringing two loaves of thanksgiving (Jerusalem) or the reminder of the meal offering (Temple court) and song, etc.[22]

Holiness is not metaphysical, something objective that exists in the universe, something that we could discover were we able to invent a 'holiness-meter' version of a Geiger counter. No, holy is what we call things, places, people, times, towards which halakhah determines a special attitude. Any other attitude, as we have seen, constitutes fetishism.

The approach I ascribe here to Maimonides will not surprise Maimonidean scholars, some of whom have dealt with various aspects of this issue, which is at the centre of my book *Maimonides' Confrontation with Mysticism*.[23] This has definitely been a minority view in the history of Jewish thought since the Middle Ages, and to see Rabbi Soloveitchik endorsing it without batting an eyelash is indeed surprising.

Jewish Philosophy beyond Halakhah

I now consider topics where I see Rabbi Soloveitchik differing from Maimonides. In the first topic, their dispute touches on an essential and fundamental question. A central idea in Rabbi Soloveitchik's thought, as noted, is that there is no extra-halakhic Jewish thought: a Jewish viewpoint is a halakhic viewpoint. Rabbi Soloveitchik mentions this notion in many of his writings, and scholars have emphasized this as a key notion in his thought. I cite several examples, all from books that Rabbi Soloveitchik published himself:

1. '[T]here is only a single source from which a Jewish philosophical *Weltanschauung* could emerge; the objective order—the Halakhah'.[24]

---

[22] Soloveitchik, *Halakhic Man*, 46–7.   [23] See ch. 3.
[24] Soloveitchik, *The Halakhic Mind*, 101. Compare further pp. 93–4: 'Rambam, the halachic

2. From his central philosophical work, *Halakhic Man*: 'The Halakhah, which was given to us from Sinai, is the objectification of religion in clear and determinate forms, in precise and authoritative laws, and in definite principles. It translates subjectivity into objectivity, the amorphous flow of religious experience into a fixed pattern of lawfulness.'[25]

3. 'The study of the Torah is not a means to another end, but is the end point of all desires. It is *the most fundamental principle* of all.'[26]

For Maimonides, by contrast, halakhah depends on the historical reality and could, in principle, have been different.[27] Given that, for Maimonides, observing the commandments is a means to an extra-halakhic end, the study of Torah (in the halakhic sense of the term 'Torah') cannot be a means to this extra-halakhic end.[28] And what is this end? The perfection of the intellect.

Maimonides' position finds expression in almost all his works. I will discuss only a few examples here. Concerning the first, Rabbi Soloveitchik not only seems to disagree with Maimonides (though there is no surprise here as almost every Jewish thinker since the Middle Ages has disagreed with Maimonides on this issue), but also seeks to enlist Maimonides in his favour. He writes:

I do not agree with those who interpret 'to know' as meaning 'to understand', indicating that each and every Jew would have to philosophize and investigate for himself all that is relevant to the existence of God. I do not believe that this is what Maimonides meant . . . I am convinced therefore that Maimonides did not mean

scholar, came nearer the core of philosophical truth than Maimonides, the speculative philosopher.'

[25] Soloveitchik, *Halakhic Man*, 59.

[26] Ibid. 87 (my emphasis). In conclusion, see the words of R. Soloveitchik's friend, Marvin Fox: 'The unifying principle in all of the Rav's works is his frequently stated conviction that the only legitimate source of Jewish doctrine is the Halakhah'; Fox, 'Unity and Structure', 49. See also Rynhold, *Two Models of Jewish Philosophy*, 61. This point merits attention. Maimonides' universalism follows from his view that human perfection is equivalent to intellectual perfection. If R. Soloveitchik holds that human perfection is equivalent to 'halakhic' perfection (in the broad meaning of 'halakhah' as philosophy), then he is not a Maimonidean universalist. To the best of my knowledge, R. Soloveitchik did not relate to this question in his writings and I do not know what his view was. Compare further the very last line in Kaplan, *Maimonides between Philosophy and Halakhah*, 239 n. 5: Maimonides, 'after all his adventures in the field of philosophy . . . came back to the Halakhah'.

[27] Horetzky, 'Maimonides and Gersonides' (Heb.), 16, refers to this idea as Maimonides' 'Copernican revolution'.

[28] R. Soloveitchik seems to have understood Maimonides' view well. For example: 'In rationalizing the commandments genetically, Maimonides developed a "religious instrumentalism". Causality reverted to teleology (the Aristotelian concept of *causa finalis*) and Jewish religion was converted into technical wisdom'; Soloveitchik, *The Halakhic Mind*, 93.

that every Jew had to become a philosopher or, in modern parlance, a theologian. I would say that 'to know' (*leida*) means that our conviction of the existence of God should become a constant and continuous awareness of the reality of God, a level of consciousness never marred by inattention; 'to believe' (*leha'amin*), on the other hand, implies no prohibition against inattentiveness. 'I believe'—but it may happen that I become distracted at times from the thing in which I believe. But in the term 'to know' (*leida*) the reference is to a state of continuous awareness—that the belief in God should cause man to be in a state of perpetual affinity, of constant orientation, God should become a living reality that one cannot forget even for a minute. This keen awareness of the existence of God should constitute the foundation of our thoughts, ideas and emotions in every kind of situation and under all conditions. Everything else inevitably depends upon this supreme article of faith.[29]

Rabbi Soloveitchik relates here to the famous sentence that opens Maimonides' *Mishneh torah*:

The basic principle of all basic principles and the pillar of all sciences is to realize that there is a First Being who brought every existing thing into being. All existing things, whether celestial, terrestrial, or belonging to an intermediate class, exist only through His true Existence.[30]

What Maimonides intended here is precisely what he wrote: the basic principle of all basic principles is the pillar of all sciences, and it is also the first of the 613 commandments, and also the first of the Thirteen Principles. And what is its content? *To know* that God exists. This sentence encompasses a long list of new notions, which will not be considered here.[31] His position here is connected to the fact that Maimonides clearly distinguished between halakhah and 'the true science of Torah' in many places. For example, at the beginning of the *Guide*, he writes:

The first purpose of this Treatise is to explain the meanings of certain terms occurring in books of prophecy. Some of these terms are equivocal; hence the ignorant attribute to them only one or some of the meanings in which the term in question is used. Others are derivative terms; hence they attribute to them only the original meaning from which the other meaning is derived. Others are amphibolous terms, so that at times they are believed to be univocal and at other times equivocal. It is not the purpose of this Treatise to make its totality understandable to the vulgar or to beginners in speculation, nor to teach those who have not engaged

---

[29] Soloveitchik, *On Repentance*, 145. See also Gotlieb, *Rationalism in Hasidic Attire* (Heb.), 119–21, for a similar approach among Habad rabbis.

[30] 'Laws of the Foundations of the Torah', 1: 1 (34*b*).

[31] See Kellner, *They Too Are Called Human* (Heb.).

in any study other than the science of the Law—I mean the legalistic study of the Law. For the purpose of this Treatise and of all those like it is the science of Law in its true sense.[32]

Another instance may be found in the parable of the palace towards the end of the *Guide*, where Maimonides, when comparing Torah scholars to men of science, favours the latter.[33]

Rabbi Soloveitchik understood this and rejected the most important of Maimonides' conclusions, that 'each and every Jew would have to philosophize and investigate for himself all that is relevant to the existence of God'.[34] Rabbi Soloveitchik was the scion of a long line of brilliant Torah scholars, none of whom had ever enquired into 'the existence of God'. If Maimonides had indeed set this requirement, then no member of the illustrious Brisk dynasty had succeeded in observing even the first commandment, at least according to Maimonides.[35] It is not hard to understand why Rabbi Soloveitchik would reject this determination.

What *is* hard to understand is Rabbi Soloveitchik's clear-cut statement in light of a footnote written by his friend, Rabbi Chaim Heller (1879–1960). On the use of the verb 'to believe' in the first positive commandment in Maimonides' *Book of the Commandments*,[36] Rabbi Heller notes in his edition: 'and

---

[32] *Guide*, introd. to pt. i (p. 5).

[33] *Guide* iii. 51 (p. 618). I hold that, in the parable, Maimonides compares Torah scholars who study only Torah and Torah scholars who are also scientists. See Kellner, *Maimonides on Human Perfection* (15–16). If my understanding is correct here, then Shem Tov ben Yosef ibn Shem Tov was mistaken in his comment ad loc.: 'Said Shem Tov: many rabbinic scholars said that this chapter had not been written by the Rav [Maimonides] and, if it had, it should have been hidden away or, better still, burnt. How could he have said that those who know the natural things rank higher than those who deal with religion and, worse still, that they are with the ruler in the inner court? If so, the philosophers who deal with natural things and with divine science rank higher than those who deal with Torah' (my translation). Clearly, then, Shem Tov knew (as did many of the 'rabbinic scholars' he mentions) that Maimonides draws a distinction between halakhah and philosophy in favour of the latter, and that he certainly does not think of halakhah as the only source for a philosophy of Torah.

[34] Soloveitchik, *On Repentance*, 145. On this matter, R. Soloveitchik follows Isaac Abrabanel, who wrote: 'Why does the Rav [Maimonides] write in the first law of the *Book of Knowledge*, "the basic principle of all basic principles and the pillar of all sciences" when it would have been fitting for him to say "one of the principles" rather than "the basic principle of all basic principles"? And how can we know whether or not this principle is the pillar of all the Gentile sciences ("of all the people who were left of the Amorites, the Hittites, the Perizzites, the Hivites, and the Jebusites, who were not of the children of Israel" (1 Kgs. 9: 20))?'; Abrabanel, *Principles of Faith*, 76.

[35] Soloveitchik's equation of the Maimonidean philosopher with the modern theologian is not accurate, in my view. The Maimonidean philosopher is closer to a contemporary physicist than to a theologian.

[36] 'By this injunction we are commanded to believe in God; that is, to believe that there is a Supreme Cause who is the Creator of everything in existence': *Book of Divine Commandments*, positive commandment 1: 1.

it seems better to translate that he has commanded us to know God'.[37] Here Rabbi Soloveitchik's friend (in New York) and teacher (in Berlin) correctly understood Maimonides' intention in 'Laws of the Foundations of the Torah', 1: 1. Rabbi Soloveitchik (tacitly) rejected Heller's view. A plausible assumption is that, as a leader of his generation, Rabbi Soloveitchik thought it inappropriate to highlight a Maimonidean position that he outright opposed.

In 1980 Rabbi Soloveitchik's son-in-law Isadore Twersky published his monumental work, *Introduction to the Code of Maimonides*. The book includes a very long chapter, almost a book in itself, entitled 'Law and Philosophy'. This chapter develops motifs first presented in a trailblazing article that Twersky published in 1967, 'Some Non-Halakhic Aspects of the *Mishneh Torah*'. For Twersky, as for all scholars of Maimonides in the world who are known to me, halakhah is definitely not the sole source of Jewish philosophy in Maimonides' eyes. Quite the contrary, as Twersky emphasized: for Maimonides, *gufei torah* (the essentials, literally *the bodies*, of Torah) rest on a philosophical basis.[38]

In another example of Jewish philosophy that goes beyond halakhah, Rabbi Soloveitchik seems to disagree with his son-in-law about Maimonides. We learn in Maimonides' 'Laws Concerning the Recitation of the Shema':

The Shema is recited twice every day, once in the evening and once in the morning, as it is said, 'Recite them when you stay at home and when you are away, when you lie down and when you get up' [Deut. 6: 7]. The time when people customarily lie down is evening and the time when people customarily get up is morning.

    What does one recite? The three paragraphs beginning with the words 'Hear' [Deut. 6: 4–9]; 'If, then, you obey' [Deut. 11: 13–21]; and 'The Lord said' [Num. 15: 37–41]. The paragraph 'Hear' is recited first because it contains commandments concerning God's unity, the love of God, and the study of God [*talmudo*] which is the basic principle on which all depends.[39] After it, 'If, then, you obey', is recited since the passage commands obedience to all the other commandments. After that, the paragraph concerning the fringes is recited, since it also contains a command to recall all the commandments.[40]

What is the meaning of the word *talmudo* in this passage? In the wake of what

---

[37] Maimonides, *Book of the Commandments* (Heb.), ed. Heller, 35.
[38] Twersky, 'Law and Philosophy', in id., *Introduction to the Code*, 356–514: 361 (emphasis in original).
[39] Cf. *MT* 'Laws of the Foundations of the Torah', 1: 1–7, particularly Law 6: 'To acknowledge this truth is an affirmative precept, as it is said, "I am the Lord thy God" [Exod. 20: 2; Deut. 5: 6]. And whoever permits the thought to enter his mind that there is another deity besides this God, violates a prohibition; as it is said "Thou shalt have no other gods before me" [Exod. 20: 3; Deut. 5: 7], and denies the essence of religion—this doctrine being the great principle on which everything depends.'   [40] *MT* 'Laws Concerning the Recitation of the Shema', 1: 1–2.

is implied by the *Leḥem mishneh* and the *Kesef mishneh*,[41] modern commentators and translators have explained *talmudo* as the study of Torah.[42] Rabbi Soloveitchik agrees with them.[43] I know of exactly two people who understood Maimonides otherwise, and took *talmudo* to mean the study of God's existence. One was Rabbi Kafih in his commentary on the *Mishneh torah*,[44] and the other was Isadore Twersky, who emphasized this point in his lectures at Harvard University.[45]

Demonstrating that Kafih's and Twersky's understanding of Maimonides is the correct one is not difficult, and I have done so elsewhere.[46] What matters here is that Rabbi Soloveitchik consistently attempts to interpret Maimonides as a halakhist rather than as a thinker.

Keneset Yisra'el

I turn now to a topic where Rabbi Soloveitchik adopts an approach that has been accepted by the majority of Jewish thinkers since the Middle Ages, including rabbis and their disciples, though at the high price of an internal con-

---

[41] The first of these classic commentaries was written by R. Abraham di Boton (1560–1606), and the second by R. Joseph Karo (1488–1575).

[42] See the commentary ad loc. of Shmuel Tanhum Rubinstein in *Mishneh torah: sefer ahavah* ('Rambam La'am' edition published by Mosad Harav Kook), and the *Yad peshutah* commentary of Nachum L. Rabinovitch. Translators of the *Mishneh torah* into English agree with this interpretation: Hyamson, in *The Book of Knowledge*, renders it as 'and studying his words'; Boruch Kaplan, in *Maimonides' Mishneh Torah*, writes 'and the study of Torah'. Unlike them, I translate 'and the study of God', as cited in the text.

[43] R. Soloveitchik hints at this in *Worship of the Heart*, ch. 7. His view comes across clearly, though indirectly, in *And From There You Shall Seek*, 92–3: 'Let us consider the way the Halakhah formulates the commandment of cleaving to God—*le-dovkah bo* (Deut. 11: 22). As was emphasized above, the Halakhah says that one should cleave to those who know Him. In other words, those who know God cleave to Him, and man achieves his goal of cleaving to God by joining together with them. But then the question simply reappears: How do those who know Him cleave to Him? The simple answer is: Through their knowledge. It is clear that the Halakhah is not referring to abstract knowledge, which is of no importance. Study is an important principle when it leads to practice (see BT *Kid.* 40b, *Sifrei* Deut. 41). The pure life in the abstract, without taking on the form of the practical life, is not the aspiration of halakhic man or the man of God. When thought is transformed into will, and will turns into practical action that incorporates lovingkindness, justice, and righteousness, then the thinking, desiring, and achieving individual arrives at the level of cleaving to God: "But let him that glories, glory in this, that he understands and knows Me, that I am the Lord who exercises lovingkindness, justice, and righteousness on the earth" (Jer. 9: 23). The goal of knowledge is moral action, and so the term "those who know Him" includes more than what we see at first glance. "Those who know Him" are men of God, with achievement and aspiration, in whom study and practice, knowledge and will are blended together in a unified spiritual entity.'

[44] And, in his wake, Makbili in *Mifal mishneh torah*.

[45] I am grateful to Diana Lobel, who told me about this.

[46] See Kellner, 'Philosophical Themes'.

tradiction. The contradiction, in my view, derives from the tension between Maimonides' views and those of most Jewish sages.

In the controversy between nominalism and realism, one of the crucial philosophical disputes of the Middle Ages, Maimonides is a nominalist and says so in many places. For example, in the *Guide* he writes:

After what I have stated before about providence singling out the human species alone among all the species of animals, I say that it is known that no species exists outside the mind, but that the species and the other universals are, as you know, mental notions and that every existent outside the mind is an individual or a group of individuals. This being known, it is also known that the divine overflow that exists united to the human species, I mean the human intellect, is merely what exists as individual intellects—that is, what has overflowed toward Zayd, Umar, Khalid, and Bakr. Now if this is so, it follows necessarily according to what I have mentioned in the preceding chapter that when any human individual has obtained, because of the disposition of his matter and his training, a greater portion of this overflow than others, providence will of necessity watch more carefully over him than over others—that is to say, providence is, as I have mentioned, consequent upon the intellect. Accordingly divine providence does not watch in an equal manner over all the individuals of the human species, but providence is graded as their human perfection is graded.[47]

'No species exists outside the mind' means that the names of the species do not denote something existing in reality beyond the individuals themselves: there are horses; there is no 'horseness'. He who says that 'the divine overflow . . . [is] united to the human species' means to say (as we saw Rabbi Soloveitchik himself saying above) that specific individuals (Zayd, Umar, Khalid, and so forth[48]) can be granted this overflow. Since 'providence is consequent upon the intellect' and there are only individual intellects, there is no providence for universals (such as *keneset yisra'el*), only for individuals.[49]

[47] *Guide* iii. 18 (pp. 474–5).

[48] One supposes that traditionalist readers of Maimonides would be surprised by his choice of names here, instead of the more traditional Reuben and Simeon.

[49] Moshe Grimberg notes (personal communication): 'It could also be understood as stating that the divine overflow does not unite with the human species, but does unite with *Knesset yisra'el*. This reading is indeed mistaken, but I'm sure that this is how more than a few will understand this passage. This mistake does make some sense—*Knesset yisra'el* is not a species or a universal, but a kind of individual made up from all the Jews (as a house is made up of bricks), and Maimonides' nominalism does not necessarily apply to it. Clearly, however, Maimonides does not make such a claim. He does not ascribe an intellect to complex entities of this kind (states or nations), if he does at all acknowledge their real existence. Furthermore, the claim that *Knesset yisra'el* is a complex individual compels us to admit that it is not a form (meaning that the Jew has no unique form, different from all other humans, as Judah Halevi claimed). Were *Knesset yisra'el* a form that applies to individuals, it would be a universal and, therefore, not real either.'

At the end of this chapter in the *Guide* Maimonides again points out (in direct reference to the matter at stake here):

> It would not be proper for us to say that providence watches over the species and not the individuals, as is the well-known opinion of some philosophic schools. For outside the mind nothing exists except the individuals; it is to these individuals that the divine intellect is united. Consequently providence watches only over these individuals. Consider this chapter as it ought to be considered; for through it all the fundamental principles of the Law will become safe for you and conformable for you to speculative philosophic opinions; disgraceful views will be abolished; and the form of providence, as it is, will become clear to you.[50]

Providence does not apply to species: providence follows from a union with the divine overflow, which unites only with (individual) intellects and not with universals. Generally, 'outside the mind nothing exists except the individuals'. Universal names are merely names. There are Jews, but there is no people of Israel as a meta-historical entity that exists beyond the existence of specific Jews. Whoever understands this will understand through it 'the fundamental principles of the Law', will correctly grasp 'speculative philosophical opinions', witness the abolition of 'disgraceful views', and clearly apprehend 'the form of providence'.

Maimonides' nominalist view is also expressed in an unexpected place:

> All that the Holy God, blessed be He, created in His universe, falls into three divisions. Some are creatures consisting of substance and form, continuously coming into being and decaying. Such are bodies of human creatures and other animals, plants, and minerals. Others are creatures consisting of substance and form which do not however like those of the first category, change, from one body to another or from one form to another, but retain their form permanently in their substance, not varying like the members of the former class. Such are the heavenly spheres and the stars placed in them. Their substance is not like other substances nor are their forms like other forms. Others again are creatures that consist of form without substance. These are the angels. For the angels are not material bodies, but only forms distinguished from each other.[51]

There are precisely three types of creature in the world:

- Specific things made up of matter and form subject to generation and corruption (meaning that they exist for a defined period).

- Specific things made up of matter and form that are not subject to generation and corruption (meaning they exist eternally or since the creation of the world, namely the spheres and the stars). They are made up of matter

---

[50] *Guide* iii. 18 (p. 476).   [51] *MT* 'Laws of the Foundations of the Torah', 2: 3.

and form, but both their matter and their form differ from those making up the first kind of beings.

- Intellects separate from matter, having no matter at all (in religious terms, angels).[52]

Beyond that, there is nothing. What is missing here? Universals and general terms. So there are Jews, but there is no *keneset yisra'el*.

The passage from *The Emergence of Halakhic Man* quoted above shows that Rabbi Soloveitchik did understand Maimonides' position well, but did not always apply it consistently. Concerning the standing of the Jewish people, not only did he deviate from Maimonides' position (coming close to the 'fetishism' of Judah Halevi and Nahmanides); he also contradicted himself.

In *On Repentance*, Rabbi Soloveitchik discusses the halakhic standing of the Jewish people: 'a "communal sacrifice" has one sole owner, exactly as does an individual offering. Who is this owner? It is the entire community of Israel, which according to the law is not the sum total or arithmetic aggregate of such and so many individuals but a single, composite personality in its own right.'[53] How are we to understand the essence of this 'single, composite personality', which stands 'in its own right'?

On the one hand, Rabbi Soloveitchik's explanation fits Maimonides' view extremely well:

This definition of *Knesset Israel* as an independent entity has no relationship to the Kabbalah where it is represented by *sefirat malkhut* nor with Hasidism (which focuses upon the special sanctity of *Knesset Israel*); we are referring to a straightforward halakhic application, which has implications in several other areas where it is necessary to distinguish between the community of Israel as an aggregate of individuals and *Knesset Israel* as an independent, integral entity.[54]

Neither kabbalah nor hasidism grasps the essence of *keneset yisra'el* correctly—these approaches go beyond what we should learn from halakhah, the only source of Jewish thought. And what should we learn from halakhah about this matter? The people of Israel, *keneset yisra'el*, *kelal yisra'el*—these names are a 'straightforward halakhic application' and do not point to an entity that exists at the objective (or even at the mystical) level. Just as a corporation is a legal fiction, *keneset yisra'el* is nothing but a halakhic fiction.

Thus far the Maimonidean Rabbi Soloveitchik. On the previous page, however, a seemingly different approach emerges: 'The right of the Jewish People to the Land of Israel is not of an individual nature; it is a right accruing

---

[52] Kellner, *They Too Are Called Human* (Heb.), ch. 8.   [53] Soloveitchik, *On Repentance*, 115.
[54] Ibid. On the scholarly disputes hinging on R. Soloveitchik's approach to kabbalah, see D. Schwartz, *Challenge and Crisis* (Heb.), 303.

to the Jewish People as a whole ... The individual Jew's right to the Land of Israel is derived from the communal prerogative of *Knesset Israel* as a metaphysical entity.'[55] *Keneset yisra'el* is perceived here as 'a metaphysical entity' and not only as part of a 'straightforward halakhic application'.

This latter approach is the dominant one in Rabbi Soloveitchik's work. Gerald (Ya'akov) Blidstein, a disciple of Rabbi Soloveitchik, sums up: 'R. Soloveitchik often returns to the assertion that the Jewish community is a metaphysical entity.'[56] Blidstein cites a typical passage from Rabbi Soloveitchik's essay 'Community':

The community in Judaism is not a functional-utilitarian but an ontological one. The community is not just an assembly of people who work together for their mutual benefit, but a metaphysical entity, an individuality; I might say, a living whole. In particular, Judaism has stressed the wholeness and the unity of *Knesset Israel*, the Jewish community. The latter is not a conglomerate. It is an autonomous entity, endowed with a life of its own. We, for instance, lay claim to *Eretz Israel*. God granted the land to us as a gift. To whom did He pledge the land? Neither to an individual, nor to a partnership consisting of millions of people. He gave it to the *Knesset Israel*, to the community as an independent unity, as a distinct juridical metaphysical person. He did not promise the land to me, to you, to them; nor did He promise the land to all of us together. Abraham did not receive the land as an individual, but as the father of a future nation. The owner of the Promised Land is the *Knesset Israel*, which is a community persona.[57]

In these formulations, Rabbi Soloveitchik moves far away from Maimonides (and from his own formulations in other places): the Jewish people is an actual ontological entity.

Conclusions: Rabbi Joseph Soloveitchik and Maimonides

We have found evidence, then, of the very close spiritual bond between Rabbi Soloveitchik and Maimonides. We also saw one instance (providence) where

---

[55] Soloveitchik, *On Repentance*, 116. See also ibid. 137: 'The Jew who believes in *Knesset Israel* is a Jew who binds himself with inseverable bonds not only to the People of Israel of his own generation but to the community of Israel throughout the ages. How so? Through the Torah which embodies the spirit and the destiny of Israel from generation to generation unto eternity.'

[56] Blidstein, *Society and Self*, 77–104. This chapter is titled 'The Jewish People'. On this issue, see also Herskowitz, 'Soloveitchik's Endorsement'.

[57] Soloveitchik, 'The Community', 7. 'Judaism has stressed the wholeness and the unity of *Knesset Israel*, the Jewish community. The latter is not a conglomerate. It is an autonomous entity, endowed with a life of its own ... However strange such a concept may appear to the empirical sociologist, it is not at all a strange experience for the halakhist and the mystic, to

he shows a deep grasp of Maimonides' approach and presents it openly and boldly. We saw another instance (the essence of holiness) where he embraces a (very!) uncommon view of Maimonides without mentioning his name, but did not publish the book in which this approach appears during his lifetime. We saw yet another instance (the negation of an extra-halakhic philosophy in Judaism) where he interprets Maimonides as agreeing with his own view. Finally, we saw his inner conflict regarding the essence of the people of Israel: on the one hand, Rabbi Soloveitchik agrees with Maimonides that the uniqueness of the Jewish people is conveyed only at the halakhic level; on the other, he speaks about metaphysical uniqueness.

How should we understand these occurrences? In my view, an appropriate answer could only come from Rabbi Soloveitchik's basic stance—a matter that is halakhically irrelevant is not truly important from a Jewish perspective. The dispute between Maimonides, on the one hand, and almost every other figure in the history of Jewish thought since the Middle Ages on the other, is thus not truly interesting or important. Rabbi Soloveitchik, as a brilliant preacher and a prominent community leader, can allow himself to say what suits his preferences and those of his audience, even if they are in conflict not only with Maimonides but at times also with himself.

whom *Knesset Israel* is a living, loving and suffering mother' (ibid. 9). Another typical saying appears in Soloveitchik, *Philosophical Essays* (Heb.), 115: *keneset yisra'el* constitutes a 'mystical individual entity'. See also D. Schwartz, *Challenge and Crisis* (Heb.), 297–305.

THREE

Rabbi Abraham Isaac Kook and the Mystification of Maimonidean Rationalism

JAMES A. DIAMOND

Rabbi Kook's Defence of Maimonides

When modern Jewish thinkers staked out their own novel ground and advanced Jewish thought in the twentieth century, they looked back and engaged a foundational Jewish canon of scriptural and rabbinic texts. Maimonides looms so large in the development of Jewish law and thought that it is no exaggeration to consider his intellectual and jurisprudential legacy an integral part of that canon.[1] Just as it is difficult to classify thought as 'Jewish' unless it engages in some way with the Hebrew Bible or the Talmud, the same can be said of thought that ignores Maimonides. To engage him involves, at the same time, a re-engagement with the biblical and rabbinic sources he interpreted, which make up the common library of authentically Jewish intellectual discourse.

One such embodiment of modern Jewish authenticity in the twentieth century is Rabbi Abraham Isaac Hakohen Kook (1865–1935). It would be hard to identify a more seminal and influential modern Jewish figure: virtually all Jewish intellectual, literary, and activist currents intersected in him, be they halakhic, mystical, poetic, midrashic, political, or philosophical. The elaborate complexity of his thought reflects the dizzying and often tormented drama of his life. His formative biography begins as a talmudic prodigy (*ilui*) in the elite yeshiva of Volozhin under the leadership of Rabbi Naftali Tsevi Yehudah Berlin, the most prominent of rabbinic scholars in his time, and to whom Chapter 1 of this volume is devoted.[2] It then evolves through his passionate spiritual and political advocacy of Zionism, his rabbinic leadership of pre-state Jaffa, a stint as a pulpit rabbi in England, the establishment of his

---

[1] For a full-length treatment of this claim spanning Jewish thought from the medieval to the modern periods, see Diamond, *Maimonides and the Shaping of the Jewish Canon*.

[2] For a concise recent biography see Mirsky, *Rav Kook*.

own independent political movement, and ultimately his work as the founder of the Chief Rabbinate under the British Mandate and the first Ashkenazi Chief Rabbi. Much like Maimonides in his day, throughout Rabbi Kook's frenetic communal career his writing rarely ceased, leaving us a prodigious record of his thought. He was constantly driven by an irrepressible urge to disclose his most intimate reflections, no matter what the consequences might be: 'I must deliberate without any restraint, to pour onto paper without limits all my heart's thought.'[3]

His was a holistic approach to the theoretical and practical dimensions of existence, and he viewed all of these aspects as integrated components in an overarching monistic urge for proximity to the divine and knowledge of it. That urge extended to the diverse trends coursing through Jewish intellectual history, and he synthesized them all to forge his own new direction.[4] This spiritual 'pluralism' was generated by the profound love he had for the totality of existence, no matter what its origins, for, as he poeticized, 'the whole of Existence whispers its secret to me'.[5] This overwhelming oneness with the world is expressed throughout his voluminous literary corpus. It is a love whose surging intensity can be sensed throughout his writing, resistant to any inhibiting force, and which 'flows directly from the depth of the holy and the wisdom of the godly soul'.[6]

Shortly before his death in 1935, Rabbi Kook published a vigorous defence

[3] *Shemonah kevatsim* 1: 295 (p. 92), cited hereafter by section (collection), page number, and paragraph. This collection introduced, for the first time, many of R. Kook's writings as they were originally conceived and arranged, as opposed to the collections edited by his son and students that were previously available. For a close examination of its importance in understanding Kook and offering a new window into his thought, particularly in terms of chronological development, see Rosenak, 'Who's Afraid' (Heb.), and Garb, 'Prophecy, Halakhah and Antinomianism' (Heb.). Unless otherwise noted all translations from Hebrew are my own.

[4] Much has been written on pluralism and tolerance in R. Kook's thought. On the issue of his openness to various philosophical schools, in accordance with his metaphysical perspective that all ideas, if developed sincerely and properly motivated, stem from the same divine source, see Ish-Shalom, 'Tolerance and its Theoretical Basis' (Heb.). Ish-Shalom shows that every idea reveals some aspect of the divine in the world for R. Kook. An outstanding example of this magnanimous theology is his simultaneous embrace of both Spinoza and Bergson, even though they are philosophically antithetical to each other (ibid. 154).

[5] See Ezra Gellman's citation of this poem and his analysis of it in 'Poetry of Spirituality', 101–16.

[6] *Hadarav*, 194. For repeated articulations of this all-embracing love see the section entitled 'Great Is My Love', 188–95. Though all-encompassing, R. Kook's approach is not egalitarian, especially considering his view on the singularity of the Jewish people that pervades his writings. For example, he commences with an uncontrollable universal love for all existence, but the intensity of that love is graded, for 'my love for Israel is more passionate, deeper'. However, unlike other kabbalistic trends, that love is immediately repatriated back into its universal tendency for, despite the greater love for Israel, 'the internal urge spreads out by the power of its love to literally everything'.

of Maimonides against an Orthodox assault by Zev Yavetz in the twelfth volume of his *History of Israel* series, which excoriated Maimonides for importing alien Greek thought into Judaism in his *Guide of the Perplexed*. This assault was nothing new in the long history of struggle and controversy over Maimonides' thought since his own lifetime. Its twentieth-century incarnation is simply a testament to the power of Maimonides' intellectual legacy, which still stirs emotions as passionate as they were eight centuries ago.

Rabbi Kook argued that Maimonides' philosophical oeuvre is at its core grounded in consummately *Jewish* conceptions of prophecy, creation, ethics, and providence. He combined this substantive defence with a kind of pluralist notion about how to achieve holiness and true faith in God: different paths and ideas are legitimate for individual spiritual needs and constitutions; the Maimonidean teaching speaks to those who are more philosophically inclined (an opinion with which Maimonides would be in complete agreement).[7] But Rabbi Kook attributes the same pluralistic understanding to Maimonides himself, whose 'daring image of a compound light stands before us like a legendary figure'.[8] He thus opposes those who would split the 'philosopher' of the *Guide of the Perplexed* from the 'rabbi' of the *Mishneh torah*. Rabbi Kook advocated an integrated Maimonides, one whose halakhic-philosophical hybrid doubly illuminates Jewish thought for a new age.

True to his reverence for the 'Jewishness' of Maimonides' thought, throughout his vast corpus Rabbi Kook often refers to Maimonidean formulations and draws on them for the purpose of formulating his own kabbalistic ones.[9] Like any scholar steeped in rabbinic thought, Rabbi Kook continued to

---

[7] For a concise summary of R. Kook's defence see Davidson, *Moses Maimonides*, 423–5; Kook's position is that 'all approaches are legitimate as long as they are guaranteed by authoritative personages; whether or not they are compatible with one another is presumably immaterial' (p. 424).

[8] 'Le'aḥduto shel harambam', R. Kook's defence of Maimonides, is by no means a wholesale endorsement of it. As Lawrence Kaplan incisively argues, Kook also profoundly distinguishes himself from his medieval predecessor, especially on the roles of the intellect and imagination. In addition there are Maimonides' exclusive versus Kook's pluralistic paths to truth, Maimonides' fixed view of existence versus Kook's evolutionary one, and what I believe is the crucial difference: Maimonides' view that only the forms exist within God as opposed to Kook's view that 'all existents and all movements exist within God'; Kaplan, 'Rav Kook and the Philosophical Tradition', 54.

[9] R. Kook's oeuvre is so thoroughly imbued with kabbalistic thought that Gershom Scholem could celebrate it as 'a veritable *theologia mystica* of Judaism equally distinguished by its originality and the richness of the author's mind' in his *Major Trends*, 354 n. 17. For a comprehensive listing of first-hand evidence of his mystical 'nature', as well as scholarship on kabbalistic influences and strains in his thought (beginning with a pioneering article by Hillel Zeitlin in 1938), see J. Meir, 'Longing of Souls' (Heb.), 775–7. His thought reflects virtually the entire spectrum of Jewish mysticism that preceded him. For a panoramic listing of those influences see Fine, 'R. Abraham Isaac Kook', 25.

engage Maimonides throughout his prolific career.¹⁰ But Maimonides' own corpus, in its thoroughly systematic nature (whether halakhic or philosophical), could not be more antithetical to Rabbi Kook's.¹¹ Writing, for Maimonides, was anything but unrestrained, often couched in language of 'great exactness and exceeding precision', devised to exclude all readers except 'the remnant whom the Lord calls'.¹² Rabbi Kook conducts his own engagement by citing the classical biblical and rabbinic sources that appear in Maimonides, and creatively reinventing them in existential and kabbalistic ways. He thus translates Maimonides' philosophy into a new philosophical mysticism.¹³ This exercise is informed by a penchant for a fusion between the overt world of philosophy and the covert one of mysticism, for the 'revealed and rational *Weltanschauung* must be united with that of the concealed mystical, and out of both, in their comprehensive profuse details, poetry will blossom, courage will strengthen, beauty will be magnified, and knowledge increased'.¹⁴

In this blending of what are often considered to be conflicting sensibilities, all dimensions of human existence—literary, ethical, aesthetic, intellectual—coalesce in an acutely augmented spiritual whole.¹⁵ Rabbi Kook, then,

---

¹⁰ For a thorough and comprehensive overview of this engagement with Maimonides and the centrality of his thought for R. Kook, particularly with respect to the *Guide*, as well as secondary literature on the subject, see U. Barak, 'Formative Influence' (Heb.), 364–70. Most relevant to the topic here is ibid. 365–6 n. 14, regarding Kook's relationship to Maimonides' halakhic oeuvre, including the *Mishneh torah*.

¹¹ See R. Kook's own self-appraisal as being in 'no sense a systematic writer', in *Igerot hare'iyah*, 2: 243, as well as the testimony of his dedicated disciple David Cohen (the 'Nazir') in his introduction to the first volume of Kook's *Orot hakodesh*. See also Fox's rationale for this apparent 'disorder', since 'the lack of system is inherent in his subject matter and in his method'; Fox, 'Rav Kook', 80.

¹² *Guide* i. 34 (p. 75), citing Joel 3: 5. Pines notes, 'systematic expositions of the Aristotelian philosophers are often dislocated and broken up . . . in a word, order is turned into disorder' (p. lvii). However, this is intentional; Maimonides is systematic in his disorder.

¹³ In a series of studies over the past few decades, David Blumenthal has argued forcefully for this as authentically characteristic of Maimonides himself. He detects a stage reached after strictly rationalist pursuit where the intellectual contemplation of God is so intense and continuous as to properly be considered mystical. For the most recent formulation see Blumenthal, 'Maimonides' Philosophical Mysticism', pp. v–xxv, and the comprehensive bibliography at pp. xxii–xxv.   ¹⁴ *Shemonah kevatsim* 1: 602 (p. 192).

¹⁵ With this reconciliation of philosophy and mysticism, R. Kook can be considered the culmination of a long relationship between philosophy and kabbalah, beginning with such rabbinic thinkers as Rabad of Posquières. Twersky describes it as 'a complex dialectical attitude of partial rapprochement and withdrawal, if not hostility' in his *Rabad of Posquières*, 300. See also Scholem's description of Moses de León's relationship with philosophy in *Major Trends*, 203, and Elliot Wolfson, *Luminal Darkness*, 51 n. 32. Attempts such as Harold Bloom's to appreciate poetry and literature through an interpretative paradigm of kabbalistic conceptions can be viewed as a practical fruition of Kook's anticipation of the 'blossoming of poetry'. See Bloom, *Kabbalah and Criticism*, where he endorses the 'excessive audacity and extravagance' of kabbalistic reading and interpretation as a model for modern readers of literature (p. 48). Within the scholarly world there has also been a 'reconciliation', due in no small part to the

did not view himself as combating or overcoming the medieval privileging of reason, whose chief exponent was Maimonides, but rather as perfecting it, and Maimonides along with it. He considered his reworking of Maimonides a natural extension of Maimonides' thought. In fact, Rabbi Kook applied the methodology he ascribed to Maimonides' appropriation of Aristotelian philosophy to his very own appropriation of Maimonidean philosophy. He claimed that Maimonides 'did not follow Aristotle and his Arabic philosophical commentators blindly, but rather investigated, distinguished, and refined the matters . . . and after it became clear that there was no contradiction to the fundamentals of the Torah and he was convinced by them, he did not hide the truth, declaring that they were his opinions, and determined it proper to explain the Written and the Oral Laws in light of them'.[16] Rabbi Kook's exegetically tortured relationship with Maimonides is thus emblematic of a vibrant engagement with Maimonides' thought by major exponents of the hasidic and kabbalistic movements.[17] Rabbi Kook systematically appropriates Maimonidean positions, only to make them transcend their own rationalist limits in a kind of meta-metaphysics.[18]

The *Guide of the Perplexed* looms large in Rabbi Kook's concerted subversion of Maimonides' rationalist grounding of the cardinal commandments to know, love, and fear God. Along with affirming God's unity, these are the very first commandments enumerated by Maimonides in his *Book of the Commandments*, and the first to be halakhically explicated in the *Mishneh torah*.[19] Rabbi Kook accomplishes his subversion through an exegesis that incorporates a metaphorical image or prooftext that appears in the *Guide*. When

studies of Elliot Wolfson. A tribute to the success of Wolfson's efforts is the inclusion of his essay on Jewish mysticism in Frank and Leaman (eds.), *The History of Jewish Philosophy*, where he succinctly states that 'it is impossible to disentangle the threads of philosophy and mysticism when examining the texture of medieval Jewish mysticism in any of its major expressions. This entanglement is both historical and ideational' (pp. 450–98, esp. 453).

[16] Kook, 'Le'aḥduto shel harambam'.

[17] Dienstag offers a survey of this engagement, whose rationale, he notes, could also be R. Kook's, for 'despite the consensus that Maimonides is a proponent of the "mastery of the intellect"' while ḥasidut reflects the emotional and poetic current of Judaism, there persists a spiritual 'proximity between them'; Dienstag, 'The *Guide of the Perplexed*' (Heb.).

[18] In this exegesis of *Mishneh torah* R. Kook bears a special affinity to Habad's engagement with this work; see Jacob Gotleib's full-length study, *Rationalism in Hasidic Attire* (Heb.). The last leader of Habad, R. Menachem Mendel Schneerson, related to *Mishneh torah* 'on two levels, a rationalist and a kabbalistic one' (ibid. 40), which echoes R. Kook's approach.

[19] In an essay he wrote about Maimonides shortly before his death, R. Kook argued that *Mishneh torah* and the *Guide* are cut from the same cloth, and aggressively criticized those who would bifurcate the two; see Kook, 'Hamaor ha'eḥad', 115–17. As Dov Schwartz concludes in his close analysis of R. Kook's defence of Maimonides against his contemporary detractors, 'Kook drew no distinction between Maimonides in the *Mishneh torah* and Maimonides in the *Guide*'; Schwartz, 'Maimonides in Religious-Zionist Philosophy', 395.

examined closely, it targets both the *Mishneh torah* and the *Guide* in order to construct a new intellectualist halakhic mysticism, as will be shown, by reinventing those commandments which form the very bedrock of Jewish law and theology.[20]

Rabbi Kook also penned an early commentary, *Orot harambam*, on the *Book of Knowledge*, the first book in the *Mishneh torah* and the most philosophically informed part.[21] This commentary is methodical but fragmentary. As with many Jewish thinkers who wanted to co-opt Maimonides in order to advance their own thought, Rabbi Kook's co-opting is more of an eisegetical reinforcement of his own thought than an objective commentary.[22] This work, combined with other reflections scattered throughout Rabbi Kook's oeuvre, is instrumental in demonstrating how what appears as endorsement and positive averment actually amounts to repudiation and reinvention. The result is a harmonization and mystification of Maimonidean rationalism.[23]

The First Commandment: *Unknowing* God

At the commencement of each section of the *Mishneh torah* Maimonides tallies all the positive and negative commandments contained therein, and so Rabbi Kook's first substantive comment on the body of the work appears on its very first positive commandment, namely 'to know that there is a God [literally a 'primary existent', *matsui rishon*]'. Its argument revolves around a hyperliteral reading of it which emphasizes 'to know *there* is a God', taking the term 'there' (*sham*) as a locational referent to another realm of knowing. Rabbi Kook identifies two crucial epistemological levels with respect to God. They consist of 'knowledge acquired through things that are possible to know, that is recognition of Him through His actions' and 'that aspect of knowledge

---

[20] If David Blumenthal is correct in his interpretation of Maimonides' thought as an intellectual mysticism, then R. Kook's commentary may in fact be more properly classified as such rather than as a 'reinvention'.

[21] Indeed, Pines has argued that Maimonides' halakhic works, including the *Book of Knowledge*, are more radical in their Aristotelian formulations than the *Guide*; see Pines, 'Philosophical Purport'.

[22] Although the near-obsession in the rabbinic world with the study of *Mishneh torah* has not abated since Maimonides' time, as Allan Nadler has shown (see his 'The "Rambam Revival"'), rabbinic engagement with the *Guide* did not enjoy the same love-affair. There was a revival of its study after a long period of neglect and suppression in the latter decades of the 18th century. Although the study here focuses on what is another example of the long-standing exegetical tradition vis-à-vis *Mishneh torah*, it will become clear that the *Guide* looms prominently in the background.

[23] Yehuda Mirsky dates this composition to some time shortly after 1903 and R. Kook's first arrival in Palestine; see Mirsky, 'Rav Kook and Maimonides', 399 n. 9.

which is impossible to know'.[24] The term 'there' refers to the latter, superior form of knowledge, but a kind which is 'hidden' (*ne'elam*). It is a rigorous and methodical kind of *not knowing* which grasps its inaccessibility by establishing 'its parameters and the reasons preventing a complete knowledge of the divinity'. It bears emphasizing that Maimonides never explicitly wrote about any kind of human knowledge other than that first type identified by Rabbi Kook, in which God is known 'through His actions', and which relates to Maimonides' theory of attributes of action.[25] His actions are all that we can affirm of God, as opposed to direct attributes, which must be negated. Every attribute that is negated from God actually takes the negater further along towards a true conception of God, 'undoubtedly com[ing] nearer to Him by one degree'.[26]

In another context Rabbi Kook draws an analogy between Maimonides' negation of attributes and his 'negation of a purpose to the universe and the negation of reasons for the details of the commandments'.[27] Rabbi Kook argues that all these—telos of creation, divine attributes, and rationale for the commandments—share in an ineffability that exceeds our limited intellects. However, he concludes, all three are treated as one class by Maimonides, 'who did not negate them intrinsically from the essence of their reality, but only from the capacity of our expression'.[28] Maimonides himself, however, argues at great length that to affirm attributes of God is tantamount to inventing an imaginary being: 'an invention that is false; for he has, as it were, applied this term to a notion lacking existence as nothing in existence is like that notion'.[29] In other words, refraining from assigning positive attributes to God is not merely a matter of human incapacity but is a truth claim. Rabbi Kook's creative reading of 'there' leaves room for what Maimonides would consider to be a distortion of reality, or even idolatry. This remarkable midrashic play on one word lets extreme Maimonidean negative theology (apophatism) accommodate a meta-reality where God resides in the fullness of positive attributes.[30]

[24] *Orot harambam*, 171.

[25] See e.g. *Guide* i. 58–9 (pp. 134–43). For a recent and typically concise exposition of Maimonides' theory of attributes of action, see Seeskin, 'Metaphysics and its Transcendence', 83–91. As he states, 'They are not descriptions of God, but descriptions of what God has made or done' (p. 87).   [26] *Guide* i. 60 (p. 144).

[27] *Shemonah kevatsim* 6: 78 (p. 213). See Tamar Ross's discussion of R. Kook's view of divine attributes, in which the theistic conception of absolute incomparability or likeness between God and the world is not 'the absolute truth but a deficient perception'. In fact one ends up with a notion of God that is diametrically opposed to that of Maimonides, for 'it is only when we associate attributes with God himself . . . that [divinity] is disclosed in a form superior to that available to intellectual understanding'; Ross, 'The Concept of God in the Thought of Rabbi Kook' (Heb.), 46.   [28] *Shemonah kevatsim* 6: 78 (p. 213).   [29] *Guide* i. 60 (p. 146).

[30] This notion of divine attributes is another formulation in a long history of kabbalistic

Although Maimonides' negative theology may end in a philosophically informed ignorance, that ignorance is what ultimately lies within the purview of the human intellect. Rabbi Kook's suggestive interpretation of 'there' broadens the narrow intellectual straits to which Maimonides confined the religious enterprise and knowledge of God, in order to allow for faith.[31] This is an extraordinarily crucial exegetical move, for it anchors the entire *Mishneh torah* in a Kookian model of *homo religiosus*, for whom an exclusively intellectual mould is stifling. Pure rationalism stunts the religious spirit in its quest for proximity to God. Rational thought alone cannot adequately accommodate holiness within the Torah and the world, according to Rabbi Kook. One needs therefore to boost reason, to 'inject the components of reason which operate on the basis of their order and nature into the highest emanation of the holy spirit, to extract them from their confined and constricted existence in which they find themselves, to their expanses, to the world of supernal freedom'.[32]

Rabbi Kook's microscopic reading of Maimonides' inaugural formulation of the first commandment in the *Mishneh torah* thus 'injects' his own existential-kabbalistic thought into what is patently an Aristotelian formulation. Maimonides meant God as a 'primary existent' (*matsui rishon*) that lies within the scope of human knowing. In supplementing the Maimonidean rational realm with a hidden one, Rabbi Kook also resolves a longstanding 'contradiction' perceived by rabbinic thought between Maimonides' formulations in his *Book of the Commandments* and in the *Mishneh torah*, namely 'to believe' in God (*leha'amin*) versus to 'know' God (*leida*) respectively. Despite possible questions about comparing a Hebrew translation from Judaeo-Arabic in the former to the original Hebrew of the latter, this distinction is essential to Rabbi Kook's systematic derationalization of the *Mishneh torah*.[33]

---

struggles with the nature of the divine *sefirot* and Maimonides' theory of negative attributes. As Idel has demonstrated, 'Maimonides' theory of negative attributes was not accepted at all by the mystics . . . they negate the attributes from the *ein sof* (the hidden God) only to attribute them to the *sefirot*.' What I have argued here regarding R. Kook is another example in a long line of mystics who, Idel claims, 'view the negative attributes as an expression of the philosopher's inability to appreciate any positive ingredients'; Idel, 'Divine Attributes and Sefirot', 112.

[31] For a lucid analysis of faith in R. Kook's thought, see ch. 1 of D. Schwartz, *Faith at the Crossroads*, esp. 27–30, where he concludes that faith for Kook must transcend 'human epistemological or intellectual capabilities', since those only render an 'epistemological illusion'.

[32] *Shemonah kevatsim* 5: 88 (p. 233). As Bergman notes, for R. Kook rational reflection only presents a fragmentary and disconnected view of reality, while only the 'non-rational faculty of his inner vision and the power of his imagination' can 'push beyond the fragmentariness of conceptual knowledge and discover the underlying principle'; Bergman, 'Rav Kook: All Reality Is in God', 125.

[33] Much ink has been spilled in the rabbinic academies on the perceived contradiction between the first commandment listed in *Book of the Commandments* in the Ibn Tibbon translation, 'to believe' in the existence of God, and that of the *Mishneh torah*, which begins with

The multivalent language, he claims, captures the totality of the commandment to know God precisely, as it is fulfilled by a 'revealed knowledge and a hidden knowledge' at once. The hidden knowledge is real knowledge. 'There' leads you to the realm in which 'belief' is operative, and is captured by the formulation in the *Book of the Commandments*: 'for that aspect of knowledge defined as not knowing is perfected afterward clearly in the form of faith'.[34]

For Rabbi Kook the hidden realm that invokes faith is a point at which 'all knowledge is vitiated, and all classifications and strict logic are absolutely nullified as it ascends conceptually, there resides the hidden *shekhinah*, and there the divine revelation flickers like light that appears through the cracks "running and returning as the appearance of a flash of lightning" [Ezek. 1: 14].'[35] It is no coincidence that Rabbi Kook cites a key verse from Ezekiel's account of the chariot. He does so in order to remystify Maimonides' naturalistic exegesis of it.[36] He thus elevates it from its scientific, logical, and empirical framework to a realm where all such criteria break down in a kind of cosmic theological black hole.[37]

The first four words of the *Mishneh torah* (following the enumeration of commandments) are *yesod hayesodot ve'amud haḥokhmot* ('the foundation of foundations and the pillar of wisdoms'). Rabbi Kook assigns these words to the two realms of knowledge that he posits: since the not-known is

---

the commandment 'to know' that Being. What Ibn Tibbon translated as 'to believe' is *itiqad*, 'to know', and therefore the *Mishneh torah* is perfectly consistent with *Book of Commandments*. See Nuriel, 'The Concept of Belief' (Heb.), 43, and Chaim Heller's first note on the first commandment in his edition of *Book of the Commandments* (Heb.), 35. See further the discussion of this issue in Ch. 2 above, on R. Soloveitchik.

[34] *Orot harambam*, 171.

[35] *Shemonah kevatsim* 6: 278 (p. 279). This closely parallels the affinity of R. Nahman of Bratslav—a major hasidic antagonist of Maimonidean rationalism—for the maxim 'the ultimate knowledge is that we do not know'; for an example see *Likutei moharan* i: 24: 8. See also Rapoport-Albert, 'Self-Deprecation'. For the most recent examination of this tenet in Bratslav thought, see Mark, *Mysticism and Madness*, 230, where his description anticipates R. Kook's formulation here: 'This knowing, yet not knowing, this attaining yet not attaining, is the ultimate knowledge.'

[36] See Davidson's decoding of Maimonides' account, which reads 'Ezekiel's vision as a figurative depiction of the universe outside of God'; Davidson, *Moses Maimonides*, 348–9.

[37] One of the most striking implications of this meta-rational realm in R. Kook's thought is his approval of the medieval Islamic *mutakallimūn*'s notion that everything that can be imagined as possible 'in truth exists' (*Shemonah kevatsim* 2: 9 (p. 256)), in stark contrast to Maimonides' deprecation of it. While Maimonides eschews and disparages their blurring of the imagination and reality, Kook approves of their position that whatever can be imagined as possible does indeed exist in the sense that 'the epistemological function of the imagination should be asserted joyfully'. See Carmy, 'Rav Kook's Theory of Knowledge', 195. See also Ish-Shalom's discussion, which presents Kook's qualified endorsement of the Kalam as one that knits together Kalam's necessary possibility with Maimonides' necessary existence to render a hybrid formulation; Ish-Shalom, *Between Rationalism and Mysticism*, 41–2.

inaccessible by science or philosophy and is therefore more sublime than its rational counterpart, it corresponds to the 'foundation of foundations' (*yesod ha-yesodot*), while that which is known corresponds to 'wisdom' or sciences (*amud haḥokhmot*). This pair, i.e. 'foundation' = knowing-of-the-not-known and 'wisdom' = knowing-of-the-known, in turn corresponds to what follows in the first four chapters of the *Mishneh torah* as the account of the chariot (*ma'aseh hamerkavah*) and the account of Creation (*ma'aseh bereshit*).[38] The latter correlates to 'the known by way of actions, that part of knowledge possible to know, while the account of the chariot images the knowledge impossible to know, the recognition of the hiddenness of the hidden'.[39] Thus, the entire section on the two most important disciplines in the Maimonidean curriculum, which together comprise the knowledge of God, are informed by Rabbi Kook's kabbalistic epistemology.

In this way Rabbi Kook tempered Maimonides' elitism, whose onerous intellectual demands exclude all but a minute number of individuals from ever fulfilling the primary commandment to know God. Rabbi Kook views scientific progress as a means of increasing worldwide familiarity with the account of the Creation, 'which progressively becomes an exoteric science that is investigated publicly'.[40] Understanding the Creation account through the exoteric sciences is a vital stage towards the more speculative and esoteric realm which is the subject matter of the chariot. The Creation account provides 'essential forces to opening the gates of the account of the chariot, that is the supernal channel, which vitalizes the senses and the desires, the cognitions and the emotions, to grasp the depth of a formidable spirituality into the origin of eternal and perfect life'.[41]

This core bi-dimensional epistemology continues in the section where Maimonides discusses the laws governing the names of God. He immediately describes those names as 'the holy, the pure' (*hakedoshim tehorim*).[42] Rabbi Kook defines 'holy' here as 'something separated and set apart beyond

---

[38] *MT* 'Laws of the Foundations of the Torah', 2: 11, describes the subject matter of the first two chapters as the 'account of the chariot', and 4: 10 dedicates chs. 3 and 4 to the subject matter of the 'account of the Beginning'. For further discussion on these two subjects in Maimonides, see Chs. 5 and 6 in the present volume, on Rabbis Wasserman and Kotler.

[39] *Orot harambam*, 171–2.

[40] *Shemonah kevatsim* 1: 597 (p. 164). R. Kook was a staunch advocate of the public dissemination of esoterica to 'all hearts', even to those 'who have not reached that measure of expansive knowledge for the acquisition of broad and deep knowledge'; Kook, *Orot hatorah*, 56. See Garb, *The Chosen Will Become Herds*, 23–9. Indeed, the very title of this book is taken from a poem by Kook that expresses the hope that his kabbalistic thought 'which had hitherto been espoused by elitist circles ("the Chosen") only, would turn into a mass movement of sorts ("the herds")' (ibid. 27).   [41] Garb, *The Chosen Will Become Herds*, 27.

[42] *MT* 'Laws of the Foundations of the Torah', 6: 1.

comprehension', while 'pure' means 'a clear comprehension untainted by false imaginings'.[43] Thus, these epithets, as objects of human contemplation somehow capturing God's being, comprise both realms.[44] Rabbi Kook then hones in on the seemingly innocuous omission of the conjunctive 'and' between the two adjectives 'holy' and 'pure' in order to corroborate his theory that knowledge of God is constituted simultaneously by a knowing and a not-knowing. The grammatical quirk indicates that the two terms are inseparable. As such they combine into 'one single notion to be pronounced in one breath: holy pure'.[45]

Rabbi Kook's attempt to make the divine epithets subsume both realms of knowledge allows him to import his 'theory' of names, in which all names bridge the distance between existence and the *ein sof*. This latter divine dimension is precisely that uppermost aspect of God within the kabbalistic sefirotic realm that is beyond all knowing, as 'they sustain everything and call all to being'.[46] But Rabbi Kook's exegetical manipulation of the *Mishneh torah*'s syntax elides Maimonides' own philosophical taxonomy of divine names, which he developed in the *Guide*. There he offers a noetic distinction between the Tetragrammaton and the other sobriquets, where the former signifies God's *essence* stripped of any association with material existence, since it is the only one midrashically privileged with having preceded the world. It therefore conveys an ontology absolutely distinct from creation.[47] It also 'is not indicative of an attribute but of simple *existence* and nothing else' (emphasis mine),[48] while all other divine names 'derive from actions'.[49] Rabbi Kook infuses all the names with the hidden dimension of 'not knowing' which transcends the essential-derivative classification, in order to incorporate the *ein sof*, or the 'hidden realm' that indiscriminately inhabits the expression or utterance of any name of God.[50] As Rabbi Kook poetically expresses in a

---

[43] *Orot harambam*, 182.

[44] R. Kook's use of these two terms, holy and pure, here parallels the different senses in which he uses 'intellect' throughout his corpus, as delineated by Ish-Shalom. At times it designates a 'secular intellect' based on reason, and at others a 'holy intellect' that signifies mystical perception; Ish-Shalom, *Between Rationalism and Mysticism*, 185.

[45] *Orot harambam*, 182.   [46] See *Shemonah kevatsim* 1: 756 (p. 241).

[47] *Guide* i. 61 (p. 149), adapting *Pirkei derabi eli'ezer*, 3.

[48] *Guide* i. 64 (p. 156).   [49] Ibid. 61 (p. 147).

[50] Due to the unsystematic nature of R. Kook's literary corpus, which consists of spiritual diaries rather than treatises, written in a stream-of-consciousness-like presentation, his thought is 'often inconsistent and paradoxical' on this and other issues. As Bokser describes it, the entries in these diaries 'read like poems, or prose-poems, and they are independent meditations, each born in the newness of the experience that continued to unfold day by day'; Kook, *Essential Writings of Abraham Isaac Kook*, 3. There are instances when Kook also resorts to distinctions between names. See e.g. *Shemonah kevatsim* 2: 5 (p. 294). Also on the distinction drawn in this passage between *elohim* and *YHVH*, see the analogy Rosenberg draws between it and Kant's

passionate paean to God: 'The limitless [*ein sof*] light inhabits the expression of the name, the expression of *elohim*, and all the names and sobriquets that the human heart conceives and contemplates as the soul ascends higher and higher.'[51] His exegetical overlay aligns Maimonides with his own theological passion.

Abraham: The Lovesick Philosopher or Lovesick Mystic

Maimonides juridically formulates the love of God, which is the third commandment, in erotic terms. Ideal love is analogous to love for a woman that is so infatuating as to exclusively occupy the mind, even while the lover is engaged in life's normally distracting routines. The historical figure emblematic of such love is Abraham. Although this is the overarching theme of the entire Song of Songs, the biblical verse that captures its obsessive single-mindedness is 'for I am sick with love' (2: 5).[52] Maimonides identifies that love with the quest for knowledge, the kind of intellectual activity that demands 'a dedication to the understanding and comprehension of those sciences and disciplines which will inform him concerning His master, as far as it lies within human capacity to understand and apprehend'.[53] We have already encountered this key verse in Chapter 1, where we examined its crucial role in the subversion of Maimonides' intellectualism by Netsiv, Rabbi Kook's teacher. It is useful to summarize the master's engagement in order to better appreciate his student's own engagement with Maimonides. Netsiv directly challenges Maimonides' reading of the verse and transforms it from a description of love's ideal state to a plea for its attainment. Netsiv understands 'sickness' in its ordinary sense as a deficiency or abnormality. The verse therefore means that 'I lack love of God . . . thus the Song reverts to prayer and supplication to attain love of God by way of Torah'.[54] This reading is a corollary of his anti-naturalist stance, since it posits human dependence on God in all of one's endeavours. No activity can be conducted nor any goal achieved independent of divine will, not even love of God. No matter how much the lover

---

phenomenon and noumenon. *Elohim* is the phenomenon, or nature, 'veiled in the essence of being', while *YHVH* is the noumenon which 'subsumes past, present, and future, transcending temporal categories'; Rosenberg, 'R. Kook and the Blind Serpent' (Heb.), 328. However, the general thrust of his thought is to avoid pigeonholing God with the various names.

[51] *Shemonah kevatsim* 1: 164 (p. 66). For a complete translation of this as a poem see Kook, *Essential Writings of Abraham Isaac Kook*, 373. R. Kook's theory of names as described here coincides with that of a mystical predecessor, Joseph Gikatilla, as described by Scholem: 'The Torah as published is completely founded and built on the tetragram; it is woven from the tetragram and its qualifying names, that is from the divine epithets which are derivable from it and emerge in it at any given moment'; Scholem, 'The Name of God', 179.

[52] *MT* 'Laws of Repentance', 10: 2–3.   [53] Ibid. 10: 11.   [54] *Metiv shir*, 28.

exerts himself, the relationship is only fully realized by the grace of the divine beloved.

Love's vehicle is philosophy for Maimonides, and the outer limits of its reach are confined to the borders of the mind. In his quest to transcend the boundaries of human reason, Rabbi Kook expands the scope of Maimonides' lovesick philosopher. For him, Song of Songs 2: 5 does not connote a philosophically obsessive mind. On the contrary, it conveys a frustration with the limits of the philosophical enterprise, for 'all that is clearly defined is profane in relation to the supernal holiness for which I yearn, "for I am sick with love"'.[55] Rabbi Kook is not extolling such love here, but rather lamenting its debilitating effects, which trap him within the empirical boundaries of existence and the theoretical capacity of the mind. He is wont to protest against the barriers of academic study: 'How difficult is study for me, how difficult it is to accommodate oneself to details!'

Rabbi Kook's exasperation with a spiritually immobilizing philosophical love, caught up as it is with examining the endless scientific minutiae of existence, spurs him to seek elsewhere in order to overcome its spiritually retardant effects. He escapes the totality of mundane human existence and allows his soul to 'roam' (shatah) in the expanses of heaven 'which neither the walls of the heart, nor of conduct, nor of ethics, or logic, or etiquette can suppress, beyond whatever can be classified, beyond all pleasure, all pleasantness and beauty, beyond all beyondness for "I am sick with love"'.[56] This soaring of Rabbi Kook's soul derationalizes Maimonides' typology of Abraham, who 'roams' the heavens in sustained philosophical reflections on the heavenly bodies which present irrefutable proof for the existence of God.[57] For Rabbi Kook, Abraham's mind does not probe and investigate the heavens as objects of reflection, but glides freely within them in a liberating flight from every dimension of earthly existence.[58]

---

[55] Shemonah kevatsim 3: 222 (p. 86); Hadarav, 42.
[56] Hadarav, 42; Shemonah kevatsim 3: 279 (p. 102).   [57] MT 'Laws of Idolatry', 1: 3.
[58] R. Kook's lovesick ideal transcends the historical condition and thus allows for piercing through the temporal to the timeless. For a penetrating discussion of kabbalistic conceptions of time that is pertinent to Kook, see the chapter 'Linear Circularity / (A)Temporal Poetics' in Wolfson, Alef, Mem, Tau. His conclusion is equally applicable to Kook in that it probes 'another dimension of temporality, a "metaphysical" as opposed to a "physical" conception of time that well applies to the eternal', or what he terms a 'time-devoid-of-time' (ibid. 81). It is no coincidence that R. Akiva is the one who declares the Song of Songs to be 'the Holy of Holies', since he is the very same one who could laugh at the sight of the Temple's ruins in anticipation of its prophetically guaranteed restoration. As Kook explains, Akiva's love was so intense as 'to leave no room for focus on the terrifying present which he appreciated as a cloud passing by the sun'. See Kook, 'Song of Songs' (Heb.), 513. This would also explain Akiva's Herculean ability to overcome intolerable physical torture as a historically contingent condition that will pass. At that scene Akiva literally sees the rays of morning light signalling a halakhically mandated time for prayer.

Paralleling Maimonides' historical reconstruction of Abraham's rediscovery of monotheism, Rabbi Kook also portrays Abraham's discovery of God after a prolonged period of idolatrous ideology that virtually effaced monotheism from human consciousness. However, Abraham *reignites* the world with God, rather than *reacquainting* it with him. Rather than prove God's existence rationally and persuade others of the same, Rabbi Kook's Abraham revitalizes the world with the life force that courses through it. Rabbi Kook writes that he 'perceives the joy, the light that is prepared for all, for all life, for every soul, the divine expanse that calls to existence "Let there be light", that calls to every detail, that is replete with happiness, greatness, height and satisfaction, goodness and strength, love and sweetness'.[59]

Abraham's Calling: Philosopher or Mystic?

The divine 'call' that permeates all of existence is reciprocated by Rabbi Kook's Abraham in a radical reorientation of what is arguably Maimonides' favourite verse, 'and he called the name of the Lord God of the world' (Gen. 21: 33).[60] Like Maimonides, Rabbi Kook seizes on the midrashic career of Abraham as a smasher of idols, an iconoclast in the most literal sense. That violence (against objects, not human beings) conveys the forceful nature of Abraham's call 'to the radiance, the one God, God of the world',[61] or, more correctly, 'everlasting God'. Rabbi Kook replaces the Maimonidean content of the call— 'the existence of the deity and the creation of the world in time by that deity being comprised in that call'[62]—with light and mystical illumination. Abraham doesn't *re-educate* humanity about two forgotten postulates, but rather *stimulates* a consciousness that had been dormant. He awakens the divine reality inherent in existence ever since the primordial divine 'call' of Creation. Maimonides' Abrahamic call is an *educational* announcement, while Rabbi Kook's is an *existential* calling, a longing for one's own innate divinity that is shared with all of existence.

[59] *Shemonah kevatsim* 1: 102 (p. 35). Rabbi Kook speaks in personal terms, and these sentiments about the expansiveness of his own soul—its capacity to embrace all of existence and penetrate to the very essence of all Being—are consistent with his self-perception as a hasidic *tsadik*. As Smadar Cherlow demonstrates in her examination of *Shemonah kevatsim*, the diaries are not simply those of a mystic but of one who considered himself possessed of all the powers, duties, and goals of a hasidic *rebbe* in line with all the connotations of the phrase *tsadik yesod olam*. See Cherlow, 'Mystical Mission' (Heb.).

[60] Abraham's calling 'in the name of the Lord, God of the world' is a reference to Gen. 21: 33, whose significance to Maimonides cannot be overstated; it is employed as the epigraph not only to the *Guide* but to virtually all his writings, as noted by Lieberman, *Hilkhot hayerushalmi*, 5 n. 7. See also Kafih's comment in his Hebrew translation of the *Guide* that this exhibits Maimonides' own perception of the *Guide* as a successor to the call begun by Abraham; *Guide* i. 1 n. 1.

[61] *Shemonah kevatsim* 1: 102 (p. 30).   [62] *Guide* iii. 29 (p. 516).

That call perpetuated by Abraham evokes another image of the Maimonidean Abraham, which picks up on Isaiah's admonishment: 'Look to the rock you were hewn from, to the quarry you were dug from, look back to Abraham your father' (Isa. 51: 1–2). For Maimonides the verse mandates an assimilation of Abraham's ethical and religious postures, to 'adhere to his religion, and acquire his character, inasmuch as the nature of a quarry ought to be present in what is hewn from it'.[63] Abraham's 'religion' was devoid of any commandments (besides circumcision) and consisted of the central monotheistic teachings regarding the unity and existence of a creator God. Abraham, in his role as 'rock' (*tsur*), resonates with its metaphorical meaning, attributed to it in Maimonides' lexicography, when referring to God in the Bible as 'the principal and efficient cause of all things other than Himself'. The human 'rock' pioneers the philosophical teaching signified by the monotheistic 'Rock'.

Rabbi Kook appropriates the same imagery of a rock and quarry, but reinvents rather than replicates Maimonides' exegesis. He encases it in an existentially kabbalistic overlay: 'From the depths of the soul will Israel call that which the rock called, from which it was hewn . . . to pursue what the universal soul of existence cries out for in its chains: "Quest for me, enquire of me, and live".'[64] In Rabbi Kook's hands the relationship of a rock and quarry builds on the link between Israel and its founding ancestor, Abraham, as a paradigm of the perpetual relationship between individual souls and the universal soul of all being. The rock excavated from the quarry bears its origins within itself. So too the human soul that originates in the divine soul of all being must seek out the origins for which it 'calls', and that merger is the ultimate destination of its soul-searching odyssey.[65]

Rabbi Kook subtly changes Abraham's proclamation, which Maimonides is so fond of citing, from the 'name of the Lord' (*YHVH*), 'God' (*el*) of the world to 'the radiance, the one God [*el*], the God [*el*] of the world'. Rabbi Kook strategically omits 'name' and substitutes the cognomen *el* for the Tetragrammaton to distinguish himself from Maimonides' philosophical construct of the call. 'Name' (*shem*) and the unique divine epithet *YHVH*, in the Maimonidean sense, tend to connote an objectification of the deity which somehow

---

[63] Ibid. i. 16 (p. 42).   [64] *Shemonah kevatsim* 1: 103 (p. 35).

[65] Zionism, for R. Kook, is a national expression of this call in a time of spiritual decline when individuals are incapable of hearing the call, and so 'it is necessary for the nation to call from its innermost being, just as a great individual does from his innermost being, and this essential call in the name of the Lord exists as a national phenomenon exclusively in Israel' (Kook, *Arpilei tohar*, 28). See Schatz [Uffenheimer], 'Utopia and Messianism' (Heb.), for a discussion of this and other passages which view this new consciousness as 'the crystallization of the messianic idea'; 21.

captures God's precise nature and essence. As opposed to all other appellations, which are derivative, YHVH is the 'original name that indicates His essence', and 'it alone is indicative of the essence without associating any other notion with it'.[66] Far too reductionist for Rabbi Kook, the very word 'name' in Hebrew denotes a term or a definition. The attempt to classify God terminologically is an exercise that would distort his boundlessness. That no epithet is adequate, and therefore that each is adequate, is expressed elsewhere in another of Rabbi Kook's God-intoxicated paeans to love for the Infinite, mentioned previously:

> I am saturated with love for God [*elohim*]. I know that what I seek, what I love, cannot be called by any name [*shem*]. How could that which is greater than everything [*hakol*], greater than the good [*hatov*], greater than the essence [*hamahut*], greater than being [*hahavayah*] be called by a name? Yet I love, and I still say I love God [*elohim*]. The limitless [*ein sof*] light inhabits the expression of the name, the expression of *elohim*, and all the names and sobriquets that the human heart conceives and contemplates as the soul ascends higher and higher.[67]

Such sentiments target the Maimonidean project regarding the names of God,[68] which classifies them according to philosophical distinctions, and which aims at limiting the proliferation of divine names. That project, for Rabbi Kook, sacrifices the relational dimension with the divine for the sake of philosophical clarity, and therefore ends in spiritual frustration.

Fear of God: Limiting Human Reason or Overcoming It?

Though Maimonides' conception of fear of God is a complex one, in the *Mishneh torah* it is defined as the result of supreme intellectual endeavour. Fear immediately follows the all-encompassing appreciation of existence inspired by love, as a deeply felt intellectual humility in the face of such a vast and complex creation. Once the intellectual goals of love are achieved, one 'immediately recoils from fear and terror. He knows he is a small, lowly, dark creature with an insignificant and limited intellect, who stands before the Perfect Intellect.'[69] As Howard Kreisel astutely notes, while love seeks union with its beloved, in the case of God 'fear serves to preserve the gap between

---

[66] *Guide* i. 61 (p. 149).
[67] *Shemonah kevatsim* 1: 164 (p. 66). For a complete translation of this as a poem see Kook, *The Lights of Penitence*, 373.
[68] See also e.g. *Shemonah kevatsim* 1: 756 (p. 241) and 1: 883 (p. 282). He also expresses the Nahmanidean kabbalistic view that the entire Torah comprises the names of God; *Shemonah kevatsim* 2: 146 (p. 335).   [69] *MT* 'Laws of the Foundations of the Torah', 2: 2.

the individual and the object of fear'. Any possibility of *unio mystica* which, left unchecked, would be the logical end of love, is thereby frustrated.[70]

For Maimonides, love is the primary driving force advancing the intellectual process to know God. Fear curbs that very same drive with a sobering humility that appreciates its own limits and is a function of it.[71] But Rabbi Kook reverses these priorities, and considers what the intellect has gained to be a substrate that can be transformed and elevated towards the ultimate goal of *unio mystica*. This is anathema to Maimonides' original curriculum, which terminates at the mind's limits.[72] For Rabbi Kook, purely rational thought cannot adequately accommodate the fullness of the holy within the Torah and the world. Fear of God is not a function of intellectual love but is rather 'a deeper wisdom based on a *Weltanschauung* that is more internal, and provides a deeper foundation for science and Torah, whether sacred [*kodesh*] or mundane [*ḥol*]'.[73]

In order to corroborate this fear-based wisdom as the only authentic wisdom, in distinction to that acquired by reason, Rabbi Kook cites Job 28: 28: 'Behold [*hen*] the fear of the Lord is wisdom'. A rabbinic play on the word *hen* renders the verse 'Only fear of the Lord is wisdom', since *hen* in Greek means 'one'.[74] By citing this rabbinic 'translation' of Job 28: 28 endorsing fear of God as the only true wisdom, Rabbi Kook reorients it as a direct assault on the Maimonidean intellectual hierarchy of reason-based fear and love. In its talmudic setting it corroborates the notion that fear is 'unique' in that it is valued by God above all else.[75] Rabbi Kook uses this rabbinic prioritization of fear to demote reason, the tool normally associated with generating wisdom.

[70] Kreisel, *Maimonides' Political Thought*, 266. Though I agree with Kreisel's position, it must be noted that Maimonides does speak of conjunction and unification with God through apprehension in *Guide* iii. 51 (pp. 618–28), though by 'God', Maimonides means the Active Intellect. For recent discussion, see Freudenthal, 'Philosophical Mysticism', esp. 123–5. Instrumental in this debate is the adoption by Maimonides of Aristotle's threefold unity of intellect which, as Freudenthal argues, in its cognitive identity between subject and object 'mysticism follows when man knows God and pantheism of some sort follows when God apprehends the world' (ibid. 122).

[71] It must be noted that, for Maimonides, humility is one of the two character traits that one must cultivate in the extreme, deviating from the normally recommended golden mean. See *MT* 'Laws of Ethical Qualities', 2: 3, and the analysis by Frank, 'Humility as a Virtue', who argues that extreme meekness is a requisite for an act of *imitatio Dei*, not the actual act.

[72] Mirsky, 'An Intellectual and Spiritual Biography', demonstrates that in *Musar avikha*, a treatise composed by R. Kook in his pre-Palestine years, he distinguishes himself from Maimonides on precisely this issue. As Mirsky articulates it: 'While for Maimonides the summit of the spiritual practice was reaching the final limit of one's intellectual abilities and finding equanimity at that stopping-point, for Rav Kook, emerging from the Kabbalistic tradition, the final end of intellectual exertion is the mix of self-realization and self-dissolution that is *devequt*' (ibid. 194).   [73] *Shemonah kevatsim* 3: 220 (p. 85).   [74] See BT *Shab.* 31b.

[75] See for example Rashi's comment on BT *Shab.* 31b on the meaning of the verse with its Greek overlay: '"*Hen*" *is fear of the Lord*—fear is unique in the world.'

Fear is not simply unique, but constitutes the ultimate reality of the world as it is anchored in the sefirotic realm of kabbalistic theology. Rational knowledge gained empirically and logically is superficial and, in Rabbi Kook's words, 'simply skirts the outer surface of ideas which in truth are not included within wisdom'.[76] Rabbi Kook thus compounds his subversion of Maimonides' valorization of human reason by a rabbinic appropriation which enlists Greek, the culture and language synonymous with rationalist thought, to undermine its own reverence for reason. What Rabbi Kook has done exegetically is to reverse the Maimonidean project: Maimonides translated Hebrew conceptually into Greek, while Rabbi Kook makes Greek speak the language of kabbalah! He thus repatriated Hebrew back to its pristine sense, inverting the route along which rationalism had previously steered it.

This inversion not only subverts Maimonides' theoretical underpinnings of fear but also extends to its practical consequences. For Maimonides, the fear invoked by the intellectual passion of love manifests itself in a patient progression through the lengthy, painstaking, and rigorously methodical pedagogical curriculum requisite for intellectual perfection. This is most vividly embodied in the biblical image of Moses covering his face at the burning bush. The seductive lure of ultimate noetic truth should not cause one to 'from the outset, strain and impel his thoughts toward the apprehension of the deity; he rather should feel awe and refrain and hold back until he gradually elevates himself. It is in this sense that it is said "And Moses hid his face for he was afraid to look upon God" [Exod. 3: 6].'[77] Fear, for Moses, translates into a supreme moment of intellectual humility in restraint of a passion that outstrips his intellectual capacity in intensity and preparedness. That humility is metaphorically signified by the gesture of hiding his face.

In distinction, Rabbi Kook expresses anguish time and again over the dangers of being mired in the details demanded by such exacting requirements, ultimately obfuscating rather than enlightening. The tedium of reasoned investigation stifles the natural rhythm of the human being: 'The heart is restless to innovate incessantly, to innovate in a gushing and flowing manner because that is the nature of the soul, that it should flow like a stream. And what holds it back? Preliminaries, information, suggestions, resolu-

---

[76] *Shemonah kevatsim* 3: 220 (p. 85). Kaplan argues that R. Kook and Maimonides move in opposite directions on the love of God: Maimonides begins with an intellectual process that becomes imbued with passion, while Kook 'begins with a passionate, intuitive, non-inferential, and non-intellectual love of God' that is intellectually refined. See Kaplan, 'Rav Kook and the Philosophical Tradition', 53, where he succinctly contrasts them as a Maimonidean 'pathos of intellect' and a Kookian 'intellectualized passion', and id., 'The Love of God'. I do not believe Kook's love ends in intellectualized passion but, as I argue here, it transcends the intellect altogether towards a 'wisdom' that has been completely decoupled from its rational basis.

[77] *Guide* i. 5 (p. 29).

tions. These are all incidental matters that cannot in any way stifle the rushing of the spirit.'[78] Systematic thought obscures the secrets submerged in one's innermost being, which are 'immeasurably more valuable than inventiveness and philosophizing by means of the labour of the intellect and efforts of thought'.[79] Rabbi Kook repeatedly expresses an existential angst that defies the philosophical quest. The determination of the needs of one's innermost being is a 'riddle' that 'cannot be solved by intellect and reason but rather by plunging deeply into the aspiration of the soul, into the very foundation of its being'.[80]

Rabbi Kook implicitly dissociates himself from Maimonides on the dangers of intellectual arrogance. This is an issue on which his position comes into focus only when considered contrapuntally to that of Maimonides, for whom the antithetical biblical model to Moses' humility at the burning bush is the 'nobles of Israel' who desired to see God (Exod. 24: 9–11). They 'were overhasty, strained their thoughts, and achieved apprehension, but only an imperfect one'.[81] Maimonides then identifies the specific nature of their misapprehension as an anthropomorphically tainted conception of God, 'inasmuch as corporeality entered into it [their apprehension] to some extent'. Any belief in God that is tainted by corporeality is, for Maimonides, tantamount to idolatry, and poses the most serious notional threat to monotheism: 'For there is no profession of unity, unless the doctrine of God's corporeality is denied.'[82]

It is no coincidence that intellectual arrogance leads to corporealization of God for Rabbi Kook as well, and thus to idolatry, but in a very different sense. Though Maimonides also acknowledges the outer limits of the human intellect, he allows for a certain intellectual proximity to God via a rigorous series

---

[78] *Hadarav*, 64.

[79] Ibid. 66. This underlies the unsystematic nature of R. Kook's corpus, which has become most evident only since the relatively recent publication of *Shemonah kevatsim*. Until its release, exposure to Kook's thought was through the lens of his disciple, David Cohen (the Nazir), whose philosophical bent led him to systematize and thematize it. A useful analogy might be talmudic law as processed through Maimonides' *Mishneh torah*, which disentangled a diffuse concatenation of subjects into an orderly whole shaped by jurisprudential theory that infuses it with new meaning. Before the publication of *Shemonah kevatsim*, Dison, '*Orot hakodesh*: Re-edited' (Heb.), perceptively attempted to restructure the Nazir's edition of one of the *Orot* collections. Her effort was informed by the detection of an imaginative, intuitive consciousness rather than a philosophical one, thus retrieving its original form.

[80] *Hadarav*, 40. Habad hasidic thought is influential here in its introduction of what Scholem identifies as 'the distinctive feature of the new school . . . that the secrets of the divine realm are presented in the guise of mystical psychology. It is by descending into the depths of his own self . . . finally he transcends the limits of natural existence'; Scholem, *Major Trends*, 341.

[81] *Guide* i. 5 (p. 30).

[82] Ibid. 35 (p. 81), and then at the conclusion of the chapter: the offensive gravity of anthropomorphism is equal to belief in 'the non-existence of the deity, in the association of other gods with Him, or in the worship of other than He'.

of logically demonstrated negations which dismiss any characteristic attribution to him and progressively allow a clearer conception of him.[83] Rabbi Kook translates the philosophically unknowable divine essence into the 'uppermost light, that is the foundation and source of all, that no knowledge can grasp'.[84] That 'light' is the *ein sof*, the apex of the sefirotic chain of being, which intellectual hubris deludes itself into thinking it can grasp. In doing so it degrades the divinity in it by forcing it 'into the imaginable, resulting in an idol and a molten image within the hiddenness of the world'.[85] This hubris ontologically affects the very fabric of existence by literally demoting its generative root in the very process of capturing it by a definition, a concretization of the indefinable.

An inflated ego causes one's own self-image to surmount the image one has formulated of God, thus interposing a barrier between the *shekhinah* (the lowest of the *sefirot*) and its 'protective light' (or its sefirotic mate *tiferet*).[86] For Maimonides, intellectual arrogance produces categorical mistakes that are particular to the mind generating them, and sabotage progress toward that individual's perfection. This ruptures the organic structure of the divine. The *shekhinah*, isolated from its co-*sefirot* by a domineering egocentrism, transforms into an object of idolatrous worship. Rabbi Kook appropriates the anthropomorphic repercussions of intellectual conceitedness identified by Maimonides, but raises the stakes inestimably by linking that arrogance to an idolatrous perversion within the sefirotic realm.[87]

In a short meditation titled 'Esoteric and Philosophical Illumination',

[83] *Guide* i. 60 (pp. 143–7).

[84] *Shemonah kevatsim* 1: 636 (p. 21). The latter locution is based on the zoharic dictum, popular with hasidic masters, *leit maḥshavah tefisah bakh kelal*, 'thought cannot grasp Him at all' (*Tikunei zohar*, introd. 17a). See E. Wolfson, *Open Secret*, 324 n. 150.

[85] *Shemonah kevatsim* 1: 636 (p. 21).

[86] R. Kook also considers it 'foolishness' to hold oneself back from creative pursuits such as learning and innovation for fear of indulging the ego, since pride can ultimately be suppressed or sacralized or nullified by repentance. See Kook, *Midot hare'iyah*, ch. 23. There are also other positive roles played by pride, such as internal spiritual perfection (*Shemonah kevatsim* 1: 831 (p. 230); 2: 206 (p. 304)); governance (2: 314 (p. 337)); national pride (2: 164 (p. 294)); and recognition of one's unique talents (1: 318 (p. 98)).

[87] In order to understand the disastrous effect of hubris, one needs to bear in mind the contrasting means and scheme of ascent towards God, which for Maimonides is intellectual, cultivating the mind to its utmost capacity in the rational pursuit of knowing God. But for R. Kook it is ultimately a mystical ascent through the various levels of *sefirot*. One acquires a degree of certainty commensurate with the sefirotic level of faith reached whose apex is, as Pachter locates it, 'the arrival from the *sefirah* of Malkhut to the *sefirah* of Binah and binding oneself to it. At this highest level one acquires the absolute certainty that is embedded in the *sefirah* of Hokhmah, and it becomes clear that at this level one exists beyond any doubt whatsoever, even beyond the shadow of a shadow of a doubt.' Therefore hubris for Kook has ontic-metaphysical consequences, while for Maimonides it causes intellectual muddledness; Pachter, 'The Kabbalistic Foundation' (Heb.), 91–2.

Rabbi Kook claims that philosophy can pierce through to the very inner recesses of the Torah, but only when the body is ethically perfected: when it is 'purified of the impurities of desire and sin, one can achieve the great light and supernal joy even through philosophical speculation on the divine'.[88] Combining a religious posture of the fear of God with rational thought 'binds the secular to the holy, rendering it easier to distinguish between holy and secular, and see that the divine light that stems from the bountiful holiness of divine revelation that belongs to "the secret of the Lord is with them that fear Him" [Ps. 25: 14] is inestimably sweeter than the constricted pleasure the human intellect can offer'. Rabbi Kook then cites Maimonides and others of the rationalist school as exemplars of this transformation of the mundane (ḥol) into the holy (kodesh), men 'who drew their divine wisdom by way of the human intellect related to philosophical metaphysics which penetrated the completeness of their spirit from the secular to the holy'. Motivation, intent, and spiritual perfection, captured by proper 'fear of God', transform the objects of rational thought into a 'holiness' that transcends their own rationality, which elevates the secular discipline of metaphysics into a meta-metaphysics of divine secrets. Philosophy naturally evolves into a superior form of mysticism in its profound appreciation of the absolute distinction between kodesh and ḥol, which is paradoxically acquired through immersion in the latter.[89]

Rabbi Kook's strategic incorporation of Psalm 25: 14, 'The secret of the Lord is with them that fear Him', is crucial here. This verse exegetically enacts the very process of transubstantiation he describes from ḥol to kodesh. This same verse also appears in Maimonides' introduction to the *Guide of the Perplexed*, but as a prooftext for an entirely different notion. There it is cited, not as a qualification of those who are adept at the science of 'secrets', but rather as an endorsement of the kind of esoteric writing requisite for conveying those secrets. In compliance with halakhic constraints on the public teaching of esoteric subject matter,[90] Maimonides warns his audience to anticipate a disjointed composition designed to exclude those who are unqualified to cope with the challenging subject matter of the text. He warns of a reading experience that elucidates at the same time as it disorients, in order that 'the truths be glimpsed and then again be concealed, so as not to oppose

[88] *Kovets ma'amarim*, 14; *Shemonah kevatsim* 6: 42 (pp. 17–18).
[89] When discussing the limitations of human intellect and philosophy R. Kook uses the term *tsimtsum*. In *Shemonah kevatsim* 6: 41 (p. 17), he restricts the utility of philosophy to 'uprooting alien principles that result from false imaginings', while the greatest joy 'is only achieved through the secrets of the Torah, which reveal to man the shining speculum of the supernal vital soul as it is'. The transition from philosophy to secret in a sense parallels a reversal of the Lurianic *tsimtsum*, or divine withdrawal, so that the fullness of the divine essence will be disclosed.   [90] BT Ḥag. 11a–b.

that divine purpose which one cannot possibly oppose and which has concealed from the vulgar among the people those truths especially requisite for His apprehension. As He said: "The secret of the Lord is with them that fear Him".[91]

Maimonides subtly changes the original divine object of fear in the verse. Since it is cited to endorse the esotericism of divine secrets, the object of fear refers back to the subject of the phrase, the 'secret'.[92] Its Maimonidean translation renders a cautionary stricture regarding the dissemination of 'secrets', that is: 'The secret of the Lord should remain with those that fear for it.' Fear for the secret's reception should guide those who have mastered it, in order to preserve its secrecy when guiding others in deciphering its meaning.[93]

What Maimonides considers an admonishment to preserve a secret's secrecy, due both to pragmatic concerns and its inherent ineffability, is reinvested by Rabbi Kook with spiritual and mystical ingredients.[94] Philosophy becomes *sod*, that is mysticism, when it is channelled through a 'fear of the Lord'. Rabbi Kook processed the verse from *ḥol* to *kodesh* in a way that mirrors what he sees as the process that leads from philosophy into mysticism.

Love and Fear of God: Reversing the Priorities

While for Maimonides knowledge achieves intellectual enlightenment and thereby increasing knowledge of God, for Rabbi Kook it transcends its own rational limits to tap into a divine realm from which it 'draws'.[95] In this case it

[91] *Guide*, introd. to pt. i (p. 7).

[92] Pines, in his translation of the *Guide*, preserves its original biblical context when translating the object of fear in the upper case ('Him') as referring to God. I believe that this distorts its meaning in its Maimonidean guise.

[93] In support of this reading, the one other instance of Ps. 25: 14 within the Maimonidean corpus appears to buttress a warning as to the sensitive nature of a letter's contents and thus an admonishment to disseminate it selectively so that it does not end up in the wrong hands. See *Epistle to Yemen*, in *Igerot harambam*, i. 167. There Maimonides explicitly articulates his 'fear': 'And though I fear much about this, I have determined that it is worth risking the danger for the public good and, in addition, I have sent it to those like you and "the secret of the Lord is with them that fear Him".' Here it is clear that the fear is for the secret and the danger lies in its dissemination.

[94] R. Kook must also wrest Ps. 25: 14 out of its original Maimonidean sense, which mandated the preservation of secrecy for the Torah's secrets by communicating them only to the trained elite, since he was a staunch advocate of their public dissemination to 'all hearts', even to those 'who have not reached that measure of expansive knowledge for the acquisition of broad and deep knowledge'; Kook, *Orot hatorah*, 56. See Garb, *The Chosen Will Become Herds*, 23–9.

[95] R. Kook is another link in the long line of kabbalists who consider philosophical thought limited in the ultimate truths it can access. See, for example, the studies of Ravitzky, 'Samuel Ibn Tibbon', and Idel, '*Sitrei Arayot*'. As Elliot Wolfson has demonstrated, one of the pioneers of this school who engaged Maimonides was Abraham Abulafia, whose own mode of transmitting mystical gnosis derives from 'a complex synthesis of the Maimonidean perspective and the

channels a *ḥesed* (grace) whose essence is its unwarrantedness. It also transforms another facet of the noetically developed relationship with God that Maimonides posits. In Maimonides' opinion, whatever aspect of the divine is gained by knowledge is a natural consequence and therefore warranted, 'for providence is consequent upon intellect and attached to it'.[96] Except for the possibility of divine intervention interrupting a prophetic process, Maimonides is in agreement with the philosophical position that once the rational, imaginative, and moral qualities are perfected a man 'will necessarily become a prophet, inasmuch as this is a perfection that belongs to us by nature'.[97] Since Rabbi Kook's notion of knowledge allows for surpassing the boundaries of reason, its objectives are not subject to any rules or mechanisms that automatically dictate their realization once certain levels of knowledge have been achieved, as they are in Maimonides' formulation. That is why Rabbi Kook reverses the priorities Maimonides sets for love and fear of God when defining them halakhically. Love is the outcome of 'comprehending [God's] actions and magnificent creations and perceiving from them an inestimable and infinite wisdom'.[98] Fear then follows this understanding when one 'immediately recoils from fear and terror. He knows he is a small, lowly, dark creature with an insignificant and limited intellect, who stands before the Perfect Intellect.'.[99]

Rabbi Kook transforms what appears to be a reflex of the ultimate goal of love[100] into a higher state of consciousness for which love sets the stage: 'From the words of our master it appears that fear of the Exaltedness is a superior level that is consequent on a perfected love.'[101] Maimonides continues with a preface that, in consonance with his definitions of love and fear, he will proceed to 'explain important principles of the works of the Master of the

---

acceptance of an oral tradition that transcends philosophical orientation'; E. Wolfson, *Abraham Abulafia*, 77–8. Kook's own hermeneutical engagement with Maimonides has roots in medieval precedents. For a different hasidic hermeneutic which views the *Guide* and the Zohar as sharing a common esoteric tradition, see the detailed treatment of the Izbica and Radzin traditions of appropriating Maimonides' *Guide* in Magid, *Hasidism on the Margin*.

[96] *Guide* iii. 17 (p. 474).
[97] Ibid. ii. 32 (p. 361). [98] *MT* 'Laws of the Foundations of the Torah', 2: 2.
[99] Ibid. As observed in n. 76, Kaplan, 'The Love of God', ably argued for R. Kook's reversal of Maimonides' directional movement of love itself, which he claims progresses from a cold intellectual love to a passionate desirous one in Maimonides, while Kook follows the reverse route from a passionate, intuitive love to an intellectually refined one. Though that may be the case with love, what I argue here is that the path towards perfection does not end there but it is ultimately a preliminary to 'fear'.
[100] Maimonides does abandon the intellectual fear formulated at the beginning of *Mishneh torah* for a more popular one afterwards, which Kreisel hypothesizes may be attributed to the fact that 'inferior forms of fear play an important role for the masses' observance of the Law'; Kreisel, *Maimonides' Political Thought*, 259. [101] *Orot harambam*, 173.

universe that will serve as an entryway [*petaḥ*] for the intellectual to love God'.¹⁰² Rabbi Kook ingeniously reinforces his reversal of Maimonidean priorities by midrashically reading *petaḥ* as referring to love. In other words, love is merely the *preliminary*, the 'entryway', for further degrees of perfection.

The significance of Psalm 36: 11, as it resonates in Rabbi Kook's inversion of fear and love, is accentuated by his distinction, posed in the same comment, between lower and higher forms of fear, corresponding to its pre-love and post-love manifestations. The former is simple fear (*yirah peshutah*), motivated by the literal fear of punishment or reprisal. The latter is a more direct fear of God (*yirat hakavod veharomemut*), uncompromised by ulterior concerns for one's own welfare. This stratification of fear, repeatedly endorsed elsewhere in Rabbi Kook's corpus,¹⁰³ is particularly pertinent to his exegetical engagement with the *Mishneh torah*. Since its self-professed intention is to provide a comprehensive guide to all of halakhah, or mandated Jewish practice, it runs the risk of cultivating an inferior form of fear caught up in the myriad of details that Jewish law involves.

This fear is best expressed by Rabbi Kook in another context, which itself climaxes in the utopian state envisioned by Psalm 36: 11. Concern with the minutiae of the commandments stems from two sources, the lower one being fear of punishment, and a much-enhanced one from 'the current of the light of life within the source of apprehension'.¹⁰⁴ That apprehension consists of a consciousness of the sanctity of the commandments, along with 'the unity of the soulful nature of Israel with all the commandments, their different classifications, and branches of their branches'.¹⁰⁵ The ascent from that elementary fear is propelled by an overarching appreciation of the entire command structure and its intrinsic relationship with the whole community of Israel. Simple fear is fragmentary, manifested by a religiosity that is itself fragmentary in its obsession with details. A practice-obsessed concern for commandments, lacking a deeply felt integrated conceptual grasp of them, amounts to a 'sham *frumkeit* [religiosity]' containing an 'alienating and foreign kernel'.¹⁰⁶ What

---

¹⁰² Here I agree with my co-author: Kellner's suggestion (citing Berman, 'Ibn Bajja and Maimonides' (Heb.), 37) that Maimonides' notion of human perfection entails two tiers of *imitatio Dei*, one 'before intellectual perfection and an imitation of God after such perfection. Put in other words, we obey God before intellectual perfection out of fear and after intellectual perfection out of love'; Kellner, *Maimonides on Human Perfection*, 39.

¹⁰³ His development of this hierarchy of fear runs throughout his writing; for a few examples see *Shemonah kevatsim* 2: 264 (p. 318) (the power of the superior fear possessed by the righteous); 2: 304 (p. 333) (the evolution from 'simple fear' to the superior form advanced by the progressive removal of doubts about reality and God); 1: 274 (p. 87); 2: 332–3 (p. 310) (the detriment of excessive simple fear); 6: 25 (p. 199) (fear that cultivates despondency and retards spirituality); 6: 272 (p. 277) (how to elevate an overwhelming crude fear to the higher form of *yirat romemut*).

¹⁰⁴ *Shemonah kevatsim* 6: 125 (p. 227). ¹⁰⁵ Ibid. ¹⁰⁶ Ibid. 5: 241 (p. 168).

must be read into Rabbi Kook's interpretation of Maimonides' epigraphic verse is the assurance he sees expressed by it in one of his meditations, that the petty legalistic attitude fuelled by 'the lower spring of fear of punishment' inevitably ascends to 'the upper spring of the light of life'.[107] In Rabbi Kook's hands the verse spiritually reinforces what is purported to be a comprehensive legal code. It inspires a love-grounded holistic fear over the legalistic religiosity it is most prone to induce.[108]

Conclusion: Hebraizing the Greek Maimonides

The method behind Rabbi Kook's approach to Maimonides, as it has been examined in this chapter, is encapsulated in his exegesis of a verse which brackets the entire *Guide*. Maimonides' analysis of the nature of Adam and Eve's post-sin awareness of their own nakedness draws a philological comparison between the 'opening' of their eyes in Genesis 3: 7 denoting that awareness, and other biblical appearances of that term, including Isaiah's messianic expectation: 'Then the eyes of the blind shall be opened' (Isa. 35: 5). Their shared 'opening' is a metaphor for 'uncovering mental vision'. It represents a perceptual, rather than a visual, development whereby some new mental consciousness is attained. In Eden it is an epistemological transition from contemplating the universal objective categories of 'true and false' to the subjective fluctuating ones of 'good and bad'.[109] If 'opening' in Eden signifies an intellectual deterioration at the beginning of the *Guide* (and the world), then the messianic 'opening' of Isaiah, as cited at the very end of the *Guide*, anticipates a progressive reversal of that intellectual descent. It acts as a supplication for the realization of its promise in the perfection of the intellect to the point where a human being's original 'mental vision' of philosophical truths is restored.[110]

For Rabbi Kook, however, this verse envisions an all-encompassing appreciation of the world that transcends the narrow and skewed views that individual perspectives produce, be they emotional or intellectual. Each of these,

[107] Ibid. 6: 126 (p. 227).

[108] For the distinctions between a primitive fear and an advanced one—the kind which only appears externally to be opposed to human autonomy in its subordination to a supreme power, but in reality 'is the motive power of life', see Ish-Shalom, *Between Rationalism and Mysticism*, 114–15 and 140–1.   [109] *Guide* i. 2 (p. 25).

[110] As Ravitzky notes, the key to understanding the messianic vision at the end of *Mishneh torah*, in which all the world is preoccupied with the knowledge of God, 'is to be found precisely in Maimonides' allegorical interpretation of the story of the Garden of Eden in the opening chapters of the *Guide*'. The true meaning of the messianic era is realized when 'the opening of human history is united with its final perfection . . . the universal redemption of the human race . . . refers in fact to man's return to his original stature represented by the human archetype'; Ravitzky, 'To the Utmost of Human Capacity', 230–3.

cultivated in isolation, tends to occlude the others and therefore render a distorted grasp of reality which bifurcates the physical and the spiritual.[111] Rabbi Kook then cites Isaiah 35: 5 as an aspiration for the kind of 'opening' where 'the scientific sea and the emotional depths will imbue every single scientific perspective and every single emotion as reality is truly constituted, for it is impossible for any spiritual creation to exist independently, it must be permeated by everything'.[112]

There can be no better example of the transformation that Maimonides' thought undergoes in Rabbi Kook's hands than their radically different conceptions of the utopian destiny of humanity. For Maimonides, the 'opening' of primal man's eyes entailed a broadening of his mental scope that signalled a deterioration in thought. The ideal future therefore envisions a *narrowing* of that 'opening', in order to revert back to the single-minded utopian state which sifts out all but the purest of philosophical thought. Rabbi Kook, however, appropriates that very image for the purpose of reversing its direction, as we have shown in relation to his commentary on the *Book of Knowledge*. Rather than a constriction, Rabbi Kook's 'opening' contemplates a *widening* that embraces all that is human, beyond the merely intellectual, 'where all opinions, emotions, and images exist in one single, organic and perfected whole',[113] so that all of reality, in the holistic fullness of its divinity, can materialize.

We now return to Rabbi Kook's vigorous defence of Maimonides, mentioned at the beginning of this chapter, against what he considered the calumny of introducing alien ideas into Judaism. There he actually calls for integrating the *Guide of the Perplexed* into the classic literary canon of Judaism. One cannot approach the *Guide* cavalierly, but is obligated 'not just to afford his words the benefit of the doubt, but to plumb its depths and to force its principles into line with those of the Torah'. Rabbi Kook in fact adheres to Maimonides' own instructions when the latter cautions his readers 'not to explain to another anything in it save that which has been explained and commented upon in the words of the famous Sages of our Law who preceded me'.[114] Maimonides means by this to restrict the public dissemination of his

---

[111] Ross understands Adam's sin as a rupture between spirit and nature; thus utopia is the restoration of the pre-sin consciousness of a 'continuum between the spiritual and the physical'; Ross, 'Immortality', 245–6.

[112] *Shemonah kevatsim* 3: 69 (p. 387). Like Maimonides, R. Kook envisions the messianic era as a universal transformation in human consciousness, but the nation of Israel has a special role in its achievement. Israel is elected in that sense to remedy the current historical 'tragedy of the world which inhabits only the edge of truth, alienated from itself and all of existence'. Schatz [Uffenheimer], 'Utopia and Messianism' (Heb.), 21.

[113] *Shemonah kevatsim* 6: 104 (p. 220). [114] *Guide*, introd. to pt. i (p. 15).

thought to that which is consistent with tradition, while confiding the novel within it to only his most astute and perplexed disciples. However, Rabbi Kook's comprehensive view of Torah, which envelops a wide spectrum of competing ideas, can embrace all of Maimonides' thought as Torah. In fact, like other serious compositions for Rabbi Kook, the *Guide* can only communicate the fullness of its ideas when coupled with those that stand ideologically opposed to it, as they clash in a reciprocal perfection of each other.

The entire spectrum of the Jewish intellectual tradition discloses itself within a parity of disparity, where 'the benefit and perfection of each book is increasingly recognizable when the aura of one critical book is combined with that of another that appears antithetical to it, for only this opposition, when brought into harmony, is what leads to completeness, for one complements the other'.[115] Rabbi Kook accomplishes this very harmonization of Maimonides with the sum of Jewish thought that converges in his own person in the twentieth century through the kind of exegesis demonstrated in this chapter. He situates himself in a continuous dialogue with Maimonides throughout his thought, 'purifying' and reintegrating him in the new philosophical mystical direction that Rabbi Kook charts for the future of Judaism.

Rabbi Kook concludes his defence by vindicating Maimonides' pivotal place within the ongoing evolution of Jewish thought, and anticipating that 'even the great book, the *Guide of the Perplexed*, will remain an eternal light within the wisdom of Israel and its Torah "like the sun of righteousness with healing in its wings" [Malachi 3: 20]'. The verse Rabbi Kook alludes to is part of a passage to which Maimonides directs his readers, substantiating the notion 'that things should be considered as they are in their final outcome and not in their beginnings'.[116] In the particular context of the *Guide* it addresses the problem which the apparent lack of justice in human affairs poses for God's omniscience. This is the very essence of Rabbi Kook's response to his opponent regarding the legitimacy of Maimonides' teachings: the troubling intrusion of foreign Greek ideas into Jewish thought, in its final outcome, will reveal itself as enlightening and enhancing Judaism rather than undermining it.

Recourse must also be had to Maimonides' lexicography in order to gain a full appreciation of Rabbi Kook's biblical allusion. The metaphorical meaning

---

[115] See discussion of this and the harmony of opposition and unity of particulars in Rabbi Kook's thought in Goldman, 'Morality, Religion, and Halakha', 202. This ontological perspective of the underlying unity between opposing systems of thought informs Kook's 'program to expand the study of Jewish thought to cover all its periods and currents' (ibid.). It would seem that on the whole, Kook restricts his 'liberal' pedagogical programme to Jewish thought and excludes that of other cultures. See e.g. *Shemonah kevatsim* 7: 10 (p. 119); 8: 124 (p. 282); 6: 193–4 (pp. 71–2); and Garb, 'Alien Culture'.   [116] *Guide* iii. 19 (pp. 477–8).

of the term 'wing' is concealment,[117] which in Rabbi Kook's hands conveys what he reiterates time and time again. Rational and critical thought is perfected by what is hidden, by the secret, for 'rationalism develops only because beyond its cognitive purview, the hidden [*nistar*] performs its noetic and ethical work . . . and in the fusing of the hidden and the critical a firm foundation is built for the supernal divine light which stands beyond all conception and recognition'.[118] Rabbi Kook's Malachi declares that Maimonides' thought comes to full fruition when channelled through the hidden science. Its *healing* lies in what is *winged*—in other words in what is concealed. Rabbi Kook deftly hebraizes Maimonides' exoteric Greek understanding of Judaism into its higher esoteric incarnation of Jewish thought.

[117] *Guide*. i. 43 (p. 94).   [118] *Shemonah kevatsim* 4: 1 (p. 131).

FOUR

Maimonides and Rabbi Kalonymus Kalman Shapira: Abandoning Reason in the Warsaw Ghetto

JAMES A. DIAMOND

The Holocaust and the Eclipse of Thought

Any book concerned with Jewish thought and theology in the twentieth century, even one such as this focusing on engagements with a medieval Jewish thinker, would be incomplete without confronting the theological implications of the Holocaust (Shoah) in some meaningful way. This was a time when suffering and loss were of such catastrophic proportions as to overwhelm previous tragedies, which had by then become paradigms of suffering for Jewish history and theology. These former crises included the destruction of the two Temples, followed by various persecutions in the diaspora such as crusades, expulsions, and pogroms. As with the classic biblical example of an innocent sufferer, Job, all these crises provoked agonizing theological protests and struggles to wrest some sense out of innocent suffering, as well as posing challenges to the justness of a God who could preside over such suffering.

However, with the Holocaust, Jewish experience and theology crossed into uncharted territory. What kind of a deity, the ultimate subject of any theology, allows, or worse, orders, the *systematic* genocide of millions of human beings, including a million children, let alone that of his 'chosen' ones? In Jewish theology, can a covenant between a people and its God survive a time when the human partner to that covenant was nearly obliterated while the divine partner stood by? Can even Maimonides' negative theology with its 'solutions' to the problems of suffering and evil in the world still be viable in the face of a God who was so consummately absent that hardly a *theos* remains about which any coherent *logos* can be conducted?[1] The question 'What would Rabbi

---

[1] Primo Levi, in his customary devastatingly clinical manner, posited it pithily: 'There is Auschwitz, so there cannot be God'; Camon, *Conversations*, 68.

Kook have thought?', had he lived another ten years, is impossible to answer, as always with such exercises. Yet it would also be inconceivable that his supreme optimism about human nature, and his belief in a harmony of all existence working its way towards an ultimate unity, would not have been, at the very least, challenged, or even shattered by the events of the Holocaust.

The Maimonidean view of evil as a 'privation' or an absence of good, and therefore not attributable to any positive act of a Creator God[2] is no longer tenable in the face of a million children systematically gassed and burned. Equally untenable is Maimonides' view that the common perception of the pervasiveness of evil that human beings inflict upon one another is an exaggerated one.[3] The Holocaust, along with numerous genocides since 1945, such as Rwanda and Darfur, all fly in the face of that claim. The murder of six million Jews is neither an illusion nor a statistical anomaly. Evil was in fact all-pervasive. Neither can the characterization of genocide as evil be dismissed as an erroneous anthropocentric view of the world, which assesses good and evil in terms of human material good. This genocide was in fact largely successful, as far as the Jewish populations in countries such as Poland are concerned. The magnitude of other atrocities committed, during 'peacetime', in Mao's China and Stalin's Russia, renders hollow Maimonides' empirical observation that 'there is no city existing anywhere in the whole world in which evil of this kind is in any way widespread or predominant'.[4]

Finally, to accept a theory of divine providence which conditions God's watchful eye on the development of one's intellect, or, in Maimonidean terms, that is 'consequent upon the intellect',[5] is not only morally problematic, but theologically offensive as well. It is tantamount to relieving God of any responsibility for the victims who fell outside the ambit of God's watchful eye because of some intellectual deficit. Surely this amounts to an obscenity, an insult to the memory of the victims, and a blasphemy against the notion of a just and good God.

An 'eclipse' of God, or the 'hiding of the face', often proposed to alleviate the theological dilemma of divine absence in some way, or worse, the positing of God's indifference to indiscriminate and innocent suffering, simply masks the severity of the theological crisis. Is there really an essential difference between a theism which rationalizes an existent God who has abandoned mankind or consciously ignored it, and an atheism which denies God's exis-

---

[2] *Guide* iii. 12 (p. 443). For a good exposition of Maimonides' position on this issue see Leaman, *Evil and Suffering*, ch. 4.   [3] *Guide* iii. 12 (p. 444).

[4] Ibid. See also *Guide* iii. 12 (p. 442), where Maimonides attributes the 'whole mistake' of being perturbed by perceived evil to the intellectually ignorant and selfish attitude that 'if something happens that is contrary to what he wishes, he makes the trenchant judgement that all that exists is an evil'.   [5] *Guide* iii. 17 (p. 474).

tence altogether? At the very least, for those who experienced that suffering and loss, is that absentee God who is oblivious to their very existence not, for all intents and purposes, non-existent? Maimonides' version of God's 'hiding of the face' (*hester panim*) is simply a corollary of the principle that providence is contingent on intellect. In ascribing that hiddenness to inadequate or imperfect human knowledge, it lays the blame on human beings and sacrifices humanity in the defence of a perfect and just God.[6] Is the erection of a barrier between God's providential concern and six million human beings because of faulty cognition really a viable option, or does it not simply deepen the insult to the victims and to a God who would hide behind such a flimsy barrier? All attempts to grapple with the theologically debilitating challenges to mind, faith, and existence posed by the Holocaust across a spectrum of genres, be they philosophical, theological, literary, or aesthetic, consistently end in darkness. We arrive at a void that lingers 'at the mind's limits', to borrow a phrase from Jean Améry, a prominent survivor.[7]

Like the black hole theorized by physicists that allows no light to escape, that darkness posed by the Holocaust is so penetrating as to have often consumed the very lives of those writers and thinkers who profoundly struggled with it.[8] Many, like Améry, drowned in the memories that drenched them.[9] One would think that the least likely place for Maimonides, the most prominent exponent of Jewish rationalism, to appear would be in the context of Holocaust theology. How could one such as he, who considered thought a supreme religious value, be helpful when struggling with an experience in which, as Emil Fackenheim wrote, 'no thought could exist', and after which thought's 'survival lies elsewhere'?[10]

Sermonizing in a Time that Defies Reason

Kalonymus Kalman Shapira (1889–1943), the Piaseczner Rebbe, heroically persevered as a hasidic master, ministering to his followers even in the face of unimaginable pain and loss, both communal and personal. He delivered sermons, published posthumously as *Holy Fire* (*Esh kodesh*), in the Warsaw

---

[6] 'It is clear that we are the cause of this "hiding of the face", and we are the agents who produce this separation'; *Guide* iii. 51 (p. 626).   [7] Améry, *At the Mind's Limits*.

[8] The list of suicides among this class is too long to be considered coincidental. That list, in addition to Améry, includes such figures as Primo Levi, Paul Celan, Bruno Bettelheim, Tadeusz Borowski, Jerzy Kosiński, and Joseph Wulf (to name but a few of the most prominent). See also Lester, *Suicide and the Holocaust*.

[9] The phrase 'drenched in memory' is borrowed from Primo Levi, who himself succumbed to drowning in it. See Levi, *The Drowned and the Saved*, 34–5.

[10] Fackenheim, *To Mend the World*, 191.

ghetto between autumn 1939 and summer 1942.[11] Shortly before his murder he transcribed and buried them in the hope that they would provide a record of the unbearable suffering of those years. Far more than a collection of Saturday morning rabbinic sermons, together they serve as a witness to the theological struggle that unrelenting torment, starvation, and death surely would provoke in a knight of faith such as Rabbi Shapira. The sermons were retrieved some years after the end of the Second World War, and together form a rare, if not wholly unique, testament to an existential struggle to wrest meaning out of evil of such magnitude as to defy all reason.[12]

Rabbi Shapira was theologizing, sermonizing, and writing in the very heart of the devastating maelstrom that raged during what he described in his own original title for his work as the 'years of rage' (*shenot haza'am*). This chapter will focus on his sermons, delivered in the shadow of the *longue durée* of Maimonidean rationalism. Maimonides becomes instrumental in projecting thought forward as it is channelled through a hasidic incarnation into perhaps the only realm that could accommodate the *za'am* (rage), a realm beyond reason. Close readings of excerpts from his sermons reveal the depths of deprivation and life lived in painful extremes, and probe this 'trans-reason' dimension of his existential predicament. His experience defies all reason, in any manifestation, whether historical, political, sociological, philosophical, or theological. Startlingly, however, Rabbi Shapira resorts to Maimonides, the father of Jewish rationalism, in order to find an entry into a realm beyond reason, when reason was no longer equipped to respond to the madness that had engulfed him and his community. Nevertheless, as the studies in this book demonstrate, far from startling is his attempt to hold on to Maimonides at any cost. Thus this hasidic *rebbe*, when faced with a phenomenon of 'radical' evil, creatively and desperately fills the hollowness of Maimonidean solutions to the problem of evil in the world with the aid of Maimonides himself.

I return to Emil Fackenheim who considered the Holocaust an evil of such metaphysical proportions as to amount to a 'rupture' within history. The Holocaust thus raises not just a theological dilemma of the sort that generated various earlier theodicies dealing with the incongruity between an omniscient, omnipotent, supremely benevolent deity on the one hand and innocent

[11] Shapira, *Esh kodesh* (Jerusalem, 1960). All translations, unless otherwise noted, are my own. Since I wrote the draft of this chapter a very valuable critical edition of the original manuscript has appeared with an extremely informative introduction by Daniel Reiser: *Rabbi Kalonymus Kalman Shapira* (Heb.). References to 'Reiser' below are to the first volume of this edition, while references to *Esh kodesh* are to the 1960 edition.

[12] See Polen, *The Holy Fire*, for a pioneering study of *Esh kodesh*. Eliezer Schweid argues that *Esh kodesh* is incomparably unique in that it documents a theological struggle contemporaneous with the oppressive conditions of the ghetto 'both as a witness to and victim of all that transpired there'; Schweid, 'The Bush Is Aflame' (Heb.), 105 and 126.

suffering on the other; it evokes an epistemological dilemma as well that challenges civilization itself and the modes of thinking it had adopted as 'civilized'.[13] To cite Fackenheim again, 'among things ruptured may be not just this or that way of philosophical or theological thinking, but thought itself'.[14] If Fackenheim's assessment is correct, it would be all the more unlikely for Maimonides, who valued intellectual apprehension above all else, to enter the realm of thinking about the Holocaust. Even a thinker like Hannah Arendt, who viewed the Holocaust as a kind of logical culmination of tendencies already present within Western civilization, expressed the breakdown of all previous categories of thinking in the face of such evil. In a moment of philosophical exasperation she opined, 'Not only are all our political concepts and definitions insufficient for an understanding of totalitarian phenomena, but also all our categories of thought and standards of judgment seem to explode in our hands the instant we try to apply them.'[15]

Just as Maimonides' *Guide* contemplates different readers, so do Rabbi Shapira's sermons. However, while Maimonides crafts his writing to meet wide disparities in intellectual capacity, Rabbi Shapira directs himself to two ontologically distinct audiences, one horizontally and the other vertically defined. On the horizontal plane he addresses his disintegrating community, offering hope, consolation, and motivation to persevere in the face of its rapidly diminishing prospects for survival. The relationship between the *rebbe* and his hasidim already opens the path towards a realm beyond reason, moored as it is in an I–Thou encounter, animated by the interface of the two, and 'impossible to attain by things related to the intellect'.[16] Vertically, the sermons direct themselves to God and assume a metaphysical tenor analogous to supplicatory or petitionary prayer. In that sense they are also desperate appeals to rouse a seemingly oblivious God to live up both to his specific biblical promise as a guardian of Israel and to his universal role as creator and architect of historical events. They are written in the same hasidic tradition that motivated other hasidic masters such as Rabbi Dov Ber of Mezhirech, who prefaced his classic work, *Magid devarav leya'akov*, with the driving force behind his setting pen to paper: 'in order to inform the entire nation of God that our God has not abandoned us even during this bitter exile sustained in this impure land, and He has sent us great and insightful *tsadikim* [righteous ones] to sustain us'.[17] Likewise, Rabbi Shapira's sermons are not simply abstruse rabbinic homilies, nor detached ruminations on the meaning of suffering, but are evoked by a life lived in pain, wholly consumed by his God

---

[13] Dan Diner captures this provocatively with his phrase *Zivilisationsbruch des Holocaust*; Diner, *Beyond The Conceivable*.
[14] Fackenheim, *To Mend the World*, 194.   [15] Arendt, 'Mankind and Terror', 302.
[16] Shapira, *Mevo hashe'arim*, 242.   [17] Dov Ber of Mezhirech, *Magid devarav leya'akov*, 3.

and his people, whose rapid deterioration we can track historically to an exact time and place. Maimonides' sole audience lives on the horizontal plane, in his own time and in the future, and the comfort he offers is far more abstract yet for him just as pressing. His *Guide* delivers intellectual salvation and advice on how to resolve a philosophical angst, the result of a distorted conception of God that might be misconstrued from the highly anthropomorphic text of the Bible. His intended audience is not a starving, decimated community targeted for death but rather philosophically troubled Jews who wish to preserve both their intellectual honesty and their dedication to the Jewish scriptures. Of course persecution, deprivation, and suffering did not begin at the start of the Second World War; they were the entrenched conditions of east European Jewish life long before.[18] Likewise, for Rabbi Shapira, engaging and reinventing Maimonides did not begin in the Warsaw ghetto.

At this point I will present an example that lays the theological groundwork for Maimonidean engagement in the ghetto. Here Rabbi Shapira totally reinvents one of Maimonides' Thirteen Principles, as filtered through the popular *Ani ma'amin* version, an anonymously authored Hebrew adaptation that has been a standard part of Jewish daily prayer-books since the middle of the sixteenth century.[19] The third principle posits God's incorporeality, asserting that 'God is not a body and . . . nothing material can attach to Him and . . . He is free of any form'. In a classic midrashic move, Rabbi Shapira re-parses the principle to mean that there is an inferior 'nothing' mode of knowing God, indulged in by those 'who only apprehend corporeal things, and corporeal matters fill their hearts and minds'.[20] That kind of knowledge partially succeeds when approaching God, because God undergoes a process of self-limitation (*tsimtsum*) that allows his divinity to inhere in the material world. Thus even the boor and ignoramus can find their way towards God through the medium of the lowest rungs of existence.

What is important for our purposes is that Rabbi Shapira reads Maimonides against the grain of what patently mandates a philosophically abstruse conception of a purely immaterial God. He thus turns the principle that privileges abstraction, and theoretical reasoning as the only means of grasping that abstraction, on its head.[21] In his hands, Maimonides' third principle

---

[18] For just one study see Heller, *On the Edge of Destruction*. The following sentence typifies the depth of Jewish economic conditions during the interwar years: 'It is difficult to convey to the western mind the squalor and misery in which large numbers of Jews lived' (ibid. 101).

[19] Shapiro, 'Ani Ma'amin', 165.   [20] Shapira, *Derekh hamelekh*, 105.

[21] Hyman views the third principle as the only wholly conceptual one which grounds the others concerning God: 'Of the five principles concerning God, that of Divine corporeality is the only one which guarantees *conceptual* knowledge of Him for all. For the masses might well affirm that God exists, is one, eternal, and solely to be worshipped and yet picture Him through

actually concretizes God in the material world and dismisses the notion that philosophy and conceptualization are the exclusive means of apprehending God. This radical overhauling of an intellectualized principle of belief chips away at Maimonides' advocacy of reason as the exclusive route towards God. In addition, by spanning what appears as an unbridgeable impasse between the corporeal world and an incorporeal Being that shares nothing in common with that world, Rabbi Shapira opens the door to calling on Maimonides once again when confronted with the theological impasse posed by the inordinate suffering of the ghetto.

Reading Maimonides out of Intense Suffering

In a passage from the third and final cycle of his sermons, Rabbi Shapira attempts to salvage some positive theological value out of what could be described as his dismally pessimistic expectation of the implosion of the world to its originating chaos. He does so by returning to his rabbinic ideational homeland and his own pre-war theology, looking beyond reason for the true plane of convergence between the human and the transcendent. That desperate reach beyond reason critically hinges on Maimonides. The following extract was delivered on the sabbath of 7 February 1942 ('Yitro'), five months before the mass deportations from the Warsaw ghetto to the death camps began:

And in addition to this, 'Go and inform them that you may know that I the Lord have consecrated you' [Exod. 31: 13], that even the very knowledge by which one experiences that one is righteous [ḥasid] is itself an integral part of divine knowledge [da'at elohim] and through it one knows. It is well known according to Maimonides, cited by the mystics [mekubalim], that God's knowledge is acquired by knowing Himself, which we have discussed previously. Consequently, God's cognizance of one's worship and righteousness is also contained in the knowledge of Himself. For a man's worship and righteousness belong to God since He grants him the will, the strength, the intellect, and the emotions to worship. And when God grants a part of His knowledge to man and through it he knows of his own worship, then he realizes that it is not his, but that everything belongs to God. Then it always appears to him that he does not do anything on his own. But he is aware that the deficiencies are his own since in truth they are his own and he causes them. Thus his heart sinks and his spirit becomes broken.

Now it is known that in Egypt, knowledge [da'at] was in exile. The letters that make up the word Pharaoh [pr'h] can be inverted to read 'the neck' [ha'oref, from

categories of the imagination. But once God is to be known as incorporeal, this knowledge can only be conceptual'; Hyman, 'Maimonides' Thirteen Principles', 137–8.

h'rp], which indicates the constriction of knowledge, preventing its dissemination. And in the present-day exile, knowledge of the attributes is in a state of exile. Worship then consists of extricating knowledge from exile. That is why it states 'And God knew' [Exod. 2: 25] and when they left Egypt it states that 'I the Lord have consecrated you' [31: 13] and when the messiah arrives, 'the world will be filled with the knowledge of God' [Isa. 11: 9]. All the sufferings then in Egypt and now, though they defy knowledge, are in any event for this purpose—to crush and override human cognition with which man thinks he cognizes and on which he relies in the sense of 'increasing knowledge increases pain' [Eccles. 1: 18]—to crush it and override it so that the divine mind can reveal itself in each and every individual internally and through the entire world.[22]

Drawing on kabbalistic notions of the human being mirroring the divine anthropos, he asserts that the usual means of acquiring knowledge, by reason or experience, must be surrendered, since they are actually obstacles to the ultimate truths of divine knowledge. In support, Rabbi Shapira paradoxically enlists what has usually been considered a supremely rationalist conception of God and man, namely Maimonides' Aristotelian conception of God as thought thinking itself.[23] Thus, for divine knowledge to enter and suffuse the world, human thought must abandon its own self. Suffering provokes an epistemological rupture, which empties the human mind of its usual modes of knowing, leading to a noetic paradigm shift in which they are replaced by a divine episteme. The human intellect, and its confidence in its own ability to make sense of the world, must in fact be abandoned to gain access to the divine mind, in order to make sense of what is an insurmountably senseless world.

This notion of displacing the intellect, or transcending it, to gain true knowledge, or knowledge from a divine perspective, has deep roots in hasidic thinking. As with Rabbi Kook, Rabbi Shapira is also emblematic of how central Maimonides, the supreme rationalist, is to a movement which largely eschewed rationalism as the path towards God and metaphysical truth. One can trace the idea that suffering plays a positive role in weakening the body, and thereby strengthening the soul, as far back as the Middle Ages to the Zohar (the canonical scripture of all subsequent Jewish mysticism). God inflicts 'sufferings of love' when he 'crushes the body to empower the soul; then the person is drawn to Him in love fittingly, the soul dominant, the body weakened'.[24] Although Maimonides does consider there to be an inverse relationship in strength between the body and the intellect, which he identifies as

[22] *Esh kodesh*, 158; Reiser, 267–8.
[23] For an excellent treatment of Aristotle's conception of how God knows, see De Koninck, 'Aristotle on God'.   [24] Zohar, i. 180b, and *Zohar: Pritzker Edition*, 93–4.

the soul, he rejects the notion of 'sufferings of love' out of hand as inconsistent with divine justice.[25] It is therefore all the more ironic to see that very notion surface in a Maimonidean guise in the nascent hasidic movement of the eighteenth century. In particular, Rabbi Shneur Zalman of Lyady (1745–1812), one of hasidism's pioneers and the founding father of the Habad hasidic dynasty, promotes a Maimonidean incarnation of the very idea that Maimonides rejects. He also repeatedly cites Maimonides' Aristotelian-influenced identification of the knower, knowing, and known, as a kind of mystical axiom which many of the 'sages of kabbalah admit'.[26] Similarly, Rabbi Nahman of Bratslav (1772–1810), the grandson of hasidism's founder, the Ba'al Shem Tov, and an outspoken critic of Maimonides, endorses a pivotal doctrine that proximity to God can only be acquired by displacing one's rational mind.[27] The fact that God is one with what he knows implies that he knows everything, because he knows himself. In other words, there is nothing that exists outside his own self. Maimonides' medieval rational epistemological theory, borrowed from Aristotle, the founding father of the Western rational philosophical tradition, ironically forms the underpinning for Habad's eighteenth-century kabbalistic acosmism, which views all of reality as a facet of God.

Indeed, Maimonides' own formulation of divine knowledge throughout all his major works, including the *Mishneh torah*[28] and the *Guide*,[29] patently lends itself to this mystical appropriation that absorbs all being into the divine Being. Some contemporary scholars might view this hasidic idea as a logical consequence of Maimonides' 'post-rational' philosophical mysticism.[30] Even

---

[25] See *Guide* iii. 24 (p. 499). For talmudic notions of 'sufferings of love', see for example BT *Ber.* 5a–b, and *Kid.* 40b.   [26] Shneur Zalman of Lyady, *Tanya: likutei amarim*, 2.

[27] For a full-length treatment of this doctrine see Mark, *Mysticism and Madness*. For R. Nahman 'removing one's rational mind (*da'at*) and casting away one's intellect (*sekhel*) represents the apex of religious worship' (ibid. 2).

[28] *MT* 'Laws of the Foundations of the Torah', 2: 10 presents the epistemological theory of the unification of the knower with the known, and then concludes that God knows the creation by knowing himself.

[29] For example, *Guide* iii. 51 (pp. 621–2) speaks of achieving a unity of divine and human intellects. See also *Commentary on the Mishnah* on *Avot* 3: 20, and introd. to *San.* 10 (p. 205). Although there are statements made in this work that indicate the capacity of the human mind for abstracting God's form, and thus adopting the logic of the identity of the knower and the known, becoming one with God, this would directly contradict other statements by Maimonides that deny the human intellect's ability to know God's essence. I agree here with Davidson's solution that the *Commentary on the Mishnah*, intended for a general audience, expresses itself loosely, and that the highest level of human knowing is of the Active Intellect, that intellect occupying the lowest rung in Maimonides' incorporeal hierarchy and the one that governs the sublunar world; Davidson, *Maimonides the Rationalist*, 64–9, 201–6.

[30] See e.g. Blumenthal, 'Maimonides' Philosophical Mysticism', and the comprehensive bibliography at pp. xxii–xxv.

some who disagree conclude that Maimonides can in fact be read as a 'pantheist of sorts': 'If, in cognition, subject and object are identical, then mysticism follows when man knows God, or ultimate reality, and pantheism of some sort follows when God apprehends the world. In either case the opposition between subject and object collapses.'[31] There is also a renowned proponent of a quasi-mystical version of this Maimonidean formulation in the non-hasidic rabbinic world of the twentieth century: Rabbi Joseph B. Soloveitchik, another prominent figure treated in this book (see Chapter 2), adapts the Maimonidean epistemological unity between the knowing, knower, and known in quasi-mystical terms, resulting in an intellectualist mysticism. However, in contrast to hasidism, Maimonides is not a stage leading towards kabbalah but, on the contrary, 'Kabbalah is a stage leading to the Maimonidean ideal which R. Soloveitchik depicts in mystical colours.'[32]

Although this is a subject that requires further discussion, for the purposes of understanding Rabbi Shapira's intent it is sufficient to appreciate the panentheistic consequence of this identity of the knower with the known, which collapses all being into a divine oneness. That unity is only manifest by way of the composite emanation of the *sefirot*. The integral sefirotic unity of attributes, knowledge, will, wisdom, and understanding with the divine essence is not, in the words of Rabbi Shneur Zalman, 'within the bounds of human comprehension'. It is an esoteric principle of faith, which 'lies beyond the intellect'.[33] If it is a mode of exercising the intellect that surpasses the limits of human comprehension, then perhaps the only way of entering that mode is to abandon the normal modes of human use of the intellect. Only then does one gain access to another noetic realm, in this case the divine one, or, more appropriately, allow its ingress into one's own mind and being.

What is particularly noteworthy about this epistemological breakthrough is the historical context of suffering that led to it. In the first cycle of sermons, Rabbi Shapira dedicates the one delivered on the sabbath designated as 'Zakhor', when the evil committed by the biblical nation Amalek is traditionally commemorated, to an exposition of how Amalekite evil seeped into the fabric of Israelite society. Rarely if ever does Rabbi Shapira refer to the Nazis or Germans by name, so it is reasonable to assume in this case that Amalek stands for the Nazis, Israel's contemporary oppressors.[34] Some exegetical

[31] Gideon Freudenthal, 'Philosophical Mysticism', 122.
[32] D. Schwartz, 'R. Soloveitchik as a Maimonidean' (Heb.), 321.
[33] Shneur Zalman of Lyady, *Tanya*, 'Sha'ar hayihud veha'emunah', 9.
[34] According to Alana Vincent, Shapira's sermon on Amalek both enables his followers 'to interpret their experiences within the narrative framework provided by the cultural memory transmitted through the regular recital of scripture', and 'buttressed the viability of the Amalek narrative as a cultural memory, a part of their own living (and lived) experience'; Vincent, *Making Memory*, 30.

ingenuity applied to biblical verse and rabbinic midrash leads him to the conclusion that the 'external wisdom', or science and philosophy, by which Amalek gained world renown, appealed to some Israelites and served to dampen (literally 'cool down') their faith in 'Torah wisdom'. The same collection of sermons reinvents Maimonides for a world gone mad, in which reason cannot cope and which it cannot fathom, by renouncing reason, the only ability that human beings share with God, according to Maimonides.[35] For Rabbi Shapira a reason-based faith is not just a watered-down one; he identifies it with the very nation considered by Jewish theology to be evil incarnate. Rabbi Shapira thus lays the groundwork for a kabbalistically revamped version of Maimonides' own means of uniting with God, which originally could be achieved precisely through the scientific appreciation of the world that Rabbi Shapira associates with Nazism.

Historically, according to Rabbi Shapira, this very phenomenon of Jewish attraction to philosophical wisdom accounts for the great catastrophe of the Spanish expulsion in the fifteenth century. Morality grounded in autonomous reason is fickle, since 'those same sciences and rationales that previously led autonomously to a beautiful ethics are now being used to justify theft, robbery, and murder, and all the other disgusting characteristics as good'.[36] The only absolute ground of human behaviour that allows for no relativism is God's word, even for those commandments normally classified as rational (*mishpatim* as opposed to non-rational *ḥukim*). Obedience to the former must be motivated by submission to the divine will, rather than conformity to reason, for 'all commandments are divine *ḥukim* whether one understands them with one's reason or not'.[37] This position is consistent with Rabbi Shapira's general approach as developed in his pre-war theology as well. For example, one of his pre-war sermons asserts: 'Anyone who performs a commandment solely because he understands it, that commandment remains incomplete, since he fulfils the commandment only as a result of his intellect and his own will, but not because of the divine will.'[38]

It is not too speculative to suggest that Rabbi Shapira envisages the Germans as the intellectual successors to the biblical nation of Amalek and the philosophers of medieval Spain. Rabbi Shapira's enemy was in fact the embodiment of the very summit of Western civilization, rationally and culturally. The nation represented at its most rational peak by the Nazi philosopher Martin Heidegger, arguably one of the greatest intellects of the twentieth century, proves Rabbi Shapira's point as no other. In fact, Rabbi Shapira explicitly identifies Germany in his pre-war writing as achieving the very heights of

---

[35] *Guide* i. 1 (pp. 21–3).   [36] *Esh kodesh*, 29–30; Reiser, 114–15.
[37] Ibid.   [38] Shapira, 'Sermon for Shabat Teshuvah 2', *Derekh hamelekh*, 611.

science and rationalism and yet, at the same time, sinking to the abysmal depths of immorality to the point of becoming 'the very worst of the civilized world'.[39] Morality becomes an arbitrary matter of human choice, Rabbi Shapira states also in his pre-war writings, unless 'even the *mishpat* of the Torah, that is laws that appear reasonable, are also really *ḥukim*. God wishes [his laws] to transcend the intellect'.[40] But later in his sermons during the war he can no longer bring himself to even utter the name 'Germany'. Its actions now qualify it as the embodiment of the demonic Amalek. Rabbi Shapira clearly parts ways with Maimonides' classification of 'rational virtues' as the 'ultimate end' of 'true human perfection' while 'moral virtues' are merely preparatory to this end.[41]

Accessing the Divine Mind by Suppressing the Human Mind

Rabbi Shapira charts history in terms of the progression and regression of knowledge, in which the integrity of knowledge is always threatened by exile or by Israel's alienation from its natural environment. Knowledge is rootless precisely when it is a product of autonomous human activity, of reason through 'which man thinks he cognizes and upon which he relies'.[42] Such knowledge is in fact alienated from its divine source, since it forms a barrier of independent common human knowledge standing between the upper and lower worlds, and thus prevents the influx of true divine knowledge. The citation of Exodus 2: 25, 'and God knew', in his 1942 sermon cited above corroborates Rabbi Shapira's epistemology, which entails the triggering of divine knowledge by displacing human knowledge. In the case of Egyptian bondage, such triggering is occasioned by the agonizing and oppressive circumstances described shortly before this phrase: 'And the children of Israel sighed by reason of the bondage, and they cried, and their cry came up unto God by reason of the bondage. And God heard their groaning, and God remembered His covenant with Abraham, with Isaac, and with Jacob. And God saw the children of Israel, and God knew' (Exod. 2: 23–5). The consequence of the natural state of divine knowing, which 'knows with a knowing that is not outside itself', is, as he explains in his pre-war thought, to render the objects of God's knowledge an integral part of his own being: 'For this is the meaning of the deep unity between Israel and their heavenly father: what emerges from us becomes a part of divinity and what emerges from the divinity becomes the

---

[39] *Derekh hamelekh*, 604.   [40] Ibid. 169.
[41] *Guide* iii. 54 (p. 635).   [42] *Esh kodesh*, 158; Reiser, 267–8.

Jew.'[43] Human reason disrupts the reciprocity of that unifying force. But when suffering overwhelms the normal course of human thought, it actually restores the harmony between Israel and its God. The physical alleviation of Israel's exilic condition at the same time remedies God's own grief at having caused it.[44] The consequences of disrupting this unifying reciprocity are dire. Since the Jews declare God's unity, exile or fragmentation impedes an efficacious unification of God. God's ontological integrity is contingent on Israel's cohesiveness.[45]

Paradoxically, the very constriction of knowledge by the despotic subjection of Israel to suffering contributes to the redemption of knowledge by its very inhibition of the normal modes of reason. The prooftext is instructive in that its original biblical context also depicts processes of divine knowledge and human knowledge moving inversely along parallel planes—divine knowledge increasing and occupying the human realm in direct proportion to the waning of human knowledge. This is precisely opposed to Maimonides' own model, which conditions God's knowledge of human beings on the extent of their knowledge of him. For Maimonides, it is the intellect which forms the bridge between the two. Using the metaphor of light for knowledge, he captures this one-to-one relationship as follows: 'Just as we apprehend Him by means of that light which He caused to overflow toward us—as it says "In Thy light do we see light" [Ps. 36: 10]—so does He by means of this selfsame light examine us.'[46] But for Rabbi Shapira, God's 'knowing' evolves from a chain of sensory and mental awareness consisting of hearing, remembering, and seeing (Exod. 2: 24–5), all evoked by the human suffering experienced below. Or in the language of verse 23, which sets the process of divine knowledge in motion, God was touched by Israel's anguish which 'rose up to Him', conveying a sensual experience of Israel's pain.

This verse, which captures the idea that true divine knowledge gained is a function of human knowledge lost, highlights Rabbi Shapira's kabbalistic transformation of Maimonidean thought. Sabbath observance, according to Exodus 31: 1, guarantees the 'knowledge' of God's consecration of Israel, 'for it is a sign between Me and you throughout the ages to know that I the Lord have consecrated you'. For Maimonides, the knowledge gained in this verse refers to the empirical insight of the 'religious communities' other than the Jews, who are witnesses to Jewish fidelity to God in sabbath observance.[47] But

[43] *Derekh hamelekh*, 479.
[44] *Esh kodesh* is very partial to the talmudic passage in BT *Ber.* 3a which depicts God in a state of constant remorse at having caused destruction and exile. See *Esh kodesh*, 20, 127, 147, and 159–60; Reiser, 102, 117, 251, and 268–9.
[45] See *Esh kodesh*, 131; 'Sermon for Hoshanah Rabah'; Reiser, 230.
[46] *Guide* iii. 52 (p. 629).   [47] Ibid. ii. 31 (p. 359).

for Rabbi Shapira this interpretation has been refuted by historical events. Those very 'communities', who are supposed to be theologically inspired by Jewish sabbath observance as a testament to monotheism are the very ones who have forced Israel into desecrating the sabbath simply in order to survive. Rabbi Shapira bears witness to 'the desecration of the sabbath by many Jews under duress because of the sufferings caused by Amalek [read Nazis]'.[48]

It is a time when Jewish devotion to God is not publicly evident, precisely because the surrounding communities are the cause of its corrosion. Rabbi Shapira attests to his distress at the widespread sabbath desecration in the ghetto, 'for many have failed the test, forced by hunger to conduct business on the marketplace on the sabbath'.[49] For Rabbi Shapira the knowledge gained is reflexive, with devotion leading to the replacement of self-knowledge by divine knowledge: 'When God grants a part of His knowledge to man, and through it he knows of his own worship, then he realizes that it is not *his*, but that everything belongs to God.'[50] In other words, man aspires to the realization that his dedication to God in truth is God's, consisting of a removal of the self in favour of God even as a subject of epistemology.

Emptying the Mind towards the Messianic Age

There are far broader ramifications to this epistemological shift that extend beyond the individual to the world as a whole. Here too there is a radical transformation of Maimonidean epistemology into a kabbalistic version. Rabbi Shapira sees the steady cumulative merging of individual consciousness with divine consciousness as progressively leading towards the messianic age. At that point all minds will meld globally with the divine, as envisioned by Isaiah, 'when the whole world will be replete with knowledge of God' (Isa. 11: 9). That same verse typifies Maimonides' messianic vision. In fact it is so paramount that he brings the *Mishneh torah* to its end with its citation. However, for Maimonides, it is God as an object of intellectual quest and contemplation that Isaiah anticipates will be the shared enterprise of all humanity. In fact, the *Mishneh torah* as a whole is bracketed by this idea: it commences with a general foundation of all human existence 'to know that there is a primary Being' (humanly imperative for all but normatively binding only on Jews) and concludes with the universal pursuit of this very foundation.

Rabbi Shapira transforms God as a universal *object* of knowledge in the

---

[48] *Esh kodesh*, 169; Reiser, 282.
[49] See *Esh kodesh*, 84 and 112; Reiser, 175 and 210. For R. Shapira's special devotion to maintaining the sanctity of the sabbath even under the harshest of conditions in the ghetto, see the testimony of the Hebrew weekly *Nerot shabat*, 'Mishpatim', 9 Feb. 1945.
[50] *Esh kodesh*, 158; Reiser, 267–8.

messianic era to a *subject* of knowledge: every human knower will reflect God's knowledge rather than his own. Divine knowledge will suffuse the world, as opposed to knowledge *about* God. Every human cognition will in fact be a divine cognition, as opposed to human cognition of the divine. There will no longer be a division between physics and metaphysics as separate epistemological disciplines, since metaphysics will overcome physics, as reflected by the divine mind, which thinks only Itself. Rabbi Shapira thus manages to elevate suffering into an instrument of messianic achievement, gradually chipping away the normal instruments of human cognition to make way for the divine mind.

The Ḥok of Senseless Suffering

Thus far we have seen how Rabbi Shapira derationalizes the worship of God. This is accomplished intellectually by emptying the mind of its mundane modes of thinking, and normatively by divorcing all of the commandments, including the 'rational' ones, from any rational sense as a motivating factor in their performance. Rabbi Shapira's version of fealty to the God of Abraham, Isaac, and Jacob, rather than to the God of the philosophers, is that Jewish faith is not anchored in reason (*ta'am* or *sekhel*) but rather in the genetic heritage of the Patriarchs.[51] This concerted effort at draining various dimensions of a Jew's relationship with God of rationality extends even further, to the very instrument of its realization, namely suffering. Rabbi Shapira posits that different grades of suffering can be classified analogously to the traditional division of commandments between rational and non-rational, or *mishpatim* and *ḥukim*: 'There are sufferings that are *mishpatim* which are comprehensible, whose goal and purpose are understood, but there are also sufferings that are in the category of *ḥukim*, whose purpose is incomprehensible, and, on the contrary, we actually witness its opposite.'[52]

Rabbi Shapira clearly addresses his own experience in the ghetto, which, by his own account, introduces a totally novel torment, one never experienced previously in the long history of Jewish suffering (not unlike Fackenheim's historical 'rupture'). Rather than succumb to a notion of useless or meaningless suffering, Rabbi Shapira sees such irrational suffering as the catalyst for faith that transcends the rational realm in kind: 'For just as reason is absent from *ḥok*, so faith transcends reason. Thus when we dedicate ourselves to God with a perfect faith that transcends reason, then even sufferings that are *ḥok*-like, become sweetened.'[53] And so when suffering reaches such extremes

---

[51] *Esh kodesh*, 138; Reiser, 240–1. [52] *Esh kodesh*, 84; Reiser, 175.
[53] *Esh kodesh*, 85; Reiser, 175.

as to push the mind towards mindlessness, the mind ascends towards a higher realm of faith beyond that of the reasoned mind. Senseless suffering can only be confronted by senseless thinking. That kind of anti-Maimonidean attitude in turn projects suffering into a higher plane where it can be tolerated. It is important to note that, at least here, Rabbi Shapira is not endorsing an old theology in which suffering increases future reward when it cannot possibly be rationalized as punishment. Rather, suffering is instrumental in sacralizing a new epistemological mode conditioned on the abandonment of reason. For Maimonides the reason-based intellect is the bridge to God, and injury is a symptom of the collapse of that bridge for both the perpetrator and the victim. The former inflicts harm out of ignorance and a 'privation of knowledge',[54] while the latter suffers harm for the same reason, becoming a 'target for every evil that may happen to befall him'.[55] However, Rabbi Shapira totally reconstructs Maimonides' intellectual bridge, enabling it to be crossed precisely when its moorings are decoupled from the intellect.

The Politics of Senseless Suffering

There is one more sermon I would like to mention in this chapter, one that moves the notion of overcoming reason from the realm of thought and law to that of history and politics. It is employed as a hermeneutical key to the biblical episode of the scouts, or spies (*meragelim*), in the desert, who were sent by Moses to reconnoitre Canaan and its inhabitants in preparation for the envisioned military campaign against them. As always, an exegetical problem fuels the ensuing discussion. In this case, Caleb's response in favour of mounting the assault does not logically refute the practical strategic arguments raised by the other scouts about the insurmountable odds posed by formidable Canaanite manpower and its invincible lines of defence. All Caleb resorts to is a rhetorical gesture, 'Let us by all means go up [advance]',[56] rather than engaging them and repudiating their logic (*sekhel*) and their reasoned argument (*divrei ta'ameihem*). Rabbi Shapira explains that Caleb's unreasoning leadership precisely captures the 'beyond reason' nature of Israelite faith, for 'it is exactly at a time when, God forbid, one cannot imagine any logical or natural possibility for salvation that one should have faith in God's salvation, and strengthen one's faith and conviction. And, on the contrary, at such a point it is preferable not to strain to discover some logical or natural perspective, since the futility of it might lead to impairing faith.'[57]

[54] *Guide* iii. 11 (p. 440). [55] Ibid. 51 (p. 625).
[56] 'Caleb hushed the people before Moses and said "Let us by all means go up and we shall gain possession of it, for we shall surely overcome it"' (Num. 13: 30).
[57] *Esh kodesh*, 55; Reiser, 144–5.

It perhaps is no coincidence that this also strikes at the very heart of Maimonides' rational approach towards geopolitical confrontations in Israel's past, particularly the occupation of Canaan. Most prominently, Maimonides logically accounts for the circuitous forty-year wandering in the desert as a necessary period of transition from the subjugated spirit of slavery to a courageous one, ready to wage war against those who stand in Israel's way in the campaign to establish a new homeland. The slave cannot instantly transform into a warrior without first 'procuring . . . the capacity to engage in wars'.[58] Indeed, Maimonides cites 'the children of Anak' (giants), the very enemy facing Caleb, the other scouts, and the Israelites, as emblematic of the need to acclimatize to the frame of mind and body required for warfare. In his *Letter on Astrology*, Maimonides extends this reasoning to account for the destruction of the Temple, the most devastating catastrophe in Jewish history before the Holocaust. If the Jewish nation had attended to all the natural scientifically proven tactics of engaging in war and self-defence, rather than relying on popularly held but false 'science', they might have averted that disaster as well, but 'they did not busy themselves with the art of war or with the conquest of lands'.[59] For Maimonides, biblical events present a model of reasoned and empirically proven strategies when confronting the various challenges posed by historical circumstances.

Rabbi Shapira's ensuing comments regarding the *benefits* of irrational suffering are revealing when juxtaposed to Maimonides' *dismissal* of suffering as a threat to the relationship with the divine (if placed in a proper intellectual perspective). In order to reinforce Israelite faith under the yoke of the Egyptians, Moses performs miraculous signs, transforming his staff into a serpent (*naḥash*) and exposing an arm riddled with skin disease (*tsara'at*). Rabbi Shapira considers that the specific nature of these signs substantively addresses Israel's dire circumstances, 'since both are from the unclean side [*sitra demeso'ava*]: the serpent represents the evil inclination and leprosy signifies impurity. Precisely these signs will buttress Israel's faith, a signal that even in the lowly depths to which they have fallen God will raise them, and the sparks will still be raised to the way they were.'[60] Rabbi Shapira draws on kabbalistic notions that view the source of evil as integral to the Godhead. Rather than the Maimonidean view of evil as an absence or a privation of good, it is sefirotically conceived. Human experience of evil as a reality is at odds with the metaphysical reality. As a result, ultimate redemption can only arrive when the

---

[58] *Guide* iii. 32 (p. 528).

[59] Alexander Marx (ed.), 'The Correspondence', 350. Ralph Lerner states, 'Astrology is here not condemned as idolatry, as the greatest transgression . . . Rather, astrology is here seen as a stupid distraction from useful and necessary actions. This political judgment is sufficient condemnation'; Lerner, 'Maimonides' Letter on Astrology', 147.   [60] *Esh kodesh*, 85; Reiser, 175.

illusion of evil is overcome and, in the words of Gershom Scholem, 'evil will no longer be evil because it will have been restored to its proper place in the union of holiness'.[61] Rabbi Shapira voices the idea that the Godhead encompasses a unified integration within itself of what human beings perceive as separate destructive and constructive forces. Human cognition based on experience sees fragmentation, but beyond human cognition there is harmony.

For Maimonides, however, intellectual failure *accounts* for suffering. Operating outside the framework of established human modes of cognition excludes human beings from the divine purview, making them vulnerable to the vicissitudes of the physical world, since 'providence is consequent upon the intellect and attached to it'.[62] Rabbi Shapira views forces like the serpent, or the evil inclination, or leprosy as apparent to the senses as distinct entities external to God, able to jolt men experientially into another realm of thought that transcends normal thought, where they all meld into a unified divine whole. Maimonides, on the other hand, views these phenomena as symbols of the same thing: the material dimension of a human being, which diverts man's attention from the noetic realm of universal truths to the physical world of subjectivity. In fact, co-opting a rabbinic maxim, he asserts that the angel of death, the evil inclination, and Satan are all metaphorical synonyms for the malaise of intellectual impoverishment.[63] The serpent too falls into this same cluster of metaphors that signify intellectual deficit.[64]

Leprosy is symptomatic of false reasoning as well, a point that Maimonides develops at the end of the *Mishneh torah*, 'Laws of Leprosy Defilement'. Leprosy is the culminating disease at the end of a chain of offences all associated with speech, which commence with idle chatter but progressively deteriorate into fundamental cognitive error about the ultimate truth in the universe.[65] For Maimonides, the problem with the biblical persona of Job, the paradigmatic innocent sufferer in the history of religion, is that even though he is morally virtuous he lacks wisdom—the trait is conspicuously absent from the initial description of Job, who 'is not said to be a wise, or a comprehending, or an intelligent man'.[66] For Rabbi Shapira, suffering propels man to a meta-rational dimension where divine thought can be accessed, while for Maimonides, suffering is a deleterious consequence of leaving the confines of rationality.

---

[61] Scholem, 'Sitra Ahra', 70–1.   [62] *Guide* iii. 17 (p. 474).   [63] Ibid. 22 (p. 489).
[64] Ibid. ii. 30 (p. 356).   [65] Diamond, 'Maimonides on Leprosy'.   [66] *Guide* iii. 22 (p. 487).

Conclusion: Wresting Meaning out of Meaningless Suffering

Emmanuel Levinas could not find meaning in and of itself within individual suffering. For him, 'the evil of pain, the harm itself is the explosion and most profound articulation of absurdity'. In other words, as he sums it up, 'intrinsically it is useless, for nothing'.[67] The only meaning that can be salvaged from suffering is the ethical obligation it imposes on others to suffer for the sufferer. The suffering for useless suffering is an imperative that affords meaning to it, 'the suffering for the useless suffering of the other person, the just suffering in me for the unjustifiable suffering in the Other, opens upon suffering the ethical perspective of the interhuman'.[68] The magnitude of suffering at Auschwitz renders all other rationalizations or theodicies insipid, and in fact calls God's existence into question, for, Levinas asks rhetorically, 'Did not the word of Nietzsche on the death of God take on, in the extermination camps, the signification of a quasi-empirical fact?'[69]

Rabbi Shapira could never tolerate a life without the continued living presence of God, and so he wrested ultimate meaning from what Levinas considered to be devoid of meaning. For divine knowledge to enter and suffuse the world, human thought must abandon its own self. Suffering achieves this by provoking an epistemological rupture, which empties the human mind of its usual modes of knowing, leading to a paradigm shift in which those normal modes of cognition are replaced by divine ones. Rabbi Shapira thus enlists Maimonides to advance what is essentially an anti-Maimonidean theology. He thus presents another extraordinary example of co-opting and adapting Maimonides for the modern age. In Rabbi Shapira's case, the Great Eagle provided a theology to cope with the most cataclysmic challenge to Jewish theology and survival in the entire history of Jews and Judaism, a challenge that Maimonides himself could never have envisioned.

[67] Levinas, 'Useless Suffering', 157–8. See also Don Seeman, 'Ritual Efficacy'.
[68] Levinas, 'Useless Suffering', 159.
[69] Ibid. 162.

FIVE

Rabbi Elhanan Wasserman on Maimonides, and Maimonides on 'Reb Elhanan'

MENACHEM KELLNER

Maimonides and Rabbi Elhanan Wasserman: Two Different Torahs?

In this chapter I discuss Maimonides' and Rabbi Elhanan Wasserman's different understandings of the nature of Torah. I then illustrate this difference by writing a 'Maimonidean' commentary on several key passages in Rabbi Wasserman's writings. I try to show that Maimonides and Rabbi Wasserman read the Torah in two different 'languages', and that the latter did not understand the 'language' of Maimonides' Torah.

The vast gap between Maimonides' world and that of Rabbi Wasserman relates to a meaningful truth concealed within the well-known Italian pun, *traduttore-traditore* (translator-traitor). Translators are well acquainted with the problems of transmitting ideas from one language to another without changing them and often even distorting them, particularly in theological contexts. I shall illustrate this with several significant examples.

In the Septuagint, through which the Torah reached the Christian world, the word 'Torah' is generally translated as *nomos* (law).[1] No wonder, then, that the founders of Christianity related to the Torah mainly as a 'dry' book of laws.[2] Many other words in the Septuagint underwent a Christianizing process, so to speak, in the transition from Hebrew to Greek. One prominent example is the pair 'faith' (Heb. *emunah*) and *pistis*—merely noting that this

---

[1] For a seminal study, see Feldman, 'The Septuagint'.

[2] It bears mention that this approach is not unknown within Judaism as well. Rashi in his commentary on Gen. 1: 1, and Sa'adyah Gaon and Nahmanides in their introductions to their commentaries on the Torah, undertake to explain that the Torah does not only contain laws. Clearly, none of them would have imagined that the Torah is *only* a book of laws as is maintained by many Christian apologists. This feature, as shown below, is particularly prominent in Nahmanides.

Greek term is the root of the word 'epistemology' will suffice to clarify that whoever reads the Torah with, as it were, Greek undertones, reads a book very different from one who reads it with the original undertones.[3] Another example: the word 'mercy' in English clearly denotes a person in a privileged position who, out of kindness, consents to help someone of lesser status. Compare this to the Hebrew equivalent *raḥamim* and its tie to *reḥem* (womb), and the fundamental difference in the 'music' accompanying these two terms becomes immediately apparent. A third example: the word 'man' in German and Yiddish is identical—*Mensch*—but their meaning is entirely different. A *Mensch* could be evil in German, but never in Yiddish. One last example, from the very beginning of all Jewish thought: does Genesis 1: 1 say, 'In the beginning . . .' or 'When God began to create . . .'?

Anyone living in more than one language will immediately grasp this. But what if we were to return to the word 'Torah' and imagine someone learning Torah from, presumably, Arabic-speaking teachers and, at the same time, also engaging in reading the Quran;[4] learning mathematics as a necessary introduction to astronomy; writing introductions to logic; coming to understand the writings of the *mutakallimūn*;[5] seeing *ma'aseh bereshit* (the account of Creation) and *ma'aseh merkavah* (the account of the chariot) as physics and metaphysics[6]—would such a person perceive the Torah essentially differently from someone studying it in Yiddish and for whom *ma'aseh bereshit* and *ma'aseh merkavah* are tied to the mysteries of kabbalah rather than to physics and metaphysics? I will argue here that these two people read very different Torahs—and that is not a trivial matter.

I will illustrate this through a comparison between Maimonides and Holocaust martyr Rabbi Elhanan Wasserman. I will try to rely on Maimonidean statements that are clear and explicit to preclude any claims that I am distorting his views or reading them tendentiously. Should I succeed, we will

---

[3] For discussions on the distortions resulting from the lack of fit between 'faith' (*emunah*) (a word related to 'loyalty' (*ne'emanut*) and to 'trust' (*emun*)) and *pistis* (a word closer to the Arabic *itiqad*, to the Hebrew *yediah* and the English 'knowledge'), see Buber, *Two Types of Faith*, and Seeskin, 'Judaism and the Linguistic Interpretation'. See also Perry, 'The Meaning of "Emunah"'. Perry's attempt to grapple with the theological problem that emerges (for Christianity) from the difference between *emunah* and *pistis* is interesting (and in my view not too successful). For the distortions that result from the confusion between 'faith' and 'knowledge' in Hebrew translations of medieval Arabic texts, see, *inter alia*, A. Kafih, 'Notes from R. Joseph Kafih' (Heb.); and Nuriel, 'The Concept of Belief' (Heb.). This issue is discussed at length, with citations of other studies, in Kellner, 'Religious Faith' (Heb.).

[4] Maimonides occasionally cites quranic verses and it is highly plausible that he knew the text itself. See W. Z. Harvey, 'Averroes and Maimonides' (Heb.), 75–83.

[5] Medieval Muslim theologians.

[6] This sentence is based on the 'Epistle Dedicatory' that opens *Guide of the Perplexed*. In the present chapter, I discuss mainly *ma'aseh bereshit*. For a comprehensive discussion of *ma'aseh merkavah* from a Maimonidean perspective, see Kreisel, 'From Esotericism to Science'.

reach the following conclusion: my colleagues and I, academic scholars of Maimonides, despite our differences, understand Maimonides better than people like Rabbi Wasserman. Now Maimonides is among the few figures of whom we can say that, if he endorsed a view, then, precisely because of his endorsement, that view will, from a Torah perspective, be considered kosher. What follows is that we, academic scholars, understand one aspect of the Torah better than Rabbi Wasserman and his colleagues (contemporary ḥaredi yeshiva heads). This is, admittedly, an arrogant conclusion that I will tone down slightly at the end of this chapter.

Rabbi Elhanan Bunem Wasserman (1874–1941) headed the Ohel Torah yeshiva in the Polish city of Baranowicze.[7] He was a distinguished disciple of Rabbi Yisra'el Me'ir Hakohen Kagan (the Hafets Hayim, 1838–1933) and the brother-in-law of Rabbi Hayim Ozer Grodzinski (1863–1940).[8] Rabbi Wasserman was among the few yeshiva heads of his time who wrote philosophical essays,[9] and is still numbered among the leading exponents of the ḥaredi world-view (at least in its 'Lithuanian' version).[10] He was an intractable zealot,[11]

---

[7] Bauer, 'Jewish Baranowicze'.

[8] R. Wasserman's life is described in Sorasky, *Or elḥanan*. The idea of writing this book came from R. Simha Wasserman, who died in 1992 and was the son of Reb Elchonon (as he was known in the world of Lithuanian yeshivas). Sorasky authored more than 100 biographies of rabbinic figures for ḥaredi readers but, unlike most of the books in this genre, this one is more a biography than a hagiography.

[9] Gershon Greenberg has written several profound studies on the thought of R. Wasserman; see 'Amalek during the Shoah' (Heb.); 'Orthodox Theological Responses'; 'Ontic Division and Religious Survival' (esp. 46–50); 'Consoling Truth'; 'Elhanan Wasserman's Response'. For other studies on R. Wasserman's thought, see Ravitzky, *Messianism* (Heb.), 234–48; Schweid, *From Ruin to Salvation* (Heb.); Horowitz, 'From the Generation of Moses' (Heb.); Brown, 'The *Da'at Torah* Doctrine' (Heb.); and id., 'The Torah as Commandment and as Promise' (Heb.).

[10] As is evident from the following interesting event. In 2008 the world experienced a profound economic crisis. The editors of the *Jewish Observer*, the organ of Agudat Yisra'el in the United States, sought a spiritual leader who would explain to their readers the religious/historical meaning of the crisis, and decided to translate an essay that R. Wasserman had written following the Great Depression of the 1930s: Wasserman, 'The Current Crisis and Its Causes'. On R. Wasserman's influence, note also that his essays on faith and heresy are the basis for J. David Bleich's introduction to his book, *With Perfect Faith*, which is otherwise entirely based on statements by the early authorities (*rishonim*).

[11] Consider this example from Sorasky, *Or elḥanan*, vol. ii, 34–5 (an account of a similar event appears in id., *Reb Elchonon: The Life and Ideals*, 383): 'During R. Elhanan's visit to America in 1938, Yosef Herzman from the Mir Yeshiva in Poland who, in his youth, had been R. Elhanan's disciple in Baranowicze, wrote to tell him that he expected to be called up by the Polish army and, since war was looming, he asked R. Elhanan to intercede for him and request yeshiva heads in America to send him an affidavit that would enable him to emigrate legally, in order to flee from danger. R. Elhanan, however, unswervingly refused to fulfill this request, and answered as follows: "I received your letter and cannot do that . . . the yeshivas in America that students can attend . . . are dangerous places for spirituality, because they are run in a free spirit, and what is the point in running away from a material danger to a spiritual danger?"' This response appears

and a fierce critic of modernity and of Zionism,[12] seeing himself as a disciple of the Hafets Hayim.[13]

R. Wasserman assumed the responsibility of leadership and, seeking to pave a philosophical path for his contemporaries, published many essays. Many of these occasional writings were compiled in his *Kovets ma'amarim*, and perhaps the most famous among them is *Footsteps of the Messiah* (*Ikveta dimeshiḥa*). He uses Maimonides' writings to support his own positions, and this chapter will show how far he went in this use. I am not accusing him, God forbid, of malicious intent. I am not even accusing him (as he does others) of an 'inadvertence equivalent to malice'.[14] Rabbi Wasserman was so sure that he was right and that his view was that of traditional Judaism that he found it inconceivable that Maimonides might not concur with his approach. I am certain that he could not but see Maimonides as a thinker who would easily fit into his yeshiva in Baranowicze.

Part One: Maimonides and R. Wasserman on *Ma'aseh Bereshit*

Let us turn now to the substance of this chapter. In this section I will relate only to one main topic: Maimonides' view of *ma'aseh bereshit*—according to Maimonides himself and according to Rabbi Wasserman—while briefly addressing related topics. If I am successful, the reader will have to admit that Maimonides and Rabbi Wasserman understand the concept of 'Torah' in very different ways and that the world of scholarship understands Maimonides (hence traditional Judaism) better than does the yeshiva world.

Let us first consider a brief passage by Rabbi Wasserman:

in Sorasky, *Or elḥanan*, vol. i, 12 (Hebrew pagination). Sorasky cites this story in praise of R. Wasserman!

[12] Particularly in his highly influential work *Footsteps of the Messiah*. On his critique of Zionism, see Menachem Friedman, 'The State of Israel', and Bacon, 'Birth Pangs of the Messiah'. *Footsteps of the Messiah* was published in a hard-to-find English translation by R. David Cooper of London under the title *Epoch of the Messiah*. I am grateful to R. Cooper's son, Mr Meir Cooper, who lent me a copy of the translation.

[13] It is not clear that the Hafets Hayim himself would have agreed with many of the acts and pronouncements of his disciple. Avinoam Rosenak notes that the Hafets Hayim and R. Kook developed a close friendship and enjoyed studying together. This friendship stood the test of time even thirty years later, in the period of R. Kook's Zionist activity. At an international conference of Agudat Yisra'el in Vienna in September 1923, the Jerusalem representatives were extremely critical of R. Kook. In protest, the Hafets Hayim left the plenary hall and no longer participated in the sessions. He did not shake hands with the Agudat Yisra'el Jerusalem delegation, who were R. Kook's enemies. Rosenak, *Rabbi A. I. Kook* (Heb.), 19–20.

[14] Hebrew: *shegagah she'olah zadon*.

The Vilna Gaon wrote about Maimonides that 'he never saw the *pardes*', thereby meaning to object to Maimonides' statement that *ma'aseh bereshit* is natural science. If Maimonides meant this literally, his words are most certainly astounding given that this *ma'aseh bereshit* is a subject studied in every high school! But in *Derashot haran, Derush* 1, he [Rabenu Nissim of Gerondi, 1320–80] excelled at explaining the depth of Maimonides' intention in a compelling interpretation, noting there that there is a revealed and a concealed natural science, and Maimonides had meant the concealed natural science, which cannot be grasped through the human intellect but only through the holy spirit. See there.[15]

Rabbi Wasserman refers here to the objection to Maimonides that the Gaon Rabbi Eliyahu ben Shelomoh of Vilna (the Vilna Gaon, 1720–97) raised in his commentary on the *Shulḥan arukh*. Maimonides had stated that *ma'aseh bereshit* is synonymous with physics (a matter I discuss at length below). Rabbi Wasserman notes (following Rabenu Nissim) that, by *ma'aseh bereshit*, Maimonides could not possibly have meant the physics studied in every high school. Definitely not! Maimonides had intended 'the concealed natural science', a science that cannot be grasped through the human intellect 'but only through the holy spirit'. Before we proceed, note that, according to Rabbi Wasserman, a non-Jew (or even a non-observant Jew such as Albert Einstein) could not have understood true natural science. Clearly, however, this could not possibly have been the view of Maimonides, who thought that Aristotle had understood true natural science, as shown below.[16]

The background to Rabbi Wasserman's view is the *Shulḥan arukh*. The passage in 'Yoreh de'ah' 246: 4 relies mainly on Maimonides' 'Laws of Torah Study', 1: 11–12,[17] and reads as follows:

A person should divide his study into three: one third the Written Torah, meaning the twenty-four [books of Scripture]; one third Mishnah, meaning the Oral Torah, including the commentaries on the Written Torah; and one third *talmud*, meaning to understand the end from the beginning, and deduce one thing from another, and compare one thing to another, and study the hermeneutical rules by which the Torah is interpreted until he knows the essence of these principles and how to deduce forbidden and allowed and so forth, from what one has learnt traditionally.

[15] Sorasky, *Or elḥanan*, vol. i, 95. All the translations of R. Wasserman's writings are my own, in collaboration with Batya Stein.

[16] Note Maimonides' praise for Aristotle in a letter to Samuel Ibn Tibbon: 'His intellect, meaning Aristotle's, is the very limit of the human intellect, except for those who have received the divine emanation and have reached the rank of prophecy, above which there is no higher'; *Igerot harambam*, vol. ii, 553 (Hebrew pagination). Worth noting in this context is also Maimonides' comment in *Guide* ii. 22 (p. 319): 'Everything that Aristotle has said about all that exists from beneath the sphere of the moon to the center of the earth [i.e. all of terrestrial physics] is indubitably correct.'

[17] On this passage, see Kellner, '*Mishneh torah*: Why?' (Heb.), and the studies cited there.

How? If one is an artisan who works at his trade three hours daily and devotes nine [hours] to the study of Torah, he should spend three [hours] in the study of the Written Torah, three in the study of the Oral Torah, and the remaining three in reflecting how to deduce one rule from another. To what does this refer? To the period when one begins learning. But after one has become proficient and no longer needs to learn the Written Torah, or be continually occupied with the Oral Torah, he should, at fixed times, read the Written Torah and the Oral Torah, so as not to forget any of the rules of the Torah, and should devote all his days exclusively to the study of *talmud*,[18] according to his breadth of mind and maturity of intellect.

Rabbi Moses Isserles (Rema, c.1520–72) comments on this:

Some say that by studying the Babylonian Talmud, which mixes Scripture, Mishnah and Gemara, one fulfils all of one's obligations.[19] And all one needs to do is study Scripture, Mishnah, and Gemara and the verses derived from them and, through them, ensure for oneself this world and a share in the world to come, but not so through the study of other sciences.[20] In any event, it is occasionally allowed to engage in the study of other sciences, so long as they are not books of heresy, and among the sages they refer to this as 'to dally in the *pardes*'. And a person should dally in the *pardes* only after he has first filled himself with meat and wine, which means he knows what is permitted and what is forbidden and the laws of the commandments.[21]

On Rema's determination, the Vilna Gaon comments:

'In any event and so forth, and among the sages they refer to this and so forth, and a person should dally and so forth.' These are the words of Maimonides, and he [Rema] explains that they refer to the four who went into the *pardes* and were

---

[18] On the actual meaning of the word *talmud* in this context, see Kasher, 'Talmud Torah' (Heb.). I obviously do not expect R. Wasserman to agree with Kasher's interpretation, and my discussions below do not rely on her approach.

[19] This view implies that someone who studies the Babylonian Talmud need not study Scripture, Mishnah, Midrash, or any other book. The well-known jest that yeshiva students know only the biblical verses that appear in the Talmud is not far from the regime that Rema tried to enforce. As Warren Zev Harvey noted to me, the pun *bavel-balel* (Babylon-mix) is already found in the Babylonian Talmud: 'What does Bavel denote? Said R. Yohanan: Mixed with Scripture, mixed with Mishnah, mixed with *talmud*' (BT *San.* 24a). The Tosafists note there: 'Rabbenu Tam explained that [studying] our Talmud exempts us from the rabbinic dictum "one should divide one's years [of study] into three: one third Scripture, one third Mishnah, and one third *talmud*" [BT *AZ* 19a]. Nevertheless, we still read every day the portion on the continual burnt offering [*korban tamid*] [Num. 28: 1–8; Lev. 1: 11] and study the mishnah "Which is the place?" [Mishnah *Zev.* 5: 1–8] and learn that "R. Ishmael says in the thirteen rules" [*Sifra*, introd.] and so forth.'

[20] I assume that Rema seeks to prevent students from studying sciences, and perhaps kabbalah as well.

[21] Rema explicitly cites Maimonides as evidence for his view: 'Maimonides, *Book of Knowledge*, end of ch. 4 of the "Laws of the Foundations of the Torah"'.

punished for it, and all were young in years except for Rabbi Akiva and Aher [Elisha b. Avuya]. In the Gemara, they said that 'many heretical books and so forth'.[22] And Rabbi Eleazar said, 'I am not old enough'.[23] But they never saw the *pardes*, neither he [Rema] nor Maimonides. And the text of the rabbi [Rema] is corrupt,[24] given that, if this is *pardes*, how could he say 'but not so [through the study of other sciences]'? And you have no greater reward than that, as it is written [*Suk.* 28a and *BB* 134a] 'a small matter the discussions of Abaye and Raba, a great matter and so forth'.[25] And it is also written there,[26] 'it is not proper to dally in *pardes* and so forth', as is written in *Ḥagigah* 13a 'the mysteries of the Torah may be conveyed and so forth', and so it seems to me.[27]

According to the Gaon, Maimonides never saw the *pardes*.[28] He explains that

---

[22] BT *Ḥag.* 15b: 'They said about Aher—when he stood up in the study house, many heretical books would fall from his lap.' For a discussion of rabbinic sayings about Elisha ben Abuyah, see Liebes, *The Sin of Elisha* (Heb.).

[23] BT *Ḥag.* 13a: 'R. Yohanan said to R. Eleazar: Come, I will instruct you in *ma'aseh merkavah*. He replied: I am not mature enough. When he was mature enough, R. Yohanan had died.'

[24] The Vilna Gaon tries to defend Rema by claiming that the text before him had been corrupt.

[25] BT *Suk.* 28a: 'Our rabbis have taught: Hillel the Elder had eighty disciples—thirty of them were worthy of the Divine Spirit resting upon them, as [it had upon] Moses our Master, thirty of them were worthy that the sun should stand still for them [as it had for] Joshua b. Nun, [and the remaining] twenty were ordinary. The greatest of them was Jonathan b. Uziel, the smallest [was] Yohanan b. Zakai. They said of R. Yohanan b. Zakai that he skipped nothing in Scripture, Mishnah, Gemara, halakhah, *agadah*, details of the Torah, details of the Scribes, inferences *a minori ad maius*, analogies, calendrical computations, *gematrias*, the speech of the ministering angels, the speech of spirits and the speech of palm-trees, fullers' parables and fox fables, a great matter or a small matter. A great matter—*ma'aseh merkavah*; a small matter—the discussions of Abaye and Rabah. To fulfil what is said, "That I may cause those that love me to inherit substance, and that I may fill their treasuries" [Prov. 8: 21]. And if the smallest of them was so great, how much more so was the greatest? They said of Jonathan b. Uziel that when he used to sit and occupy himself with the study of Torah, every bird that flew above him was immediately burnt.' For a discussion of this text, see Kellner, *Maimonides on the 'Decline of the Generations'*, 13–14, and Twersky, *Introduction to the Code*, 494–6.

[26] The Vilna Gaon refers here to the determinations of Maimonides himself in *MT* 'Laws of the Foundations of the Torah', 4: 13.

[27] BT *Ḥag.* 13a: '"Nor upon the *merkavah* in the presence of one." R. Hiyya taught: But chapter headings may be conveyed to him. R. Zera said: Chapter headings may be conveyed only to the head of a court and to one whose heart is troubled . . . R. Ammi said: The mysteries of the Torah may be conveyed only to one who possesses five attributes [Isa. 3: 3]: The captain of fifty, and the honourable man, and the counsellor, and the cunning artificer, and the skilful enchanter.' The 'captain of fifty' hints at a man's age, the 'honourable man' at his standing in society, the 'counsellor' at his wisdom, and the 'cunning artificer' and 'skilful enchanter' at one who understands things one should not talk about and knows how to hold his tongue.

[28] See the other famous comment of the Vilna Gaon on Maimonides: 'many incantations appear in the Gemara and he [Maimonides], because he was drawn to cursed philosophy, wrote that witchcraft and names and incantations and devils and amulets are all a sham, but he has already been found to be wrong [lit. 'hit on the head'], since we found many stories in the Gemara according to names and witchcraft' (commentary on *Shulḥan arukh*, 'Yoreh de'ah',

Elisha ben Avuya became a heretic ('many heretical books would fall from his lap') even though he was not young. The Gaon conveys reservations about Rema's formulation (in terms more respectful than those he uses to convey his reservations about Maimonides), and asks: how can Rema be opposed to the study of *ma'aseh bereshit* and *ma'aseh merkavah* (which for him are mystical knowledge), when they are 'a great thing'?

Now let us reconsider the passage from Rabbi Wasserman cited above. He cannot accept the Vilna Gaon's critique of Maimonides at face value.[29] He notes that this critique would have been justified had Maimonides indeed meant that *ma'aseh bereshit* and physics are identical. Relying on Rabenu Nissim, however, Rabbi Wasserman determines that the natural science that Maimonides had identified as *ma'aseh bereshit* is not the natural science studied 'in every high school' but the concealed (that is, I take him to mean, the kabbalistic) natural science, and that is what Maimonides had intended. This natural science cannot be grasped by a human intellect (such as that of a non-Jew like Aristotle) but solely through the holy spirit.

Before we examine what Maimonides himself said, let us see precisely what it is that Rabenu Nissim said:[30]

> What is *ma'aseh bereshit* is indeed a matter requiring extensive explanation. For Maimonides, of blessed memory, said ['Laws of the Foundations of the Torah', 4: 10–11] that *ma'aseh bereshit* is natural science. Major contradictions are involved here because, when we speak of the elements [earth, water, air, fire] and of the more complex [entities] derived from them, we find nothing requiring concealment and suppression. Moreover, if it is so, we should know the limits wherein to stay without revealing [this knowledge] to the multitudes because, unquestionably, nothing regarding nature and its explanation should remain concealed and suppressed. Rather, it merits revelation to all given that, as we know, the science of medicine and the science of agriculture and shepherding draw on natural science. Hence, those who dwell in towns without walls [Esther 9: 19; i.e. farmers] always study *ma'aseh bereshit*.[31]

'Laws of Diviners and Wizards', 179: 13). On the Vilna Gaon on this matter, see Shohat, 'The Vilna Gaon' (Heb.), and Dienstag, *Relation of Elijah Gaon* (Heb.).

[29] For further attempts to 'save' Maimonides (in the early modern period), see Nadler, 'The "Rambam Revival"'.

[30] N. Gerondi, *Derashot haran*, 23–4 (my translation throughout).

[31] In a footnote (ibid. 24 n. 147), Gerondi's editor, Aryeh Feldman, cites sentences that were added in some of the manuscripts: 'and know it. But neither can we say that *ma'aseh bereshit* is not natural science, given that *ma'aseh bereshit* relates entirely to the sublunar world rather than the superlunar one, because that would be *ma'aseh merkavah*. If *ma'aseh bereshit* is not natural science and its concerns, then what is it? And that is the matter that makes for confusion and requires explanation.'

Rabenu Nissim asks: if *ma'aseh bereshit* is merely natural science—that is, what we call today the natural sciences—why the need for hiding it? Every doctor and every farmer is a natural science expert! He answers:

And the answer is that *ma'aseh bereshit* is unquestionably natural science, but not of the kind that people acquire by study but rather of the kind that is hidden from study and can only be acquired through divine emanation. This is so because all existents have two active forces, one that follows their matter, and one that follows their form, which is their essence. And the forces that follow their matter will be understood through study and through apprehension of their accidents, but those that follow their form cannot possibly become known through study, only through what experience brings to light. And even when we come to know these forces through experience, we will not know them in general. We know that pepper heats, and we know that it heats because the element of fire is dominant in it, since it follows its matter. But even though we know that only human beings laugh and that a magnet draws iron, we know this from experience, but we do not know the cause because they follow their form, and this gate shall be shut [Ezek. 44: 2] to all seekers of wisdom and human learning alone will not open it. The activities which follow from the matter of the thing, as compared to those which follow from the thing itself, are as a drop in the bucket [Isa. 40: 15], because these are drawn from the truth of the thing and its essence and follow from its accidents, which follow from its truth, while these—the forces drawn from its form—depend on the givers of the form or whatever [other] giver. This subject of philosophical investigation [*iyun*] cannot be apprehended solely by human wisdom; rather, its apprehension is outside the realm of possibility.[32]

Rabenu Nissim endorses a philosophical distinction between matter and form and explains that the natural science that is not *ma'aseh bereshit* relates to questions dealing with matter (physics, chemistry, biology, and so forth). These are questions studied empirically and open to the human intellect— everyone's intellect. But there are issues we come to know through experience (that only humans laugh, that magnets attract iron, and so forth), yet we do not grasp the reasons for them, and our understanding of them is very limited compared to our understanding of material things. This realm, which is hidden from our day-to-day awareness, is the concealed part of *ma'aseh bereshit*, as Rabenu Nissim goes on to say:

And this is what Solomon said in his wisdom [Eccles. 7: 23–4]: 'All this have I proved by wisdom: I said, I will be wise; but it was far from me. That which is far off, and exceedingly deep, who can find it out?' When he said that wisdom was far from him and then said 'that which is far off', you should not think that, when saying this

---

[32] Ibid.

wisdom was far off, he was only referring to the apprehension of future things while able to judge the truth of what had already been. Rather, [what he meant to say is] I found what was over and done with also exceedingly deep and I do not know its cause. He learned that this is so from those who know wisdom, which is why he said, 'All this I have proved by wisdom.' Because all the wise [mithakmim] have already admitted that, for knowledge about the essence of things and the actions that follow from them, no enquiry will suffice. That is why Maimonides, of blessed memory, laughed at Galen when he said he does not know why man laughs, and said it would be impossible for him to know the cause of it, since it follows from man's being and form.[33] *Ma'aseh bereshit*, then, is the true natural science. Instead of the subject that the wise [mithakmim] speculate [yitpalsefu] about, *ma'aseh bereshit* is knowledge about the true essence of things, following and drawing on the givers of form, which are the separate intellects that can only become known through divine prophetic emanation. The science of *ma'aseh bereshit*, therefore, is close to and borders on *ma'aseh merkavah* and second to it in rank, because both these sciences entail apprehension of the incorporeal entities, namely, the separate intellects.[34]

Ma'aseh bereshit, then, as the true natural science, is not the one studied in the high schools of Athens, Girona, or Baranowicze. Knowledge of it, which includes knowledge of the 'givers of form'—that is, the separate intellects[35]—is attained solely through 'divine prophetic emanation'.

Rabbi Wasserman, like Rabenu Nissim, insists that *ma'aseh bereshit* is not synonymous with the physics studied 'in every high school'. The difference between Rabenu Nissim (as well as his disciple, Rabbi Hasdai Crescas[36]) and

---

[33] N. Gerondi, *Derashot haran* (p. 28 n. 159), where Feldman notes: 'Maimonides, *Sefer pirkei mosheh birefuah*, 7: 72 (Muntner ed., 106)'. The text to which Feldman refers is quoted here from an English version (*Maimonides, Medical Aphorisms*): 'Says Moses: This statement is correct because laughter is a specific characteristic of human beings. It is well known that each specific property belongs to the generic form, regardless of whether it belongs to the species of animals or plants or minerals. There is no way to give a reason for this. Therefore, one should not look for it in any way, neither regarding laughter nor any other specific property'; see *Maimonides: Medical Aphorisms*, 41.

[34] N. Gerondi, *Derashot haran*, 28. This sentence is based on Maimonides' account in his introduction to the *Guide* (pp. 8–9), using some of the same language. For the text, see below. One wonders if R. Nissim here is casting aspersions on the *mithakmim*, which could be understood to mean 'wise in their own eyes'. Note that he also cited the verse from Ecclesiastes, and was absolutely sure that he was interpreting Maimonides correctly.

[35] On this role of the separate intellects in medieval philosophy, see Goldstein, 'Dator Formarum'.

[36] In *Or hashem*, iv. 10, Hasdai Crescas (d. 1412) followed his teacher and sharply criticized Maimonides ('some of the wise men in our nation') for equating *ma'aseh bereshit* with natural science and *ma'aseh merkavah* with the science that comes after ('meta-') nature. For an illuminating study, see W. Z. Harvey, *Rabbi Hasdai Crescas* (Heb.), 127–34. For other examples of this critique of Maimonides, see Hansel, 'Philosophy and Kabbalah'.

Rabbi Wasserman hinges on Maimonides' view. Rabenu Nissim seemingly claimed that Maimonides had been wrong to equate *ma'aseh bereshit* with revealed natural science. Rabbi Wasserman, who apparently could not bring himself to say such a thing, determined instead that Maimonides had not equated *ma'aseh bereshit* with physics. What is the view of Maimonides himself on this issue? I will consider several texts.

The Mishnah, in *Ḥagigah* 2: 1, reads:

> One does not expound upon forbidden sexual relations in the presence of three, nor upon *ma'aseh bereshit* in the presence of two, nor upon the *merkavah* in the presence of one, unless that one were wise and understood on his own. All who look upon four things, it were better they had not come into the world: what is above, what is below, what is in front, and what is behind. All who are not protective of the honour of their master, it were better they had not come into the world.

This famous text informs us, *inter alia*, that the rabbis had a secret, esoteric Torah. In the context of the present discussion, we need not clarify the essence of this Torah but only acknowledge its existence.[37] Maimonides discusses the issue at length, and here I relate only to some of his comments on this passage in his *Commentary on the Mishnah*:

> Hear *from me* what has become clear to *me* according to *my* understanding on the basis of what *I have learned* from the words of the sages, and it is that they call *ma'aseh bereshit* natural science[38] and enquiry into the beginning of creation. By *ma'aseh merkavah* they mean the divine science,[39] it being speech on the generality of existence and on the existence of the Creator, His knowledge, His attributes, that all created things must necessarily have come from Him, the angels, the soul, the intellect attached to humans, and what is after death. Because of the importance of these two sciences, the natural and the divine—and they were justly considered important—they warned against teaching them as the mathematical sciences are taught. It is known that each person by nature desires all the sciences,[40] whether he be an ignoramus or a sage. [It is further known] that it is impossible for a person to begin the study of these two sciences and direct his thought towards them without the appropriate premises and without entering the stages of the science; they therefore forbade this and warned against it. And they said, seeking to frighten one who directs his thought towards *ma'aseh bereshit* without [appropriate] premises, 'all who look upon four things . . .'. And they [also] said, seeking to restrain one who would direct his thought towards divine matters and examine them with his unaided imagination without ascending the rungs of the sciences, 'all who are not

---

[37] For a valuable study of classic and medieval Jewish esotericism, see Klein-Braslavy, *King Solomon* (Heb.).   [38] Arabic: *al-'ilm al-tiba'i*.   [39] Arabic: *al-'ilm al-ilahi*.

[40] Based on the opening sentence of Aristotle, *Metaphysics*: 'All humans by nature desire to know.'

protective of the honour of their master [it were better they had not come into the world]'. 'It were better they had not come into the world'—means that removing such a person from the ranks of humanity and classifying him as another species of animal would be better for existence than his being a human because he wishes to know something in an inappropriate manner and in a way unsuited to its nature, for only one who is ignorant of the nature of existence would seek to imagine what is above and what is below. When a man empty of all knowledge seeks to use his corrupt imagination in order to know what is above the heavens and below the earth, and imagines [reaching] them to be like ascending to the attic of a house, and also [to know] what was before the creation of the heavens and what will be after they are no longer, he will certainly be brought to madness and desolation. Examine this wonderful expression, said with divine help, 'all who are not protective of the honour of their master', intended to mean, all who are not protective of their intellects, for the intellect is the honour of God [*kevod hashem*]. Since he does not know the value of this matter that was given to him, he is abandoned to his desires and becomes as an animal. Thus, they said, 'Who is he who is not protective of the honour of his Master?—He who transgresses secretly' [BT Ḥag. 16a, Kid. 40a], and they said elsewhere, 'adulterers do not commit adultery until the spirit of madness enters them' [*Midrash tanḥuma*, 'Naso' 5]. This is the truth, for while one craves any of the desires, the intellect is not perfected. This matter is raised here since he said above 'these are bodies of Torah', and therefore mentioned the matters that are the principles of 'bodies of Torah'. Already in the Talmud they forbade teaching them publicly, expressly prohibited it, and commanded that the individual should teach them to himself by himself and should not pass them on to another, deriving this [prohibition] from a parable on Solomon's saying on this matter [S. of S. 4: 11]: 'honey and milk are under thy tongue'.[41]

Maimonides uses two Arabic terms—*al- 'ilm al-tiba 'i* and *al- 'ilm al-ilahi*—in order to explain the terms in the Mishnah, *ma'aseh bereshit* and *ma'aseh merkavah*. These are the accepted Arabic terms for translating the Greek terms *physica* and *metaphysica*. Maimonides even details the contents of *ma'aseh merkavah*: 'it being speech on the generality of existence,[42] and on the existence of the Creator,[43] His knowledge, His attributes, that all created things must necessarily have come from Him,[44] the angels,[45] the soul, the intellect

---

[41] For the translation and discussion of this passage, see Kellner, 'Maimonides' Commentary'.   [42] i.e. ontology.   [43] Proofs of the existence of God.

[44] Meaning precisely 'that all created things must necessarily have come from Him' and not necessarily the creation of the universe. In the Middle Ages, even those who denied that the universe was created generally agreed that God logically precedes the universe.

[45] That is, the separate intellects. R. Wasserman may have been familiar with the following sentence from *Guide* ii. 6 (p. 262): 'Now a chapter making it clear for us that the angels are not bodies occurs previously in this Treatise. This is also what Aristotle says. But there is a difference in the terms; for he speaks of separate intellects, and we speak of *angels*.'

attached to humans,[46] and what is after death'. These, precisely, are the issues included in medieval metaphysics.[47] Why, then, should we think that when Maimonides comes to deal with *ma'aseh bereshit*, a topic more accessible and less dangerous than *ma'aseh merkavah*, he would suddenly change gears, as it were, and intend 'the concealed natural science, which cannot be grasped through the human intellect but only through the holy spirit'?

Another instance of Maimonides equating *ma'aseh bereshit* with physics appears in the first chapters of the *Mishneh torah*. At the end of chapter 4, we read:

The topics connected with these five precepts, treated in the above four chapters, are what our wise men called *pardes*, as in the passage, 'Four went into the *pardes*' [BT Ḥag. 14*b*]. And although those four were great men of Israel and great sages, they did not all possess the capacity to know and grasp these subjects clearly. Therefore I say that it is not proper to dally in the *pardes* till one has first filled oneself with bread and meat; by which I mean knowledge of what is permitted and what is forbidden, and similar distinctions in other classes of precepts. Although these last subjects were called by the sages 'a small thing' (when they say, 'a great thing, *ma'aseh merkavah*; a small thing, the discussion of Abaye and Raba'), still they should have the precedence. For the knowledge of these things gives primarily composure to the mind. They are the precious boon bestowed by God, to promote social well-being on earth, in order to inherit life in the world to come. Moreover, the knowledge of them is within the reach of all, old and young, men and women, those gifted with great intellectual capacity as well as those whose intelligence is limited.[48]

At the end of chapter 2, Maimonides clarifies that the material discussed in chapters 1 and 2 of 'Laws of the Foundations of the Torah' is what the sages, in our *mishnah* in Ḥagigah, called *ma'aseh merkavah*: 'What has been said on this topic in these two chapters is but a drop in the ocean, compared with what has to be elucidated on this subject. The exposition of all the principles included in these two chapters is what is called *ma'aseh merkavah*.'[49] He wants to make sure that we understand that he alludes here to the same *ma'aseh merkavah* concerning which the authors of Ḥagigah 2:1 enjoined public teaching. He goes on and says:

The ancient sages enjoined us only to discuss these subjects privately, with one individual, and then only if he be wise and capable of independent reasoning. In this case, the heads of the topics are communicated to him, and he is instructed in a minute portion of the subject. It is left to him to develop the conclusions for himself and to penetrate to the depths of the subject. These topics are exceedingly profound;

---

[46] The reference is apparently to the Active Intellect.
[47] See the classic article by H. A. Wolfson, 'The Classification of Sciences'.
[48] *MT* 'Laws of the Foundations of the Torah', 4: 13.   [49] Ibid. 2: 11–12.

and not every intellect is able to grasp them. Solomon, in his wisdom, said, in regard to them, by way of parable: 'The lambs will be for thy clothing' [Prov. 27: 26]. Thus have the sages said, in the exposition of this parable, 'matters that deal with the mystery of the universe shall be for thy garment, that is, for thee alone; do not expound them in public'. So too, Solomon said concerning these topics 'Let them be for thee alone and not for strangers with thee' [Prov. 5: 17]. And he further said concerning these subjects 'Honey and milk are under thy tongue' [S. of S. 4: 11]. This text the ancient sages have thus explained, 'The things that are like milk and honey shall be under thy tongue.'[50]

Maimonides then relates to the content discussed in chapters 3 and 4, writing:

The matters just discussed are like a drop in a bucket, and are very deep, but are not as deep as those treated in the first and second chapters. The exposition of the topics dealt with in the third and fourth chapters is termed *ma'aseh bereshit*. Our ancient sages enjoined us that these matters are not to be expounded in public, but should be communicated and taught to an individual privately.[51]

What, then, are the matters discussed in chapters 3 and 4 of the 'Laws of the Foundations of the Torah'? Chapter 3 relates to what is called today 'astronomy': the spheres, stars, planets, and also the four elements (earth, water, air, fire). In chapter 4, Maimonides continues the discussion of the four elements ('chemistry' in today's language) and, in greater detail, discusses the difference between matter and form and explains (in contemporary scientific terms) the essence of the soul.

Maimonides opened the discussion with the following introduction:

This God, honoured and revered, it is our duty to love and fear; as it is said 'Thou shalt love the Lord, thy God' [Deut. 6: 5], and it is further said 'Thou shalt fear the Lord, thy God' [Deut. 6: 13].

And what is the way that will lead to the love of Him and the fear of Him? When a person contemplates His great and wondrous works and creatures and from them obtains a glimpse of His wisdom which is incomparable and infinite, he will straightway love Him, praise Him, glorify Him, and long with an exceeding longing to know His great Name; even as David said 'My soul thirsteth for God, for the living God' [Ps. 42: 3]. And when he ponders these matters, he 'immediately recoils from fear and terror. He knows he is a small, lowly, dark creature with an insignificant and limited intellect, who stands before the Perfect Intellect.' And so David said, 'When I consider Thy heavens, the work of Thy fingers—what is man that Thou art mindful of him?' [Ps. 8: 4–5]. In harmony with these sentiments, I shall explain some large, general aspects of the Works of the Sovereign of the Universe, that they may serve the intelligent individual as a door to the love of God, even as our sages have remarked in connection with the theme of the

[50] *MT* 'Laws of the Foundations of the Torah', 2: 12.   [51] Ibid. 4: 10.

love of God, 'Observe the Universe and hence, you will realize Him who spake and the world was.'[52]

Maimonides clarifies here that the aim of his discussions in the first chapters of the 'Laws of the Foundations of the Torah' is to help those reading his book to love and fear God by contemplating the 'great and wondrous works and creatures' of the Holy One, blessed be he, in order to obtain a glimpse of his 'wisdom which is incomparable and infinite'. And what are these great and wondrous works and creatures? God's actions in the world he created, that is, *ma'aseh bereshit* and *ma'aseh merkavah*, which a person can recognize when contemplating God's creation. The 'person' here includes the Greek non-Jew from whom Maimonides learned these issues.

We find no insight here based on the holy spirit, as Maimonides himself clarifies in his introduction to Part III of *Guide of the Perplexed*:

in that which has occurred to me with regard to these matters, I followed conjecture[53] and supposition; *no divine revelation has come to me to teach me* that the intention in the matter in question was such and such, nor did I receive what I believe in these matters from a teacher. But the texts of the prophetic books and the dicta of the sages, together with the speculative premises that I possess, showed me that things are indubitably so and so. Yet it is possible that they are different and that something else is intended.[54]

And if this is true concerning *ma'aseh merkavah*, all the more so concerning *ma'aseh bereshit*!

A third place where Maimonides explains the nature of *ma'aseh bereshit* and *ma'aseh merkavah* is his introduction to the *Guide of the Perplexed*:

God, may His mention be exalted, wished us to be perfected and the state of our societies to be improved by His laws regarding actions. Now this can come about only after the adoption of intellectual beliefs, the first of which being His apprehension, may He be exalted, according to our capacity. This, in its turn, cannot come about except through divine science, and this divine science cannot become actual except after a study of natural science. This is so since natural science borders on divine science, and its study precedes that of divine science in time as has been made clear to whoever has engaged in speculation on these matters. Hence God, may He be exalted, caused His book to open with the Account of the Beginning [*ma'aseh bereshit*], which, as we have made clear, is natural science. And because of

---

[52] Ibid. 2: 1–2.

[53] In Arabic, *hads*. On this term in Maimonides' thought, see Eran, '*Hads* in Maimonides' (Heb.). See also the long discussion in the translation of the *Guide* by Michael Schwarz, ii. 22 n. 9 (p. 331).

[54] *Guide* introd. to pt. iii (pp. 415–16). Since there is no holy spirit here, Maimonides admits that he may be wrong in his understanding of the 'texts of the prophetic books and the dicta of the Sages'.

the greatness and importance of the subject and because our capacity falls short of apprehending the greatest of subjects as it really is, we are told about these profound matters—which divine wisdom has deemed necessary to convey to us—in parables and riddles and in very obscure words. As [the sages], may their memory be blessed, have said: 'It is impossible to tell mortals of the power of the Account of the Beginning. For this reason Scripture tells you obscurely: In the beginning God created, and so on.' They thus have drawn your attention to the fact that the above-mentioned subjects are obscure. You likewise know Solomon's saying [Eccles. 7: 24]: 'That which was is far off, and exceeding deep; who can find it out?' That which is said about all this is in equivocal terms so that the multitude might comprehend them in accord with the capacity of their understanding and the weakness of their representation, whereas the perfect man, who is already informed, will comprehend them otherwise.[55]

Very simply, then, *ma'aseh bereshit* is identical to natural science. To observe the commandments seriously, what is required is knowledge of the commander (as far as possible), which is attainable through the study of metaphysics. One can study metaphysics only after studying physics, and that is why the Torah opens with *ma'aseh bereshit*, namely physics, using a language that we would today call mythical.

To sum up so far: contrary to what Rabenu Nissim and Rabbi Wasserman thought, Maimonides did indeed equate *ma'aseh bereshit* with physics, and saw no need for the holy spirit in the study of this science, which is accessible to non-Jews and not only to Jews.

So what *is* the mystery here? Why did the rabbis determine that 'one does not expound upon forbidden sexual relations in the presence of three, nor upon *ma'aseh bereshit* in the presence of two, nor upon the *merkavah* in the presence of one, unless that one were wise and understood upon his own'? What actually is the 'big deal'? Anyone asking this question forgets that, according to Aristotle, his physics proved that the world is not created but eternal and that, according to Aristotle, his metaphysics proved that God is not personal, not a creator, not revealed, and entirely passive. Maimonides strenuously tried to overcome these obstacles and understood that not every Jew would endeavour, as he had, to understand the truth that the god of Aristotle is the God of Abraham, Isaac, and Jacob.

Let us remember Maimonides' summary of his discussion on the creation of the world in the *Guide of the Perplexed*:

Know that with a belief in the creation of the world in time, all the miracles become possible and the Law becomes possible, and all questions that may be asked on this

---

[55] *Guide*, introd. to pt. i (pp. 8–9). For discussion, see Kellner, 'Rashi and Maimonides'.

subject, vanish. Thus it might be said: Why did God give prophetic revelation to this one and not to that? Why did God give this Law to this particular nation, and why did He not legislate to the others? Why did He legislate at this particular time, and why did He not legislate before it or after? Why did He impose these commandments and these prohibitions? Why did He privilege the prophet with the miracles mentioned in relation to him and not with some others? What was God's aim in giving this Law? Why did He not, if such was His purpose, put the accomplishment of the commandments and the non-transgression of the prohibitions into our nature? If this were said, the answer to all these questions would be that it would be said: He wanted it this way; or His wisdom required it this way. And just as He brought the world into existence, having the form it has, when He wanted to, without our knowing His will with regard to this or in what respect there was wisdom in His particularizing the forms of the world and the time of its creation—in the same way we do not know His will or the exigency of His wisdom that caused all the matters, about which questions have been posed above, to be particularized. If, however, someone says that the world is as it is in virtue of necessity, it would be a necessary obligation to ask all those questions; and there would be no way out of them except through a recourse to unseemly answers in which there would be combined the giving the lie to, and the annulment of, all the external meanings of the Law with regard to which no intelligent man has any doubt that they are to be taken in their external meanings. It is then because of this that this opinion is shunned and the lives of virtuous men have been and will be spent in investigating this question. For if creation in time were demonstrated—if only as Plato understands creation—all the overhasty claims made to us on this point by the philosophers would become void. In the same way, if the philosophers would succeed in demonstrating eternity as Aristotle understands it, the Law [Arabic: *al-sharia*] as a whole would become void, and a shift to other opinions would take place.[56]

Anyone studying Aristotelian physics at the medieval Cairo High School of

---

[56] *Guide* ii. 25 (p. 330). The entire discussion appears in *Guide* ii. 13–35 (pp. 281–330). Worth mentioning in this context is also the beginning of Maimonides' discussion on the creation of the world in *Guide* ii. 13 (p. 284). He summarizes Aristotle's position as follows:

He thinks furthermore that this whole higher and lower order cannot be corrupted and abolished, that no innovation can take place in it that is not according to its nature, and that no occurrence that deviates from what is analogous to it can happen in it in any way [that is, no miracles]. He asserts—though he does not do so textually, but this is what his opinion comes to—that in his opinion it would be an impossibility that will should change in God or a new volition arise in Him [that is, no Torah from heaven]; and that all that exists has been brought into existence, in the state in which it is at present, by God through His volition; but that it was not produced after having been in a state of nonexistence [that is, there is no voluntary creation, not even in Plato's restricted sense]. He thinks that just as it is impossible that the deity should become nonexistent or that His essence should undergo a change, it is impossible that a volition should undergo a change in Him or a new will arise in Him. Accordingly it follows necessarily that this being as a whole has never ceased to be as it is at present and will be as it is in the future eternity.

Science will be persuaded that the world is eternal and, consequently, 'the Law as a whole would become void'—a sufficient reason for making sure that *ma'aseh bereshit* is not taught in high schools. Modern physics in a high school would seem to be far less threatening in this sense.

Maimonides' philosophy, then, includes both physics and metaphysics—and they are foundations of bodies of Torah (as in his commentary on *Ḥagigah* quoted above).[57] A Maimonidean Torah scholar, then, must study the sciences to be considered a 'true' Torah scholar. Is it at all conceivable that Rabbi Wasserman could agree with such a statement? Let us also remember that the 'mysteries of the Torah' (as the Gemara in *Ḥagigah* 13*a* refers to *ma'aseh bereshit* and *ma'aseh merkavah*) are, according to Maimonides, open to every intelligent person without the holy spirit. The Torah, then, has indeed been given to every person in the world, and not only to Jews,[58] a notion that Rabbi Wasserman would find truly outrageous!

In this context, it will suffice to mention the view that Nahmanides (with whose school Rabenu Nissim sympathized) formulates in the introduction to his *Commentary on the Torah*:

> The Torah . . . preceded the creation of the world,[59] and needless to say, it preceded the birth of Moses our Teacher. It has been transmitted to us by tradition that the Torah was written with letters of black fire upon a background of white fire.[60] . . . Thus everything that has been said prophetically concerning *ma'aseh merkavah* and *ma'aseh bereshit*, and was transmitted about them to the sages, together with the four forces in the sublunar world: the force of minerals, the force of earthly vegetation, the animal and rational souls, all of them were transmitted to Moses, including the nature of their creation, their essence, their powers and functions, and the disintegration of those of them that are destroyed. All of this was written in the Torah, explicitly or by implication. Now our sages have already said: 'Fifty gates of understanding were created in the world, and all were transmitted to Moses with one exception, as it is said, "Thou has made him but little lower than the angels" [Ps. 8: 6]' [BT *RH* 21*b*].[61]

As it is unquestionable that Rabbi Wasserman agreed with these statements, so is it unquestionable that Maimonides could not support them.[62] Rabbi Wasserman's Torah preceded the world, and the world is therefore made fit

---

[57] Twersky was the first to point out the importance of this determination: physics and metaphysics are *yesodot gufei torah*. See id., *Introduction to the Code*, 361.

[58] Hirshman, *Torah for the Entire World* (Heb.), 271. The main points of this book are summarized in id., 'Rabbinic Universalism'.

[59] On this idea, see Kellner, 'Did the Torah Precede the Cosmos?' (Heb.).

[60] JT *Shek.* 6: 1; Rashi on Deut. 33: 2.

[61] I cite (with emendations) Chavel (trans.), *Ramban: Commentary*, vol. i, Gen., p. 8.

[62] I have discussed these matters at length in 'Did the Torah Precede the Cosmos?' (Heb.).

for the Torah and not vice versa. Maimonides' Torah, by contrast, describes what actually happened (and could have happened differently), rather than what must have happened and could not have happened otherwise. We learn this from Maimonides' 'scandalous' discussion on the matter of sacrifices,[63] stating that God 'was forced'[64] to command the sacrifices due to the spiritual weakness of the people of Israel at the time of the Exodus (unlike Judah Halevi, who saw all of them as prophets), rather than because God was genuinely interested in sacrifices.[65]

The status of the commandments is also related to this issue. Again, so as not to repeat myself,[66] I will merely note the following: according to Maimonides, the commandments could have been different (the prohibition on mingling wool and linen (sha'atnez), for example, is contingent on the non-necessary historical fact that idolatrous priests at the time of Abraham wore garments made of wool and linen[67]), and they shape a social reality rather than reflect true distinctions in the ontology of existence. Rabbi Wasserman would probably have scornfully rejected these determinations.

Rabbi Wasserman, then, did not understand Maimonides—which is not at all surprising,[68] and he is obviously not the only one.[69] Not only did he

---

[63] Guide iii. 32 (pp. 526–7).

[64] In the words of Isaac Abrabanel in his commentary on Jer. 7. See Kellner, 'Maimonides' Moses' (Heb.). [65] See Kellner, Maimonides' Confrontation, 140–54.

[66] Ibid., ch. 2, and id., 'Rabbis in Politics' (Heb.). See also the illuminating discussions of Yohanan Silman on these questions: 'Halakhic Determinations' (Heb.); 'Commandments and Transgressions' (Heb.); 'Introduction to the Philosophical Analysis'; and Halakhic Instructions (Heb.). [67] See Guide iii. 37 (p. 544).

[68] Note that Maimonides views the Torah of Moses as a species in the genre of 'Torahs'. What separates the Torah of Moses from other Torahs is that it is genuinely divine. Thanks to an anonymous friend, who gave me a digital version of the Arabic text of Guide of the Perplexed, I was able to discover that Maimonides uses the expression 'sharia of Moses' ten times in the Guide (as opposed to the expression al-torah, which appears ninety-seven times). Imagine R. Wasserman writing 'The Bible of Moses, may he rest in peace' instead of 'the Torah of Moses', and you will understand the meaning of this fine distinction. On the expression 'sharia of Moses' in Maimonides, see Nuriel, 'On the Meaning' (Heb.), and Kraemer 'Naturalism and Universalism', esp. 49–52. Note that contemporary physics does not lead to metaphysical insights (my thanks to Yitzhak Lifschitz who pointed this out to me), a fact that hinders R. Wasserman's understanding of Maimonides. Furthermore, note that Maimonides was aware of the difficulty of drawing borders between physics and metaphysics 'since natural science borders on divine science, and its study precedes that of divine science in time' (Guide, introd. to pt. i (p. 9)). For further discussion, see Gad Freudenthal, 'Maimonides on the Scope of Metaphysics'. Finally, note also that, for R. Wasserman, proving the existence of God poses no problems. His God is so immanent in his world that it is simply a pity to waste energy on proofs of his existence. By contrast, Maimonides invests great effort in the proofs of God's existence. Hence, even if today's physics were to lead to metaphysics, and if metaphysics were to lead to proofs of God's existence, R. Wasserman would have considered this effort superfluous.

[69] The late Shlomo Sprecher of New York pointed out to me some astounding statements of R. Moshe Feinstein (Igerot mosheh, 'Yoreh de'ah', ii. 141). These statements are an attempt to

not understand Maimonides as the latter understood himself; there is no way in which he could have understood him. Yeshiva study as practised by Rabbi Wasserman and his cultural heirs is ahistorical and completely oblivious to cultural and intellectual influences. In that world, Rabbi Wasserman and Maimonides had to live in the same culture and speak the same language (Yiddish?), since they had to breathe the same Torah culture which transcends history. Living ahistorically, Rabbi Wasserman could not have been aware that his use of a term like *ma'aseh bereshit* carries with it the baggage of eight hundred years of kabbalistic thought. In his eyes (if not in the eyes of Rabenu Nissim Gerondi or of Hasdai Crescas, as we shall see soon), the term as used in Mishnah Ḥagigah, in Maimonides' writings, and in his own studies must mean the same thing. Torah study is an insular experience divorced from its material surroundings and immune from non-Jewish thinking or contributions.

This matter should be understood in the context of a charming urban legend about a student of the great teacher Nehama Leibowitz who once suggested an interpretation of a verse. Nehama rejected it outright and the student protested: 'What about the "seventy faces of Torah"!' Nehama resolutely answered: 'Seventy yes, seventy-one—no.' Rabbi Wasserman would agree: seventy faces of Torah, yes, seventy-one, no—and it is unquestionable that, in his view, the Maimonides I have presented here is one of the seventy-one (rather than one of the seventy kosher ones). No one will question that Maimonides understood the Torah. But who understands Maimonides? I have tried to show here that academic scholars understand him better than his commentators in the yeshiva world. In other words, we, the professors, understand this facet of the Torah better than many rabbis and halakhists.

But, and there is always a but, I think that Maimonides also held 'seventy faces, yes, seventy-one, no'. And, indeed, it is highly plausible that, in Maimonides' view, Rabbi Wasserman's view on the essence of the Torah—a Torah without physics or metaphysics but with kabbalah—is the seventy-first rather than one of the seventy kosher ones.[70]

---

force Maimonides to agree with what is acceptable in Feinstein's circles concerning the nature of angels. He had already been preceded by Maimonides' commentators, but the literal meaning of the *Mishneh torah* laws cited in this passage confutes Feinstein's interpretation, as do Maimonides' explicit statements in *Guide* ii. 6 (pp. 261–5). On angels in Maimonides' thought, see Kellner, *Maimonides' Confrontation*, ch. 8.

[70] The following excerpt from the beginning of his *Epistle on Resurrection* will suffice:

When I applied myself to this task, I realized that it was not correct to strive to explain the ramifications of the religious law, and to leave its roots neglected, unexplained, and its essentials undiscussed, providing no guidance. This is especially urgent since I have met some who think that they are among the sages of Israel—by God, they indeed know the way

As we know, there have been attempts, as it were, to exclude Maimonides from the *beit midrash*, up to and including the burning of his books in the Middle Ages, and simply ignoring many of his writings in today's yeshiva world; but apparently, Maimonides would also have been happy to exclude Rabbi Wasserman from his own *beit midrash*.[71] What should a Jew (and not necessarily a scholar) conclude from this? Probably that there are more rooms in the palace of Torah than either Maimonides or Rabbi Wasserman imagined.

Part Two: Four Essays by Rabbi Wasserman about Maimonides

My presumption is that, at present, there is hardly any Jewish group that fails to see Maimonides as its spiritual forefather. Rabbi Wasserman surely falls into that category. In this section I will attempt to trace his use of Maimonidean thought by writing a 'Maimonidean' commentary on four of his essays in which Maimonides plays a central role. I translate the texts and add my commentary in a series of footnotes. By way of providing leadership for Jews dispersed over Europe and the globe, Rabbi Wasserman published many essays on issues of communal concern. Most of these occasional writings were compiled in his *Kovets ma'amarim*. Below are the first four essays from the first volume. All deal with matters of belief, and all were written in what could be called a 'Maimonidean spirit'. Rabbi Wasserman uses Maimonides' writings to support his own positions, and this discussion will show how far he went in his use of Maimonides.

---

of the Law since childhood, and they battle in legal discussions—but they are not certain if God is corporeal, with eyes, hands, and feet, as the Bible says, or if He has no body. Others, whom I have met in some lands, assert positively that He is corporeal and call anyone who thinks differently a nonbeliever, name him a heretic and Epicurean. . . . When I learned of these exceedingly deficient folk and their doubts, who, although they consider themselves sages in Israel, are in fact the most ignorant, and more seriously astray than beasts, their minds filled with the senseless prattle of old women [sic] and noxious fantasies, like children and women, I concluded that it was necessary that I clearly elucidate religious fundamentals in my works on law. I determined not to teach these basic truths in the idiom of inquiry, since examination of these roots requires skills in many fields, of which, as I pointed out in the *Guide*, the learned in Torah know nothing. (trans. A. S. Halkin, *Crisis and Leadership*, 212)

[71] Maimonides' treatment at the hands of ArtScroll's publishers exemplifies the first phenomenon; Maimonides' oft-expressed disdain for many of his rabbinic contemporaries exemplifies the second. See, for example, the previous note.

1. Essay on Belief: 'Examples of Literal Explanations'[72]

'And that you seek not after your own heart' [Num. 15: 39],[73] this is heresy and so forth [BT *Ber.* 12*b*].[74] The cause of heresy is seemingly the corruption of reason and of the intellect,[75] but knowledge resides in the person's head rather than in the heart,[76] so the warning should have said 'and that you seek not after your own reason and your own heads'. Yet we often find in Scripture that wisdom is ascribed to the heart, as 'for my heart has seen much of wisdom' [Eccles. 1: 16],[77] 'the wise in heart will receive commandments' [Prov. 10: 8].[78] This connection of wisdom to the heart requires explanation.

Maimonides wrote in the *Book of the Commandments*, 'The first positive commandment is to know and believe in the Holy One, blessed be He', and so forth.[79] And we must understand how the commandment to believe can be

---

[72] Throughout these extracts, the sources supplied in square brackets are by the editor, Menahem Tsevi Goldbaum. I have spelled out abbreviations and, in the footnotes, I cite in full the scriptural verses and rabbinic sayings that R. Wasserman cites in abridged form.

[73] 'And it shall be to you as a fringe, that you may look upon it, and remember all the commandments of the Lord, and do them; and that you seek not after your own heart and your own eyes, after which you go astray.'

[74] 'Why did they include the section of fringes [in *keriat shema*]? R. Judah b. Habiba said: Because it makes reference to five things: the precept of fringes, the exodus from Egypt, the yoke of the commandments, [a warning against] the opinions of the heretics, and the hankering after sexual immorality and the hankering after idolatry. The first three, we grant you, are obvious: the yoke of the commandments, as it is written [Num. 15] "That ye may look upon it and remember all the commandments of the Lord"; the fringes, as it is written: "That they make for themselves fringes", and so forth; the Exodus from Egypt, as it is written: "Who brought you out of the land of Egypt". But where do we find [warnings against] the opinions of the heretics, and the hankering after immorality and idolatry? It has been taught: "After your own heart": this refers to heresy; and so it says [Ps. 14], "The fool hath said in his heart, There is no God". "After your own eyes"—this refers to the hankering after immorality; and so it says [Judg. 14], "And Samson said to his father, Get her for me, for she is pleasing in my eyes". "After which ye use to go astray": this refers to the hankering after idolatry; and so it says [Judg. 8], "And they went astray after the *be'alim*".'

[75] Meaning that an uncorrupted, healthy, and perfect intellect will, by itself, reach true belief. This approach is important to R. Wasserman, who wishes to accuse those who believe in falsehood of fraudulence. He disagrees in this regard with Maimonides, for whom true belief results from a strenuous intellectual effort. See the 'Epistle Dedicatory' to his student at the opening of the *Guide*, and also the parable of the palace in *Guide* iii. 51 (p. 618).

[76] A determination attesting that R. Wasserman is a man of the modern world, despite his strong opposition to it.

[77] 'See, I have acquired great wisdom, surpassing all those who were before me in Jerusalem: for my heart has seen much of wisdom and knowledge.'

[78] 'The wise in heart will receive commandments: but a prating fool shall be punished.'

[79] 'Believing in God. By this injunction we are commanded to believe in God; that is, to believe that there is a Supreme Cause Who is the Creator of everything that is in existence. It is contained in His words (exalted be He): "I am the Lord thy God, who brought thee out of the land of Egypt" and so forth [Exod. 20: 2].' Chavel (trans.), *Book of Divine Commandments*, 1. On the issue of belief versus knowledge in Maimonides, see Ch. 2 in the present volume.

among the positive commandments—this would make sense with respect to one of the commandments to act [*ḥovat ha'evarim*],[80] which depend on a person's will to act or desist from action, while faith in God, may He be blessed, and in His Torah is, in any event, in God's hands.[81] You cannot have it both ways: if he does have faith, he need not be commanded to believe, and if, God forbid, faith has been cut off from his heart,[82] he is incapable of bringing it back and is, as it were, entirely compelled in this regard, since he is coerced by his heart. And from the Torah we see that the offence of heresy is extremely grave, even more than idolatry, since an idolater must be judged in court, with witnesses and a warning,[83] whereas heretics are cast into a well and not brought up,[84] anywhere and at all times, without a need for a warning or for a Sanhedrin decision. And the same applies to a [sincere] believer in idolatry who is willing to die for it, or to one sacrificing his son to Moloch. At first glance, he deserves to be judged as compelled, since his belief in idolatry is so strong that he sacrifices his son to it, and his punishment should therefore be more lenient than that imposed on one who believes in God and simply commits an offence. In the Torah, however, we find the opposite, because the offence of idolatry is extremely grave, and Maimonides writes that we only find the expression 'jealousy' in the Torah in reference to idolatry—jealous and vengeful.[85]

[80] Here R. Wasserman adopts the terminology of Bahya ibn Pakuda. Bahya's *Duties of the Heart* is one of the very few philosophical works he mentions.
[81] R. Wasserman was apparently unaware of the book *Or hashem* by Hasdai Crescas or of the discussion about it in Isaac Abrabanel's *Principles of Faith*. Crescas raises the question considered here in the preface to his book, and Abrabanel relates to Crescas' discussion in ch. 4 of his own book. See Kellner's translation of *Principles of Faith*, chs. 4 and 17.
[82] The default option for a healthy and uncorrupted person, then, is to believe.
[83] See Mishnah *San.*, ch. 6, on the four types of capital punishment. [84] BT *AZ* 26b.
[85] *Guide* i. 36 (p. 82): 'Know that if you consider the whole of the Torah and all the books of the prophets, you will find that the expressions *wrath, anger,* and *jealousy* are exclusively used with reference to *idolatry*. You will also find that the expressions, *enemy of God* or *adversary* or *hater* are exclusively used to designate an idolater.' The discussion here shows that R. Wasserman held that Maimonides too believes that heresy is an offence graver than idolatry and that heresy means atheism. He did not relate to Maimonides' own definitions of heresy in *MT* 'Laws of Repentance', 3: 8:

Three classes are deniers of the Torah; he who says that the Torah is not of divine origin—even if he says of one verse or of a single word, that Moses said it of himself—is a denier of the Torah; likewise, he who denies its interpretation, that is the Oral Torah, and repudiates its reporters, as Zadok and Boethus did; he who says that the Creator changed one commandment for another, and that this Torah, although of divine origin, is now obsolete, as the Nazarenes and Muslims assert. Everyone belonging to these classes is a denier of the Torah.

R. Wasserman may have refrained from dealing with these definitions because they focus on the denial of the Torah rather than on the denial of God's existence. It is strange that he ignores the fact emerging from *Guide* i. 35–6 (pp. 79–85) (on one chapter of which he relies here), stating that idolatry is a far graver offence than 'heresy' (in R. Wasserman's sense).

Moreover, belief is among the commandments incumbent on all Jews as soon as they reach maturity[86]—that is, a boy at age 13 and a girl at age 12.[87] Yet we know that, on matters of belief, the greatest philosophers have failed, such as Aristotle, of whom Maimonides[88] said that his intellect ranks only below prophecy and thereby meant that, except for prophecy and the holy spirit,[89] he was the wisest of all sages in the world. Yet he failed concerning belief or, at least, his wisdom did not suffice to attain true belief. How, then, can the holy Torah compel all youths to attain with their limited reason more than Aristotle, when we know that the Holy One, blessed be He, does not deal imperiously with His creatures?[90]

Furthermore, the descendants of Noah were commanded to observe seven commandments.[91] If they failed to observe them, they would surely be punished for it in the world to come. Let us imagine a Noachide, all his life a

---

[86] R. Wasserman appears to be following Maimonides, as he understood him, and determines that there are commandments regarding belief. He could not have known that Maimonides actually set commandments on matters of knowledge rather than belief (on this issue, see below). He could have known that many distinguished figures (such as Crescas) challenged Maimonides on this question, but he could not have known that the Maimonidean determination that there are principles of belief in Judaism is an absolute innovation in the history of the Jewish religion. See Kellner, *Dogma in Medieval Jewish Thought* and *Must a Jew Believe Anything?*

[87] BT *Nid.* 45b.

[88] Letter to R. Samuel Ibn Tibbon, *Kitvei harambam*. Following is the relevant section of the letter:

> Be careful not to study the works of Aristotle without the commentaries on them, the commentary of Alexander [of Aphrodisias, end of the 2nd cent.], or the commentary of Themistius [317–87], or the commentary of ibn Rushd [Averroes, 1126–98]. . . . The books of Aristotle are the sources and foundations for these compositions on the sciences. They are not understandable, as we have mentioned, except with the commentaries on them, [namely,] the commentary of Alexander or Themistius or the commentary of ibn Rushd. . . . The discourse of Plato, the teacher of Aristotle, in his books and compositions, contains enigmas and parables and are also superfluous for an intelligent man; for the books of his pupil Aristotle cover all that was composed previously. *His opinion—I mean to say, the opinion of Aristotle—is the ultimate of human opinion, save for those who received the divine overflow, so that they attained the rank of prophecy, which is the highest rank.*

Kraemer, *Maimonides: The Life and World*, 442–3 (my emphasis).

[89] R. Wasserman appears to be quoting inaccurately here. According to Maimonides (see the note above), Aristotle reached one rung below prophecy. According to R. Wasserman's Maimonides, Aristotle reached one rung below the holy spirit. According to Maimonides, the holy spirit is one rung below prophecy itself (*Guide* ii. 45, pp. 398–40). According to R. Wasserman, then, the Aristotle of Maimonides is less talented than Aristotle according to Maimonides himself. Maimonides viewed Aristotle and King Solomon on the same rung (one below actual prophecy). For a discussion of prophecy and the holy spirit in Maimonides' thought, see Lasker 'Sub-Prophetic Inspiration' (Heb.). On King Solomon in Maimonides' thought, see Klein-Braslavy, *King Solomon* (Heb.).

[90] BT *AZ* 3a.

[91] BT *San.* 56a: 'The sons of Noah were given seven precepts, viz. [prohibition of] idolatry, adultery, murder, robbery, [and] flesh cut from a living animal, and establishing courts of law.' On this, see Novak, *The Image of the Non-Jew*.

drunkard and a shepherd,[92] who comes to the heavenly court and is sentenced to hell for failing to fulfil the seven commandments. He will then scream: 'How should I have known that I am to observe the seven commandments?' Ostensibly, his claim is entirely justified, but he will still be found guilty. All these matters require an explanation.

But when we consider this, we will find that the belief that the Holy One, blessed be He, created the world is self-evident to every thinking person who is not a fool, and there is no need for any philosophy to reach this understanding.[93] This is what [Rabenu Bahya's] *Duties of the Heart* says in the 'Treatise on the Unity of God', ch. 6:

Some people have said that the world was formed by chance, without a Creator, God forbid. I wonder how such a thought can occur. Had someone said about a waterwheel used to water a field that it was made without the artisan's intention, we would have thought him a fool, mad, and all the rest. It is well known that no signs of wisdom will be found in things lacking a purposeful intention, and were a man to suddenly spill some ink on a clear sheet of paper, no orderly writing could ever come from it. Were an orderly piece of writing be brought to us and were someone to say that ink was spilt by itself on the paper and turned into writing, we would think him a fool, and so forth.[94]

How could a rational person say about the entire creation that it happened by itself after we see at every step signs of deep and unfathomable wisdom? How much wondrous wisdom is there in the structure of a human body and in the arrangement of its limbs and powers, as all doctors and surgeons will attest! And how can one say about such a wondrous machine that it was built by itself without prior intention? Anyone saying about a clock that it came about by itself would surely be thought mad. And all these matters are to be found in the *midrash* (*Batei midrashot*, vol. ii: *Midrash temurah hashalem* 1: 5):

A heretic once came to Rabbi Akiva. Said the heretic to Rabbi Akiva: Who created the world? Rabbi Akiva said to him: The Holy One, blessed be He. Said the heretic: Show me something clear [proof]. Said Rabbi Akiva to him: Who wove your garment? Said the heretic: A weaver. Rabbi Akiva said to him: Show me something clear [proof]. In the same words, Rabbi Akiva said to his disciples: As the garment

---

[92] There is more than a suggestion of bestiality here. See BT *AZ* 22b.

[93] This determination would probably surprise Maimonides, who strenuously sought to prove that the world was created. He finally admitted that to prove that the world was created is impossible (*Guide* ii. 25, p. 329), and was forced to limit himself to the statement that it cannot be proved that it was not.

[94] R. Wasserman appears to have been quoting from memory. See Ibn Pakuda, *Duties of the Heart*, trans. Mansoor, 120; trans. Kafih (Heb.), 57.

attests to the weaver, and the door to the carpenter, and the house to the builder, so the world attests to the Holy One, blessed be He, who created it. So far the *midrash*.⁹⁵

And were we to imagine that a person possesses all his faculties from the moment of his birth, we would still fail to grasp his amazement at suddenly seeing the heavens and their hosts and the earth and all that is upon it. And then if we were to ask this man to answer our question—has the world he is now seeing for the first time emerged by itself without any prior intention or is it the work of a wise creator?—he will then consider and, unquestionably, will answer that this is a work of wonderful wisdom and sublime order, as explained in Scripture [Ps. 19: 2], 'The heavens declare the glory of God',⁹⁶ 'But while I am still in my flesh' [Job 19: 26].⁹⁷ And if so, the opposite is quite astonishing—how could great philosophers foolishly say that the world was created by chance?⁹⁸

We found the solution to this riddle in the holy Torah that reveals to us all that is obscure, where it is written [Deut. 16: 19], 'neither take a bribe, for a bribe blinds the eyes of the wise'.⁹⁹ And a bribe, according to the law of the Torah, is as much about a penny as about theft, interest, and so forth. And this law is incumbent on everyone, including 'the wisest of all men'¹⁰⁰ and even on a righteous man like Moses, may he rest in peace. Were we to imagine that he took a bribe of a penny, the eyes of his mind would be blinded, and he could not judge fairly. At first glance, it seems amazing to say about Moses and Aaron that, for some profit that they might have enjoyed from one of the litigants, they changed their minds and perverted justice. But the Torah attested that it was so, and 'the testimony of the Lord is sure' [Ps. 19: 8].¹⁰¹ It must therefore be clarified that this is the law of nature over the powers of the human soul,¹⁰² because the will influences the mind. All is obviously according to the measure of the will and the measure of the mind—the influence

---

⁹⁵ This is not precisely the formulation in the *midrash* that has reached us.

⁹⁶ 'The heavens declare the glory of God; and the firmament proclaims his handiwork.'

⁹⁷ 'But whilst I am still in my flesh, though it be after my skin is torn from my body, I would see God.'

⁹⁸ The philosopher that Maimonides grapples with, Aristotle, never claimed that the world 'was created by chance'. Aristotle stated that the world is eternal and was never created at all. See *Guide* ii. 13 (pp. 281–5) and ii. 25 (pp. 327–30). I assume that R. Wasserman would have found this fine distinction meaningless.

⁹⁹ 'Thou shalt not wrest judgement; thou shalt not respect persons, neither take a bribe, for a bribe blinds the eyes of the wise, and perverts the words of the righteous.'

¹⁰⁰ This description usually refers to King Solomon.

¹⁰¹ 'The Torah of the Lord is perfect, restoring the soul: the testimony of the Lord is sure, making wise the simple.'

¹⁰² Note that, in a move rather unusual for him, R. Wasserman resorts here to an idea ('law of nature') that is not explained in rabbinic sources. I found close to a dozen uses of the expression 'law of nature' in the Bar Ilan Responsa Project, all dating from R. Nissim onwards.

of a limited will on a great mind will be small and on a small mind will be greater, and of a great one even more so. Some effect, however, will always be felt, and even the most limited of wills will, in some way, be able to affect a greater mind. And we found in the second chapter of *Ketubot* [105b] that our rabbis, of blessed memory, felt that any gain that might have reached them from some person could immediately have biased them to suggest 'he could have pleaded thus and so forth', and said about this, 'May all those who take bribes be destroyed!'[103] See very wonderful things there.

Now, let us see. If the judgement of our rabbis, of blessed memory, who were as angels in the breadth of their knowledge and in their holy virtues,[104] could become biased by a gift, all the more so individuals who are engrossed in the cravings of this world, who are bribed by the evil inclination telling them—a free world is before you, do as your heart wishes.[105] How great is the power of this coarse touch to blind the eyes of their mind, because on a matter that a man has been bribed, he will be unable to recognize the truth if it contradicts his wishes and, in this regard, he is as drunk. And wisdom, when one is drunk, will not serve even the greatest of sages. It is no longer puzzling, then, that philosophers refuted the creation of the world because, however great their intellect, their craving for the pleasures of this world is even greater, and such a bribe can prejudice a person to say that two times two is not four but five.[106] No power or intellect will enable a person to know the

---

[103] 'A man once brought a gift of the first fleece to R. Ishmael b. Elisha [who was a priest]. R. Ishmael asked him, "Where are you from?" "From such and such a place", he replied. "And between that place and here there was no other priest to whom the first fleece could be given?" "I have a lawsuit", replied the other, "and I thought that at the same time I come for the lawsuit I would bring it to the Master". He said to him, "I am unfit to try your action", and he refused to receive the gift and appointed two rabbis to try his action. As he was arranging this matter, R. Ishmael thought: "Had he wished, he could have pleaded thus or, if he preferred, he might have pleaded thus." "May all those who take bribes be destroyed!", he exclaimed. "If I—who did not take the gift and, had I taken it, I would only have accepted what is mine by right—am inclined in his favour, all the more so those who accept bribes."'

[104] BT *Shab.* 112b: 'If the earlier scholars were sons of angels—we are sons of men, and if the earlier scholars were sons of men—we are like asses, and not even like the asses of R. Hanina b. Dosa and R. Pinhas b. Jair, but like all other asses.' BT *Eruv.* 53a: 'R. Johanan further stated: The hearts of the ancients were like the door of the *ulam* [the Temple's large chamber], but that of later generations was like the door of the *heikhal* [the Temple's smaller chamber], while ours is like the eye of a fine needle. The ancients—R. Akiva, the later generations—R. Eleazar b. Shammoa. Some say: ancients—R. Eleazar b. Shammoa, later generations—R. Oshaia Beribi. And we are like the eye of a fine needle. And we, said Abaye, are like a peg in a wall as regards Gemara. And we, said Raba, are like a finger in wax as regards logical argument. We, said R. Ashi, are like a finger in a pit as regards forgetfulness.'

[105] R. Wasserman relies here on the idea of the decline of the generations. It is plausible to assume that Maimonides was not acquainted with this idea and also that, had he been, he would have rejected it. See Kellner, *Maimonides on the 'Decline of the Generations'*.

[106] R. Wasserman accuses the philosophers who denied the creation of the world (as did

truth if he is prejudiced on the matter at stake, but if knowing the truth goes against a person's will, even a greater intellect will lack power to show him the light.[107]

In themselves, then, the principles of faith[108] are simple and necessary for anyone who is not a fool, and their truth is unquestionable, indeed only insofar as the person is not prejudiced, meaning that he is free from the cravings of this world and its desires. The cause of heresy and apostasy, then, is not the corruption of the intellect as such but rather the person's desire for earthly cravings, which blinds his mind.[109]

The Torah's warning 'And that you seek not after your own heart—this is heresy'[110] is now perfectly clear. The person is warned to quash and subdue his wishes so that the intellect may be free from the inclinations of the will and thus able to recognize the truth obvious to any rational being—that the Holy One, blessed be He, created the world. As Rabbi Akiva said, the world attests that it was created by the Holy One, blessed be He. Heresy has absolutely no room in a person's intellect, only in his will for his cravings.[111] Had his cravings not reached the rung of coarseness, he could not possibly have come to a mistake of heresy or idolatry, and his offence—in allowing his cravings so to overwhelm his reason that he fails to recognize this simple truth—is therefore unbearable. The commandment to believe means preventing his passions from overwhelming his reason, and faith will then necessarily ensue.[112] And

---

Aristotle) of moral corruption. According to Maimonides, high moral perfection is a condition for intellectual advancement; see, for example, *Guide* i. 34 (pp. 76–7): 'For it has been explained, or rather demonstrated, that the moral virtues are a preparation for the rational virtues, it being impossible to achieve true, rational acts—I mean perfect rationality—unless it be by a man thoroughly trained with respect to his morals and endowed with the qualities of tranquillity and quiet.' For Maimonides, then, it was impossible to think of Aristotle as morally corrupt.

[107] Liron Hoch commented to me that, according to Maimonides, perplexity is a stage on the way to belief. According to R. Wasserman, perplexity leads to heresy.

[108] R. Wasserman adopts the Maimonidean determination that there are principles of faith in the Torah; Kellner, *Dogma in Medieval Jewish Thought*, ch. 1. His claim in the continuation of this sentence that 'the principles of faith are simple and necessary for anyone who is not a fool' is surprising, given the debates around Maimonides on resurrection of the dead.

[109] This entire discussion again indicates that, according to R. Wasserman, an atheist cannot be moral.

[110] BT *Ber.* 12b. R. Wasserman seemingly fails to separate the verse from its commentary.

[111] The default option, then, is to believe with perfect faith, and those who do not can only blame themselves. Yisrael Ben-Simon pointed out to me that, to some extent, this view resembles Maimonides' explanation for sacrifices brought for inadvertent transgressions (*Guide* iii. 41, pp. 563–4; *MT* 'Laws of Offerings for Transgressions Committed through Error', 5: 6). For a discussion, see Kellner, *Maimonides' Confrontation*, 52–66.

[112] An illuminating comparison is that between R. Wasserman and Isaac Abrabanel, who grapples with the same question (how can belief be commanded?) but reaches a different answer. See Abrabanel, *Principles of Faith*, ch. 11.

one need not strain to attain faith but only remove the reasons for its corruption, and it will come by itself.[113] And even the ignorant Noachide,[114] through the power of his reason, can recognize that the world attests that it was created by the Holy One, blessed be He. Very simply, every action performed by a rational person has a purpose, and since creation was the action of a Creator, may He be blessed, it most certainly has a purpose. A drunkard, then, will be unable to justify himself by claiming he had believed heaven and earth were created for the purpose of drinking spirits and getting drunk. Simply, the purpose of all creatures is to fulfil their Creator's will.[115] Hence, he should have recognized that his purpose in coming into the world was to fulfil the will of his Creator and he should have asked and enquired what God's will is.[116] And for this he deserves to be punished, as they said,[117] 'the Noachide is liable for the death penalty', since he should have acquired instruction and he did not.

This is also the reason for the grave punishment imposed for the offence of idolatry, because if the human intellect were free from its will, it could not go astray after idolatry. Belief in idolatry reached it because of the growing craving to engage in the idolaters' abominations, as they said,[118] 'Israelites[119] engaged in idolatry only that they might openly satisfy their incestuous lusts.'

And they say that the *gaon ba'al hatumim*[120] was asked by a Gentile sage: It is written in the Torah [Exod. 23: 2], 'to incline after a multitude',[121] 'for you

---

[113] According to R. Wasserman, attaining faith is simple and natural; according to Maimonides, it is hard and complex, as evident in his tireless efforts to prove the existence of God, the non-corporeality of God, and that God is one, as well as in his endeavour to refute Aristotle's claims concerning the eternity of the world. R. Wasserman's statements suggest that Maimonides wasted his time writing *Guide of the Perplexed* and it would have been far wiser of him to write a *musar* book.

[114] The natural state for a non-Jew according to R. Wasserman? Apparently so.

[115] The purpose of the universe is for humans to worship God through the commandments. For Maimonides, the commandments are a tool for attaining 'the welfare of the soul and the welfare of the body'; *Guide* iii. 27 (p. 510). Like any tool, it is theoretically possible to exchange it for others. For further discussion, see Kellner, 'Rabbis in Politics' (Heb.) and 'Did the Torah Precede the Cosmos?' (Heb.).

[116] Unlike Maimonides, who holds that we should ask about and enquire into the nature of God (through tools accessible to human beings in general and not only to Jews), while God's will is conveyed in his commandments and openly revealed in Scripture and in the Oral Law. To help us understand God's will, Maimonides wrote the *Mishneh torah*. Note that Maimonides' halakhic responsa are not widely studied in Lithuanian yeshivas since they are brief, without the *lomdus* and the casuistry beloved of R. Wasserman and his spiritual partners. I am grateful to Eliezer Zitronenbaum for this and the previous note.   [117] BT *BK* 92a.   [118] BT *San.* 63b.

[119] This word is missing in the standard printed editions of the Talmud.

[120] R. Jonathan Eybeschütz (1690–1764), author of the book *Urim vetumim*. Apparently R. Wasserman did not follow R. Jacob Emden (1697–1776) and, later, Gershom Scholem, in regarding Eybeschütz as a Shabatean.

[121] 'Thou shalt not follow a multitude to do evil, neither shalt thou speak in a cause to incline after a multitude to pervert justice.'

were the fewest of all peoples' [Deut. 7: 7].[122] So why will you not accept our faith? And the *gaon* answered that majority rule applies only to matters that are in dispute and not to certainties as, for example, if nine shops sell kosher meat and one does not and meat of unknown provenance is found, we follow the majority, but if it is known to be from the minority, the majority does not help.[123] And so with us, we have no doubt about the truth of our faith, and the majority will not be able to change our minds (as noted by Rabbi Moses Sofer [the Hatam Sofer, 1762–1839] in *Torat mosheh*). And this explanation is true and clear.

But according to what was explained above, there is no room for this question in any event, since the rule 'to incline after a multitude' is meant for judges, all of whom are qualified to deal with a matter not involving a conflict of interests. But if a majority of the judges have a conflict of interests and a minority does not, we follow the minority. And on matters of faith and religion, one can only know the truth when free from all the cravings of this world, and such people are not to be found at all in any nation, only among the sages of Israel, who are as holy as God's angels. And even if among the sages of other nations there once were people free from the cravings of this world, they were fewer than few as opposed to our holy sages, of blessed memory, who were in the thousands and the tens of thousands, as has been taught[124]— many prophets arose for Israel, double the number of [the Israelites] who came out of Egypt, but the prophecy that was not required for future generations was not written down, and so too after them, in the generations of the *tana'im* and the *amora'im* [the sages of the Mishnah and Talmud]. Hence, this very law—'to incline after a multitude'—means that we must abide by what we have received from our masters, of blessed memory, who were the only ones qualified to deal with matters of faith, since their minds were free from any inclinations of the will.[125] And this question resembles that of a man who goes past a tavern, where a hundred drunkards wallow in waste, and they ask him: 'We are a hundred people and you are one, so why will you not do like us?' The same applies here, and except for the sages of Israel, the whole world are those drunk with their passions, as they have taught,[126] 'There is no free individual, except for he who occupies himself with the study of Torah', because without studying Torah it is impossible for any person to be free from the evil inclination that bends his mind to his desires.[127]

---

[122] 'The Lord did not set his love upon you, or choose you, because you were more in number than any people; for you were the fewest of all peoples.' [123] BT *Pes.* 9b. [124] BT *Meg.* 14a.
[125] R. Wasserman apparently chose to ignore a well-known rabbinic saying, 'The greater the man, the greater his evil inclination' (BT *Suk.* 52a). [126] Mishnah *Avot* 6: 2.
[127] This approach contradicts Maimonides' statement at the end of *MT* 'Laws of the Sabbat-

And from the first principle—belief in God—follows, as a necessary consequence, the second principle—Torah from heaven.[128] This is a simple matter because, given that the purpose of all creatures is to do God's will and given that no power in the human mind can fathom God's mind and apprehend what is His will, may He be blessed, should God not tell us His will, creation would have no purpose.[129] How can humans do God's will if they do not know what His will is? It was thus absolutely imperative for the Holy One, blessed be He, to announce and reveal to humans what His will is and what He desires from them by revealing His *shekhinah* [Divine Presence] to the world, and that is the Torah from Heaven.[130] What necessarily also follows is the belief in the coming of the messiah,[131] because after we clearly found that all existents were created to do His will, may He be blessed, and we see everywhere in the world precisely the opposite, that all are engrossed and drowning in a sea of passions and none 'understood and sought God', as it is written [Ps. 14: 2],[132] creating heaven and earth for such people was obviously worthless. We must therefore necessarily surmise that what is written [Isa. 40: 5],

---

ical Year and Jubilee' by stating that non-Jews and non-observant Jews cannot be released from the evil inclination and are doomed to be corrupt (in fact, it also includes Jews who do not observe the Torah and the commandments according to the way acceptable to R. Wasserman such as, for instance, Zionists, may the Lord have mercy). For a discussion of Maimonides' statements in *MT* 'Laws of the Sabbatical Year and Jubilee', 13: 13, see Kellner, *They Too Are Called Human* (Heb.), ch. 6.

[128] It is obvious from this that R. Wasserman took Albo's *Sefer ha'ikarim* to be the classic statement of Jewish dogma. According to Albo, Judaism has three fundamental dogmas: existence of God, Torah from heaven, and divine retribution.

[129] This statement implies that the purpose of creation is observance of the commandments, making the existence of non-Jews rather puzzling. R. Wasserman disagrees with Maimonides, who stated in *Guide* iii. 13 (p. 448) (the text is cited in n. 141 below) that one should not seek a purpose for creation and that the commandments are a tool for bringing humans to true perfection, meaning intellectual perfection. It is a plausible assumption that R. Wasserman viewed Rashi's exegesis of Gen. 1: 1 (that the world was created in order to give the Torah—that is, all of the commandments—to the people of Israel) as the normative interpretation of Judaism, and he could ascribe no other outlook to Maimonides. On Maimonides and Rashi on this question, see Kellner, 'Rashi and Maimonides'.

[130] The revelation of the *shekhinah* means Torah from heaven. For discussions on Maimonides' understanding of the concept of *shekhinah*, see Kellner, *Maimonides' Confrontation*, ch. 6, and Diamond, *Converts*, ch. 6.

[131] Interestingly, R. Wasserman disagrees here with several thinkers, beginning with Nahmanides, not to speak of the *amora* R. Hillel, all of whom played down the significance of dogmatic belief in the coming of the messiah. See Kellner, *Dogma in Medieval Jewish Thought*, 213–17.

[132] 'The Lord looked down from heaven upon the children of men, to see if there were any that understood, and sought God.'

'And the glory of the Lord shall be revealed'[133] will come to be, 'And the Lord shall be king over all the earth' [Zech. 14: 9].[134] Amen and amen.

2. Essay on Belief: 'Contemplation: Wondrous and Simple'[135]

The sin of idolatry, then, is the gravest[136] of all sins—but should it not be the opposite, since the sin of idolatry is less grave because an apology can be offered stating—what could he have done? And, given that he was mistaken, should not his punishment be less harsh?[137]

All this will indeed be understood after proper contemplation, because knowledge about matters of belief is a very easy thing and neither wisdom nor philosophy are required in its regard. It is indeed among the first intelligibles [*muskalot rishonot*],[138] as it says in *Duties of the Heart*,[139] that wisdom found in

---

[133] 'And the glory of the Lord shall be revealed, and all flesh shall see it together: for the mouth of the Lord has spoken it.'

[134] 'And the Lord shall be king over all the earth: on that day the Lord shall be one, and his name One.'

[135] Although the gist of this composition appears in the previous essay, I have included it because of the changed formulations and the innovations in the content. In my comments, I relate only to matters that do not appear in the first essay.

[136] In the continuation of the text in *Guide* i. 36 (pp. 84–5), Maimonides actually determines that believing in God's corporeality is a sin graver than idolatry:

Know accordingly, you who are that man, that when you believe in the doctrine of the corporeality of God or believe that one of the states of the body belongs to Him, you provoke His jealousy and anger, kindle the fire of His wrath, and are a hater, an enemy, and an adversary of God, much more so than an idolater. If, however, it should occur to you that one who believes in the corporeality of God should be excused because of his having been brought up in this doctrine or because of his ignorance and the shortcomings of his apprehension, you ought to hold a similar belief with regard to an idolater; for he only worships idols because of his ignorance or because of his upbringing: 'They continue in the custom of their fathers' [BT Ḥul. 13a]. If however, you should say that the external sense of the biblical text causes men to fall into this doubt, you ought to know that an idolater is similarly impelled to his idolatry by imaginings and defective representations. Accordingly there is no excuse for one who does not accept the authority of men who inquire into the truth and are engaged in speculation if he himself is incapable of engaging in such speculation. I do not consider as an infidel one who cannot demonstrate that the corporeality of God should be negated. But I do consider as an infidel one who does not believe in its negation; and this particularly in view of the existence of the interpretations of Onqelos and of Jonathan ben Uziel, may peace be on both of them, who cause their readers to keep away as far as possible from the belief in the corporeality of God.

For further discussion, see W. Z. Harvey, 'The Incorporeality of God' (Heb.), 74–9, and Kasher, 'Between the Idolater and the Believer' (Heb.).

[137] What emerges here is that R. Wasserman contrasts belief in God with idolatry. In his view, idolatry is seemingly equivalent to atheism. By contrast, in *Guide* i. 36 (pp. 82–5), Maimonides contrasts heresy with *itiqad* and ignorance with *'ilm*. See Stroumsa, 'Was Maimonides an Almohad Thinker?' (Heb.), 161.   [138] See Maimonides, *Logical Terms*, ch. 8.

[139] Bahya ibn Pakuda, *Book of Direction to the Duties of the Heart*, 'Treatise on the Unity of God'.

the order of a book attests that it has an author, and one thinking that ink was perhaps spilt and that it was thus written by itself will be thought mad. This matter is clarified in what our sages, of blessed memory, told of a heretic, who asked Rabbi Akiva who created the world. And he said to him: The Holy One, blessed be He. Said he: Show me some proof. Said he: The garment attests to the weaver. Said he: As the garment attests to the weaver so the world attests to the Creator.

And we should see that deriving from Rabbi Akiva's first intelligible is also the first intelligible, namely, the principle [*yesod*] of 'Torah from Heaven', since it is clear a person never does anything without reason but invariably for some purpose.[140] The beast goes from place to place to fulfil its purpose—the pleasure of eating the hay; the child pursues his amusements for his purpose—his pleasure; and so too the entire endeavour of traders and artisans—for the purpose of money. It is a basic principle that all agents act for some purpose and, obviously, all the more so the Creator, who created humans with a great aim.[141]

[140] R. Wasserman's text here seems a bit confused. For the point being made, see *Guide* iii. 13 (p. 448): 'Now I will explain that in all schools this question is abolished. I say then that in the case of every agent who acts with a purpose, the thing he has done must necessarily have some end with a view to which it has been done. According to philosophic speculation, this is clear and is not in need of demonstration.'

[141] Here, R. Wasserman disagrees with Maimonides, who explicitly stated in *Guide* iii. 13 (pp. 450–2, 454, 456):

[A]ccording to our opinion and our doctrine of the production in time of the world as a whole after nonexistence, this question is obligatory—I mean that it is obligatory to seek out the finality of all that exists. It is likewise thought that the finality of all that exists is solely the existence of the human species so that it should worship God, and that all that has been made has been made for it alone so that even the heavenly spheres only revolve in order to be useful to it and to bring into existence that which is necessary for it. . . . However, if this opinion is carefully examined, as opinions ought to be carefully examined by intelligent men, the flaw in it becomes clear. This result is achieved through posing to him who believes this opinion the following question: the final end being the existence of man, is the Creator able to bring him into existence without all these preliminaries, or was it possible for him to be brought into existence only after they were carried out? If someone answers that this is possible and that, for instance, God was able to bring man into existence without there being a heaven, the following question may be posed. What is the utility for him of all these things, which are in themselves not the final end, but exist for the sake of a thing that could have existed without all of them? Even if the universe exists for the sake of man, and the final end of man is, as has been said, to worship God, a question remains to be asked regarding the final end of his worship. For He, may He be exalted, would not acquire greater perfection if He were worshipped by all that He has created and were truly apprehended by them, nor would He be attained by a deficiency if nothing whatever existed except Him. If the answer is given that this is not with a view to His perfection, but to our perfection, for that is the most excellent thing for us—namely, our perfection—the same question follows necessarily: namely, what is the final end of our existence with that perfection? Necessarily and obligatorily the argument must end with the answer being given that the final end is: God has wished it so, or: His wisdom has

Moreover, as is well known, all that humans fashion, create, and do, is made to satisfy the desire of the person making it because one wishes every action and every machine created and operated by humans should do their will, as a rich man who builds a city and allots it to the inhabitants wishes them to be subject to him. Accordingly, given that the Holy One, blessed be He, created humans, he obviously wishes them to do His will and that presents a difficulty—how can humans do God's will if they do not know what His will is? In particular, given that God's will has no boundary and no limit, how can the creature imagine his Creator's will without knowing what He wishes?

Given that belief is a simple matter,[142] it is entirely impossible for a person to think (mistakenly) that his position is correct, because no mistake is possible in this regard. As for the many who have erred on this matter, the reason for their mistake is different—it is not due to the depth of the concept but to the transgression of the one apprehending, because we clearly know that mistaken views follow from wilful wrongdoing.[143] The greater the wrongness in this view (which, allegedly, is inadvertently mistaken), the greater the indication of 'wilful wrongdoing', denoting that his vices overwhelmed him and he is a coarser wrongdoer. Belief itself, however, is obvious to reason, and only confusion in the impure heart leads to confusion in a person's pure brain as well, so that a positive commandment on matters of belief is extremely pertinent since it is assumed in the first intelligible, as we explained.

The Holy One, blessed be He, was therefore very stringent on the matter of idolatry and heresy,[144] and the Torah wrote 'jealous' in this regard given that the mistake derives from wilful wrongdoing, since 'the touch blinded his eyes'[145] and he did not see the light of truth.

---

required this to be so. And this is the correct answer... And we shall seek for it no cause or other final end whatever. Just as we do not seek for the end of His existence, may He be exalted, so do we not seek for the final end of His volition, according to which all that has been and will be produced in time comes into being as it is.

As Yisrael Ben-Simon noted to me, R. Wasserman does what Maimonides forbade: he infers from the human intellect and projects it onto God. Maimonides would resolutely object to this inference and to the conclusion drawn from it.

[142] Such a non-Maimonidean formulation!

[143] To some extent, Maimonides could have agreed with this view: he holds that the perfection of the intelligibles cannot be attained without first attaining moral perfection. But an abyss separates him from R. Wasserman in this regard since, for Maimonides, a person may attain moral perfection without the commandments.

[144] Again, R. Wasserman apparently equates idolatry and atheism.

[145] The expression 'blinded his eyes' is found dozens of times in rabbinic literature.

3. The Corruption of Concepts[146]

According to Maimonides,[147] the believer in corporeality is a heretic, and Rabad [R. Abraham b. David of Posquières, 1125–98] wrote[148] that many of the 'good and great'[149] erred on this because of *agadot* that corrupt concepts. And I heard in the name of our honoured teacher and rabbi, the Gaon Rabbi Hayim Halevi of Brisk of blessed memory,[150] that Maimonides held that inadvertence[151] is not pertinent on matters of heresy because a non-believer cannot, under any circumstances, be part of the community of Israel.[152] He [R. Hayim] is quoted as saying, '*der vos is nebekh an apikoires is oikh an apikoires*'.[153] It appears that he must be right, since all heretics and all idolaters are mistaken. You cannot be more mistaken than one who sacrifices his child to Moloch, and such a one is punished with death. There is a problem, however: a baby in the cradle has no belief either, but is still part of the community of Israel, and one who had been a captive among idolaters brings a sacrifice to atone for his unwitting transgression and is not considered a heretic,[154] and we know that

---

[146] From 'Examples of Literal Explanations of *Agadot*' (Heb.), 12: 8–9.

[147] *MT* 'Laws of Repentance', 3: 7: 'Five classes are termed heretics: He who says that there is no God and the world has no ruler; he who says that there is a ruling power but that it is vested in two or more persons; he who says there is one ruler, but that He is a body and has form; he who denies that He alone is the First Cause and Rock of the Universe; likewise, he who renders worship to any one beside Him, to serve as a mediator between the human being and the Lord of the Universe. Whoever belongs to any of these five classes is termed a heretic.'

[148] Ad loc. This is his gloss: '[H]e who says there is one ruler, but that He is a body and has form—why did he call such a one a heretic, and many better and greater than him followed this view according to what they saw in Scripture, and even more so according to what they saw in *agadot*, which corrupt concepts.' [149] R. Wasserman's formulation omits here 'than him'.

[150] R. Hayim Soloveitchik (1853–1918).

[151] On this issue, see Kellner, 'Inadvertent Heresy' (Heb.).

[152] Ostensibly, this sentence conveys Maimonides' position accurately ('ostensibly' because 'belief' for R. Wasserman is not the same as 'belief' for Maimonides). See the ending of the Thirteen Principles:

When all these foundations are perfectly understood and believed in by a person he enters the community of Israel and one is obligated to love and pity him and to act towards him in all the ways in which the Creator has commanded that one should act towards his brother, with love and fraternity. Even were he to commit every possible transgression, because of lust and because of being overpowered by the evil inclination, he will be punished according to his rebelliousness, but he has a portion [of the world to come]; he is one of the sinners of Israel. But if a man doubts any of these foundations, he leaves the community [of Israel], denies the fundamental, and is called a sectarian, *epikoros*, and one who 'cuts among the plantings'. One is required to hate him and destroy him. About such a person it was said, 'Do I not hate them, O Lord, who hate Thee?' [Ps. 139: 21]'.

I have analysed this crucial statement in several contexts. See 'Could Maimonides Get into Rambam's Heaven', and *Must a Jew Believe Anything?*, 173–4.

[153] Which can be paraphrased as 'One who became a heretic without meaning to do so is still a heretic.' For a discussion, see Shapiro, *Limits of Orthodox Theology*, 12. [154] BT *Shab.* 68b.

God exempts one who was coerced, including for lack of belief.¹⁵⁵ And we must say [*veyesh lomar*] that, as explained above, the foundations of belief are necessary and human reason as such leaves no room for heresy. Only the human desire for immorality diverts a person's reason to err on simple and necessary things, and a person's inadvertence is therefore equivalent to malice.¹⁵⁶ But one who says idolatry is allowed is mistaken and not liable to death because he holds that his action is permitted by the Torah.¹⁵⁷

When saying that '*agadot* corrupt concepts', Rabad perhaps meant that they [*agadot*] are not per se mistaken but the error is in deferring to them. Hence, allowing a mistake to exculpate means that inadvertence is taken into account in heresy as well, thereby settling the objection concerning Rabbi Hillel: 'There shall be no Messiah for Israel, because they have already enjoyed him in the days of Hezekiah.'¹⁵⁸ Could one say, God forbid, that Rabbi Hillel was excluded from the community of Israel because he denied one of the principles of religion? According to what was explained, then, we must assume that Rabbi Hillel said so because he erred in his understanding of Scripture and, as one who thinks (mistakenly) 'that his position is correct', is guilty [only] of inadvertence. That is why Rabbi Joseph said there, 'May God forgive Rabbi Hillel [for saying so].'¹⁵⁹ And Maimonides holds that mistakes on the matter of corporeality are in their own minds and not because of *agadot*¹⁶⁰ since, had they been clearheaded, *agadot* would not have misled them and they would have found ways of reconciling the *agadot* with the concepts to avoid contradictions.

On this matter, we should explain the objection raised in the Gemara:¹⁶¹ 'Is

---

¹⁵⁵ In other words God exempts the one who is coerced, including on matters of faith. See BT *Ned.* 27a. See further Kellner, *Must a Jew Believe Anything?*, ch. 6.

¹⁵⁶ BT *San.* 103b.

¹⁵⁷ Cf. *Guide* ii. 35–6 (pp. 367–73). Maimonides certainly does not agree that there is any room for leniency on inadvertence concerning matters of belief. For further discussion, see Kellner, 'Inadvertent Heresy' (Heb.). Actually, I do not understand R. Wasserman here.

¹⁵⁸ BT *San.* 99a: 'R. Hillel said: There shall be no Messiah for Israel, because they have already enjoyed him in the days of Hezekiah. R. Joseph said: May God forgive R. Hillel [for saying so]. Now, when did Hezekiah flourish? During the First Temple. Yet Zechariah, prophesying in the days of the Second, proclaimed [Zech. 9], "Rejoice greatly, O daughter of Zion, shout, O daughter of Jerusalem, behold, thy king cometh unto thee! He is just, and having salvation, lowly, and riding upon an ass, and upon a colt the foal of an ass."'

¹⁵⁹ Rashi comments: 'The Holy One, blessed be He, will forgive him, since he said wrong things.'

¹⁶⁰ This interpretation of Maimonides is extremely problematic. Maimonides strenuously endeavoured to distance the multitude from literal readings of Scripture and from *agadot* that 'corrupt concepts'.

¹⁶¹ BT *Ber.* 33b: 'R. Hanina further said: Everything is in the hand of heaven except the fear of heaven, as it says, "And now, Israel, what does the Lord thy God require of thee but to fear" [Deut. 10: 12]. Is the fear of heaven such a small thing? Has not R. Hanina said in the name of R.

the fear of heaven such a small thing? And they said, "Yes; for Moses it was a small thing."' And we need to explain what is meant by 'a small thing', given that this text is not meant solely for Moses but for the whole of Israel, and for them it is no small thing.[162] According to the explanation, the foundations of belief are necessary but the desire of humans for immorality diverts their reason. As such, belief is very easy to attain yet it is also very difficult because the will affects reason and misleads it. According to the one objecting,[163] given that it is in fact difficult to attain the fear[164] [that follows belief],[165] this is no 'small thing'. And the one responding to the objection said that we see how, for Moses, fear was a small thing because his desires did not rule him but he them. And we learn from this that, were it not for the person's desires, the fear of the One who holds every living soul in His hand is a small thing.[166] It is thus pertinent to say 'a small thing' given that, in itself, it is not hard to attain.

4. Degrees of Belief[167]

'And he believed in the Lord; and he accounted it to him for righteousness' [Gen. 15: 6]—see Nahmanides ad loc.[168] And Rashi's commentary raises a question—what is new in this, and why should he not have believed in what he had heard from the Holy One, blessed be He? A similar difficulty emerges concerning what is written about the people that, after the parting of the sea, they 'believed in the Lord, and in his servant Moses' [Exod. 14: 31].[169] Had they

---

Simeon b. Yohai, the Holy One, blessed be He, has in His treasury nought except a store of the fear of heaven, as it says, "The fear of the Lord is His treasure!" [Isa. 33: 6]? Yes; for Moses it was a small thing. As R. Hanina said, to illustrate with a parable, if a man is asked for a big article and he has it, it seems like a small article to him; if he is asked for a small article and he does not have it, it seems like a big article to him.'

For Maimonides on the fear of heaven, see his letter to Obadiah (*Igerot harambam*, i. 436) and the eighth of his 'Eight Chapters' (= introd. to *Commentary on the Mishnah, Avot*).

[162] See Shmuel Eidels (Maharsha), *Ḥidushei agadot*, on BT *Ber.* 33b.
[163] In the passage from BT *Ber.* 33b.
[164] Maimonides did not think it was so hard, but that it required investing effort in matters that R. Wasserman definitely considered a waste of time, as well as dangerous (*MT* 'Laws of the Foundations of the Torah', 2: 1–2).
[165] I do not know whether the words in parentheses are R. Wasserman's or the editor's. What *is* clear is that they do not reflect the view of Maimonides, who sees fear as a stage on the way to faith (*MT* 'Laws of the Foundations of the Torah', 2: 1–2) rather than vice versa.
[166] Fear according to Maimonides reflects acknowledgement of the divine wisdom evident in nature rather than dread of a frighteningly powerful ruler.
[167] From 'Examples of Literal Explanations of *Agadot*' (Heb.), 12: 10–11.
[168] Chavel (trans.), *Ramban: Commentary*, vol. i, 197.
[169] 'And Israel saw that great work which the Lord did upon Egypt: and the people feared the Lord, and believed in the Lord, and in his servant Moses.'

not believed till then, after seeing the ten plagues? But we read that already in Egypt, 'the people believed' [Exod. 4: 31]?

And at the end of *Makot* [24b],[170] when they saw a fox coming out from the Holy of Holies, they began to weep and Rabbi Akiva was merry when he saw that the prophecy had been fulfilled. And the difficulty appears here again— surely even before seeing the fox emerging he had not doubted that the prophets' words would be fulfilled, so what was added now that he was merry?

Seemingly, then, although all Israel are believers as is promised in the Torah, 'and trust you ever after' [Exod. 19: 9],[171] they differ in their degree of belief. (And about those who were found to be heretics among us, Maimonides wrote in the *Epistle to Yemen* that there are no Jews whose ancestors had not been present at Mount Sinai,[172] as Radak [R. David Kimhi] writes on

[170] There, it is written: 'Once again they were going up to Jerusalem together and, as they reached Mount Scopus, they ripped their clothes. As they came to the Temple Mount, they saw a fox coming out from the Holy of Holies. They began to weep and R. Akiva was merry. They said to him, why are you merry? Said he: Why are you weeping? Said they to him: A place of which it was once said, "And the stranger that comes near shall be put to death" [Num. 1: 51] has now become the haunt of foxes and we should not weep? Said he to them: Therefore am I merry, for it is written, "And I took to myself faithful witnesses, namely Uriah the priest and Zechariah the son of Jeberechiah" [Isa. 8: 2]. What is the connection between Uriah and Zechariah? Uriah lived during the times of the first Temple and Zechariah lived during the second Temple! The Holy Writ linked the [later] prophecy of Zechariah to the [earlier] prophecy of Uriah. Of Uriah, it is written, "Therefore shall Zion for your sake be ploughed as a field" [Mic. 3: 12]. Of Zechariah it is written, "Thus said the Lord of Hosts, 'Old men and old women shall yet again dwell in the streets of Jerusalem'" [Zech. 8: 4]. So long as Uriah's prophecy had not been fulfilled, I feared that Zechariah's prophecy might not be fulfilled. Now that Uriah's prophecy has been fulfilled, it is certain that Zechariah's prophecy will also be fulfilled. Said they to him: Akiva, you have comforted us! Akiva, you have comforted us!'

[171] 'And the Lord said to Moses, Lo I will come to you in a thick cloud, [in order that the people may hear when I speak with you,] and so trust you ever after. And Moses told the words of the people to the Lord.'

[172] I do not know whether this parenthetical comment was R. Wasserman's or the editor's. Be that as it may, it correctly reflects Maimonides' view in the *Epistle to Yemen*:

So rely upon these true texts, O our brethren, and be not alarmed by the succession of persecutions and the power over us or the weakness of our community [*kalima*]. All this is to test and purify, so that only the saints and the pious of the seed of Jacob our father, the pure and chaste seed, will adhere to our religion, those of whom it is said: 'And among the remnant those whom the Lord shall call' [Joel 3: 5]. The verse explains that they are few, they being people whose ancestors were present at Mount Sinai and heard the speech from the Almighty, raised their right hands for the covenant of God, and registered themselves to obey and accept, saying, 'We will do, and we will obey' [Exod. 24: 7]. They imposed this upon themselves and their descendants, as it says: 'For us and our children forever' [Deut. 29: 28]. God, the Exalted, has guaranteed—He is a sufficient guarantor—and notified us that all those who were present at the Gathering at Mount Sinai justify and believe in the prophecy of Moses our Master and all that he revealed, they and their descendants and their descendants' descendants throughout time. So God, the Exalted, said: 'Lo I will come to you in a thick cloud, [in order that the people may hear when I speak with you,] and so trust you ever after' [Exod. 19: 9]. Therefore, let everyone know who deviates from this religion of

Ezekiel.)¹⁷³ Belief is like a ladder, placed on the ground and its head reaching heaven,¹⁷⁴ with thousands upon thousands of rungs one above the other. It would seem that if a person's belief reaches the rung of the senses and he believes as if he were actually seeing with his own eyes, he has already reached the highest rung and no one in the world could believe more. Yet it is not so— belief in God's word should be stronger than the sense of sight because one's sense could actually be misled by a deceptive trick and so forth, but God's word stands forever and could never be flawed at all.

Since what is written in the Torah can have no part, none whatsoever, of deceit, God forbid,¹⁷⁵ the Torah will not attest 'and he believed' unless one has reached the highest and most perfect rung of faith, one that flesh and blood could not go beyond as long as it is found within the material body. Should any part be missing from this rung, the text will not say 'and they believed'. Possibly, then, this is what 'and he believed in the Lord' means, that it was at that moment that he reached the perfection of belief attainable in reality. And so concerning the parting of the sea—their belief reached the highest rung only at that moment. And so concerning Rabbi Akiva, who was merry when he saw that fox because, at that moment, belief reached in him the rung of the senses, and before seeing it, his belief had been slightly less. Were you to question and say—how can one say about Rabbi Akiva that his belief had been slighter than his sight, see what Raban Yohanan ben Zakkai said to his disciples [BT *Ber.* 28*b*]: 'May the fear of Heaven be upon you like the fear of flesh and blood. Know that one who commits a transgression says, I hope no man will see me.'

*

His that was revealed at that great assembly that he is not an offspring of these people. This is what they (peace be on them) say concerning the one who doubts: 'His ancestors were not present at Mount Sinai' [e.g. BT *Ned.* 20*a*].

I suggest that these statements do not reflect Maimonides' true view and were written in light of the circumstances, but a discussion of this issue would not be appropriate here. I see Maimonides writing persuasively here, not descriptively. For details on this understanding of several passages in his writings, see Kellner, *They Too Are Called Human* (Heb.), ch. 8.

¹⁷³ Apparently referring to what Kimhi wrote on Ezek. 6.

¹⁷⁴ On Maimonides' interpretation of Jacob's dream (extremely incongruent with R. Wasserman's world view), see Klein-Braslavy, 'Maimonides' Interpretation of Jacob's Ladder' (Heb.), and Eisenmann, '"A Ladder"' (Heb.).

¹⁷⁵ Maimonides holds that in the Torah there are more than a few 'necessary beliefs', but he would not want to refer to them as 'lies'. Clearly, however, verses that ascribe anger to God, for example, do not convey truth in any straightforward sense. The same is true, obviously, of verses anthropomorphizing God. For discussions on this matter, see Kasher, 'The Myth of the "Angry God"' (Heb.), and Diamond, 'Maimonides on Leprosy'.

Thus Rabbi Wasserman and his commentary on Maimonides. On the one hand, no surprises. Jolene Kellner has noted more than once that Maimonides serves as a Rorschach test: everyone looking at the inkblots on the pages of his works sees a different picture. Rabbi Kafih conveyed a similar idea in a letter to Michael Schwarz: 'In my view, Maimonides resembles a mirror. Whoever stands before it sees his own image, and so with Maimonides—he has many faces, and each one infuses his own flavour.'[176] But even in an amusement park fun-house mirror, some connection is still discernible between the person facing the mirror and the image reflected in it. I have tried to show here that the Wassermanian image of Maimonides is far removed from the original. This was predictable: how could Rabbi Wasserman, whose Torah (studied in Yiddish) reflects eight hundred years of misgivings and suspicions about the culture surrounding him, grasp in depth the Torah that Maimonides (apparently) studied in Arabic, reflecting a positive attitude towards a fifteen-centuries-old tradition of Greek wisdom?[177] I submit that this comment is not only extremely significant but also explains why my critique of Rabbi Wasserman here misses the point. His Maimonides is not the Maimonides of academic scholarship (or, as I tried to show, not the Maimonides of Maimonides either). One who studies Torah in Yiddish, in an environment rejecting the very possibility of the wide world ever contributing to its apprehension, approaches it in a very different way from one who studies it in Arabic, expecting to gain knowledge and insights from a surrounding culture capable of enriching his understanding.[178] Since Rabbi Wasserman would reject this determination as abhorrent, he would not relate to my current critique.

A rabbinic tradition already in existence in the Middle Ages claimed that, when studying Maimonides, the *Guide of the Perplexed* should be ignored. This approach is evident in Responsum 45 of Rabbi Yitshak ben Sheshet Perfet (1326–1408), known as Rivash, where he determines that Maimonides did not write the *Guide of the Perplexed* out of inner conviction but in order to

---

[176] Cited in *Guide*, trans. Schwarz, vol. ii (p. 752).

[177] For a prominent example of the difference between them, one may consider whether R. Wasserman would have been willing to write the following sentence: 'If the philosophers would succeed in demonstrating eternity as Aristotle understands it, the Law [al-sharia] as a whole would become void, and a shift to other opinions would take place'; *Guide* ii. 25 (p. 330).

[178] On this Seth Kadish comments (personal communication): 'This isn't just a traditional community that views outsiders and their ideas with apprehension (his "environment"). Rather, it's the conscious creation of an ideology that despises modernity. It's not just eight centuries of misgivings. More important than those eight centuries are just a couple of generations of modernity's mortal threat to continuity. R. Elhanan doesn't simply reflect his environment, rather he is actively trying to create a *new* environment.' I have no problem seeing the matter in this light as well.

draw closer those who had grown distant. In this sense, Rabbi Wasserman actually resembles Shlomo Pines (as well as Pines' friend, Leo Strauss). In the introduction to his English translation of the *Guide*, Pines notes that Maimonides' concern with halakhah was for him only an 'avocation'(!).[179] According to Pines, then, someone seeking to understand Maimonides truly and deeply should ignore his halakhic writings. This is Rabbi Wasserman's view, only the other way around: since Maimonides' philosophical concern was at best merely a hobby, his philosophical writings should not be considered when trying to understand his positions correctly and in their full depth.

But if all this is true, an interesting issue surfaces, tying the above discussion to politics. According to Maimonides, it is extremely hard to prove the existence of God, that he is one, and that he is not a body (see the introduction to the second part of the *Guide*[180]), and, generally, to demonstrate the creation of the world (be it *ex nihilo* or *ex materia*—see *Guide* ii. 25) is impossible. What, then, is the proper reaction to a person who does not know that God exists or who acknowledges God's existence but casts doubt on the creation of the world and, consequently, does not observe the commandments? The answer is clear: such a person must be educated with cords of love.[181] Maimonides' entire endeavour, then, can actually be seen as an educational enterprise.

How was Rabbi Wasserman supposed to react to a reality of non-observant Jews? In his view, non-observance is precisely what leads to lack of faith in God. The knowledge that God exists, that he created the world, and that he gave us the Torah and its commandments is simple and clear—so much so that anyone denying the existence of God and the creation of the world does so only in order to enjoy this world without curb or restraint. What is the proper reaction to such individuals? Should we draw away from them altogether, or—if we have the power—force them to observe the commandments, that is, relate to them politically? Rabbi Wasserman supported the former view; many who think of themselves as his followers—in entirely different circumstances—support the latter one.

---

[179] *Guide*, p. cxvii. In the Hebrew translation of this introduction, Shlomo Pines downplayed this meaning and rendered the word as 'profession' (*miktso'a*). See Pines, *Studies in the History of Jewish Philosophy* (Heb.), 158. On Pines as an interpreter of Maimonides, see W. Z. Harvey, 'The Return of Maimonideanism'. On Leo Strauss on Maimonides, see Kellner, 'Strauss's Maimonides' (Heb.).

[180] It should be remembered that Abraham sought to understand (*shotet beda'ato*) for forty years before he reached the right conclusion. See *MT* 'Laws of Idolatry', 1: 3.

[181] Hos. 11: 4: 'I drew them with human cords, with leading strings of love: and I was to them as they that lift off the yoke from their jaws, and I held food out to them.' See Maimonides, *Teshuvot harambam*, at the end of §268. For a discussion of the harsh statements that Maimonides uttered on heretics, apostates, and renegades, see Kellner, *Dogma in Medieval Jewish Thought*, ch. 1.

SIX

Each Generation and Its Maimonides: The Maimonides of Rabbi Aharon Kotler

MENACHEM KELLNER

IN THIS CHAPTER I analyse the way in which Rabbi Aharon Kotler (1891–1962) presented Maimonides' thought. Rabbi Kotler played a crucial role in the shaping of the *haredi* world view in the twentieth century.[1] To each generation its exegetes, to each commentator his Maimonides; in twentieth-century Orthodox Judaism, different elements have endorsed Maimonides as an authority granting legitimacy. As noted above in the Introduction, both the Lubavitcher Rebbe (Menachem Mendel Schneerson, 1902–94) and the 'Leibowitzer Rebbe' (Yeshayahu Leibowitz, 1903–94), as is well known, considered themselves Maimonides' contemporary spokesmen. The dovish Meimad movement in Israeli politics adopted him, as did their hawkish religious-Zionist opponents, while a pale kabbalistic hue colours the Maimonides of Rabbi Joseph B. Soloveitchik. No wonder, then, that Rabbi Kotler too understands Maimonides as if he were a supporter of his own positions.

---

[1] R. Kotler was born in Svislač, Poland, and died in the USA. He was the son-in-law of R. Isser Zalman Meltzer (1870–1953), was considered a prodigy, and became a prominent leader in Agudat Yisra'el circles in Europe. He reached the USA during the Second World War and played an important role in the Va'ad Hahatsalah (rescue committee). He founded and led Beth Medrash Govoha in Lakewood, New Jersey, and became a leader of the world Agudat Yisra'el movement after the Holocaust. For biographical details, see Sherman, *Orthodox Judaism in America*, 122–3. Thanks to my friend Professor Gershon Greenberg, I succeeded in obtaining a book about R. Kotler (among many other figures) that has been boycotted in the *haredi* world and is now difficult to obtain: Kaminetzky, *The Making of a Godol* (pp. 296–314 discuss R. Kotler). On the controversies surrounding this book, see Assaf, *Caught in the Thicket* (Heb.), 33–4, and Shapiro, 'Of Books and Bans'. On R. Kotler's endeavours on behalf of European Torah scholars during and after the war, see Zuroff, *Response of Orthodox Jewry*, 136, 151, 244. On the yeshiva R. Kotler founded, see Finkelman, 'Haredi Isolation', and Lewitter, 'A School for Scholars'. Finkelman, 'Haredi Isolation', 76 n. 3, contains an extensive bibliography of writings about R. Kotler, most of them hagiographical. Finkelman is also the author of three other important studies on R. Kotler: 'An Ideology', 'On the Limits of American Jewish Social Engineering', and 'War with the External World' (Heb.).

I will argue that not only does Rabbi Kotler read Maimonides as if the Great Eagle had grown up in east European yeshivas (which is not at all startling), but he also loads (*ma'amis*)[2] upon Maimonides notions that, ostensibly, he should have known are entirely alien to him.[3] Rabbi Kotler's disciples compiled his lectures, *shiurim*, letters, eulogies, and other occasional writings in the four volumes of *Mishnat rabi aharon*.[4] We will examine several of Rabbi Kotler's references to Maimonides in these writings.

Innovation and Independent Enquiry in Torah Study

In *Mishnat rabi aharon*, Rabbi Kotler invokes Maimonides when he discusses how one should understand the Torah:

At the end of 'Laws of Trespass', Maimonides writes: 'It is fitting for man to meditate upon the laws of the holy Torah and to comprehend their full meaning to the extent

---

[2] I adopt this formulation following R. Israel Salanter (1810–83), since R. Kotler studied in the Keneset Yisra'el yeshiva in Slobodka, which was inspired by the *musar* (ethical self-improvement) movement founded by R. Salanter. R. Israel often used this expression, apparently aware that he had at times 'loaded' upon rabbinic writings notions unintended by the sages. See Pachter (ed.), *Writings of R. Israel Salanter* (Heb.), 115, 133, 234. Interestingly, R. Israel, like R. Kotler after him, interprets Maimonides in ways suited to his own views. See e.g. ibid. 129–30, and editor's note 19 ad loc. I am grateful to my friend Professor Pachter, who drew my attention to this matter. Isadore Twersky's comment merits mention in this context: 'It is interesting to page through great books of ḥasidism as well as basic books of the Musar movement to see the extent to which the use of Maimonides is selective and strategic, in line with the notion of *philosophia perennis*.' See his article, 'On Maimonides' (Heb.). In this context, it should be noted that, in the four volumes of *Mishnat rabi aharon*, R. Kotler relies on a broad range of rabbinic sources. He cites very sparingly from the halakhic literature of the *rishonim*, and almost completely ignores the literature of medieval kabbalah and philosophy. One outstanding exception is Baḥya ibn Pakuda, *The Duties of the Heart*, though R. Kotler uses it as an ethical rather than as a philosophical text. He cites Halevi's *Kuzari* a few times and Albo's *Sefer ha'ikarim* once. Of Maimonides' works, R. Kotler cites only the *Mishneh torah*, but almost entirely ignores the first four chapters of the 'Laws of the Foundations of the Torah'. Closer attention is paid to medieval ethical literature (particularly Y. Gerondi, *Sha'arei teshuvah*). R. Kotler often cites several *aharonim* (authorities who lived after the publication of the *Shulḥan arukh*): R. Moses Hayim Luzzatto (1707–46) appears in the indexes, but not prominently, while the Vilna Gaon and R. Hayim of Volozhin are cited more frequently. At the centre, however, as is fitting for a Slobodka graduate, are *musar* figures: R. Yosef Zundel of Salant (1786–1866), R. Israel Salanter, R. Simha Zissel of Kelm (1824–98), and R. Nathan Tsevi Finkel, the Alter of Slobodka (1849–1927).

[3] For an enlightening discussion of the way Maimonides was 'absorbed' in eastern Europe in the modern era, see Nadler, 'The "Rambam Revival"'.

[4] All the volumes appeared in Lakewood, published in 1988–2005 by Machon Mishnat Rabbi Aharon. His disciples also published his novellae on Maimonides' *Mishneh torah* in two volumes: *Al harambam hilkhot shekhenim* (Jerusalem, 1975), and *Ḥidushim uve'urim* (Jerusalem, 1986). The discussions in these books are solely halakhic and do not shed light on R. Kotler's use of Maimonides' thought.

of his ability. Nevertheless, a law for which he finds no reason and understands no cause should not be trivial in his eyes. "Let him not break through to rise up against the Lord" [Exod. 19: 24]; nor should his thoughts concerning these things be like his thoughts concerning profane matters. Come and consider how strict the Torah was in the law of trespass! Now if sticks and stones and earth and ashes became hallowed by words alone as soon as the name of the Master of the Universe was invoked upon them, and anyone who comported with them as with a profane thing committed trespass and required atonement even if he acted unwittingly, how much more should man be on guard not to rebel against a commandment decreed for us by the Holy One, blessed be He, only because he does not understand its reason; or to heap words that are not right against the Lord; or to regard the commandments in the manner he regards ordinary affairs.'[5]

The explanation is that the divine Torah is broader than the land and deeper than the sea. If a man approaches the Torah with the limited tools of his intellect and appreciates it in the measure of his trivial intellect, then, as it were, he is lowering the Torah to the rank and grasp of his intellect, and you could have no greater profanation and betrayal of the sacred . . . A man cannot evaluate the Torah according to his own grasp, and he must accept the explanation of our sages on every word and letter of the Torah. Because the language of the Torah is not our habitual language, nor are its concepts our own, and understanding it demands great apprehension and the study of Torah for its own sake in holiness and purity and faithful transmission from one to another, which is why only through the rabbis' chain of transmission . . . can we understand something of the holy Torah's words in the measure of our own apprehension. Maimonides' words touch on every matter in the Torah—halakhah and *agadah*, law and story—and one cannot appreciate any of them according to his intellect. Most particularly, one must beware of the Torah's stories, where very serious errors are possible, and these errors undermine the foundations of the people of Israel.[6]

Rabbi Kotler learns two things from Maimonides: (1) there is no room in Jewish tradition for essential changes, and (2) the Torah is not to be approached solely with intellectual tools and we must always rely on rabbinic tradition.[7] I will argue that Maimonides' true endeavour must indeed appear to Rabbi Kotler as 'lowering the Torah to the rank and grasp of his intellect, and you could have no greater profanation and betrayal of the sacred'. I will relate to several sources in four of Maimonides' works in order to show that he held

---

[5] *MT* 'Laws of Trespass', 8: 8. For a discussion of this law, see Henshke, 'On the Question of Unity' (Heb.), and, in great detail, ch. 8 in Kellner and Gillis, *Maimonides the Universalist*.

[6] *Mishnat rabi aharon*, vol. iii, 173. On the meaning of expressions such as 'the foundations of the people of Israel' (*yesodot am yisra'el*), see Kellner, *Maimonides' Confrontation*, ch. 7. Without doubt, R. Kotler understands this expression in terms that are clearly non-Maimonidean.

[7] For a particularly strict formulation of this view, see *Mishnat rabi aharon*, vol. iv, 30.

that we definitely can, and even need to, approach the Torah with intellectual tools, as well as evaluating its words according to human apprehension. Indeed, it may at times be impossible to obtain the 'explanation of our sages on every word and letter of the Torah'—both because there is no rabbinic explanation on the matter at stake and because these explanations are insufficient or even mistaken.

I will relate first to essential innovations on extremely important matters. Mishnah Ḥagigah, at the end of chapter 1, reads:

[Laws about] release from vows hover in the air and have nothing to rely upon. Laws about the sabbath, festival offerings, and trespasses are as mountains hanging by a hair—little Scripture and many laws. Laws about the Temple service, about purity and impurity, and about forbidden sexual relations do have something to rely upon —they are most assuredly bodies of Torah.

This *mishnah* seems to be here because of its reference to the festivals. It also refers to forbidden sexual relations, and it is apparently for this reason that the next *mishnah* (2: 1) was attached to this text:[8]

One does not expound upon forbidden sexual relations in the presence of three, nor upon *ma'aseh bereshit* in the presence of two, nor upon the *merkavah* in the presence of one, unless that one were wise and understood upon his own. All who look upon four things, it were better had they not come into the world: what is above, what is below, what is in front, and what is behind. All who are not protective of the honour of their master, it were better had they not come into the world.

This famous *mishnah* informs us, *inter alia*, that rabbinic sages had a mysterious, esoteric Torah. In the present context, we need not clarify the essence of this Torah but merely acknowledge its existence.[9] The Babylonian Talmud relates to this esoteric Torah as 'mysteries of the Torah'.[10] In the introduction to part iii of *Guide of the Perplexed*, Maimonides relates to this identification and writes:

We have already made it clear several times[11] that the chief aim of this Treatise is to explain what can be explained of the Account of the Beginning [*ma'aseh bereshit*] and the Account of the Chariot [*ma'aseh merkavah*], with a view to him for whom this Treatise has been composed. We have already made it clear that these matters belong to the mysteries of the Torah,[12] and you know that [the sages], may their memory be blessed, blame those who divulge the mysteries of the Torah. They, may

[8] For a discussion, see Halperin, *The Merkabah in Rabbinic Literature*.
[9] For an illuminating discussion of classic Jewish esotericism, see Klein-Braslavy, *King Solomon* (Heb.). See further the discussion of this passage above, in Ch. 5.   [10] BT Ḥag. 13a.
[11] In the notes to his exemplary Hebrew translation of the *Guide*, Michael Schwarz refers the reader to ii. 2 and 29 (pp. 252–4 and 336–8). See also *Guide*, introd. to pt. i (p. 6).
[12] Schwarz refers to *Guide* i. 33 and 34 (pp. 70–9).

their memory be blessed, have already made it clear that the reward of him who conceals the mysteries of the Torah, which are clear and manifest to the men of speculation, is very great.... They have already made it clear how secret the Account of the Chariot was and how foreign to the mind of the multitude. And it has been made clear that even that portion of it that becomes clear to him who has been given access to the understanding of it, is subject to a legal prohibition against its being taught and explained except orally to one man having certain stated qualities,[13] and even to that one only the chapter headings may be mentioned. This is the reason why the knowledge of this matter has ceased to exist in the entire religious community, so that nothing great or small remains of it. And it had to happen like this, for this knowledge was only transmitted from one chief to another and has never been set down in writing.[14]

In other words, knowledge of these mysteries of the Torah 'has ceased to exist in the entire religious community, so that nothing great or small remain[ed] of it' in Maimonides' times because this knowledge 'was only transmitted from one chief to another and has never been set down in writing'.

Maimonides announces that he may have succeeded in rediscovering the lost tradition—without teachers and without revelation, but rather through the independent interpretation of Scripture and resorting to personal insights:

If this is so, what stratagem can I use to draw attention toward that which may have appeared to me as indubitably clear, manifest, and evident in my opinion, according to what I have understood in these matters? On the other hand, if I had omitted setting down something of that which has appeared to me as clear, so that that knowledge would perish when I perish, as is inevitable, I should have considered that conduct as extremely cowardly with regard to you and everyone who is perplexed. It would have been, as it were, robbing one who deserves the truth of the truth, or begrudging an heir his inheritance. And both those traits are blameworthy. On the other hand, as has been stated before, an explicit exposition of this knowledge is denied by a legal prohibition, in addition to that which is imposed by judgement. In addition to this there is the fact that in that which has occurred to me with regard to these matters, I followed conjecture[15] and supposition; no divine revelation has come to teach me that the intention in the matter in question was such and such, nor did I receive what I believe in these matters from a teacher. But the texts of the prophetic books and the dicta of the sages, together with the speculative premises that I possess, showed me that things are indubitably so and so. Yet it is possible that they are different and that something else is intended.[16]

---

[13] Schwarz refers to the introd. to pt. i (pp. 16–17) and i. 33 (pp. 70–2).

[14] *Guide*, introd. to pt. iii (p. 415).

[15] In Arabic, *ḥads*. On this term in Maimonides' thought, see Eran, '*Ḥads* in Maimonides' (Heb.). See also the long discussion in Schwarz (trans.), *Guide* (Heb.) ii. 22 n. 9.

[16] *Guide*, introd. to pt. iii (pp. 415–16).

Notwithstanding this hesitation, Maimonides writes that his explanation of the account of the chariot was guided and driven by God:

> Now rightly guided reflection[17] and divine aid[18] in this matter have moved me to a position, which I shall describe. Namely, I shall interpret to you that which was said by Ezekiel the prophet, peace be on him, in such a way that anyone who heard that interpretation would think that I do not say anything over and beyond what is indicated by the text, but that it is as if I translated words from one language to another or summarized the meaning of the external sense of the speech. On the other hand, if that interpretation is examined with a perfect care by him for whom this Treatise is composed and who has understood all its chapters—every chapter in its turn—the whole matter, which has become clear and manifest to me, will become clear to him so that nothing in it will remain hidden from him. This is the ultimate term that it is possible to attain in combining utility for everyone with abstention from explicit statements in teaching anything about this subject—as is obligatory.
>
> After this introduction has preceded, apply your mind to the chapters that will follow concerning this great, noble, and sublime subject, which is a stake upon which everything hangs and a pillar upon which everything is supported.[19]

Maimonides again clarifies here that his understanding of 'this great, noble, and sublime subject' 'has become clear and manifest to me' thanks to independent enquiry and had not been transmitted to him by a teacher nor reached him through 'the explanation of our sages on every word and letter of the Torah', as Rabbi Kotler insists.[20]

In his *Commentary on the Mishnah*, Maimonides emphasizes that his understanding of our *mishnah* in Ḥagigah had not relied on ancestral tradition. He resorts to expressions unusual for him (or for any traditional Jewish exegete):

---

[17] i.e. guided by God (Schwarz).

[18] Since Maimonides explicitly notes in the previous passage that he had not understood this through a divine revelation, I see no particular significance in this statement beyond its nature as a 'religious' saying and an expression of humility.   [19] *Guide*, introd. to pt. iii (p. 416).

[20] I find support for my understanding of Maimonides here in Isaac Abrabanel. Addressing Maimonides' interpretation of Ezekiel's vision of the Chariot, Abrabanel writes: 'And the rabbi unquestionably saw in the verses all or most of what I have noted, but he relied so much on his own view and his own enquiries that, after deciding that was the truth and that is what should be, he did not fear and thought of changing the verses or, perhaps thinking that the problem in Ezekiel was a corrupted theoretical enquiry, he may have held that all was in any event his own thought, may God protect us from such a notion!'; Abrabanel, 'Arguments Drawn from the Verses' (Heb.), included in the often reprinted Warsaw 1872 edition of the *Guide*. I am grateful to Liron Hoch, who referred me to this passage. On the question of whether Maimonides indeed thought that Ezekiel's enquiry might have been 'corrupted', see Rosenberg, 'On Biblical Exegesis' (Heb.), esp. 148–9, and W. Z. Harvey, 'How to Begin to Study' (Heb.).

Hear *from me* what has become clear to *me* according to *my* understanding on the basis of what *I have learned* from the words of the sages, and that is that they call *ma'aseh bereshit* the natural sciences and the enquiry into the beginning of creation. By *ma'aseh merkavah* they mean the divine science, it being speech on the generality of existence and on the existence of the Creator, His knowledge, His attributes, that all created things must necessarily have come from Him, the angels, the soul, the intellect which links with humans, and existence after death. Because of the importance of these two sciences, the natural and the divine—and they were justly considered important—they warned against teaching them as the mathematical sciences are taught. It is known that each person by nature desires all the sciences, whether he be an ignoramus or a sage. [It is further known] that it is impossible for a person to begin the study of these sciences, and direct his thought towards them, without the appropriate premises, and without entering the stages of science; they therefore forbade this and warned against it. They sought to frighten one who directed his thought towards 'the account of the beginning' without [appropriate] premises, as he said, 'All who look upon four things . . . '. They [also] sought to restrain one who would direct his thought towards and would examine divine matters with his unaided imagination, without ascending the rungs of the sciences and said, [with reference to such people,] 'all who are not protective of the honour of their master, [it were better had they not come into the world].'[21]

Here, too, Maimonides emphasizes (more resolutely and less hesitantly than in the *Guide*, perhaps because he is younger?) that his explanation of the sages' meaning in such expressions as 'the account of the beginning' and 'the account of the chariot' is not based on a tradition he had received but on what had become clear to *him* according to *his* understanding on the basis of what *he had learned* from the words of the sages. Maimonides, as is well known, repeats this explanation in the *Mishneh torah*, there too without expressing any reservations:

The topics connected with these five precepts, treated in the above four chapters, are what our wise men called *pardes* (Paradise), as in the passage 'Four went into *pardes*' [BT Ḥag. 14]. And although those four were great men of Israel and great sages, they did not all possess the capacity to know and grasp these subjects clearly. Therefore, I say that it is not proper to dally in *pardes* till one has first filled oneself with bread and meat; by which I mean knowledge of what is permitted and what forbidden, and similar distinctions in other classes of precepts. Although these last subjects were called by the sages 'a small thing' (when they say 'A great thing, *ma'aseh merkavah*; a small thing, the discussion of Abaye and Rava'), still they should have precedence. For the knowledge of these things primarily gives composure to the mind. They are the precious boon bestowed by God, to promote social well-being on

[21] Kellner, 'Maimonides' Commentary' (emphasis added).

earth, in order to inherit life in the world to come. Moreover, the knowledge of them is within the reach of all, young and old, men and women; those gifted with great intellectual capacity as well as those whose intelligence is limited.[22]

At the end of chapter 2, Maimonides clarifies that the material discussed in chapters 1 and 2 of 'Laws of the Foundations of the Torah' is what the sages had called *ma'aseh merkavah* in our *mishnah* in Ḥagigah. He writes:

What has been said on this topic in these two chapters is but a drop in the ocean, compared with what has to be elucidated on this subject. The exposition of all the principles included in these two chapters is what is called *ma'aseh merkavah*.

The ancient sages enjoined us only to discuss these subjects privately, with one individual, and then only if he be wise and capable of independent reasoning. In this case, the heads of the topics are communicated to him, and he is instructed in a minute portion of the subject. It is left to him to develop the conclusions for himself and to penetrate to the depths of the subject. These topics are exceedingly profound; and not every intellect is able to grasp them. Solomon, in his wisdom, said, in regard to them, by way of parable: 'The lambs will be for thy clothing' [Prov. 27: 26]. Thus have the sages said, in the exposition of this parable, 'matters that deal with the mystery of the universe shall be for thy garment, that is, for thee alone; do not expound them in public'. So too, Solomon said concerning these topics, 'Let them be for thee alone and not for strangers with thee' [Prov. 5: 17].

And he further said concerning these subjects, 'Honey and milk are under thy tongue' [S. of S. 4: 11]. This text the ancient sages have thus explained, 'The things that are like milk and honey shall be under thy tongue.'[23]

In chapter 4, Maimonides relates to the issues discussed in chapters 3 to 4:

The matters just discussed are like a drop in a bucket, and are very deep, but are not as deep as those treated in the first and second chapters. The exposition of the topics dealt with in the third and fourth chapters is termed *ma'aseh bereshit* [cosmogony]. Our ancient sages enjoined us that these matters are not to be expounded in public, but should be communicated and taught to an individual privately.[24]

Several points emerge from the discussion so far. Maimonides argues that the sages had used for the field known in Greek as physics the term *ma'aseh bereshit*, and for the field known in Greek as metaphysics the term *ma'aseh merkavah*. He also argues that, after Jews had forgotten these equivalences (physics = *ma'aseh bereshit* and metaphysics = *ma'aseh merkavah*), he rediscovered them by himself. What is unquestionable is that Maimonides explains the essence of the 'mysteries of the Torah' without relying on rabbinic tradition, and relies on his own intellect. As he says on this matter, 'I followed conjec-

[22] *MT* 'Laws of the Foundations of the Torah', end of ch. 4.
[23] Ibid. 2: 11–12. [24] Ibid. 4: 10.

ture and supposition; no divine revelation has come to teach me that the intention in the matter in question was such and such, nor did I receive what I believe in these matters from a teacher. But the texts of the prophetic books and the dicta of the sages, together with the speculative premises that I possess, showed me that things are indubitably so and so.' Hence, Maimonides could not possibly have agreed with Rabbi Kotler's use of these formulations when he stated that 'every matter in the Torah—halakhah and *agadah*, law and story . . . one cannot appreciate any of them according to his intellect. Most particularly, one must beware of the Torah's stories, where very serious errors are possible, and these errors undermine the foundations of the people of Israel.'

Opponents could argue that Maimonides had no option but to formulate an independent stand on this specific matter since rabbinic tradition had been severed and was unknown. This argument collapses in the light of two facts:

1. Maimonides categorically determines:

    But since all these rules have been established by sound and clear proofs, free from any flaw and irrefutable, we need not be concerned about the identity of their authors, whether they were Hebrew prophets or gentile sages. For when we have to deal with rules and propositions which have been demonstrated by good reasons and have been verified by sound and flawless proofs, we rely upon the author who has discovered them or has transmitted them only because of his demonstrated proofs and verified reasoning.[25]

2. Maimonides also relies on his own view on highly significant matters of which it cannot be said that rabbinic tradition had been severed as, for example, the nature of divine providence. In the *Guide* he deals with several possible opinions about divine providence over existents, and numbers five views. He opens his explanation of the fifth one as follows:

    The fifth opinion is our opinion, I mean the opinion of our Law. I shall let you know about it what has been literally stated in the books of our prophets and is believed by the multitude of our scholars; I shall also inform you of what is believed by some of our latter-day scholars; and I shall also let you know what I myself believe about this.[26]

In this surprising text, Maimonides explicitly states that his view of providence—a matter that Rabbi Kotler claims is entirely learned from 'the Torah's stories, where very serious errors are possible, and these errors undermine

[25] *MT* 'Laws Concerning the Sanctification of the New Moon', 17: 24.
[26] *Guide* iii. 17 (p. 469).

the foundations of the people of Israel'[27]—is not identical to 'the opinion of our Law'. And he indeed adds a sixth opinion on providence, his own, and opens as follows:

> As for my own belief with regard to this fundamental principle, I mean divine providence, it is as I shall set it forth to you. In this belief that I shall set forth, I am not relying upon the conclusion to which demonstration has led me, but upon what has clearly appeared as the intention of the book of God and of the books of our prophets. This opinion, which I believe, is less disgraceful than the preceding opinions and nearer than they to intellectual reasoning.[28]

In his detailed later discussion of his view, Maimonides uses the following expressions: 'which I believe . . . I for one believe . . . I do not by any means believe . . . all this is in my opinion . . . according to me, as I consider the matter . . . I was impelled to adopt this belief'.

We need not enter here into the fascinating question of how Maimonides viewed the connection between his own view of providence and the 'opinion of our Law' and what indeed was his view.[29] For our present concern, it is enough to draw attention to the fact that, on a topic that Rabbi Kotler views as related to 'the foundations of the people of Israel' that could be undermined by errors of understanding, Maimonides again relies on his own view rather than on rabbinic tradition, and even hints that his view differs from that of (at least some of) the sages.

Maimonides' Universalism versus Stipends to Torah Scholars

As is well known,[30] Maimonides claims that there are several important subjects on which rabbinic sages did not issue compelling rulings (such as the order of events in the days of the messiah).[31] There are also important subjects on which some rabbinic sages issued mistaken rulings (for example, astrol-

---

[27] Later in the chapter, Maimonides explicitly states that we learn the notion of divine providence from stories: 'And all the stories figuring [in Scripture] concerning Abraham and Isaac and Jacob are an absolute proof of there being an individual providence' (*Guide* iii. 17 (p. 472)).

[28] *Guide* iii. 17 (p. 471).

[29] On the relationship between Maimonides' view and that of the Torah, see D. Schwartz, *Faith and Reason* (Heb.), 142, and in greater detail, id., *Central Problems*, 136–48. Mordechai Cohen focuses on this question in 'Maimonides' Disagreement'. On Maimonides' view of providence, see Dienstag, 'Maimonides on Providence' (Heb.). See also Diesendruck, 'Samuel and Moses ibn Tibbon'; Raffel, 'Providence as Consequent'; and Diamond, 'Maimonides on Leprosy'.

[30] At least to those who have read Kellner, *Maimonides on the 'Decline of the Generations'*.

[31] *MT* 'Laws of Kings and Wars', 12: 1–2: 'All similar expressions used in connection with the

ogy),[32] and there are others on which their view is not compelling (for example, concerning the sanctification of the month).[33] Though I do not offer a view here on whether Rabbi Kotler is right in his outlook on Jewish tradition, in the previous section I think that I have succeeded in showing that he had not fully understood Maimonides when he ascribed to him his own stance. This is not a surprising finding, since we have no reason to assume that Rabbi Kotler was well acquainted with the passages of the *Guide* that I have analysed here or with their historical context. I therefore turn now to a case where Rabbi Kotler's commentary upends Maimonides, as it were, in a context that, at least partly, was well known to him.

In *Mishnat rabi aharon*, Rabbi Kotler cites the end of the 'Laws of the Sabbatical Year and Jubilee', 13: 12–13:[34]

Why was the tribe of Levi granted no right to a share in the Land of Israel and in its spoils, together with his brothers? Because they were set apart to worship the Lord, to serve Him, and to teach His upright ways and His righteous judgements to the many, as it is said, 'They shall teach Jacob Thine ordinances, and Israel Thy law' [Deut. 33: 10]. They were consequently set apart from the ways of the world: they may not wage war as do the rest of Israel, they have no share in the land, and they may acquire nothing for themselves by physical force. They are rather the host of the Holy Name, as it is said 'Bless, Lord, His host' [Deut. 33: 11]. It is He, blessed

---

messianic age are metaphorical. In the days of the King Messiah the full meaning of those metaphors and their allusions will become clear to all . . . Some of our sages say that the coming of Elijah will precede the advent of the messiah. But no one is in a position to know the details of this and similar things until they have come to pass. They are not explicitly stated by the prophets. Nor have the rabbis any tradition with regard to these matters. They are guided solely by what the scriptural texts seem to imply. Hence there is a divergence of opinion on the subject.'

[32] 'What we have said about this from the beginning is that the entire position of the stargazers is regarded as a falsehood by all men of science. I know that you may search and find sayings of some individual sages in the Talmud and midrashim whose words appear to maintain that at the moment of a man's birth, the stars will cause such and such to happen to him. Do not regard this as a difficulty, for it is not fitting for a man to abandon the prevailing law and raise once again the counterarguments and replies (that preceded its enactment). Similarly it is not proper to abandon matters of reason that have already been verified by proofs, shake loose of them, and depend on the words of a single one of the sages from whom possibly the matter was hidden. Or there may be an allusion in those words; or they may have been said with a view to the times and the business before him. (You surely know how many of the verses of the holy Law are not to be taken literally. Since it is known through proofs of reason that it is impossible for the thing to be literally so, the translator [Aramaic Targum] rendered it in a form that reason will abide.) A man should never cast his reason behind him, for the eyes are set in front, not in back' (Maimonides, 'Letter on Astrology', 472).

[33] See the quotation above from *MT* 'Laws Concerning the Sanctification of the New Moon', 17: 24.

[34] R. Kotler cites this law in *Mishnat rabi aharon*, vol. iv, 42 and 82. In both places, he omits the expression *kol ba'ei ha'olam*. He also mentions this law in vol. i, 75, and vol. ii, 202.

be He, who acquires for them, as it is said, '[And the Lord spoke to Aaron, Thou shalt have no inheritance in their land, neither shalt thou have any part among them]: I am thy portion and thine inheritance [among the children of Israel]' [Num. 18: 20].

Not only the tribe of Levi, but each and every individual of those who come into the world [*kol ba'ei ha'olam*], whose spirit moves him and whose knowledge gives him understanding to set himself apart in order to stand before the Lord, [to serve Him, to worship Him, and to know Him, who walks upright as God created him to do, and releases himself from the yoke of the many foolish considerations which trouble people][35]—such an individual is as consecrated as the Holy of Holies, and his portion and inheritance shall be in the Lord forever and evermore. The Lord will grant him in this world whatsoever is sufficient for him, the same as He had granted to the priests and to the Levites. Thus indeed did David, upon whom be peace, say, 'O Lord, the portion of mine inheritance and of my cup, Thou maintainest my lot' [Ps. 16: 5].[36]

As to whom Maimonides is referring to when he says *kol ba'ei ha'olam*, Rabbi Kotler writes:

These are most assuredly [*vehem hem*] the Torah scholars of the generation who are exclusively devoted to Torah because, from the day that the Temple was destroyed, the Holy One, blessed be He, has nothing in His world but the four cubits of halakhah [BT *Ber.* 8*a*]. And that is in place of the Temple service and to tending the needs of the Temple, which had been done by the Levites.

In a brilliant hermeneutical move, Rabbi Kotler enlists Maimonides as a supporter of his Lakewood yeshiva.[37] How does he do that? Maimonides says of the one who fulfils all that he prescribes, that 'his portion and inheritance shall be in the Lord'. Asks Rabbi Kotler: what is the Lord's portion in our world? And he answers: since the Temple was destroyed, God's portion in the world is only 'four cubits of halakhah'. Specifically, we are dealing here with 'each and every individual of those who come into the world'. What world? The world of the Holy One, blessed be He. And what is the world of the Holy One, blessed be He? Rabbi Kotler answers: 'From the day that the Temple was destroyed, the Holy One, blessed be He, has nothing in His world but the four cubits of halakhah.' Furthermore, one who meets Maimonides' conditions is

---

[35] In R. Kotler's version, instead of the passage in brackets: 'and so forth'.

[36] *Mishnat rabi aharon*, vol. iii, 147.

[37] He also enlists (a very fitting term in this context) Maimonides as a supporter of his and his camp's struggle against the Israel Defence Forces' conscription of yeshiva students. For a discussion on the use of this Maimonidean law in the controversy on the military service of yeshiva students, see Hartum, 'Enlistment of Levites' (Heb.). See also S. Cohen, *The Sword or the Scroll?*, 100–1, and Stadler and Ben-Ari, 'Other-Worldly Soldiers?'.

'consecrated as the Holy of Holies'. But, 'from the day that the Temple [the place of the Holy of Holies] was destroyed, the Holy One, blessed be He, has nothing in His world but the four cubits of halakhah'. So who are *kol ba'ei ha'olam* who merit public sustenance precisely as the public had once sustained the tribe of Levi? 'These are most assuredly the Torah scholars of the generation who are exclusively devoted to Torah.'

Rabbi Kotler's use of Maimonides' formulation here raises several problems:

- Whenever Maimonides uses the expression 'each and every individual' (*kol ba'ei ha'olam*) in the *Mishneh torah*, he clearly intends all human beings generally rather than specifically Jews.[38]

- Maimonides was categorically opposed to public support for Torah scholars.

- In the introduction to his *Commentary on the Mishnah*, Maimonides cites a version of the *gemara* in BT *Berakhot* different from that familiar from the printed editions—'The Holy One, blessed be He, has nothing in His world but the four cubits of halakhah'—without the words 'from the day the Temple was destroyed'.

- Maimonides interprets this *gemara* in a way incompatible with Rabbi Kotler's stance.

- It is a well-founded assumption that Rabbi Kotler's 'Torah scholars of the generation who are exclusively devoted to Torah' are not devoted to the same Torah that Maimonides sought to impart to the generations that followed him.

Let us consider each of these points separately.

Regarding the identity of *ba'ei ha'olam*, the following merits attention. The *Mishneh torah* is divided into fourteen books. The seventh, the *Book of Agriculture*, and only the seventh book, is divided into precisely seven sections. The last section ('Laws of the Sabbatical Year and Jubilee') is divided into thirteen chapters. The thirteenth chapter is itself divided (in the printed versions) into thirteen laws.[39] Our text, then, is exactly in the middle of the

[38] See Blidstein, 'Spreading the Faith' (Heb.). Blidstein notes: 'Maimonides is very fond of the midrashic idiom "*ba'ei olam*" or "*kol ba'ei olam*", and uses it to denote humanity, usually in a spiritual or cultural context' (p. 86 n. 7). He points to our law from MT 'Laws of the Sabbatical Year and Jubilee' and to 'Laws of Repentance', 3: 3 and 6: 3; 'Laws of the Scroll of the Torah', 10: 1; and 'Laws of Sanhedrin', 12: 3. 'Laws of Kings and Wars', 8: 10 should also be added (as Blidstein hints in ibid., n. 8). For a fuller discussion, see Kellner, *They Too Are Called Human* (Heb.), ch. 6, and Kellner and Gillis, *Maimonides the Universalist*, ch. 7.

[39] In all the critical editions based on manuscripts (Joseph Kafih; *Yad peshutah* of R. Rabinovitch; the Shabse Frankel edn.; *Rambam meduyak* of R. Sheilat; and the one-volume version of

entire work—at the end of the seventh book, at the end of the seventh section of that book, at the end of its thirteenth chapter. I am far from being a supporter of Straussian numerology,[40] but it is hard to believe that our text is in its special place by chance.

And what do we find in this special place? Perhaps the most emblematic expression of Maimonides' universalism—each and every individual human being, if endowed with a generous spirit and with understanding, can stand before the Lord, serve him, and worship him. Such a person, if he learns 'to know him', and walks upright 'as God created him',[41] is 'as consecrated as the Holy of Holies', and will have a share in the world to come and adequate sustenance in this world. Such a person sees the Lord as his portion and his cup and, consequently, the Lord will 'maintain his lot', that is, will grant him a share in the world to come.

We can hardly blame Rabbi Kotler for being unaware of Maimonides' universalism. Rabbi Kotler was educated in a Jewish tradition—and was undoubtedly sure that Maimonides was an integral part of this tradition— which

the *Mishneh torah* by Yohai Makbili), this law is no. 13. But this numbering is only the one common in the printed versions, adopted by these editors for the reader's convenience. Maimonides did not number the laws in the *Mishneh torah*, and the manuscripts and printed versions are not uniform in this regard. It would be nice if our law were no. 13 according to Maimonides himself as well, but that is clearly not the case. Maimonides' willingness to cooperate with people inclined to 'play' with numbers may have been limited.

[40] Strauss, 'How to Begin to Study', p. xiii; Kraemer, 'An Intellectual Portrait', 20 and 42.

[41] In my view, there is a hint here of Maimonides' rejection of original sin, a rejection related to his universalism. All human beings were created by God to walk upright and, thus, are not stained by original sin. Note that the Gemara in BT *AZ* 22b (and parallel versions) ascribes a kind of 'original sin' to non-Jews when it says: 'Said Mar Ukba b. Hama: Because heathens frequent their neighbours' wives, and should one by chance not find her in, and find the cattle there, he might use it immorally. You may also say that even if he should find her in he might use the animal, as a Master has said: Heathens prefer the cattle of Israelites to their own wives, for R. Johanan said: When the serpent came unto Eve he infused filthy lust into her. If that be so [the same should apply] also to Israel! When Israel stood at Sinai that lust was eliminated, but the lust of idolaters, who did not stand at Sinai, did not cease.' Maimonides cites this *gemara* and writes: 'Among the amazing dicta whose external meaning is exceedingly incongruous, but in which—when you obtain a true understanding of the chapters of this Treatise—you will admire the wisdom of the parables and their correspondence to what exists, is their statement: "When the Serpent came to Eve, it cast pollution into her. The pollution of [the sons of] Israel, who had been present at Mount Sinai, has come to an end. [As for] the pollution of the nations who had not been present at Mount Sinai, their pollution has not come to an end." This too you should follow up in your thought'; *Guide* ii. 30 (pp. 356–7). Given that, in Maimonides' thought, the serpent symbolizes the imagination and imagination is not exclusive to non-Jews, what emerges is that a Jew who does not study Torah is no less 'polluted' than a non-Jew. On the serpent as a symbol of the imagination, see Klein-Braslavy, *Maimonides' Interpretation of the Adam Stories* (Heb.), 213–17. For a detailed discussion of this saying in the Gemara, of Maimonides' interpretation of it and his commentators, see Kellner, *They Too Are Called Human* (Heb.), 40–52.

accepted as obvious that an essentialist difference prevails between the Jewish people and the nations of the world (obviously in favour of the former). Nevertheless, Rabbi Kotler definitely knew that the basic meaning of the phrase *kol ba'ei ha'olam* in rabbinic texts is *everyone* in the world, and not only Jews.[42] Moreover, he could have known that, whenever Maimonides himself uses this expression, he means human beings in general.[43] He was also familiar with this expression from the *piyut* (liturgical poem) *Unetaneh tokef*.[44]

We lend power to the holiness of this day, for it is tremendous and awe-filled, and on it your kingship will be exalted, your throne will be established in loving-kindness, and you will sit on that throne in truth.

It is true that you are the one who judges, and reproves, who knows all, and bears witness, who inscribes, and seals, who reckons and enumerates. You remember all that is forgotten. You open the book of records, and from it, all shall be read. In it lies each person's insignia.

And with a great shofar it is sounded, and a thin, silent voice shall be heard and the angels shall be alarmed, and dread and fear shall seize them as they proclaim: Behold! The Day of Judgement on which the hosts of heaven shall be judged, for they too shall not be judged blameless by you, and *all creatures [kol ba'ei olam]* shall parade before you as a herd of sheep. As a shepherd herds his flock, directing his sheep to pass under his staff, so you shall pass, count, and record the souls of all living, and decree a limit to each person's days, and inscribe their final judgement.

Rabbi Kotler unquestionably knew the source of this *piyut* in Mishnah *Rosh hashanah* 1: 2:

At four seasons [divine] judgement is passed on the world: at Passover in respect of produce; at Pentecost in respect of fruit; at new year all creatures pass before God like children of *maron*, as it says, 'he fashions their hearts alike; he considers all their deeds' [Ps. 33: 15]; and on Tabernacles judgement is passed in respect of rain.[45]

---

[42] Hirshman, *Torah for the Entire World* (Heb.).

[43] See above, n. 38. I will cite here two examples of Maimonides' sayings on the subject: 'For this reason, but a single man was created, to teach us that if any man destroys a single life in the world, Scripture imputes it to him as though he had destroyed the whole world; and if any man preserves one life, Scripture ascribes it to him as though he had preserved the whole world. Furthermore, all human beings are fashioned after the pattern of the first man, yet no two faces are exactly alike. Therefore, every man may well say, "For my sake the world was created"' (*MT* 'Laws of Sanhedrin', 12: 3); and 'Moreover, Moses, our teacher, was commanded by God to compel all human beings to accept the commandments enjoined upon the descendants of Noah' (*MT* 'Laws of Kings and Wars', 8: 10).

[44] <http://www.sefaria.org/Unetaneh_Tokef.1?lang=en>. On the text itself, see Golinkin, 'Do "Repentance, Prayer and Tzedakah Avert the Severe Decree"?'.

[45] Maimonides' interpretation of this *mishnah* definitely calls for further enquiry, but this is not the place for it. He writes: 'At four seasons [divine] judgement is passed on the world: at

Nor is there any doubt that Rabbi Kotler understood the meaning of the verse cited in the Mishnah. Below is the verse in its textual context (Ps. 33: 10–16):

The Lord brings the counsel of the nations to naught: he makes the devices of the peoples to be of no effect. The counsel of the Lord stands forever, the thoughts of his heart to all generations. Happy is the nation whose God is the Lord; and the people whom he has chosen for his own inheritance. The Lord looks down from heaven; he beholds all the sons of men. From the place of his habitation he looks upon all the inhabitants of the earth; 'he who fashions their hearts alike; who considers all their deeds'.

The psalmist draws a distinction between the chosen people and 'all the sons of men', which parallels 'all the inhabitants of the earth'. The Mishnah states that all human beings are judged on Rosh Hashanah, and the author of *Unetaneh tokef* knew that too. I do not know whether Rabbi Kotler wanted his readers to learn from his interpretation of the expression *kol ba'ei olam* that the author of the *piyut* had meant that only Jews are judged on Rosh Hashanah (excluding non-Jews). However, he clearly failed to interpret correctly Maimonides' intention in his use of the expression *kol ba'ei olam* in the 'Laws of the Sabbatical Year and Jubilee'.

Rabbi Kotler uses this Maimonidean law to argue that 'the Torah scholars of the generation who are exclusively devoted to Torah' are most assuredly the contemporary tribe of Levi, and to hint that they are entitled 'to sustenance for [themselves] as [God] had granted to the priests and to the Levites' at the time of the Temple. The fact that Rabbi Kotler is absolutely convinced (and also wishes to convince us!) that the Jewish community must provide financial support for students at yeshivas and *kolels* is not surprising. But it is certainly unexpected to enlist Maimonides in this cause. Maimonides' strong words in his commentary on Mishnah *Avot* 4: 6 are well known,[46] and he sums up his view in his commentary on Mishnah *Nedarim* 4: 3: 'And I wonder about great individuals who, blinded by greed, denied the truth and assigned themselves stipends for ruling and studying, relying on flimsy evidence. And we shall speak about this matter in its place in treatise *Avot*.' And he specifically rules on this matter in 'Laws of Torah Study', 3: 1:

One however who makes up his mind to study Torah and not work but live on

Passover in respect of produce and so forth—on produce regarding what will happen to it, mishaps and whether there will be much or little. And the children of *maron*, the flock, a translation of sheep, means that people are considered and they are judged—to health, sickness, and death, and life, and other human issues. And what is revealed here is explained, as you will see, but what is hidden is without doubt extremely difficult' (*Commentary on the Mishnah*, ad loc.).

[46] Mordechai Friedman, 'Maimonides, Zuta, and the Muqaddams' (Heb.), 497–9.

charity, profanes the name of God, brings the Torah into contempt, extinguishes the light of religion, brings evil upon himself and deprives himself of life hereafter, for it is forbidden to derive any temporal advantage from the words of the Torah. The sages said, 'Whoever derives a profit for himself from the words of the Torah is helping on his own destruction' [*Avot* 4: 17]. They have further charged us 'Make not of them a crown wherewith to aggrandise thyself, nor a spade wherewith to dig' [*Avot* 4: 7]. They likewise exhorted us 'Love work, hate lordship' [*Avot* 1: 10]. 'All study of the Torah, not conjoined with work, must, in the end, be futile, and become a cause of sin' [*Avot* 2: 2]. The end of such a person will be that he will rob his fellow creatures.

Maimonides' view is controversial—that is also well known.[47] Rabbi Kotler ignores Maimonides' explicit statements and the storm that they generated, and puzzlingly enlists him in support of a view contradicting Maimonides himself.

For this 'enlistment', as noted, Rabbi Kotler quotes from part of the Gemara in BT *Berakhot* 8a: 'These are most assuredly the Torah scholars of the generation who are exclusively devoted to Torah because, from the day that the Temple was destroyed, the Holy One, blessed be He, has nothing in His world but the four cubits of halakhah. And that is in place of the Temple service and to tending the needs of the Temple, which had been done by the Levites.' Following is the full passage from the Gemara:

Raba said to Rafram ben Papa: 'Let the master please tell us some of those fine things that you said in the name of Rabbi Hisda on matters relating to the synagogue!' He replied: 'Thus said Rabbi Hisda: What is the meaning of the verse: "The Lord loves the gates of Zion [*tsiyon*] more than all the dwellings of Jacob?" [Ps. 87: 2]? The Lord loves the gates that are distinguished [*metsuyanim*] through halakhah more than the synagogues and houses of study. And this conforms with the following saying of Rabbi Hiyya ben Ami in the name of Ula: "Since the day that the Temple was destroyed, the Holy One, blessed be He, has nothing in this world but the four cubits of halakhah alone." So said also Abaye: At first I used to study in my house and pray in the synagogue. Since I heard the saying of Rabbi Hiyya ben Ami in the name of Ula—"Since the day that the Temple was destroyed, the Holy One, blessed be He, has nothing in His world but the four cubits of halakhah alone"— I pray only in the place where I study. Rabbi Ami and Rabbi Asi, though they had thirteen synagogues in Tiberias, prayed only between the pillars where they used to study.'

So far as I know, Maimonides quotes this talmudic passage only once in all his works—the introduction to his *Commentary on the Mishnah*:[48]

---

[47] See Kanarfogel, 'Compensation for the Study of Torah'.
[48] In Sheilat's edition (*Hakdamot harambam lamishnah*), 55; in Kafih's bilingual edition, 68.

And since they [the sages], may their memory be blessed, knew this matter and knew that all they said was clear and forthright—they urged and warned against contempt for them and said [BT *Eruv.* 21b and *Git.* 57b]: 'Whoever mocks the words of the sages is punished with boiling hot excrement.' And there is no greater boiling hot excrement than foolishness, which diverts one to mock. Hence, you will never find anyone mocking them unless he is driven by greed and favours emotions, as one of those whose heart has never been brightened by clear lights. And since they knew the truth of their words, spent their days with them and commanded to toil over them during the night and at the end of the days, they made an aim of them as they are and said [*Ber.* 8a]: 'The Holy One, blessed be He, has nothing in His world but the four cubits of halakhah alone.' Consider this statement because, if you study it literally—you will see that it is definitely far from the truth, as if the four cubits of halakhah alone were the aim and all other wisdom and knowledge was thrust aside. And at the time of Shem and Eber[49] and those who followed him, when there was no halakhah—we would think that God had nothing in the world. But if you study the inner meaning of these words, you will see a wondrous wisdom and will find it including a great many intelligibles. And I will explain it to you so that it may serve as a metaphor for all else that you will find, so study it properly.

The version Maimonides cites here is known from various manuscripts[50] and also from *Sefer halakhot gedolot*,[51] and we have no sure way of knowing whether Maimonides knew the 'standard' version and preferred this one or knew only the one he cites. But since the standard version appears in the work of Rabbi Isaac Alfasi, it is plausible that Maimonides knew both versions and preferred the one he cited. We have no way of knowing, however, whether he compared the two versions and chose the one he cited because he thought it conceptually preferable or simply found it technically preferable.[52] Be that as it may, Rabbi Kotler cannot use the 'standard' version if he means to interpret Maimonides through it.

What Maimonides *does* say is entirely unsuited to the line of thought that Rabbi Kotler ascribes to him. The literal meaning of 'The Holy One, blessed be He, has nothing in His world but the four cubits of halakhah alone'—

---

[49] According to several sources, Shem, Noah's son, and Eber, Noah's grandson, founded 'the *beit midrash* of Shem and Eber', where the Patriarchs studied Torah. See e.g. BT *Mak.* 23b, *Gen. Rabbah* 52 (11), 62 (3), 63 (6), and *S. of S. Rabbah* 6 (6). Maimonides mentions this legend in *Guide* ii. 41 (p. 388) and calls Shem and Eber 'prophets' in *Guide* ii. 39 (p. 379).

[50] *Dikdukei soferim*, ad loc.   [51] *Sefer halakhot gedolot*, 'Laws of Blessings', ch. 5 (vol. i, 52).

[52] I maintain that Maimonides had philosophical reasons for preferring the version he cited. According to the standard version, the cessation of sacrifices led to a kind of break between us and our Father in Heaven, a break that is to be corrected by studying Torah instead of offering sacrifices. Since Maimonides determines that God's commandment of sacrifices is due to the 'second intention' rather than to what could be called 'the original divine plan' (*Guide* iii. 32 (pp. 526–7)), he would obviously not be happy with the standard version. For details, see Kellner, *Maimonides' Confrontation*, 140–54.

which is the text that Rabbi Kotler builds upon—is 'definitely far from the truth', since it is impossible that 'the four cubits of halakhah alone were the aim and all other wisdom and knowledge was thrust aside' (an entirely plausible option for Rabbi Kotler!). Maimonides advances an interesting claim to prove that the literal reading is unacceptable: if the literal reading is correct, then, at the time of the Patriarchs—'when there was no halakhah'—the Holy One, blessed be he, had no place in his world. This claim is interesting because it supports the view that, according to Maimonides, the Patriarchs did not observe the commandments, but this is not our concern here.[53]

At the end of the passage I cited from the introduction to the *Commentary on the Mishnah*, Maimonides promises to explain Rabbi Ula's dictum. Concluding this at some length, Maimonides determines:

From all we have said it is already clear that the end of everything in the world of generation and corruption is a perfect being who incorporates both wisdom and action, as we said. And after we have learned these two things—wisdom and action —from what they said, may their memory be blessed, and from what they explained and from what they hinted, it is indeed true what was said, 'The Holy One, blessed be He, has nothing in His world but the four cubits of halakhah alone.'[54]

Observing the commandments (and not necessarily only studying them) enables a person to bring to perfection (each at his own level) that which differentiates him 'from other animals', that is, 'the mental representation of the intelligibles. And the noblest of the intelligibles—the representation of the unity of God, may He be glorified and exalted, and what is related to this from the divine [wisdom], since all other wisdoms are studied only to apprehend the divine wisdom.'[55] Maimonides, then, draws a conclusion very distant from that of Rabbi Kotler: studying halakhah is important because it enables us to study the natural sciences (in the medieval sense of the term), which enables us to study the divine science—metaphysics.[56]

The Essence of Torah Study

This matter leads us directly to the last point requiring discussion in the present context. I claimed above[57] that Rabbi Kotler's 'Torah scholars of the generation who are exclusively devoted to Torah' are not devoted to the same Torah

[53] Kellner, 'Rashi and Maimonides'.
[54] See *Hakdamot harambam lamishnah*, 60.   [55] Ibid. 57.
[56] Maimonides' stance, viewing halakhah as a means (indeed a very important one) rather than an end in itself, has been persistently contested. For a discussion, see Kellner, 'Rabbis in Politics' (Heb.). For an example of the resentment evoked by this stance, see Shem Tov ibn Shem Tov, *Sefer ha'emunot*, pt. i, ch. 1, 7a, and, generally, Peleg, 'A Critique of Jewish Rationalism' (Heb.).   [57] See above, Ch. 5 on R. Elhanan Wasserman.

that Maimonides sought to impart to the generations that followed him, and I must now address this point.

First, what does Rabbi Kotler say? In a discussion titled 'On the Virtue of the Oral Law' (*Bema'alat torah shebe'al peh*)[58] we find:

> The Gemara—which is the Oral Law—is the interpretation of the Written Law, and this interpretation too was given to Moses at Sinai, with principles and with the thirteen rules for expounding the Torah, and we have no Written Law without the Oral Law. But it has already been clarified in the letters of the *gaon* Rabbi Israel Salanter[59] that, for us, the Mishnah and the commentaries of the *rishonim* and the *posekim* [halakhists] are as the Written Law, while the study of them through casuistry [*pilpul*] and inference is called *gemara*.[60]

This passage conveys an extremely conservative approach—'the Mishnah and the commentaries of the *rishonim* and the *posekim*' become Written Law, making any notion of historical influences affecting them inconceivable, and 'the study of them through casuistry [*pilpul*] and inference' becomes Oral Law, *gemara*, making any notion of disputing the commentaries of the *aharonim* entirely implausible. Moreover, Rabbi Kotler defines *gemara* here (resorting to a Maimonidean idiom, as we will immediately see) as 'study . . . through casuistry [*pilpul*] and inference'.

Rabbi Kotler later clarifies that he relies here on Maimonides:

> And it is also explained in Maimonides' commentary[61] on the *gemara* in [tractate] *Kidushin*, 'one should always divide his years into three—a third to Scripture, a third to Mishnah, and a third to *talmud*'—and Maimonides explains in 'Laws of Torah Study' that Scripture is the Written Torah, Mishnah is the Oral Torah, including all

---

[58] *Mishnat rabi aharon*, vol. iv, 30. The piece is subtitled: 'Speaking to generous supporters of Torah'.

[59] The publisher added here: '*Or yisra'el*, 18'. Here is the relevant passage: 'The codification of the Talmud sealed our path to understand the Torah and issue halakhic rulings from the Written Law according to the thirteen exegetical principles given at Sinai. Instead, we look only at the Talmud to draw from it knowledge of God's Torah and his ways. Even the greatest and most knowledgeable Torah scholar has no other way—only seek out and reveal its mysteries. And nothing can be added to the Talmud or subtracted from it. Hence, the Talmud for us is like the study of the Written Torah for the rabbinic sages, and our study of the Written Torah is like the study of the alphabet at the time of the rabbinic sages, through which we come to study the Talmud. And the books of *rishonim* and *aharonim* [for us] are like the study of the Mishnah for the rabbinic sages.' In my humble opinion, R. Salanter is making a much more modest claim here than the one R. Kotler makes in his name. See Salanter, *Or yisra'el*, ch. 18. (I corrected the text according to Pachter, *Writings of R. Israel Salanter* (Heb.), 246.)

[60] Later R. Kotler writes: 'And things that were new to sages of a past generation, for the generation that follows they are already Mishnah' ('On the Virtue of the Oral Law' (*Bema'alat torah shebe'al peh*), *Mishnat rabi aharon*, vol. iv, 30).

[61] R. Kotler does not literally mean a commentary here, but the text from *MT* 'Laws of Torah Study' about to be cited immediately below.

the Gemara and the *ge'onim*, and *talmud* is to understand the end from the beginning, through deduction, and through comparison, that is, clarifying things in depth according to the methods of study, 'dealing only with those who rule according to religion and halakhah'.[62] And he also wrote: 'This plan applies to the period when one begins learning. But after one has become proficient and no longer needs to learn the Written Law, or continually be occupied with the Oral Law, he should, at fixed times, read the Written Law and the traditional dicta, so as not to forget any of the rules of the Torah, and should devote all his days exclusively to the study of *talmud*, according to his depth of mind and maturity of intellect.' We thus learn from Maimonides that, in our time, knowledge of the Gemara is as knowledge of the Mishnah, so that even if one knows it all by heart, one should not rule relying solely on this knowledge, as they said,[63] 'Anyone issuing a halakhic ruling relying on his memory is counted as reckless.' And as it is impossible to make a clear halakhic ruling from the Mishnah without knowing the negotiations in the Gemara, so is it impossible to issue a ruling in our time relying on the Gemara when lacking [knowledge of] the ways of study and reasoning in the *rishonim* and the *posekim*.

Thus far Rabbi Kotler's view relying on Maimonides. And what exactly did Maimonides write in 'Laws of the Study of Torah', 1: 11–12?

The time allotted to study should be divided into three parts. A third should be devoted to the Written Torah; a third to the Oral Torah; and the last third should be spent in reflection, deducing conclusions from premises, developing implications of statements, comparing dicta, studying the hermeneutical principles by which the Torah is interpreted, till one knows the essence of these principles, and how to deduce what is permitted and what is forbidden from what one has learnt traditionally. This is termed *talmud*.

For example, if one is an artisan who works at his trade three hours daily and devotes nine hours to the study of the Torah, he should spend three of these nine hours in the study of the Written Law, three in the study of the Oral Law, and the remaining three in reflecting on how to deduce one rule from another. The words of the prophets are comprised in the Written Law, while their exposition falls within the category of the Oral Law. The subjects styled *pardes* [esoteric studies] are included in *talmud*. This plan applies to the period when one begins learning. But after one has become proficient and no longer needs to learn the Written Law, or continually be occupied with the Oral Law, he should, at fixed times, read the Written Law and the traditional dicta, so as not to forget any of the rules of the Torah, and should devote all his days exclusively to the study of *talmud*, according to his depth of mind and maturity of intellect.

---

[62] The expression appears in BT *Yoma* 26b.
[63] The publisher added here: '*TDE* [*Tana devei eliyahu*] *Zuta*, ch. 16'.

Note that, as usual, Maimonides' messages here are meant simultaneously for several different audiences.[64] Someone reading this law as if it had been written by a typical yeshiva head will understand that Maimonides expects the advanced student to 'devote all his days exclusively to the study of Talmud' and will therefore think that Maimonides upholds a Jewish curriculum centred on the study of the Mishnah and the *posekim*. Without a doubt, this is how Rabbi Kotler read this law. But was this indeed Maimonides' intention? The answer is probably not, for good reasons.[65]

Maimonides clarifies that the beginner must divide his time into three:

- Written Torah (including 'the words of the prophets').
- Oral Torah[66] (including 'their exposition'[67]).
- *Talmud*.

And what is *'talmud'* ('Gemara' according to the version used by Rabbi Kotler)? Maimonides explains: 'deducing conclusions from premises, developing implications of statements, comparing dicta, studying the hermeneutical principles by which the Torah is interpreted, till one knows the essence of these principles, and how to deduce what is permitted and what is forbidden from what one has learnt traditionally'. And Maimonides adds, incidentally: 'The subjects styled *pardes* [esoteric studies] are included in *talmud*.' Maimonides thus draws a distinction here between *'talmud'* and the Oral Torah. And what is *talmud*? Maimonides tells us, as if it were obvious, that the *talmud* concept includes 'the subjects styled *pardes*'. Readers of this statement certainly know that, for Maimonides, *pardes* is the account of Creation and the account of the chariot; the former is Aristotelian physics and the latter is metaphysics.[68] Rabbi Kotler probably knew this. He added words to Maimon-

---

[64] On this Maimonidean style of writing, see Henshke, 'On the Question of Unity' (Heb.), and Kellner, 'Literary Character'.

[65] For a broader discussion, see Kellner, '*Mishneh torah*: Why?' (Heb.).

[66] For a clarification of this expression in Maimonides' halakhic thought, see Blidstein, 'Maimonides on "Oral Law"', and id., 'Oral Law as Institution'.

[67] On this expression, see the introduction to the *Mishneh torah*: 'All the precepts which Moses received on Sinai were given together with their interpretation, as it is said . . . "The Torah" refers to the Written Torah; "and the commandment" to its interpretation. God bade us fulfil "the Torah" in accordance with "the commandment". This commandment refers to that which is called the Oral Torah.' See *Book of Knowledge*, 1b. See also the third commandment included in *MT* 'Laws of Rebellious Elders': 'not to add to the Torah either in regard to the precepts in the Written Torah or in regard to their exposition which we have learnt by tradition' (ibid. 33a).

[68] Maimonides, as noted above, defines the term *pardes* at the end of ch. 4 in *MT* 'Laws of the Foundations of the Torah'. See also the discussion above on his references to *ma'aseh bereshit* and *ma'aseh merkavah*, and his commentary on Mishnah Ḥag. 2: 1.

ides' statement (in brackets), provoking a suspicion that he had understood Maimonides' intention precisely and sought to 'defuse' it:

And he added, 'This plan applies to the period when one begins learning. But after one has become proficient [and his knowledge of Torah is perfect] . . . he should, at fixed times, read the Written Law and the traditional dicta, so as not to forget any of the rules of the Torah, and should devote all his days exclusively to the study of *talmud*, according to his depth of mind and maturity of intellect.'[69]

Rabbi Kotler's interpolation 'and his knowledge of Torah is perfect' solves a problem for him. Only one whose 'knowledge of Torah is perfect'—when such a creature is obviously not to be found in this world!—should learn *pardes*. If this was Rabbi Kotler's intention, he seems to have understood the 'dangers' lurking in Maimonides' view, and acted to neutralize them.

Another strange point in Rabbi Kotler's statement merits attention: 'And Maimonides explains in the "Laws of Torah Study" that Scripture is the Written Torah, Mishnah is the Oral Torah, including all the Gemara and the *ge'onim*.' And we should not ignore his statement cited above: 'for us, the Mishnah and the commentaries of the *rishonim* and the *posekim* [halakhists] are as the Written Law, while the study of them through casuistry [*pilpul*] and inference, is called *gemara*.' Gemara, the Oral Torah, thus includes the *aḥaronim*. Rabbi Kotler thereby greatly expands the scope of 'Torah from heaven'. But Maimonides' second premise in his introduction to his *Book of Commandments* is well known: 'Commandments that were derived from the thirteen hermeneutical rules are not counted.' Maimonides greatly restricted the scope that Rabbi Kotler expanded, a restriction that Nahmanides, as we know, strongly opposed in his glosses on the *Book of Commandments*. Nahmanides opens his gloss on the second premise as follows:

In the second premise, the rabbi, of blessed memory, decreed that whatever is learned through one of the thirteen rules for expounding the Torah or by the principle of inclusion should not be counted among the commandments given to Moses at Sinai and should not be called a commandment from the Torah, nor should anything attached to one of these thirteen rules be counted. Yet, if the Gemara explicitly notes that it is from the Torah, it should be counted, and if it is not explicitly noted, one should count it as rabbinic.[70]

Nahmanides concludes this very long gloss as follows:

And this, in brief, is what I meant to write on this premise. I know that many rulings in the Gemara contradict his view. This book of the rabbi, of blessed memory, is most sweet and altogether lovely except for this premise, which uproots views

---

[69] *Mishnat rabi aharon*, vol. iv, 30.   [70] Nahmanides, *Glosses* (Heb.), 29.

deeply set in the Talmud and brings down Gemara strongholds. This is a shocking issue for those learning Gemara, may it be forgotten and go unmentioned.[71]

Rabbi Kotler nevertheless reads Maimonides as if he had been in agreement with Nahmanides! There is no other way of understanding his argument that Maimonides had included in the Oral Law not only the Mishnah, and not only the Gemara, but also the words of the *ge'onim*.[72]

In sum, we have shown that Rabbi Kotler's use of 'Laws of the Sabbatical Year and Jubilee' 13: 13 serves his own aims, but is far from faithful to Maimonides' intentions.

Conclusion: How did Rabbi Kotler Read Maimonides?

So where are we? I have analysed three sources where Rabbi Kotler rather puzzlingly relies on Maimonides. The first source relates to the role of innovation and independent enquiry in matters of faith, the second deals with universalism and with stipends to Torah scholars, and the last relates to the essence of Torah study. Concerning the first, it is quite plausible that Rabbi Kotler did not delve into the texts that I have discussed (*Guide of the Perplexed* and the *Commentary on the Mishnah*), which were not part of the yeshiva 'syllabus' in his time. Concerning the second, Rabbi Kotler may not have been aware of the universal messages in Maimonides' writings, but it is simply impossible that he was not familiar with Maimonides' 'scandalous' pronouncements on stipends to Torah scholars. As for the third—the study of 'science' as part of Torah study—Maimonides' views can hardly be said to have gone unnoticed by Rabbi Kotler: he interprets or corrects them in a way attesting that he understood their 'problematic' nature, and it is hard to believe that he probed the 'Laws of Torah Study' and simply skipped the 'Laws of the Foundations of the Torah'.

The fact that Rabbi Kotler reads a different Maimonides from the one I read is not exactly surprising. But we saw that, at least in one case, he 'loads'

---

[71] Nahmanides, *Glosses* (Heb.), 51. Entering the discussion between Maimonides and Nahmanides on this matter seems pointless. The subject has been analysed at length, both in halakhic works (Bacharach, *Ḥavat ya'ir*, §195) and in the research literature. See Blidstein, *Studies in Halakhic and Aggadic Thought* (Heb.); id., 'Tradition and Institutional Authority' (Heb.); and id., '"Even if He Tells You Right Is Left"' (Heb.). See also id., 'Oral Law as Institution'; Henshke, 'The Basis of Maimonides' Concept' (Heb.); and Sinclair, 'Legal Thinking' (Heb.). Moshe Halbertal discusses this matter at length and in depth in his *By Way of Truth* (Heb.), 43–66. Note that Maimonides and Nahmanides are in dispute on other issues related to the one here: the nature of the sages' faith and the decline of the generations. On the former, see Kellner, 'Rabbis in Politics' (Heb.); on the latter, see id., *Maimonides on the 'Decline of the Generations'*.

[72] The reader should note that Nahmanides' position widens the authority of rabbis and *posekim*, while that of Maimonides restricts it. See Kellner, 'Rabbis in Politics' (Heb.).

upon Maimonides a view that he must have known was not his—and also one that many of his listeners or readers must also know was not that of Maimonides. That is definitely surprising. Moreover, we saw another instance wherein Rabbi Kotler 'loads' upon Maimonides a view of Nahmanides that explicitly contradicts Maimonides' own view. That is also extremely surprising.

What is happening here? In my view, there are several options:

- Rabbi Kotler did not know Maimonides' views.

- Rabbi Kotler did know Maimonides' views but understood them as compatible with those of thinkers who disputed him.

- Rabbi Kotler's writing is 'political'—he adapted his sources to what his audience could (or would?) absorb. Advocates of this claim could draw support from Maimonides, who unquestionably did so himself.[73]

The first option seems flimsy to me. Rabbi Kotler had been known as a prodigy in his youth, was chosen as a son-in-law by one of the most outstanding rabbis of the time, Rabbi Isser Zalman Meltzer, began teaching at the young age of 22 at the famous Kletzk yeshiva, and was renowned in the east European rabbinic world before the Holocaust. For such a person not to know the dispute between Maimonides and Nahmanides on the definition of a commandment from the Torah is inconceivable, just as it is inconceivable that he was unaware of Maimonides' blunt and forthright assertions against public support for Torah scholars. Simply impossible!

The second option splits into two sub-options: (1) Rabbi Kotler 'loaded' upon Maimonides an interpretation that would make him more acceptable in his own world, or (2) Rabbi Kotler was so immersed in his own ideology that he was unable to read Maimonides' assertions as they are.[74] I find the second sub-option very appealing. Rabbi Kotler played a significant role in shaping an approach that has crystallized over the last two centuries—the spectrum of ideas somewhat simplistically described as the *haredi* world-view. In his perception, this world-view is Judaism, and it is simply impossible for Maimonides to depart so radically from this 'consensus'.

On the other hand, the third option gains credibility from the fact that most of Rabbi Kotler's *Mishnat rabi aharon* was addressed to 'popular' audiences (students, teachers, patrons) rather than to his illustrious scholarly

---

[73] There is another option, which I completely reject: that R. Kotler tried to lead his readers astray. I cannot for one moment imagine that a man of R. Kotler's eminence would consider such behaviour.

[74] On this option among leading twentieth-century Torah scholars, see Shapiro, *Limits of Orthodox Theology*, 157–8.

colleagues and yeshiva heads. I have no way of deciding. Several conclusions nevertheless emerge from the discussion. Maimonides is apparently so important that his support cannot be dispensed with, even when seemingly coerced. Otherwise, why does Rabbi Kotler seek his help? I have tried to show here that it would have been easier for him to shape his world-view without Maimonides, but he still 'insists' on using him. The second conclusion relates to the fact, as noted in Chapter 5, that, for his readers, Maimonides constitutes a kind of Rorschach test—everyone looks at the inkblots on the page and sees a different picture. In this chapter we have seen two dramatically different pictures of Maimonides: that of Rabbi Aharon Kotler and that of a fairly typical academic interpreter of Maimonides. I leave it up to the reader to decide which picture is a better representation of the original.

SEVEN

What, Not Who, Is a Jew: Halevi–Maimonides in Those Days, Rabbi Aviner and Rabbi Kafih in Our Day

MENACHEM KELLNER

THE STORY is told of an east European Jew in the nineteenth century who decided to convert to Christianity. He returns home from the ceremony a Christian in all respects. The next day our former Jew rises early and starts to put on tefillin. His wife yells at him: 'Fool! Yesterday you converted and today you put on tefillin?' Our newly baptized Christian smacks himself on his head and expostulates in Yiddish: '*A goyishe kop!*' ('What a Gentile head I have!').

This joke reflects an ideological position which is not at all funny: that non-Jews are more stupid than Jews, and hence, a Jew who converts to another religion lowers his intelligence. This attitude depends upon a more basic view, according to which there is some inherent, even ontological, difference between Jews and all others. According to this view, the gulf between Jew and non-Jew is so deep and broad that it takes a miracle to bridge it[1] (or perhaps it can never actually be bridged).[2]

The view that Jews and non-Jews are distinguished by some inborn, metaphysical quality is widespread in contemporary Judaism, and not only in Orthodox circles.[3] Indeed, this view is so widespread that most people who

---

[1] Those who hold these views have a hard time understanding and explaining *halakhot* concerning conversion to Judaism, but where there is a will there is a way. See the discussions in Wijnhoven, 'The Zohar and the Proselyte', and E. Wolfson, *Venturing Beyond*, 165–85.

[2] Lasker, in 'Proselyte Judaism', argues that, according to Halevi, even in the messianic era proselytes will remain distinct from born Jews. Lasker is the author of the well-known quip that, according to Halevi and those like him, the distinction between Jew and non-Jew (and even between Jew and proselyte) is a matter of hardware, while, for Maimonides and those like him, it is one of software only.

[3] Readers are invited to check themselves: if you laughed at the joke at the opening of the chapter, then you should ask yourself if you believe that there is an inherent difference between Jews and non-Jews.

hold it are actually unaware of the fact that they hold a controversial position, one deeply debated throughout the history of the Jewish tradition, at least from the Middle Ages on. In this chapter, I will seek to illuminate one aspect of this controversy. First I will illustrate the debate as it is expressed by two prominent Israeli Orthodox rabbis, and then elucidate the roots of the debate in the medieval controversy over the nature of Jews and Judaism as found in the writings of Judah Halevi and Moses Maimonides.

Rabbi Shlomo Aviner

In the world of contemporary Orthodox Zionism in Israel (*dati le'umi*) the voice of Rabbi Shlomo Aviner is heard loudly and clearly, through his many books, lectures, Internet activities, and, especially, the multitude of 'sabbath leaflets' (*alonei shabat*) to which he contributes. Rabbi Aviner was born in France in 1943 and immigrated to Israel in 1966. He earned degrees in mathematics and engineering and is an officer in the Israel Defence Forces reserves. He studied in Yeshivat Merkaz Harav Kook in Jerusalem, and is considered to be a disciple of the late Rabbi Tsevi Yehudah Kook (1891–1982).[4] Rabbi Aviner is the rabbi of the West Bank settlement Beit El and head of the yeshiva Ateret Kohanim in the Muslim Quarter of the Old City. Although he is considered a political hawk, Rabbi Aviner broke with many of his rabbinic colleagues and counselled soldiers not to disobey orders in connection with the Gaza withdrawal of 2005. This independent stand aroused considerable controversy in the world of Orthodox Zionism, earning him many enemies.[5]

One of the issues to which Rabbi Aviner often returns is the special nature of the Jewish people. Thus we find him writing:

We are the chosen people [*am segulah*[6]], not because we received the Torah, but, rather, we received the Torah because we are the chosen people.[7] This is so since the Torah is so apt to our inner nature. Each nation has a special nature, character, public psychology, unique divine character, and the Master of the Universe formed this special nation: 'This people which I formed for Myself, they will tell My praise'

---

[4] On R. Kook, see Aran, 'The Father, the Son, and the Holy Land'; Held, 'What Zvi Yehudah Kook Wrought'; Inbari, *Messianic Religious Zionism*; D. Schwartz, *Challenge and Crisis* (Heb.); Seeman, 'God's Honor'; and id., 'Violence, Ethics, and Divine Honor'.

[5] There was even an Internet site (http://aviner.net) devoted to attacking R. Aviner (accessed 19 Apr. 2015), which has since disappeared. On Aviner, see Inbari, *Messianic Religious Zionism*, 59–64.

[6] Though based on a biblical idiom, a check of the Bar Ilan Responsa Project database shows that this expression appears only 113 times in the entire body of Jewish literature covered by the database, and became popular only in the Middle Ages.

[7] Here R. Aviner reflects Halevi, *Kuzari* ii. 56.

[Isa. 43: 21]. There are those who claim against us that we are 'racist'. Our answer to them is . . . if racism means that we are different from and superior to other nations, and by this bring blessings to other nations,⁸ then indeed we admit that we differ from every nation, not by virtue of skin colour, but from the aspect of our soul-like nature [hateva hanishmati shelanu], the Torah describing our inner contents.⁹

In this typical passage Rabbi Aviner presents his position in the clearest possible fashion and takes issue with his opponents. Let us look more closely at his words. The people of Israel are the chosen people. Why and how? Rabbi Aviner discusses two possibilities: the descendants of Abraham, Isaac, and Jacob received the Torah and in consequence they became the chosen people, or the descendants of Abraham, Isaac, and Jacob were the only humans capable (*mesugalim*) of receiving the Torah. Receiving the Torah was a consequence of their already having been the chosen people (*am segulah*). In presenting these alternatives R. Aviner accomplishes several ends: he admits (barely, it seems to me) that there is controversy on the issue, takes a stand on this controversy, and hints that the opposing view ought not to be taken seriously, since he does not deign to argue against it.

Rabbi Aviner insists that the Torah is appropriate to the inner nature of the Jewish people: 'Each nation has a special nature, character, public psychology, unique divine character, and the Master of the Universe formed this special nation—"This people which I formed for Myself, they will tell My praise" [Isa. 43: 21].' In making this claim he reifies the notion of 'nation' and establishes that there are nations defined and demarcated from each other by their inner natures. In so doing he adopts the views of nineteenth-century German Romanticism and foists that ideology on Judaism.¹⁰ The Jewish people, he

---

⁸ How does Israel bring blessings to other nations? In his commentary on Halevi's *Kuzari* i. 108, R. Aviner writes: 'The Torah is the greatest divine light, and it belongs only to Israel, and from Israel drops of sanctity drip to each and every nation, according to its stature and state [*inyano*].' Aviner returns to this theme often. Thus, for example, in answer to a question asked of him on the Internet ('Why should we be a nation?') on a website that has since disappeared, he wrote: 'Indeed, what is the need for a special nation? But, just as a human being needs a heart, thus the human race needs a heart-like nation. Rabbi Judah Halevi wrote that the people of Israel are the heart of humanity [*Kuzari* ii. 36]. Not a heart which is disconnected [from the rest of humanity], not a condescending heart, not a heart frozen in a refrigerator, but a living heart which causes vitality to flow to all the limbs. Just as the heart's love is the love of all the limbs, thus love of the people of Israel is in essence love of all that is human. When we extend ourselves in our national efforts, in strengthening the settlement of the people of Israel in its land, in strengthening its army and state, we are essentially working for the good of all humanity. This is not egoistical love, but universalist love.'

⁹ *Iturei kohanim*, 174 (Sivan 5759 (1999)). My thanks to R. Dr Ronen Lubitch for bringing this source to my attention.

¹⁰ In this, R. Aviner follows in the footsteps of his teacher, R. Tsevi Yehudah Kook, who follows in the footsteps of his father, R. Abraham Isaac Kook (to a great degree). The elder Rav Kook, in turn, appears to follow in the footsteps of his teachers, Hegel and other Romantic

teaches, has an inner nature unique to it, a nature to which the Torah is particularly appropriate.[11] A number of things follow from this: to begin with, Rabbi Aviner takes a position on a tannaitic debate over whether the Torah was ultimately intended for all human beings (*kol ba'ei olam*) or just for Israel.[12] He further raises a metaphysical problem about the conversion of non-Jews to Judaism: how can a person whose inner nature is not Jewish receive the Torah?[13] He also forces himself to adopt a particularist stance concerning the messianic era: if the Torah is appropriate only for those whose inner nature is Jewish, then the essential difference between Jew and non-Jew must be preserved in the days of the messiah. Rabbi Aviner thus once again takes a stand in a controversial matter, without even admitting that there is a controversy on the issue.[14]

Rabbi Aviner is not only the rabbi of a settlement in Samaria, and not only the founder and head of a yeshiva deeply identified with the hopes for the actual construction of a third Temple; he is also a man of the wider world. Born during the Holocaust, brought up and educated in France, he holds academic degrees. He knows what sort of an outcry his words are likely to arouse, and hence hastens to assure us that he is not a racist, at least not in the accepted sense of the word: 'If racism means that we are different from and superior to other nations, and by this bring blessings to other nations, then indeed we admit that we differ from every nation, not by virtue of skin colour, but from the aspect of our soul-like nature, the Torah describing our inner contents.' His self-confessed racism is not biological—Jews come in all skin shades. No, his racism is spiritual. Jews are indeed superior to other nations,

---

thinkers. On this intellectual pedigree, see Fischer, 'Self-Expression and Democracy', esp. 66–126, 217–34. For a recent and very useful English-language study of the elder R. Kook, see Mirsky, *Rav Kook*.

[11] I tried to translate R. Aviner's usages back into rabbinic Hebrew with no success. His ideas, I submit, largely come from outside Jewish tradition and cannot easily be traced to rabbinic texts.

[12] On this debate, see Hirshman, *Torah for the Entire World* (Heb.). Hirshman summarizes the points in this book in his article, 'Rabbinic Universalism'.

[13] I am aware of the many solutions offered for this problem (see above, n. 1). For R. Aviner (and before him Halevi, not to mention the authors of the Zohar), conversion presents a problem. For Maimonides, in contrast, there is no problem that needs to be solved. Once, while teaching an introductory course in Judaism at a leading university in the United States, I mentioned the possibility of conversion to Judaism. Two of the students, both of them daughters of Baptist ministers, were surprised and asked, 'How is it possible to choose to be chosen?' Apparently it is Halevi, and not Maimonides, who is taught in Baptist Sunday Schools in the USA.

[14] See Kellner, *Maimonides on Judaism*; id., *Maimonides' Confrontation*, ch. 7; and id., 'Maimonides' "True Religion"'. I wonder how R. Aviner would react if he heard me pointing out to my students that the Patriarchs and even Moses (before Sinai) were not Jews, but at most Noachides.

but their superiority is connected to their unique Jewish souls, souls whose 'operating instructions' are written in the Torah. This superiority brings nothing but blessings to all other nations.

I think that fairness demands that we point out that Aviner is doing himself a disservice here. There is no doubt that he accepts the possibility of conversion to Judaism.[15] Thus, despite what he says about himself, he cannot be a racist in any contemporary sense of the term. He seems to be using 'racism' here as shorthand for essentialism.[16]

Rabbi Aviner is willing to accept the consequences of his position on Jewish superiority. In a book aimed at soldiers in the Israeli army he writes:

Death is ritual impurity [*tumah*] since its essence is the diminishment of the divine vitality in created entities. The measure of ritual impurity matches the measure of the departure of this divine vitality. Gentile graves in an enclosure do not cause ritual impurity according to the basic law [*ikar hadin*] since their souls are not so holy and the difference between their bodies without a soul and their bodies with a soul is not all that great. Therefore the departure of the soul in their case does not constitute so terrible a crisis. And so also the opposite: the graves of the righteous do not impart ritual impurity (according to some perspectives, if not according to settled halakhah)[17] because their bodies are holy and there is [thus] no diminishment of the divine manifestation [in them] with the departure of the soul. Jewish graves do impart ritual impurity since their souls are holy; however, their bodies without a soul are not holy and, therefore, the departure of the soul is the terrible crisis of the departure of the divine vitality from the body—and this constitutes the ritual impurity of death.[18]

According to this text (which I find horrifying), the difference between a live Jew and a dead Jew is immense; the difference between a live non-Jew and a dead non-Jew is much smaller.[19] Rabbi Aviner neither says nor even implies that the killing of a non-Jew is a light matter, but will all his readers understand that?[20] It is not my intention here to cry out against rabbinic irresponsibility, but, rather, to illustrate a certain, unfortunately widespread, view concerning the inner nature of the Jewish people.

---

[15] See, for example, Aviner, 'Converts' (Heb.).

[16] See Kellner, *Maimonides' Confrontation*, 26–31.

[17] R. Aviner cites as his sources Zohar i. 168a, and *Midrash mishlei* on Prov. 9: 2.

[18] Aviner, *Meḥayil el ḥayil*, 230, cited by Ahituv, 'State and Army' (Heb.), 466. For a view similar to that of R. Aviner, see Hayim ibn Attar (1697–1743), *Or haḥayim* on Lev. 20: 26 and Num. 19: 2.

[19] Compare R. Aviner's words in his commentary on the *Kuzari* (i. 136): 'In that we are the *segulah* of humanity, we are also the heart of humanity. We are more human than the others.' See also p. 302. For others who hold this view that Jews are 'more human' than non-Jews, see below, n. 61.

[20] Bear in mind that this text is addressed to teenage inductees into the Israeli army.

Rabbi Joseph Kafih

Rabbi Aviner represents one branch of Orthodox Zionism which often appears to dominate public discussion in Israel (and, so far as I can judge, in North America as well). But other branches exist, and I will deal with one of them here. I do not refer to the Meimad movement (and the political party which grew out of it), led by figures such as Professor Aviezer Ravitzky and Rabbi Michael Melchior—dealing with them would make my job far too easy.[21] Rather, I propose to discuss the views of another student from Yeshivat Merkaz Harav Kook, the rabbi, rabbinic court judge, and scholar Rabbi Joseph Kafih (1917–2000).[22]

In 1958 Prime Minister David Ben-Gurion turned to fifty 'Jewish sages' and sought their opinions on the nature of Jewish identity.[23] Among them was Rabbi Kafih. In the course of his reply to Ben-Gurion he wrote:

What is the meaning of the term 'Jew'? It must be stated that the term does not denote a certain race. Perhaps it is wrong to use the word 'race' so as not to mimic the modern-day racists and their associates, as according to the perception of the Torah, there are no different races in the world. In order to uproot this theory, the Torah felt compelled to provide extensive details of the lineage of all the peoples in the world so as to attribute them to a single father and a single mother. Thus it might be more proper to say that the term 'Jew' does not denote a certain tribe, or in other words, does not indicate the descendants of Abraham, Isaac, and Jacob in the limited sense of the phrase. We know beyond any doubt that throughout the generations, many people of different nations became intermixed with the Israelites.[24]

We are witness here to a position radically different from that of Rabbi Aviner, based upon a dramatically different starting point. Rabbi Kafih takes with ultimate seriousness the biblical claim that all human beings are created in the image of God and that we are all equally descendants of Adam (and Eve), of Noah (and Mrs Noah). The apparently tiresome list of 'begats' in the book of Genesis serves a religious/ethical end: to emphasize that we all trace our lineage back 'to a single father and a single mother'. There is no Jewish people

---

[21] For an entry into this phenomenon, see Fischer, 'Self-Expression and Democracy', 35–43.

[22] R. Kafih, it must be noted, was himself a student at Yeshivat Merkaz Harav Kook in the 1940s (as was the author of this chapter in 1962–3), and maintained a warm and friendly relationship with R. Tsevi Yehudah Kook. He was very close to R. Ya'akov Moshe Harlap (1882–1951), the head of the yeshiva between the two rabbis Kook. R. Kafih was not a student of R. Tsevi Yehudah's and was by no means a '*merkaznik*' as the term is understood today, i.e. an ideological follower of R. Tsevi Yehudah.

[23] Ben-Rafael (ed.), *Jewish Identities*. For background, see Waxman, 'Giyur'.

[24] R. Kafih's letter may be found in Ben-Rafael, *Jewish Identities*, 247–53 (this paragraph is on p. 247).

in the tribal-biological sense of the word, as if all Jews shared the same genetic material inherited from Abraham, Isaac, and Jacob. The House of Israel contains many individuals with no biological connection to the Patriarchs at all. Rabbi Kafih understood this well, and also knew that myriads of non-Jews are the descendants of the Patriarchs.[25]

In the continuation of his answer to Ben-Gurion, Rabbi Kafih defines the term 'Jew' as 'a nation constituted by a particular religion'. The Jew is thus defined by the Torah,[26] and not by some inner nature which distinguishes Jews from the rest of humanity. We see here a position diametrically opposed to that of Rabbi Aviner.

Rabbi Aviner versus Rabbi Kafih—Judah Halevi versus Maimonides (1)

What has happened? Both of these rabbis are identified with Orthodox Zionism; both were trained in non-rabbinical pursuits (Rabbi Kafih worked for years as a goldsmith; Rabbi Aviner trained as an engineer); both served in rabbinical posts; and both studied in Yeshivat Merkaz Harav Kook and were close to the late Rabbi Tsevi Yehudah Kook.[27]

It appears to me that there are at least two fundamental theological differences between the two figures, differences which explain their substantial disagreement about the nature of the Jewish people. The basis for their theological disagreement lies in the medieval figures who largely framed their understandings of Judaism: Judah Halevi and Maimonides. I will mention one of these differences briefly, and then move on to a more detailed analysis of the second. Many of the discussions in my book *Maimonides' Confrontation with Mysticism* relate to a debate between Halevi and Maimonides concerning the nature of the Torah. According to Halevi the commandments of the Torah reflect an antecedent reality. This is a consequence of what Y. Tzvi Langermann has termed Halevi's 'hyper-realism'.[28] Halakhic distinctions, according to Halevi, are consequences of actual distinctions in the cosmos, part of the inner nature of the universe. Sanctity, for example, is an actual characteristic

---

[25] According to some scholars, this includes contemporary Palestinians. See Parkes, *Whose Land?*

[26] This calls to mind Sa'adyah Gaon's famous comment: 'The nation of the children of Israel is a nation only by virtue of its laws'. See his *Book of Beliefs and Opinions*, iii. 7 (p. 158). R. Kafih's definition is in Ben-Rafael, *Jewish Identities*, 249.

[27] We should note that thinkers associated with Yeshivat Merkaz Harav Kook need Maimonides' naturalist messianism to make their own religious Zionist stance possible, while at the same time strongly preferring Halevi's non-naturalist ideas about the people and Land of Israel.

[28] See Langermann, 'Science and the Kuzari', 495.

of holy places, things, people, and times. If we could invent a 'sanctity counter' it would ping every time its wand came near something holy, just as a Geiger counter pings when exposed to radioactivity. We cannot see, hear, feel, taste, or smell radioactivity, and before the Curies no one even knew that it existed, but we now know it to be an integral part of the physical universe. Similarly, for figures like Judah Halevi, we cannot see, hear, feel, taste, or smell sanctity, but it is certainly an integral part of the (meta-)physical universe. Just as radioactivity can have serious consequences even though we are not aware of it through our senses, so also sanctity can have serious consequences (think of the closing scenes of the film *Indiana Jones and the Ark of the Covenant*), even though we are not aware of it through our senses (although some Jews, who have contact with what Halevi called *al-amr al-ilahi/ha'inyan ha'elohi*, can be aware of it—on this term, see below). Against this background we can understand how and why Halevi understands the universe as a system of essences and why he sees nations, for example, as actual separate entities, distinguished by their inner essences.

Maimonides opposes this view. He saw the commandments of the Torah as constituting social reality, not as reflecting antecedent metaphysical reality. Halakhah in his eyes is the name given to a set of laws which create an institution called 'Judaism'.[29] These laws are contingent, 'arbitrary', not in the sense that they are not expressions of God's wisdom and benevolence, but in the sense that they could have been different (as is proved, for example, by the way Maimonides explains God's command to offer sacrifices[30]). These laws are reasonable in the sense that they do not contradict reason, but are not rational in the sense that reason makes them necessary.[31] Violation of these laws can carry with it very serious consequences, up to and including the death penalty, but such violation carries with it no consequences on the ontological plane. Fulfilment of these commands in and of itself does not grant one a share in the world to come.

It is fair to say that the world of Maimonides is much less 'enchanted' than that of Halevi. In Maimonides' disenchanted universe human beings are simply human beings, and what distinguishes groups of them from each other are not essences, but talents, history, hopes, commitments, and differing beliefs.

We might characterize the distinction I am drawing here in a fairly simple way: Halevi did not know the Zohar and kabbalah, but his world was close to

[29] Maimonides may very well have been the first Jewish thinker to conceive of 'Judaism' as a religion constituted by a body of doctrines and laws. See Melamed, *Dat: From Law to Religion* (Heb.), and Batnitzky, *How Judaism Became a Religion*.
[30] *Guide* iii. 32 (pp. 529–31), and Kellner, *Maimonides' Confrontation*, 140–8.
[31] See J. Jacobs, *Law, Reason, and Morality*.

that of kabbalah.³² Maimonides also did not know the Zohar and kabbalah but, unlike Halevi, he would certainly have had profound reservations about them (to put the matter mildly) had he known of them.

There is no reason in the world to suspect that Rabbi Aviner would have any doubts about the traditional ascription of the Zohar to the *tana* Simeon bar Yohai, and that kabbalistic literature is authoritative and sacred. Rabbi Kafih, on the other hand, was the grandson and student of Rabbi Yihye Kafih (1850–1932), the founder of the Dor De'ah movement in Yemen (which fervently opposed the Zohar and kabbalah). Rabbi Joseph Kafih was circumspect in his comments about his grandfather's battles, but there are grounds to believe that his position was not all that different from his grandfather's.³³

Rabbi Aviner versus Rabbi Kafih—Judah Halevi versus Maimonides (2)

A discussion on the contribution of kabbalah to the debate we have isolated here between Rabbis Aviner and Kafih on the nature of the Jewish people can safely be left to others.³⁴ Here I wish to focus on another debate between them: Rabbi Aviner's Jewish thought is decisively influenced by Judah Halevi in the context of a usually unarticulated polemic against Maimonides. Rabbi Kafih's Jewish thought is decisively and admittedly influenced by Maimonides.³⁵

Rabbis Kafih and Aviner both dealt with Halevi's *Kuzari*, Rabbi Kafih as a translator,³⁶ Rabbi Aviner as a commentator. Rabbi Kafih added notes to his translation (some of them quite sharp), in some of which he emphasizes the

---

³² Halevi certainly influenced the worlds of kabbalah. See E. Wolfson, *Through a Speculum*, 294–6.

³³ On R. Kafih see Bar-Asher, 'In Memoriam' (Heb.). On the controversy surrounding his grandfather, see Y. Tobi, 'Who Wrote *Sefer emunat hashem?*' (Heb.). R. Kafih avoided controversy, and in his published works made no reference to the storm surrounding his grandfather, which created much anguish within the Yemenite community. He did write a short book when he was 17 years old, *Sihat dekalim* (published after his death), in which his reservations about kabbalah come through clearly. On the expression *sihat dekalim*, see BT *Suk.* 25*a*. On R. Kafih's reluctance to involve himself in controversies over kabbalah, see Tobi, 'The Nature of Judaism' (Heb.).

³⁴ See Hallamish, 'The Attitude Towards the Gentile Nations' (Heb.). See also the book by Elliot Wolfson cited above (n. 1). Two additional and very important studies on this subject are J. Gellman, 'Jewish Mysticism and Morality', and Balk, 'The Soul of a Jew'.

³⁵ For an early but still useful discussion of the controversy between Halevi and Maimonides on these issues, see Ben-Sasson, 'The Uniqueness of Israel' (Heb.) (155–64 on Halevi and 178–96 on Maimonides). The debate between Halevi and Maimonides is one of the central themes of Kellner, *Maimonides' Confrontation*. It should be recalled that over the generations Halevi's views were amplified in kabbalah; R. Aviner's Halevi is read through that prism.

³⁶ His translation was only published in 1997, but as he notes in the introduction, was completed many years earlier.

differences between Maimonides and Halevi,[37] and even hints at his reservations concerning some of Halevi's views.[38] It is apparent that Rabbi Aviner, in contrast, identifies with the *Kuzari*, and one even gets the impression that he sees himself as an authoritative interpreter of the text—Halevi's interpreter in our world, as it were.

Rabbi Kafih's attitude towards Maimonides is different: while it is as clear as day that he had the highest regard for 'the Great Eagle' and invested years of his life in translating and commenting on many of Maimonides' works, he would certainly have had reservations about being called a 'Maimonidean' and would have rejected (with great annoyance, one suspects) the idea that he was Maimonides' representative in our world, or even his authorized interpreter. In a personal letter to Michael Schwarz, who was then embarking on a new translation of the *Guide of the Perplexed* into Hebrew, Rabbi Kafih wrote, 'Maimonides in my view is like a mirror. Everyone who stands opposite him sees his own reflection. Maimonides has many facets [*panim*], and each person sees the facet he wants to see [*to'em bo et ta'amo*].'[39] Despite this open-mindedness, it is hard not to see in Rabbi Kafih's monumental oeuvre of Maimonidean translations and commentaries (which earned him the Israel Prize in 1969) an attempt to understand and present Maimonides in terms which would have found favour in the eyes of the Great Eagle himself.

Halevi and Rabbi Aviner

In the introduction to his commentary on the *Kuzari*, Rabbi Aviner emphasizes that the book is 'holy and pure, expressing the essentials of the faith of Israel and of the Torah'.[40] He even characterizes the book as 'the Holy of Holies',[41] 'nourished by completely, absolutely holy sources'.[42] In contrast to the *Kuzari*, Rabbi Aviner explains that 'one can take portions of the *Guide of the Perplexed*, translate them to other languages, and no one would notice that

[37] For example, 26 n. 70; 35 n. 88; 223 n. 24.
[38] For example, ibid. 11 n. 27, where R. Kafih expresses wonder at Halevi's claim that proselytes do not become the equal of born Jews.
[39] Cited by Michael Schwarz on p. 752 of his Hebrew translation of the *Guide*.
[40] Aviner, commentary on the *Kuzari*, i. 51.   [41] Ibid. 52.
[42] Ibid. 61. R. Aviner's comment must raise the eyebrows of anyone familiar with the work of scholars such as Pines, Lobel, and Krinis, who have documented Halevi's extensive use of Shi'ite ideas and motifs. See Pines, 'Shi'ite Terms'; Lobel, *Between Mysticism and Philosophy*; and Krinis, 'The Arabic Background'. See further Krinis, *God's Chosen People*. Worthy of note in this regard is the comment attributed to the Vilna Gaon: 'The *Kuzari* is holy and pure. The principles of Jewish faith and Torah depend upon it'; Shohat, 'The Faith of our Father Abraham' (Heb.), 196.

it is a Jewish work. But concerning the *Kuzari*, this is impossible! The *Kuzari* is all Jewish, head to toe.'⁴³

What did Judah Halevi write that so excited Rabbi Aviner? According to Judah Halevi, the difference between Israel and the nations is so essentialist that even proselytes remain a people apart, not wholly and completely absorbed into Israel. In *Kuzari* i. 26 the king asks, 'If this be so, then your belief is confined to yourselves?'⁴⁴ In the next paragraph he receives the following answer:

The Rabbi: Yes; but any Gentile who joins us unconditionally shares our good fortune, without, however, being quite equal to us. If the Law were binding on us only because God created us, the white and the black man would be equal, since He created them all. But the Law was given to us because He led us out of Egypt, and remained attached to us, because we are the pick of mankind.⁴⁵

It should be recalled that this speech was addressed to a non-Jewish king who would ultimately convert to Judaism. Halevi returns to this issue towards the end of the first treatise of the *Kuzari* (i. 115), and in connection with the process of conversion writes:

Those, however, who become Jews do not take equal rank with born Israelites, who are specially privileged to attain to prophecy, whilst the former can only achieve something by learning from them, and can only become pious and learned, but never prophets.⁴⁶

What keeps the proselyte from achieving the ultimate religious perfection (prophecy)?⁴⁷ According to Halevi (and, following him, Rabbi Aviner) that

---

⁴³ Aviner, commentary on the *Kuzari*, i. 56. By contrast, R. Kafih called the *Guide* a holy book (see p. 17 in the introduction to his translation), but not in any absolute sense. See Farhi, 'Rabbi Joseph Kafih's Introduction' (Heb.).

⁴⁴ Translations from the *Kuzari* here are those of Hartwig Hirschfeld (<https://en.wikisource.org/wiki/Kitab_al_Khazari>).

⁴⁵ On the status of proselytes in the thought of Halevi see Lasker, 'Proselyte Judaism'. On the issue of the apparent racism in this passage, see below in nn. 47 and 76.

⁴⁶ The issue of the status of proselytes in Judaism is not directly relevant here. Halevi's approach stands in dramatic contrast to that of Maimonides, especially as enunciated in his famous letters to Obadiah the Proselyte. See Kellner, *Maimonides on Judaism*, ch. 6, and, importantly, Diamond, *Converts*. It should be noted that R. Kafih, in his answer to Ben-Gurion (Ben-Rafael, *Jewish Identities*, 249), understands the various laws that discriminate against proselytes as designed to encourage proselytes to intermarry with born Jews and thus as quickly as possible become fully part of the House of Israel. R. Aviner, in contrast, takes Halevi's stance and deepens it, saying, for example, that 'the very jump [*kefitsah*] from the level [*madregah*] of Gentile to that of Jew is giant in and of itself' (commentary on the *Kuzari*, i. 302).

⁴⁷ It should be recalled that very few Jews by birth reach this status, according to Halevi. Thus, his discrimination between those born as Jews and proselytes is largely theoretical. Yisrael Ben-Simon pointed out to me that, for Halevi, prophecy is not a natural phenomenon (as it is for Maimonides), but is entirely a consequence of God's choosing the prophet—God causes the

which marks off the Jewish people (and unites them) is their descent from the Patriarchs. Thanks to this patrimony, the Jewish people enjoy a unique asset, a 'divine influence' or *al-amr al-ilahi* in the *Kuzari*'s original Arabic (*inyan ha'elohi* in Ibn Tibbon's Hebrew translation and *davar elohi* in the translations of Rabbi Kafih and Michael Schwarz).[48] This special property (*segulah*) enables the Jewish people properly to fulfil God's commandments and to aspire to prophecy. It is literally hereditary, and shared only by actual descendants of the Patriarchs. Thus, we find Halevi writing:

The details can be demonstrated from the lives of Adam, Seth, and Enosh to Noah; then Shem and Eber to Abraham; then Isaac and Jacob to Moses. All of them represented the essence and purity of Adam on account of their intimacy with God. Each of them had children only to be compared to them outwardly, but not really like them, and, therefore, without direct union with the divine influence. The chronology was established through the medium of those sainted persons who were only single individuals, and not a crowd, until Jacob begat the Twelve Tribes, who were all under this divine influence. Thus the divine element reached a multitude of persons who carried the records further.[49]

In Halevi's narrative, Adam was created in the image of God, and granted by God a special property, *al-amr al-ilahi*. This trait was passed to only two of his progeny, Abel and Seth, but not to Cain and his other descendants. Abel was killed by Cain, who was jealous that Abel had received *al-amr al-ilahi* and was destined to inherit the land that would be called Israel. Abel died before passing *al-amr al-ilahi* to any progeny. Seth, however, was enabled to pass it on to Enosh, from whom it passed to Noah, and from Noah to Shem and Eber, and from Shem and Eber to their descendant/disciple, Abraham. Abraham had only one son who was worthy to inherit *al-amr al-ilahi*—Isaac. Isaac, like his father Abraham, had only one son who was worthy to inherit *al-amr al-ilahi*—Jacob.[50] Jacob, unlike his father and grandfather, passed on *al-amr*

prophet to prophesy thanks to God's goodness and will. Thus, according to Halevi, it follows that proselytes cannot achieve prophecy, not only because they do not have the *inyan ha'elohi*, but because God chooses not to bestow prophecy upon them. It should be noted that in connection with this issue as well, R. Aviner moves Halevi into realms he never intended to reach. Halevi's theories are not racist in the modern sense of the term. The *inyan ha'elohi* is a potential that only Jews can actualize, but in actuality very few Jews succeed in doing so. A Jew who has not actualized this potential is in no way superior to a non-Jew. For an enlightening discussion of these issues, see Jospe, 'Teaching Judah Halevi', 112. Jospe presents Halevi's theory as a rationalist ('scientific' in contemporary terms) attempt to explain historical phenomena—that prophecy is found only among Jews, that miracles were worked for the Jewish people, and that they have survived despite all that has happened to them. My teacher, Steven Schwarzschild, sought to present Halevi's theories in what he called 'biologicist' but not racist terms in his posthumous article, 'Proselytism and Ethnicism'. See also Bodoff, *The Binding of Isaac*.

[48] On this term see Lobel, 'A Dwelling Place', 103, and Krinis, *God's Chosen People*, 189–223.
[49] *Kuzari* i. 47.
[50] See *Kuzari* i. 95 and iii. 21.

al-ilahi to all his children, the Children of Israel (Jacob) and thus was the chosen people (*am segulah*) constituted.

Once a nation worthy of carrying *al-amr al-ilahi* was created, it was possible to give that nation the Torah. This claim perplexed the Khazar king, who asked, why God could not have given the Torah to all nations (i. 102)? To this, Halevi's spokesperson in the dialogue answers:[51]

> The Rabbi: Or would it not have been best for all animals to have been reasonable beings? Thou hast, apparently, forgotten what we said previously concerning the genealogy of Adam's progeny, and how the spirit of divine prophecy rested on one person, who was chosen from his brethren, and the essence of his father. It was he in whom this divine light was concentrated. He was the kernel, whilst the others were as shells which had no share in it.[52] The sons of Jacob were, however, distinguished from other people by godly qualities, which made them, so to speak, an angelic caste. Each of them, being permeated by the divine essence, endeavoured to attain the degree of prophecy, and most of them succeeded in so doing. Those who were not successful strove to approach it by means of pious acts, sanctity, purity, and intercourse with prophets. Know that he who converses with a prophet experiences spiritualization during the time he listens to his oration. He differs from his own kind in the purity of soul, in a yearning for the [higher] degrees and attachment to the qualities of meekness and purity. This was a manifest proof to them, and a clear and convincing sign of reward hereafter. For the only result to be expected from this is that the human soul becomes divine, being detached from material senses, joining the highest world, and enjoying the vision of the divine light, and hearing the divine speech. Such a soul is safe from death, even after its physical organs have perished. If thou, then, findest a religion the knowledge and practice of which assists in the attainment of this degree, at the place pointed out and with the conditions laid down by it, this is beyond doubt the religion which insures the immortality of the soul after the demise of the body.

When we recall that, according to the narrative in the *Kuzari*, these words were spoken to a king who had already proved that he was righteous enough to receive messages from on high,[53] and ends up converting to Judaism, with much of his nation, the chutzpah of these words literally takes one's breath away. There is a qualitative difference between animals and human beings;

---

[51] *Kuzari* i. 103. I purposely ignore the scholarly debate over whether the '*ḥaver*' in the *Kuzari* always represents Halevi's views or not. For an entry into the discussion, see D. Schwartz, *Central Problems*, 137, and the sources cited there.

[52] Those who possess the *inyan ha'elohi* (whether or not it is expressed, or only dormant) are consistently compared to the kernel (*garin*) as opposed to the shell (*kelipah*); see *Kuzari* i. 95, i. 103 (our passage here), and ii. 14. Certain kabbalistic ideas reverberate in the ears of contemporary readers exposed to these texts.

[53] See Eisen, 'The Problem of the King's Dream'.

similarly, there is a qualitative difference between human beings *simpliciter* and Jews![54] Relative to other humans, Jews are like angels.[55] Even those Jews who do not reach the rank of prophecy are purified by their exposure to it.

In one specific case, the revelation of the Torah at Sinai (*ma'amad har sinai*), the entire nation of Israel achieved prophecy. On this Halevi wrote:

> The Rabbi: Bear with me a little while that I show the lofty station of the people. For me it is sufficient that God chose them as His people from all nations of the world, and allowed His influence to rest on all of them, and that they nearly approached being addressed by Him.[56] It even [*sic*] descended on their women, among whom were prophetesses, whilst since Adam only isolated individuals had been inspired till then. Adam was perfection itself, because no flaw could be found in a work of a wise and Almighty Creator, wrought from a substance chosen by Him, and fashioned according to His own design.[57]

According to Halevi, then, Israel received the Torah at Sinai because only they, of all the peoples of the earth, could receive it—only they had inherited *al-amr al-ilahi*, which made receipt of the Torah possible. In my view, Rabbi Aviner is correct in emphasizing this aspect of Halevi's thought, despite the fact that it is hard to find any specific text in which the claim is explicitly made. One possible passage on which to base this claim is in *Kuzari* ii. 56, where Halevi writes:

> If there were no Israelites there would be no Torah. They did not derive their high position from Moses, but Moses received his for their sake. The divine love dwelt among the descendants of Abraham, Isaac, and Jacob. The choice of Moses, however, was made in order that the good fortune might come to them through his instrumentality.[58]

The Torah, which, according to one rabbinic legend was written 974 generations before creation, waited after creation for another 26 generations in order to be given to the people of Israel.[59] Before the constitution of this special nation, there was simply no one to whom the Torah could be given. In his

---

[54] R. Aviner emphasizes this point time and again in his writings.

[55] Compare *Kuzari* iv. 3, where Halevi, basing himself on Lev. 19: 2 ('You shall be holy, for I, the Lord, your God, am holy'), maintains that the nation of Israel is meant to be for other nations as angels are for human beings. Compare the discussion of Maimonides' use of this verse in Kellner, *Maimonides' Confrontation*, 90.

[56] In a note to this passage, R. Kafih draws attention to Maimonides' contrasting view (*Guide* ii. 32 (p. 363)) that God spoke only to Moses at Sinai—the nation of Israel did not achieve prophecy at Sinai. [57] *Kuzari* i. 95.

[58] See also *Kuzari* iii. 1, where Israel is called the nation destined for prophecy. For Maimonides' contrasting view, see Kellner, 'Maimonides' Moses' (Heb.).

[59] For a discussion of this midrashic motif, and Maimonides' position concerning it, see Kellner, 'Did the Torah Precede the Cosmos?' (Heb.).

writings, Rabbi Aviner continually emphasizes this point and cites Isaiah 43: 21 ('This people which I formed for Myself, they will tell My praise') repeatedly in support.[60] With the Exodus from Egypt, he argues, something new was constituted in the world, a superhuman, angelic nation.[61]

Rabbi Aviner sees himself as a disciple of Judah Halevi. To my mind, Rabbi Aviner's Halevi reached him through Hegel, Rabbi Abraham Isaac Hakohen Kook, and through the latter's son, Rabbi Tsevi Yehudah Kook.[62] Each of these added a layer of his own to the Halevian base, but there is no doubt that the base exists. It also appears to me that Rabbi Aviner sees himself as Halevi's representative in our world. Rabbi Kafih, on the other hand, would never present himself as Maimonides' representative in our day—despite which I see him as faithful to Maimonides and his thought. I would go as far as to say that Rabbi Kafih is more faithful to his teacher than Rabbi Aviner is to his, but that is the topic of another discussion, and it may indeed just reflect my desire to protect Halevi from his followers.

Maimonides and Rabbi Kafih

An excellent way to enter into the worlds of Maimonides and of Rabbi Kafih[63] is through one specific law in the *Mishneh torah*, a law whose placement figuratively shouts out *darsheni*, 'examine me closely'. We discussed this law

---

[60] It is interesting to note that Maimonides did not cite this verse even once in all his writings. See R. Kafih's very useful *The Bible in Maimonides* (Heb.). It is even more interesting to note that Halevi does not cite this verse in the *Kuzari*.

[61] This is Aviner's view, not Halevi's. Among other sources, it probably draws from Judah Lowe, the Maharal of Prague (d. 1609), who held that at Sinai the image of God was diminished among the nations of the world, leaving only Jews as fully formed in the image of God. See, for example, Lowe, *Netsaḥ yisra'el*, vol. i, 305. For discussion, see Kleinberger, *Maharal's Educational Thought* (Heb.), 37–42. I was surprised to find an echo of the Maharal's view, that non-Jews are in some sense less formed in the image of God than Jews, in an article written by one of the heads of New York's Yeshiva University. See Schachter, 'Women Rabbis?', 20, where R. Schachter, distinguished professor of Talmud and *rosh kolel* at Yeshiva University, writes, as if it is totally uncontroversial: 'Hashem [God] created all men *B'Tzelem Elokim* [in the image of God], and *Bnai Yisrael* [Jews] with an even deeper degree of this *Tzelem Elokim*—known as *Banim LaMakom* [children of the Omnipresent].'

[62] This is true, but perhaps not totally fair. R Aviner certainly draws his inspiration from the *Kuzari*, but also, and importantly, from the Zohar, from kabbalistic literature, and from the Maharal—in short from a whole tradition of thinkers who emphasize the innate and essentialist superiority of Jews over non-Jews. In this connection, I personally regret to say, he swims with the stream, R. Kafih against it. Compare Isadore Twersky's comment: 'In many respects, R. Judah Halevi, Nahmanides, and the Maharal constitute a special strand of Jewish thought —threefold, yet unified'; Twersky, 'Maimonides and Eretz Israel', 261.

[63] On R. Kafih's attitude towards Maimonides see the comments of Michael Schwarz in vol. ii of his new Hebrew translation of the *Guide* (pp. 749–52). R. Kafih's devotion to Maimonides

briefly in the previous chapter, and will look at it more closely here. As already noted, Maimonides divided his *Mishneh torah* into fourteen books. The seventh book is itself divided into seven sections (and is the only book divided into precisely that number of sections). The seventh section is itself divided into thirteen chapters. The thirteenth of these chapters is itself (in all printed editions) divided into thirteen paragraphs (*halakhot*). Thus, the thirteenth *halakhah* of the thirteenth chapter of the seventh section of the seventh book of the *Mishneh torah* marks the precise midpoint of that work.

The number thirteen is, of course, significant in Judaism generally,[64] but has special significance for Maimonides. Not only did he promulgate thirteen principles of Judaism, but in *MT* 'Laws of Circumcision', 3: 9, he emphasizes the fact that the word 'covenant' (*berit*) is found precisely thirteen times in the account of Abraham's circumcision (Gen. 17).[65] The number seven is significant in many human societies, and not just in Judaism (Judah Halevi to the contrary—see *Kuzari* ii. 20); according to Leo Strauss (1899–1973) it is of particular significance to Maimonides.[66] I am in general no enthusiast for Straussian numerology, but this case seems too contrived not to have some significance.

What does Maimonides write in the text numbered 7/7/13/13, the exact midpoint of the *Mishneh torah*? Before citing the text, a bit of background is necessary. The Torah separates the tribe of Levi from the other tribes, and it is given special tasks, among which are serving in the Temple and the teaching of Torah. It is for this reason that Levi, unlike the other tribes, was given no portion in the Land of Israel (Num. 18: 20; Deut. 18: 1–2), God being their portion, as it were. Because they had no portion in the inheritance of the land, and in order to free them to serve in the Temple and to teach Torah throughout the land, they were meant not to work for their livings, but to be supported by the rest of Israel. It is against that background that Maimonides writes:

---

finds expression in almost every page of his writings. This is also demonstrated, if by nothing else, by his monumental efforts to edit and translate Maimonides' writings. See also the enlightening (and moving) article by Y. Tzvi Langermann, 'Mori Yusuf'. It is worthy of note that R. Kafih had two pictures on the walls of his study: that of his grandfather, R. Yihye Kafih, and the traditional portrait of Maimonides. See Amar and Seri (eds.), *Memorial Volume* (Heb.).

[64] The talmudic rabbis deduce thirteen attributes of divine mercy from Exod. 34: 6–7 (BT *RH* 17b) and count thirteen principles of halakhic exegesis (*Sifra*, introd.). Thirteen is best known as the age at which Jewish males reach their majority.

[65] Abrabanel discusses various other reasons for Maimonides' use of precisely thirteen principles in his *Principles of Faith*, ch. 10.

[66] Strauss, 'How to Begin to Study', in the Pines translation of the *Guide*, pp. xi–lvi and xiii. On the significance of the number seven in Maimonides see Kraemer, 'An Intellectual Portrait', 20 and 42. On Maimonides' fascination with numbers, see Gillis, *Reading Maimonides' Mishneh Torah*, 192–4 and 294–5.

Not only the Tribe of Levi, but each and every individual human being, 'whose spirit moves him' [Exod. 35: 21] and whose knowledge gives him understanding to set himself apart in order 'to stand before the Lord, to serve Him, to worship Him' [see Deut. 11: 13; Josh. 22: 5; Isa. 56: 6], and to know Him, who walks upright as God created him to do,[67] and releases himself from the yoke of the many foolish considerations which trouble people—such an individual is as consecrated as the Holy of Holies,[68] and his portion and inheritance shall be in the Lord forever and ever. The Lord will grant him adequate sustenance in this world, the same as He had granted to the priests and to the Levites.[69] Thus indeed did David, peace upon him, say, 'O Lord, the portion of mine inheritance and of my cup, Thou maintainest my lot' [Ps. 16: 5].[70]

It is natural that Maimonides, unlike Halevi, would see non-Jews as people who could become as sanctified as the Holy of Holies in the Temple.[71] Even individuals who have no tolerance for Judaic universalism admit that Maimonides was 'tainted' by it. There is no need to deal here with the many aspects of Maimonides' universalism—the subject has been treated at length in the scholarly literature.[72] Here I wish to deal with another issue. What

---

[67] I wonder if this expression ought to be read as an implied critique of notions of original sin? Such notions are not only native to Christianity, but also attracted a number of (post-Maimonidean, kabbalistic) Jewish figures. As I argued in *Maimonides' Confrontation*, Maimonides looked for opportunities to battle what I call 'proto-kabbalah'. Whether or not the text here reflects that tendency demands separate study. For a recent study on expressions of the notion of original sin in Jewish exegesis, see Cooper, 'A Medieval Jewish Version'. For studies on the notion among Jewish philosophers, see Lasker, 'Original Sin' (Heb.), and Schechterman, 'The Doctrine of Original Sin' (Heb.).   [68] 1 Chron. 23: 13 and 25, and other places in Scripture.
[69] Based on Isa. 66: 21 ('And from them likewise I will take some to be levitical priests, said the Lord'). For a fascinating discussion of how this verse has been read (and should be read), see Roth, 'Moralization and Demoralization', in id., *Is There a Jewish Philosophy?*, 128–43. I take this opportunity to point out that this article originally appeared in *Judaism*, 11 (1962), 291–302, at the invitation of its then editor, my teacher Steven Schwarzschild. Schwarzschild exercised his privilege as editor to add notes in defence of Kant, Hermann Cohen, and Moritz Lazarus.
[70] I cite the translation of Isaac Klein, *Book of Agriculture*, 403.
[71] For Maimonides on this, see Kellner, *Maimonides on Judaism*, id., *Maimonides' Confrontation*, and id., *They Too Are Called Human* (Heb.). It is worth noting that R. Kafih takes the universalist message of Maimonides' decision here at face value and as the simple meaning of the text. In his notes to this text in his commentary on *Mishneh torah* he takes strong issue with those who seek to (mis)use Maimonides to justify the *kolel* system so prevalent in the Orthodox Jewish world today. On this use of Maimonides, see Ch. 6 in this volume on R. Aharon Kotler.
[72] For texts and discussion, see Kellner, *Maimonides' Confrontation*, ch. 7. It should be noted that one can find isolated statements in Maimonides' works which seem to indicate that he held that Jews have inborn admirable traits lacking in non-Jews. Sheilat makes much of these in his book, *Between the Kuzari and Maimonides* (Heb.). In Kellner, *They Too Are Called Human* (Heb.), ch. 8, I take up Sheilat's examples (and others), proving that with one possible exception none of them represent retreats from Maimonides' consistent view that all human beings are equally created in the image of God and that there is no inherent, metaphysical difference between Jew and non-Jew.

brought Maimonides to adopt his universalist positions? The simplest answer is that he correctly understood and represented the teachings of Torah. In a context such as this, however, we cannot be satisfied with such an answer, however true we may think it to be.

The philosophical basis of Maimonides' universalism is to be found in his adoption of a definition of human beings as rational animals. Once Maimonides accepts this definition, he accepts its universalist consequence—all rational beings are created in the image of God. Thus we find in the very first chapter of the *Guide*:[73]

The term *image* [*tselem*], on the other hand, is applied to the natural form, I mean to the notion in virtue of which a thing is constituted as a substance and becomes what it is. It is the true reality of the thing in so far as the latter is that particular being. In man that notion is that from which human apprehension derives. It is on account of this intellectual apprehension that it is said of man: 'In the image of God created He him' [Gen. 1: 27] . . . That which was meant in the scriptural dictum, 'Let Us make man in Our image' [Gen. 1: 26], was the specific form, which is intellectual apprehension, not the shape and configuration.

Anyone who correctly uses his intellectual faculties is a human, created in the divine image.[74] Maimonides buys this universalism at a very high price: harsh elitism.[75] In terms of their humanity, Maimonides does not distinguish in principle among nations;[76] in terms of their fundamental humanity, he does not even distinguish between men and women.[77] But he certainly distinguishes the intellectually perfected (from among all the nations) from the intellectually unperfected (from among all the nations). In his eyes, a morally upright non-Jewish philosopher is more human than a Jewish philosophical ignoramus, whatever his talmudic learning and outward signs of learning may be. This view is generally thought to be the result of Maimonides' famous 'parable of the palace' in *Guide* iii. 51 (pp. 618–20).

Maimonides expressed this view of humanity throughout his life, beginning with his youthful treatise *Logical Terms*, continuing through his

---

[73] *Guide* i. 1 (p. 22). He also accepts its elitist consequence: individuals who do not exercise their rational faculties are less human than those who do. On this, see Kellner, *Maimonides' Confrontation*, 1, 16, 221, 227, and 238.

[74] Including Star Trek's Lieutenant Commander Data?

[75] See Kellner, *Maimonides' Confrontation*, 16.

[76] As a consequence of the near-universal acceptance of the theory of climes in the Middle Ages, Jewish thinkers thought of inhabitants of the far South (Africans) and of the far North (pale 'Turks') as less than fully human. It appears that at least some versions of this theory allowed for descendants of these individuals to achieve full humanity if they are brought up in more salubrious climes—in other words, this is not necessarily what would today be called a racist doctrine. See Melamed, *The Image of the Black*, 129–34.   [77] See Kellner, 'Misogyny'.

Commentary on the Mishnah and the *Mishneh torah*, and finding repeated expression in the *Guide of the Perplexed*.[78] Humans are born as animals; if they do not become rational (i.e. correctly exercise their rational faculty) they remain animals. Maimonides adopted a theory, attributed in the Middle Ages to Aristotle, called the doctrine of the acquired intellect.[79] According to this view, we turn ourselves from potential humans to actual humans by acquiring conceptual knowledge ('intellecting intelligibles' in the strange language of medieval philosophers as translated into English, or *haskalat muskalot* in Hebrew). One who does not 'acquire' an intellect in this fashion remains a potential human being only.[80]

According to Maimonides, there is nothing inborn, nothing inherited from the Patriarchs, which distinguishes Jews from non-Jews. Thus, he cannot be asked, 'What is a Jew?', since on the level of essence, a Jew is a human being, and nothing more. But he can certainly be asked, 'Who is a Jew?' To this question he offers a non-essentialist answer: a Jew is a human being who (correctly) accepts certain doctrines, doctrines included as part of his Thirteen Principles.[81] Sons and daughters of the Jewish people (as well as proselytes) are called upon to create their Jewish identity intellectually. According to Maimonides, being a Jew is a challenge, not a gift. According to Judah Halevi, on the other hand, the Jew is definitely distinguished from the non-Jew by his or her essential nature. One's Jewish identity is handed to the Jew on a silver platter once he or she is born to a Jewish mother. Being a Jew is God's gracious gift to the *segulah* of humankind.

Halevi and Maimonides are both elitists. Halevi's elitism is based on the spiritual superiority of Jews over non-Jews. Maimonides' elitism is based on the superiority of the morally upright and intellectually perfected philosopher over the immoral ignoramus. Before rushing to congratulate Maimonides on his enlightened universalism, it must be recalled that on his view only true intellectuals (Jews and non-Jews alike) achieve life after death and a share in the world to come—the rest of humanity (Jews and non-Jews alike) is simply cut off (*karet*) and disappears. According to Halevi, on the other hand, a non-

---

[78] For details and texts, see Kellner, *Maimonides on Judaism*, ch. 2; id., *Maimonides' Confrontation*, 15–17; and id., *They Too Are Called Human* (Heb.), throughout and ch. 1 in particular.

[79] This issue has been widely studied. For an overview, see Davidson, *Alfarabi*. For the Maimonidean context, see W. Z. Harvey, 'Crescas' Critique' (Heb.).

[80] It is important to remember that for Maimonides (and not only for him), intellectual perfection assumes antecedent moral perfection. In his wildest nightmares he could not have conceived of an unrepentant Nazi like Martin Heidegger being considered a great thinker; see Kellner, *Maimonides' Confrontation*, 63.

[81] On Maimonides' Thirteen Principles and the subset of those he thought were really dogmas, see Kellner, *Maimonides' Confrontation*, 233–8, and the literature cited there.

Jew can become a *ḥasid*, a saintly person, and, it would appear, achieve a share in the world to come.

Rabbi Aviner and Rabbi Kafih (once more, and for the last time)

Rabbis Kafih and Aviner disagree on how to define Jewish identity in our day. Rabbi Kafih, following Maimonides, negates the essentialist view of Rabbi Aviner (and of his master, Halevi) and adopts a view which may be called, following E. E. Urbach, 'historical-relativist'.[82] There is no doubt that in the world of contemporary (Orthodox) religious Zionism today Rabbi Aviner's views on our issue dominate. Rabbi Kafih's views on this matter are barely known and, it is probably fair to say, would surprise even many who see themselves as his disciples.

It seems to me that the debate as carried on in Israel today is largely between imported views. Rabbi Aviner, following in the footsteps of the two rabbis Kook, imposes upon Halevi views whose source is in nineteenth-century German Romanticism. Many who oppose such positions are themselves deeply influenced by twentieth-century liberal democracy. Personally, I prefer the latter to the former, and not only because of the xenophobia and sometimes downright hatred of and disdain for non-Jews found in some of the followers of the interrelated Halevi-kabbalah-Maharal-Habad-Kook-Aviner schools of thought,[83] but because, as I have argued elsewhere, the Maimonidean perspective expresses a form of self-confidence I find lacking in the opposed views.[84]

Rabbi Joseph Kafih, on the other hand, represents a Jewish-Maimonidean position, untouched by European thought of the last centuries. Of course, were I willing to start a whole new essay, I could ask: where are Maimonides' views from? After all, he was deeply influenced by his master, Rabbi Aristotle! True enough, but in our issue he uses Aristotle only to illuminate what it means to be created in the image of God. In his own eyes, and in those of Rabbi Kafih, and as I tried to prove in my books *Maimonides' Confrontation with Mysticism* and *They Too Are Called Human*, Maimonides' views on the question 'What/Who is a Jew?' derive from the Torah, which, after all, does teach that all human beings are created in the image of God.

---

[82] See Urbach, *The Sages*, 541–6. I prefer the expression 'historical-halakhic'.

[83] It is important to note that while kabbalistic particularism can lead to the sort of hateful xenophobia found in the writings of Yitzchak Ginsburgh and his disciples (on which see Inbari, *Jewish Fundamentalism*, 131–40), it does not have to. One can find expressions of universalism in kabbalistic and hasidic texts if one searches for them.

[84] See Kellner, 'We Are Not Alone'.

AFTERWORD

Tradition versus Traditionalism in the Contemporary Study of Maimonides

SETH AVI KADISH

THE PREMIER DEBATE in medieval Jewish philosophy was about the God of Maimonides and the nature of the Torah. Jewish philosophy until Maimonides led up to that debate, and Jewish philosophy from Maimonides on largely *was* that debate. The debate never really ended, and most of the prominent rabbinic figures from modern times who are discussed in this book echo what was for them a *maḥloket rishonim* (an argument among earlier post-talmudic authorities). Some of them, however, relate to Maimonides in a way that differs from the way in which other *rishonim* related to him.

It should be emphasized that the medieval debate about the philosophy of Maimonides was not just any *maḥloket rishonim*. Rather than an argument about a particular law or principle within the Torah, it was a fundamental dispute about what the Torah *is*. As such, it cannot be resolved by applying the tools of halakhic decision-making. Any later thinker who grapples with Maimonides and the debate that surrounded him will be forced to come to grips with his own fundamental views about the nature of the Torah.

How well did the rabbis studied in this book understand Maimonides, and how do they fit into the classic debate about him? The seven chapters of this work exhibit a range of possibilities. Some thinkers try to liberate themselves from the influence of Maimonides' ideas, others try to build on those ideas or expand them in ways that Maimonides himself did not (and with which he would probably have disagreed), while still others advance patently non-Maimonidean positions by attributing them to none other than Maimonides. Members of the last group rewrite Maimonides in their own image, and it can be hard to tell whether they realize this or not.

The first rabbi (Netsiv) and one of the last (Aviner) studied here—who frame the book both chronologically and conceptually—work to liberate themselves from Maimonides' philosophical approach, or at least move beyond it. Chapter 1 studies Netsiv, head of the Volozhin yeshiva, who takes on Maimonides in a way that is a striking reminder of the classic medieval debate. Medieval Jewish philosophy was typically written as exegesis: ideas were argued, but the arguments for or against them were never enough, because to pass muster as *Jewish* ideas they also needed to be powerful—or at least credible—interpretations of the Jewish canon. Maimonides himself was perhaps the greatest master of this art, as he brilliantly recast the entire corpus of biblical and rabbinic law and lore in accordance with his philosophy. But many of his opponents were highly talented as well. Netsiv, in the nineteenth century, brings these opponents to mind in the way he chose to oppose Maimonides' intellectualism: not through intellectual argumentation, but through a new commentary on the Song of Songs that promoted a worldly, communal ideal as opposed to a rarefied intellectualism. When the woman in the Song says 'I am sick with love', Maimonides takes it as a positive, even ideal, obsessiveness with the intellect. Netsiv, however, refuses to idealize sickness or condone any sort of obsession. Too much emphasis on the mind harms what is truly important to God, namely worldly responsibilities and community leadership. The latter call for moderation, not obsession.

In Netsiv we have a *rosh yeshivah* with a clear, hard-headed view about what Maimonides thought and meant. He opposes the Maimonidean approach in a way that is both powerful and nuanced, by writing a careful, original allegorical reading of the Songs of Songs that is consciously meant to undermine Maimonidean exegesis. Much the same may be said about Rabbi Shlomo Aviner's basic view of Maimonides, as cited in the final chapter: Aviner openly states that the *Guide of the Perplexed* does not feel like an authentic Jewish work, as opposed to the *Kuzari*, to whose positions he is far closer. But while Netsiv's view of Maimonides is conveyed through creative interpretation that takes on Maimonides' own interpretation with the aim of replacing it, Aviner's view—as described here—is simply stated. Aviner has published volumes that interpret some of Maimonides' writings, and it would be worth exploring how rich or nuanced those interpretations are as a topic for further study: do his explanations of Maimonides grapple in a sophisticated way with what he considers to be Jewishly inauthentic views, or do they simply find ways to reduce Maimonides' views to Aviner's own as far as possible? Be that as it may, both Netsiv and Aviner, as presented in this volume, echo voices in the medieval debate who openly considered aspects of Maimonides' thought to be inauthentic as interpretations of the Torah.

Other figures studied here were disturbed by Maimonides' approach, but chose to build on it rather than reject it. That is the core difference between Netsiv and his student, Rabbi Kook (Chapter 3): while the former designed his exegesis as a conscious *alternative* to that of Maimonides, the latter chose to *include* Maimonides' thought as a crucial pillar within a much larger edifice.

Rabbi Kook tried to accomplish this with integrity towards Maimonides: he saw himself as working towards a more complete understanding of the Torah by incorporating the truths he found in Maimonides' rigorous and systematic thought, just as Maimonides himself took the truths he previously found in Aristotelian philosophy and incorporated them within the Torah. But the greater truth is reached, for Rabbi Kook, by reaching past Maimonides and continuing into realms that go beyond the intellect. This approach is different from that of Netsiv in method, but the two are similar in that they both allow Maimonides to speak on his own terms, at least in principle.

For Rabbi Kalonymus Kalman Shapira (Chapter 4), unlike Rabbi Kook, the human intellect is no pillar at all, but rather an obstacle. Science, philosophy, and the intellectual culture of Europe proved themselves to be worse than empty to the inhabitants of the Warsaw ghetto. This bitter realization for Rabbi Shapira is paradoxically based upon a Maimonidean notion which, he acknowledges, was adopted in the Jewish mystical tradition: God is thought thinking itself. But rather than man conjoining with God through his intellect, as Maimonides would have it, Rabbi Shapira reaches the opposite conclusion: human intellectual activity is false activity that prevents the divine mind from infusing the world. Intense suffering helps bring redemption precisely because it destroys intellectual hubris. In this argumentation, along with further exegesis by Rabbi Shapira as described in Chapter 4, we find, as for Netsiv, interpretations of the Torah that are nuanced alternatives to those of Maimonides. And as for Rabbi Kook, the truth is found when one goes beyond the intellect. Such mystical extensions of Maimonides that have roots within his writings are also echoes of the medieval debate (as the chapter points out). Nevertheless, Rabbi Shapira seems less concerned with providing alternatives, or with understanding Maimonides in order to venture beyond him, than he is with helping his followers use hasidic thought to grapple with the realities they face. If Maimonides is cited or implied in these sermons of Rabbi Shapira, it is not for his own sake.

Rabbi Soloveitchik (Chapter 2), like Netsiv and Rav Kook, discusses Maimonidean themes in his writings, but he struggles less with them. He shows an overall affinity with Maimonidean ideas and ideals, which he sometimes presents plainly and sometimes reinterprets. But at times, as shown in the chapter's final example of the essence of the people of Israel, there are still Maimonidean ideas that he struggles with. Thus Rabbi Soloveitchik's approach to Maimonides is shown to be an eclectic one, reminiscent of participants in the medieval discussion who deeply admired Maimonides and adopted many of his ideas, but were not committed to his system as a whole, either in its details or in its principles.

In the discussions of Rabbi Elhanan Wasserman (Chapter 5) and Rabbi Aharon Kotler (Chapter 6) we encounter a powerful new phenomenon that leaves the medieval debate behind. These rabbis do not oppose Maimonides or try to move beyond him, nor do they embrace Maimonidean ideas. Instead, they forcefully promote decidedly anti-Maimonidean notions by attributing them to none other than Maimonides himself. Maimonides' rabbinic authority is used to bolster their rhetoric.

This in no way means, as the relevant chapters take pains to point out, that these rabbis were being dishonest or subversive. It means, rather, that they could not conceive that a towering rabbinic figure like Maimonides could have stood for anything other than the *haredi* outlook that they championed. This ideological way of reading Maimonides differs from typical discussion among the *rishonim*: they normally rejected Maimonides' views when they disagreed with them, rather than turning those views into their own. Immersion in a rabbinic culture distant from that of the Middle Ages and unfamiliar with its nuances is one way to explain how it was conceivable for these rabbis to read Maimonides in such anti-Maimonidean ways. But other figures studied in this book were also far removed from the Middle Ages, and for the most part they did not force Maimonides' views into their own moulds. If Rabbi Elhanan Wasserman and Rabbi Aharon Kotler couldn't conceive of Maimonides standing outside their ideologies, then further explanations are needed.

First of all, personality should be taken into consideration. A comparison with Netsiv may enlighten us on this point: the chapter about him shows clearly that he was not an ideologue by nature. At one point it emphasizes how, if Netsiv exhibited principled consistency about anything at all in his thought, it was in his consistent rejection of all forms of extremism. Furthermore, Netsiv was a great scholar in the sense that he was able to read things and understand them in a balanced way through their context. He read Maimonides with an open mind, understood him quite well, and as a consequence he reacted to Maimonidean exegesis and thought on their own terms, even when he rejected them. Thus he was the opposite of an ideologue, whose basic inclination is to read the canon he reveres as an exact reflection of his own ideology.

Beyond personal tendencies, we might consider that, in general, preoccupation with ideology is a modern phenomenon. A traditional society has little need for it. But the traditional Jewish societies of pre-modern times and the traditional*ism* of twentieth-century *haredi* Judaism are not the same thing at all.

A tradition can feel threatened and even react to threats. It remains a living tradition as long as its internal values and ideas endure (even if they are in tension with each other), and as long as its internal conversation continues. A tradition is even capable of understanding elements of itself in context (what we would call 'historically'). It does not do so as a primary value, as its goals are not academic, but nor does it squelch such notions when they prove meaningful.

This is a far cry from the kind of yeshiva study with which figures such as Rabbi Elhanan Wasserman and Rabbi Aharon Kotler are associated. The latter's yeshiva is animated by a traditionalism that has no room for context and history, no place for non-Jewish knowledge, and no ability to view the Torah sages of the past as anything other than examples of its own traditionalism. This is a very specific phenomenon that developed within a segment of the Jewish world in the twentieth century. However, most of this book's seven chapters deal with figures who are *not* clearly part of that phenomenon, such as Netsiv, Soloveitchik, Kook, Shapira, Kafih, and Aviner. They all share a basic capacity to understand Maimonides' thought as something other than how they themselves understand the Torah.

To use Netsiv as a counter-example yet again: in his time, the Jewish world of eastern Europe was arguably still traditional to a large degree (as opposed to traditional*ist*), and he seems to have had the personality and mind to match. He was well aware of modernity and reacted to it, but rejection of modernity was *not* the central thing that moved him, nor did he turn the absolute and total rejection of modernity into the yardstick by which all Torah truth is measured. That is rather what ideologues like Rabbis Wasserman and Kotler did in a generation when modernity had already become an implacable threat to Torah in their eyes.

This had an impact on the respective ways in which they understand Maimonides: Netsiv is a reminder of the traditional opposition to Maimonides among his medieval opponents. They understood him perfectly well and consequently rejected his positions to one degree or another. They might have disagreed about just how radical he was, but that important and controversial nuance was not ultimately the main issue for them. Their central questions were about his more explicit ideas in context: were they authentic interpretations of the Torah, and to what degree should his views and his works therefore be accepted or rejected? Like them, and in light of them, we may say that Netsiv is a very traditional—as opposed to traditionalist—reader of Maimonides. But for Rabbis Wasserman and Kotler, as opposed to Netsiv, such questions never even occur (despite their heavy reliance on Maimonides in theological areas). For them Maimonides is a precursor of their own traditionalism, and as such his positions need only be elaborated and explained, never questioned or rejected.

In this book, the contours of the medieval debate come back to life best in Chapter 7: Rabbi Aviner consciously prefers Halevi as a 'truer' Jewish alternative to Maimonides, a preference which indicates clear awareness of Maimonides' philosophical bent. Rabbi Aviner is presented in contrast to Rabbi Joseph Kafih, who was not only an expert translator and exegete of Maimonides but also sympathized deeply with his views, and might legitimately be considered his follower. It is not hard to hear an echo of the medieval opposition to Maimonides in Rabbi Aviner, and to see a late reflection of the Maimonidean Jews and Maimonidean Judaism of medieval Spain and Provence in Rabbi Kafih. But those sounds and images are lost entirely in the Maimonides of Rabbis Wasserman and Kotler.

In the studies of Rabbis Wasserman and Kotler, this book claims that modern scholars understand Maimonides better than they did, and this claim is expanded to the 'yeshiva world' that is associated with them. For the two rabbis themselves, that claim is proven beyond all doubt in an entertaining and edifying way. If it is also true of their kind of yeshivas in general, then that is because such institutions are incapable of reading Maimonides in context, and thus cannot conceive of him as having been anything other than what they are. That is their ideology, and it is an ideology of anachronism.

But there is a far deeper anachronism that must be mentioned in a book like this. Many people today tend to think (as mentioned in the Wasserman chapter) that to find radical or anti-traditional views in Maimonides is peculiar to 'academic' study, while to understand Maimonides as a traditional thinker is typical of 'yeshiva' study. But, historically, this was not the case at all! To accuse Maimonides of misrepresenting the tradition—in part or in whole, and whether he can be excused for it or not—was what *traditional* scholars typically did in the Middle Ages. It was the *traditional* reading of Maimonides that found him to be dangerously in error in ways that potentially falsify the Torah. Emblematic of that reading is Moses Nahmanides (Ramban), a major medieval Jewish thinker, arguably of equal intellectual and rabbinic stature to Maimonides, who understood Maimonides' positions precisely and challenged them head on with strenuous critiques. Rather than smoothing over any differences, Nahmanides accentuates them, often prefacing his opposition to Maimonides by such caustic attacks as 'these opinions contradict the biblical text and it is forbidden to listen to them let alone believe them'.

In other words, what modern academics do is actually to read Maimonides the way the *rishonim* did (albeit with a commitment to systematic rigour), while what many yeshivas do today—namely reading Maimonides as if he were a traditionalist—is actually an anti-traditional reading of Maimonides. It derives from basic ignorance of how the *rishonim* debated Maimonides.

A similar thing is true for the topic of esotericism in Maimonides' thought. To ask the question briefly and plainly: did Maimonides, in his heart of hearts, accept the God of Aristotle, rather than the God of Israel, as true? This question, as I have bluntly put it, does not account for the bulk of discussion about Maimonides' thought among the *rishonim*. But it was nevertheless an important question with which they dealt at times, and all of them were aware of it. It often lurks in the background when less controversial issues are discussed. Many of his profoundest critics (such as Nahmanides, Rabbi Shelomoh ben Aderet (Rashba; 1235–1310), and Hasdai Crescas) understood Maimonides to be innocent of this charge, while some of his most devoted followers accepted the God of Aristotle as an esoteric Maimonidean truth. The tension surrounding this question affected the intellectual atmosphere when the *rishonim* discussed Maimonides.

Today, discussion of Maimonides' esotericism is considered to be something reserved for academia, rather than how Maimonides is studied traditionally. That, too, is an anachronism based on ignorance of the medieval discussion. It is fascinating that, of the eight rabbis studied in this book's seven chapters, not one of them deals overtly with esotericism. A traditionalist, ideological reading of Maimonides, like that of Rabbis Wasserman and Kotler, is unlikely to address such a problem. As for the rest, in this too we might say that they echo the general approach of the *rishonim* by not homing in directly on the most controversial question of all about Maimonides.

In the final chapter of this book, Maimonides is compared to a mirror or an inkblot: one looks in a mirror and sees oneself, or one looks at an inkblot and sees something unique to oneself. So too Maimonides: many of his modern readers cast him in their own image, or see what they want to see in him. But these metaphors best fit those who want to embrace Maimonides' thought as their own. Others, who are willing to reject his views, or who read him in context on his own terms with a sympathetic or critical eye, can sometimes see beyond the mirror or the inkblot. When they do so, they continue the traditional, centuries-long discussion of Maimonides as active participants.

The two authors of this book are academic scholars of Maimonides. They also identify with Orthodox Judaism and maintain personal and communal connections with the contemporary world of yeshiva study. As scholars of Maimonides' philosophy—and not just his jurisprudence—they chose to examine eight Orthodox rabbis of the modern period who dealt with theology and not just halakhah, finding that their theological orientation forced them to engage Maimonides. These rabbis might use him, rewrite him, expand him, adopt him, or reject him, but they could not be apathetic about him. The same might be said of our two authors.

Bibliography

❖

Works by the Authors Studied in This Book
Maimonides
The following editions have been cited throughout; all other translations are by the authors of this book. Published translations have occasionally been emended without comment where a more literal rendering was required in order to make a point, and in cases of slight disagreement with the translator.

The Book of the Commandments [Sefer hamitsvot], ed. Chaim Heller (Jerusalem, 1946). *The Book of Divine Commandments (Sefer ha-Mitzvoth of Moses Maimonides)*, trans. Charles B. Chavel (London, 1940, repr. Jerusalem, 2000).

Commentary on the Mishnah [Mishnah im perush rabenu mosheh ben maimon], ed. and trans. from Arabic Joseph Kafih, 3 vols. (Jerusalem, 1963–7).

'Eight Chapters' [Shemonah perakim] (introd. to commentary on Mishnah *Avot*), trans. in Raymond L. Weiss and Charles E. Butterworth (eds.), *Ethical Writings of Maimonides* (New York, 1975), 83–95.

Epistle on Resurrection, trans. into English in A. S. Halkin, *Crisis and Leadership: Epistles of Maimonides* (Philadelphia, 1985), 211–45.

Guide of the Perplexed [Arabic: Dalalat al-ḥa'irin; Heb.: Moreh nevukhim], English trans. from the Arabic by Shlomo Pines (Chicago, 1963); Hebrew trans. Joseph Kafih (Jerusalem, 1972); Hebrew trans. Michael Schwarz, 2 vols. (Tel Aviv, 2002); Hebrew edition with commentaries (Warsaw, 1872).

Hakdamot harambam lamishnah [Maimonides' Introductions to the Mishnah], ed. Isaac Sheilat (Jerusalem, 1992).

Igerot harambam [Maimonides' Epistles], ed. and trans. Isaac Sheilat (Jerusalem, 1977).

'Letter on Astrology', trans. into English in I. Twersky (ed.), *A Maimonides Reader* (New York, 1974), 463–73.

Maimonides: Medical Aphorisms: Treatises 6–9, ed. and trans. Gerrit Bos (Provo, Utah, 2007).

Teshuvot harambam [Maimonides' Responsa], ed. Joshua Blau, 4 vols. (Jerusalem, 1957–61) (available on the Bar Ilan Global Jewish Database).

Mishneh torah
The Book of Knowledge, trans. Moses Hyamson (Jerusalem, 1962, repr. 1974).

The Code of Maimonides, 13 vols. (New Haven, 1949–2004): *The Book of Agriculture*, trans. Isaac Klein (1979); *The Book of Judges*, trans. Abraham M. Hershman

(1949); *The Book of Love*, trans. Menachem Kellner (2004); *The Book of Temple Service*, trans. Mendel Lewittes (1957).

Maimonides' Mishneh Torah, trans. Boruch Kaplan, 28 vols. (New York, 1988).

Mifal mishneh torah, ed. Yohai Makbili (Haifa, 2008).

Mishneh torah, ed. Shabse Frankel, 15 vols. (Jerusalem, 2000).

Mishneh torah: sefer ahavah, with commentary by Shmuel Tanhum Rubinstein (Rambam La'am) (Jerusalem, 1958).

Naftali Tsevi Yehudah Berlin (Netsiv) (Chapter 1)

The Commentary of Rav Naftali Tzvi Yehuda Berlin to Shir Hashirim, trans. Dovid Landesman (Kefar Hasidim, 1993).

Emek hanetsiv, 3 vols. (Jerusalem, 1959–61).

Ha'amek davar (Jerusalem, 1999).

Meshiv davar (Vienna, 1866).

Rinah shel torah (Jerusalem, 2002). Includes *Metiv shir* and *She'er yisra'el*.

Joseph B. Soloveitchik (Chapter 2)

'And From There You Shall Seek' (Heb.), *Hadarom*, 47 (1978), 1–83. English version: *And From There You Shall Seek*, trans. Naomi Goldblum (Jersey City, NJ, 2008).

'The Community', *Tradition*, 17 (1978), 7–24.

The Emergence of Halakhic Man (Jersey City, NJ, 2005).

Halakhic Man, trans. Lawrence Kaplan (Philadelphia, Pa., 1983).

The Halakhic Mind: An Essay on Jewish Tradition and Modern Thought (New York, 1986).

On Repentance in the Thought and Oral Discourses of Rabbi Joseph B. Soloveitchik, ed. Pinchas Peli (Jerusalem, 1980).

Philosophical Essays [Divrei hagut veha'arakhah] (Jerusalem, 1982).

Worship of the Heart: Essays on Jewish Prayer, ed. Shalom Carmy (Hoboken, NJ, 2003).

Abraham Isaac Kook (Chapter 3)

Arpilei tohar (Jerusalem, 1983).

The Essential Writings of Abraham Isaac Kook, ed. Ben Zion Bokser (New York, 1988).

Hadarav: perakim ishiyim, ed. Ron Sarid, 3rd edn. (Ramat Gan, 2002).

'Hamaor ha'ehad', in *Ma'amarei hare'iyah* (Jerusalem, 1984), 115–17.

Igerot hare'iyah [Letters], 2 vols. (Jerusalem, 1943).

Kovets ma'amarim (Tel Aviv, 1935); originally published in *Hayesod*, 26 (29 Dec. 1932).

'Le'aḥduto shel harambam: ma'amar meyuḥad', in Zev Yavetz, *Toledot yisra'el*, vol. xii (n.p., n.d.), 211–19; repr. in *Ma'amarei hare'iyah* (Jerusalem, 1984), 105–12.

The Lights of Penitence, The Moral Principles, Lights of Holiness, Essays, Letters, and Poems, ed. and trans. Ben Zion Bokser (New York, 1978).

Ma'amarei hare'iyah, ed. Elisha Aviner [Langauer] and David Landau (Jerusalem, 1984).

Midot hare'iyah (Jerusalem, 1985).

Orot hakodesh, ed. David Cohen (Jerusalem, 1963).

Orot harambam, in Jacob Filber (ed.), *Le'oro: iyunim bemishnat rabenu avraham yitsḥak hakohen kuk* [Commentary] (Jerusalem, 1995); repr. in Moshe Zuriel (ed.), *Otserot hare'iyah*, 2nd edn., 5 vols. (Rishon Lezion, 2001).

Orot hatorah (Jerusalem, 1950).

Shemonah kevatsim, 2 vols. (Jerusalem, 2004).

'Song of Songs' (Heb.), republished in H. Hamiel (ed.), *In His Light: Studies in the Thought of Rabbi Abraham Isaac Hakohen Kook* [Be'oro: iyunim bemishnato shel harav avraham yitsḥak hakohen kuk] (Jerusalem, 1986), 511–13.

Kalonymus Kalman Shapira (Chapter 4)

Derekh hamelekh (Jerusalem, 2011).

Esh kodesh (Jerusalem, 1960).

Mevo hashe'arim (Jerusalem, 1962).

'Parashat mishpatim', *Nerot shabat* (Jerusalem, 9 Feb. 1945).

Rabbi Kalonymus Kalman Shapira: Sermons from the Years of Rage: The Sermons of the Piaseczno Rebbe from the Warsaw Ghetto, 1939–1942 [Derashot mishenot haza'am], ed. Daniel Reiser, 2 vols. (Jerusalem, 2017).

Elhanan Wasserman (Chapter 5)

'Contemplation: Wondrous and Simple' (Heb.), *Ḥayenu* [weekly organ of the Ohel Torah Yeshiva, Baranowicze] (Winter 5689 [1929]).

'The Current Crisis and its Causes: Seeking Reasons and Finding Resolution, Based on an Essay by Rabbi Elhanan Bunim Wasserman, הי"ד, published in *Koveitz Ma'amarim*', *Jewish Observer* (Nov. 2008), 8–9.

Epoch of the Messiah [Ikveta dimeshiḥa], trans. David Cooper (London, 1948).

'Examples of Literal Explanations of *Agadot*' (Heb.), in id., *Kovets he'arot*, ed. Menahem Tsevi Goldbaum, vol. i (Jerusalem, 2006).

Kovets ma'amarim [anthology of essays and letters], ed. Simcha Bunem Wasserman (Jerusalem, 1963).

Aharon Kotler (Chapter 6)

Mishnat rabi aharon, 4 vols. (Lakewood, NJ, 1988–2005).

Mishnat rabi aharon al harambam hilkhot shekhenim [Mishnat Rabbi Aharon on Maimonides' Laws of Neighbours] (Jerusalem, 1975).

Mishnat rabi aharon: ḥidushim uve'urim be'omek hasugyot vedivrei haparshanim veharambam [Mishnat Rabbi Aharon: Novellae and Explanations on Fundamental Problems and on Maimonides' Commentators] (Jerusalem, 1986).

Joseph Kafiḥ (Chapter 6)

Hamikra barambam: Mafte'aḥ lifesukei hamikra barambam [The Bible in Maimonides: index of biblical verses] (Jerusalem, 1972).

Siḥat dekalim [Conversation of Palm Trees], ed. Uri Melamed (Jerusalem, 2005).

Shlomo Aviner (Chapter 7)

Commentary on Judah Halevi's *Kuzari*, 3 vols. (Beit El, n.d.).

'Converts' (Heb.), Sifriyat Hava website (2 Sept. 2012) <http://www.havabooks.co.il/article_ID.asp?id=1185> (accessed 18 Apr. 2018).

Meḥayil el ḥayil [on military ethics] (Beit El, 1999).

Other Works

ABRABANEL, ISAAC B. JUDAH, 'Arguments Drawn from the Verses Themselves' (Heb.), in Maimonides, *Guide of the Perplexed* [Moreh nevukhim] (repr. Warsaw, 1872).

—— *Principles of Faith* [Rosh amanah], trans. Menachem Kellner (London, 1982).

AGRANOVSKY, GENRICH, and SID LEIMAN, 'Three Lists of Students Studying at the Volozhin Yeshivah in 1879', in Michael Shmidman (ed.), *Turim: Studies in Jewish History and Literature Presented to Dr Bernard Lander*, vol. ii (New York, 2008), 1–24.

AHITUV, YOSEF, 'State and Army According to the Torah: Realism and Mysticism in the Circles of Merkaz Harav' (Heb.), in Aviezer Ravitzky (ed.), *Religion and State in Twentieth-Century Jewish Thought* [Dat umedinah bahagut hayehudit beme'ah ha'esrim] (Jerusalem, 2005), 449–57.

ALBO, JOSEPH, *Sefer ha'ikarim* [Book of Principles], ed. Isaac Husik (Philadelphia, 1930) (available in the Bar Ilan Global Jewish Database).

ALTSHULER, MOR, 'Rabbi Joseph Karo and Sixteenth-Century Maimonidean Messianism', in James T. Robinson (ed.), *The Cultures of Maimonideanism: New Approaches to the History of Jewish Thought* (Leiden, 2009), 191–210.

AMAR, ZOHAR, and HANANEL SERI (eds.), *Memorial Volume for Rabbi Joseph ben David Kafiḥ* [Sefer zikaron larav yosef ben david kafiḥ] (Ramat Gan, 2001).

AMÉRY, JEAN, *At the Mind's Limits: Contemplations by a Survivor on Auschwitz and Its Realities*, trans. Sidney Rosenfeld and Stella P. Rosenfeld (Bloomington, Ind., 1980).

ARAN, GIDEON, 'The Father, the Son, and the Holy Land: The Spiritual Authorities of Jewish-Zionist Fundamentalism in Israel', in R. Scott Appleby (ed.), *Spokesmen for the Despised: Fundamentalist Leaders of the Middle East* (Chicago, 1997), 294–327.

ARENDT, HANNAH, 'Mankind and Terror', in ead., *Essays in Understanding 1930–1954: Formation, Exile, and Totalitarianism* (New York, 1994), 297–306.

ASSAF, DAVID, *Caught in the Thicket: Crises and Confusion in the History of Hasidism* [Ne'eḥaz basevakh: pirkei mashber umevukhah betoledot haḥasidut] (Jerusalem, 2006).

BACHARACH, YA'IR, *Ḥavat ya'ir* [responsa] (Lemberg, 1894) (available on the Bar Ilan Global Jewish Database).

BACON, GERSHON C., 'Birth Pangs of the Messiah: The Reflections of Two Polish Rabbis on Their Era', *Studies in Contemporary Jewry*, 7 (1991), 86–99.

BAHYA B. JOSEPH IBN PAKUDA, *Book of Direction to the Duties of the Heart*, trans. Menahem Mansoor (London, 1971); Heb. trans. Joseph Kafih (Jerusalem, 1973).

BALK, HANAN, 'The Soul of a Jew and the Soul of a Non-Jew: An Inconvenient Truth and the Search for an Alternative', *Hakirah: The Flatbush Journal of Jewish Law and Thought*, 16 (2013), 47–76.

BAR-ASHER, MOSHE, 'In Memoriam: Rabbi Joseph Kafih—Scholar and Spiritual Leader' (Heb.), *Pe'amim*, 84 (2000), 5.

BAR-ILAN, MEIR, *From Volozhin to Jerusalem* [Mivolozhin ad yerushalayim] (Tel Aviv, 1971).

—— *Rabbi of Israel* [Raban shel yisra'el] (New York, 1943).

BARAK, URIEL, 'The Formative Influence of the Description of the First Degree of Prophecy in the Guide on the Perception of *The Beginning of Redemption* by Rabbi A. I. Kook's Circle' (Heb.), in Avraham Elqayam and Dov Schwartz (eds.), *Maimonides and Mysticism: Presented to Moshe Hallamish on the Occasion of his Retirement* (= *Da'at*, 64–66) (Ramat Gan, 2009), 361–415.

BATNITZKY, LEORA, *How Judaism Became a Religion: An Introduction to Modern Jewish Thought* (Princeton, NJ, 2011).

BAUER, YEHUDA, 'Jewish Baranowicze in the Holocaust', *Yad Vashem Studies*, 31 (2003), 95–151.

BEN-RAFAEL, ELIEZER (ed.), *Jewish Identities: Fifty Intellectuals Answer Ben-Gurion* (Leiden, 2002).

BEN-SASSON, HAIM HILLEL, 'The Uniqueness of Israel According to Twelfth-Century Thinkers' (Heb.), *Perakim*, 2 (1969–74), 145–218.

BENOR, EHUD, *Worship of the Heart: A Study in Maimonides' Philosophy of Religion* (Albany, NY, 1995).

BERDYCZEWSKI, MIKHAH YOSEF, 'Netsiv's Song of Songs' (Heb.), *Hatsefirah*, 25 (Tevet 5648 (1888)), 2.

BERGMAN, SHMUEL HUGO, 'Rav Kook: All Reality Is in God', in id., *Faith and Reason: Modern Jewish Thought* (New York, 1976), 122–41.

BERMAN, LAWRENCE V., 'Ibn Bajja and Maimonides' [Ibn bajah veharambam] (Ph.D. diss., Hebrew University of Jerusalem, 1959).

BIALIK, HAYIM NAHMAN, 'The Yeshiva Student (HaMatmid)', in *Shirot Bialik: A New and Annotated Translation of Chaim Nachman Bialik's Epic Poems*, ed. Steven Jacobs (Columbus, Ohio, 1987), 31–2.

BLEICH, J. DAVID, *With Perfect Faith* (New York, 1983).

BLIDSTEIN, GERALD J. (YA'AKOV), '"Even if He Tells You Right Is Left": On the Power of Institutional Authority in Halakhah and Its Limits' (Heb.), in id., *Studies in Halakhic and Aggadic Thought* [Iyunim bemaḥshevet hahalakhah veha'agadah] (Be'er Sheva, 2004), 315–38.

—— 'Maimonides on "Oral Law"', *Jewish Law Annual*, 1 (1978), 108–22.

—— 'Oral Law as Institution in Maimonides', in Ira Robinson (ed.), *The Thought of Moses Maimonides* (Lewiston, Maine, 1990), 167–82.

—— *Society and Self: On the Writings of Rabbi Joseph B. Soloveitchik* (New York, 2012).

—— 'Spreading the Faith as a Goal of War in the Doctrine of Maimonides' (Heb.), in Avriel Bar-Levav (ed.), *Peace and War in Jewish Culture* [Shalom umilḥamah batarbut hayehudit] (Jerusalem, 2006), 85–97.

—— *Studies in Halakhic and Aggadic Thought* [Iyunim bemaḥshevet hahalakhah veha'agadah] (Be'er Sheva, 2004).

—— 'Tradition and Institutional Authority: On the Concept of Oral Law in Maimonides' Thought' (Heb.), in id., *Studies in Halakhic and Aggadic Thought* [Iyunim bemaḥshevet hahalakhah veha'agadah] (Be'er Sheva, 2004), 135–53.

BLOOM, HAROLD, *Kabbalah and Criticism* (New York, 2005).

BLUMENTHAL, DAVID, 'Maimonides' Philosophical Mysticism', in Avraham Elqayam and Dov Schwartz (eds.), *Maimonides and Mysticism* (= *Da'at*, 64–66) (Ramat Gan, 2009), pp. v–xxv.

BODOFF, LIPPMAN, *The Binding of Isaac, Religious Murder & Kabbalah: Seeds of Jewish Extremism and Alienation?* (Jerusalem, 2005).

BRILL, ALAN, 'Dwelling with Kabbalah: Meditation, Ritual, and Study', in Adam Mintz and Lawrence Schiffman (eds.), *Jewish Spirituality and Divine Law* (New York, 2005), 127–62.

BROWN, BENJAMIN, 'The *Da'at Torah* Doctrine: Three Stages' (Heb.), in Yehoyada Amir (ed.), *The Path of the Spirit: The Eliezer Schweid Jubilee Volume* [Derekh haruaḥ: sefer hayovel le'eli'ezer shveid], vol. ii (Jerusalem, 2005), 537–600.

—— 'The Torah as Commandment and as Promise: The Duty of Faith According to the Hazon Ish' (Heb.), in Benjamin Ish-Shalom (ed.), *In the Ways of Peace: Studies in Jewish Thought Presented to Shalom Rosenberg* [Bedarkhei shalom: iyunim behagut yehudit mugashim leshalom rosenberg] (Jerusalem, 2007), 377–97.

BUBER, MARTIN, *Two Types of Faith: A Study of the Interpenetration of Judaism and Christianity*, trans. Norman P. Goldhawk (Syracuse, NY, 2003).

CAMON, FERDINANDO, *Conversations with Primo Levi*, trans. John Shepley (Evanston, Ill., 1989).

CARMY, SHALOM, 'Rav Kook's Theory of Knowledge', *Tradition*, 15 (1975), 193–203.

CHAVEL, CHARLES B. (trans.), *Ramban: Commentary on the Torah*, 5 vols. (New York, 1971).

CHERLOW, SMADAR, 'Rav Kook's Mystical Mission' (Heb.), *Da'at*, 49 (2002), 99–135.

COHEN, MEIR SIMHAH OF DVINSK, *Meshekh ḥokhmah*, ed. Yehuda Kupperman (Jerusalem, 1997).

COHEN, MORDECHAI, 'Maimonides' Disagreement with "the Torah" in His Interpretation of Job', *Zutot*, 4 (Leiden, 2004), 66–78.

COHEN, STUART, *The Sword or the Scroll? Dilemmas of Religion and Military Service in Israel* (Amsterdam, 1997).

COOPER, ALAN, 'A Medieval Jewish Version of Original Sin: Ephraim of Luntshits on Leviticus 12', *Harvard Theological Review*, 97 (2004), 445–60.

CRESCAS, HASDAI, *Or hashem* (Jerusalem, 1990).

DAVIDOWITZ, TEMIMA, 'Characteristic Aspects in the Exegesis of the Netsiv of Volozhin' (Heb.), in Ronelah Merdler (ed.), *Anthology: Selected Articles in Jewish Studies* [Igud: mivḥar ma'amarim bemada'ei hayahadut] (Jerusalem, 2005), 85–102.

DAVIDSON, HERBERT A., *Alfarabi, Avicenna, and Averroes on Intellect* (New York, 1992).

—— *Maimonides the Rationalist* (Oxford, 2011).

—— *Moses Maimonides: The Man and His Works* (Oxford, 2005).

DE KONINCK, THOMAS, 'Aristotle on God as Thought Thinking Itself', *Review of Metaphysics*, 47 (1994), 471–515.

DIAMOND, JAMES, *Converts, Heretics, and Lepers* (Notre Dame, Ind., 2007).

—— 'Maimonides on Leprosy: Illness as Contemplative Metaphor', *Jewish Quarterly Review*, 96 (2006), 95–122.

—— *Maimonides and the Shaping of the Jewish Canon* (New York 2014).

DIENSTAG, JACOB ISRAEL, 'The *Guide of the Perplexed* and the *Book of Knowledge* in Hasidic Literature' (Heb.), *Abraham Weiss Jubilee Volume* (New York, 1964), 307–30.

—— 'Maimonides on Providence: Bibliography' (Heb.), *Da'at*, 20 (1988), 17–28.

—— *Relation of Elijah Gaon to the Philosophy of Maimonides* [Ha'im hitnaged hagra lemishnato hafilosofit shel harambam?] (New York, 1949).

DIESENDRUCK, ZVI, 'Samuel and Moses ibn Tibbon on Maimonides' Theory of Providence', *Hebrew Union College Annual*, 11 (1936), 341–66.

DINER, DAN, *Beyond the Conceivable: Studies on Germany, Nazism, and the Holocaust* (Berkeley, Calif., 2000).

DISON, YONINA, '*Orot hakodesh*: Re-edited and Organized According to Four Motifs' (Heb.), *Da'at*, 24 (1990), 41–86.

DOV BER OF MEZHIRECH, *Magid devarav leya'akov*, ed. Rivka Schatz-Uffenheimer (Jerusalem, 1990).

EIDELS, SHMUEL (MAHARSHA), *Ḥidushei agadot*, in standard edns. of the Babylonian Talmud.

EISEN, ROBERT, 'The Problem of the King's Dream and Non-Jewish Prophecy in Judah Halevi's Kuzari', *Journal of Jewish Thought and Philosophy*, 3 (1994), 231–47.

EISENMANN, ESTY, '"A Ladder Set up on the Earth and the Top of It Reached to Heaven": Jacob's Dream and Maimonides' Self-Image' (Heb.), *Akdamot*, 6 (1999), 47–58.

ELKOUBY, JOSEPH, 'The Love of God and the Fear of God in the Thought of Maharal of Prague', in Meir Seidler (ed.), *Rabbinic Theology and Jewish Intellectual History: The Great Rabbi Loew of Prague* (New York, 2013), 44–53.

ELON, MENACHEM, 'The Values of a Jewish and Democratic State: The Task of Reaching a Synthesis', in Alfred Kellermann, Kurt Siehr, and Talia Einhorn (eds.), *Israel among the Nations* (The Hague, 1998), 177–226.

ELYAKIM, NISIM, 'Netsiv's Autonomy in His Interpretation of Legal Verses in the Torah' (Heb.), *Shma'atin*, 150 (2002), 94–113.

—— *Netsiv's Ha'amek davar: Hermeneutical Rules and Tools in the Exegesis of 'Peshat'* [Ha'amek davar lanetsiv: midot vekhelim befarshanut hapeshat] (Rehovot, 2003).

ERAN, AMIRA, '*Ḥads* in Maimonides and Rabbi Judah Halevi' (Heb.), *Tura*, 4 (1966), 117–46.

ETKES, IMMANUEL, 'A Shtetl with a Yeshiva: The Case of Volozhin', in Steven Katz (ed.), *The Shtetl: New Evaluations* (New York, 2007), 39–52.

—— and SHLOMO TIKOCHINSKI (eds.), *Memoirs of the Lithuanian Yeshivas* [Yeshivot lita: pirkei zikhronot] (Jerusalem, 2004).

FACKENHEIM, EMIL, *To Mend the World: Foundations of Post-Holocaust Jewish Thought* (New York, 1994).

FARHI, YOSEF, 'Rabbi Joseph Kafih's Introduction to the *Guide*' (Heb.), *Mesorah leyosef*, 7 (2012), 119–49.

FEINSTEIN, MOSHE, *Igerot mosheh* [responsa] (Bar Ilan Global Jewish Database).

FELDMAN, LOUIS H., 'The Septuagint: The First Translation of the Torah and Its Effects', in id. (ed.), *Judaism and Hellenism Reconsidered* (Leiden, 2006), 53–69.

FINE, LAWRENCE, 'R. Abraham Isaac Kook and the Jewish Mystical Tradition', in

Lawrence J. Kaplan and David Shatz (eds.), *Rabbi Abraham Isaac Kook and Jewish Spirituality* (New York, 1995), 23–40.

FINKELMAN, YOEL, 'Haredi Isolation in Changing Environments: A Case Study in Yeshiva Immigration', *Modern Judaism*, 22 (2002), 61–84.

—— 'An Ideology for American Yeshiva Students: The Sermons of R. Aharon Kotler, 1942–1962', *Journal of Jewish Studies*, 58/2 (2007), 314–32.

—— 'On the Limits of American Jewish Social Engineering: Ironic Reflections on Prof. Mordecai M. Kaplan and R. Aharon Kotler', *Contemporary Jewry*, 28 (2008), 58–83.

—— 'War with the Outside World: Rabbi Aharon Kotler' (Heb.), in Benjamin Brown and Leon Nissim (eds.), *The Gedolim: The Men who Shaped Haredi Judaism in Israel* [Hagedolim: ishim she'itsvu et penei hayahadut haharedit beyisra'el] (Jerusalem, 2017), 402–29.

FISCHER, SHLOMO, 'Self-Expression and Democracy in Radical Religious Zionist Ideology' (Ph.D. diss., Hebrew University of Jerusalem, 2007).

FOX, MARVIN, 'Rav Kook: Neither Philosopher nor Kabbalist', in Lawrence J. Kaplan and David Shatz (eds.), *Rabbi Abraham Isaac Kook and Jewish Spirituality* (New York, 1995), 78–87.

—— 'The Unity and Structure of Rabbi Joseph B. Soloveitchik's Thought', *Tradition*, 24 (1989), 44–65.

FRAENKEL, CARLOS, 'Theocracy and Autonomy in Medieval Islamic and Jewish Philosophy', *Political Theory*, 38 (2010), 340–66.

FRANK, DANIEL, 'Humility as a Virtue: A Maimonidean Critique of Aristotle's Ethics', in Eric L. Ormsby (ed.), *Moses Maimonides and His Time* (Washington, DC, 1989), 89–99.

FREUDENTHAL, GAD, 'Maimonides on the Scope of Metaphysics alias Ma'aseh Merkavah: The Evolution of his Views', in Carlos del Valle, Santiago García-Jalón, and Juan Pedro Monferrer (eds.), *Maimónides y su época* (Madrid, 2007), 221–30.

FREUDENTHAL, GIDEON, 'The Philosophical Mysticism of Maimonides and Maimon', in Idit Dobbs-Weinstein, Lenn E. Goodman, and James Allen Grady (eds.), *Maimonides and His Heritage* (Albany, NY, 2009), 113–52.

FRIEDMAN, MENACHEM, 'The State of Israel as a Theological Dilemma', in Baruch Kimmerling (ed.), *The Israeli State and Society: Boundaries and Frontiers* (Albany, NY, 1989), 165–215.

FRIEDMAN, MORDECHAI A., 'Maimonides, Zuta, and the Muqaddams: A Story of Three Bans' (Heb.), *Zion*, 70 (2005), 473–528.

GARB, JONATHAN, 'Alien Culture in the Circle of Rabbi Kook', in Howard Kreisel (ed.), *Study and Knowledge in Jewish Thought* (Be'er Sheva, 2006), 253–64.

—— *The Chosen Will Become Herds: Studies in Twentieth-Century Kabbalah* (New Haven, 2009).

GARB, JONATHAN, 'Prophecy, Halakhah and Antinomianism in the *Shemonah kevatsim* by Rabbi Kook' (Heb.), in Ze'ev Gries et al. (eds.), *Shefa Tal: Studies in Jewish Thought and Culture Presented to Beracha Zak* [Shefa tal: iyunim bemaḥshevet yisra'el uvetarbut yehudit mugashim liverakhah zak] (Be'er Sheva, 2004), 267–77.

GELLMAN, EZRA, 'Poetry of Spirituality', in Lawrence J. Kaplan and David Shatz (eds.), *Rabbi Abraham Isaac Kook and Jewish Spirituality* (New York, 1995), 88–119.

GELLMAN, JEROME, 'Jewish Mysticism and Morality: Kabbalah and Its Ontological Dualities', *Archiv für Religionsgeschichte*, 9 (2008), 23–35.

—— 'Radical Responsibility in Maimonides' Thought', in Ira Robinson, Lawrence Kaplan, and Julien Bauer (eds.), *The Thought of Moses Maimonides* (Lewiston, NY, 1991), 249–65.

GERONDI, NISSIM, *Derashot haran*, ed. Aryeh Leib Feldman (Jerusalem, 2003).

GERONDI, YONAH, *Sha'arei teshuvah* [Gates of Repentance] (Jerusalem, 1967).

GILLIS, DAVID, *Reading Maimonides' Mishneh Torah* (Oxford, 2015).

GOLDMAN, ELIEZER, 'Morality, Religion, and Halakha,' in Eliezer Goldman, Avi Sagi, and Daniel Statman (eds.), *Expositions and Inquiries: Jewish Thought in Past and Present* [Meḥkarim ve'iyunim: hagut yehudit ba'avar uvahoveh] (Jerusalem, 1996), 265–305.

GOLDSTEIN, HELEN TUNIK, 'Dator Formarum: Ibn Rushd, Levi b. Gerson, and Moses b. Joshua of Narbonne', in Isma'il Raji al Faruqi and Abdullah Omar Nasseef (eds.), *Essays in Islamic and Comparative Studies* (Washington, DC, 1982), 107–21.

GOLINKIN, DAVID, 'Do "Repentance, Prayer and Tzedakah Avert the Severe Decree"?', *The Schechter Institutes* website (Sept. 2005), <http://www.schechter.edu/do-repentance-prayer-and-tzedakah-avert-the-severe-decree/>.

GOTLIEB, JACOB, *Rationalism in Hasidic Attire: Habad's Harmonistic Approach to Maimonides* [Sekhaltanut bilevush ḥasidi: demuto shel harambam beḥasidut ḥabad] (Ramat Gan, 2009).

GREENBERG, GERSHON, 'Amalek during the Shoah: Jewish Orthodox Thought' (Heb.), in Yehoyada Amir (ed.), *The Path of the Spirit: The Eliezer Schweid Jubilee Volume* [Derekh haruaḥ: sefer hayovel le'eli'ezer shveid], vol. ii (Jerusalem, 2005), 891–913.

—— 'Consoling Truth: Eliezer Schweid's *Ben Hurban Le-Yeshua*: A Review Essay', *Modern Judaism*, 17 (1997), 297–311.

—— 'Elhanan Wasserman's Response to the Growing Catastrophe in Europe: The Role of Ha'gra and Hofets Hayim Upon His Thought', *Journal of Jewish Thought and Philosophy*, 10 (2000), 171–204.

—— 'Ontic Division and Religious Survival: Wartime Palestinian Orthodoxy and the Holocaust (Hurban)', *Modern Judaism*, 14 (1994), 21–61.

—— 'Orthodox Theological Responses to Kristallnacht: Chayyim Ozer Grodzensky ('Achiezer') and Elchonon Wasserman', *Holocaust and Genocide Studies*, 3 (1988), 431–41.

HALBERTAL, MOSHE, *By Way of Truth: Nahmanides and the Creation of Tradition* [Al derekh ha'emet: haramban viyetsiratah shel masoret] (Jerusalem, 2006).

HALKIN, ABRAHAM S., 'Ibn Aknin's Commentary on Song of Songs', in Saul Lieberman (ed.), *Alexander Marx Jubilee Volume*, English section (New York, 1950), 389–424.

HALLAMISH, MOSHE, 'The Attitude Towards the Gentile Nations in the World of the Kabbalists' (Heb.), in Aviezer Ravitzky (ed.), *From Rome to Jerusalem: Joseph Barukh Sermoneta Memorial Volume* [Meromi liyerushalayim: sefer zikaron leyosef barukh sermonetah] (Jerusalem, 1998), 289–311.

HALPERIN, DAVID, *The Merkabah in Rabbinic Literature* (New Haven, Conn., 1980).

HANSEL, JOELLE, 'Philosophy and Kabbalah in the Eighteenth Century: Moses Hayyim Luzzatto, Commentator of Maimonides', in Martin F. J. Baasten and Reinier Munk (eds.), *Studies in Hebrew Literature and Jewish Culture Presented to Albert van der Heide on the Occasion of his Sixty-Fifth Birthday* (Dordrecht, 2007), 213–27.

HARRIS, JAY M., *How Do We Know This? Midrash and the Fragmentation of Modern Judaism* (Albany, NY, 1995).

HARTUM, MENACHEM IMMANUEL, 'Enlistment of Levites and Scholars According to Halakhic Sources' (Heb.), in Yehezkel Cohen, *Enlistment According to Halakhah: On IDF Exemptions to Yeshiva Students* [Giyus kehalakhah: al shiḥrur talmidei yeshivot mitsahal] (Jerusalem, 1993).

HARVEY, STEVEN, 'Maimonides in the Sultan's Palace', in Joel Kraemer (ed.), *Perspectives on Maimonides: Historical and Philosophical Studies* (Oxford, 1991), 70–3.

HARVEY, WARREN ZEV, 'Aggadah in Maimonides' Mishneh Torah', *Dine Israel*, 24 (2007), 197–207.

—— 'Averroes and Maimonides on the Obligation of Philosophic Contemplation (*itibār*)' (Heb.), *Tarbiz*, 58 (1988), 75–83.

—— 'How to Begin to Study the *Guide of the Perplexed* i: 1' (Heb.), *Da'at*, 21 (1988), 21–3.

—— 'The Incorporeality of God in Maimonides, Rabad and Spinoza' (Heb.) in Sarah O. Heller-Wilensky and Moshe Idel (eds.), *Studies in Jewish Thought* [Meḥkarim behagut yehudit] (Jerusalem, 1989), 63–78.

—— 'A Portrait of Spinoza as a Maimonidean', *Journal of the History of Philosophy*, 19 (1981), 151–72.

—— *Rabbi Hasdai Crescas* (Heb.) (Jerusalem, 2010).

—— 'Rabbi Hasdai Crescas' Critique of Philosophical Happiness' (Heb.), in *Proceedings of the Sixth World Congress of Jewish Studies*, vol. iii (Jerusalem, 1977), 143–9.

HARVEY, WARREN ZEV, 'The Return of Maimonideanism', *Journal of Jewish Social Studies*, 42 (1980), 249–68.

—— 'Sex and Health in Maimonides', in Samuel S. Kottek and Fred Rosner (eds.), *Moses Maimonides: Physician, Scientist, and Philosopher* (Northvale, NJ, 1993), 33–9.

HAYIM IBN ATTAR, *Or haḥayim* [commentary on the Torah] (Benei Berak, 2001) (available on the Bar Ilan Global Jewish Database).

HELD, SHAI, 'What Zvi Yehudah Kook Wrought: The Theopolitical Radicalization of Religious Zionism', in Michael Morgan and Steven Weitzman (eds.), *Rethinking the Messianic Idea in Judaism* (Bloomington, Ind., 2015), 229–55.

HELLER, CELIA STOPNICKA, *On the Edge of Destruction: Jews of Poland Between the Two World Wars* (Detroit, Mich., 1994).

HENSHKE, DAVID, 'The Basis of Maimonides' Concept of Halakhah' (Heb.), *Jewish Law Annual* [Shenaton hamishpat ha'ivri], 20 (1995–7), 103–49.

—— 'On the Question of Unity in Maimonides' Thought' (Heb.), *Da'at*, 37 (1997), 37–51.

HERSKOWITZ, DANIEL, 'Rabbi Joseph B. Soloveitchik's Endorsement and Critique of Volkish Thought', *Journal of Modern Jewish Studies*, 14 (2015), 373–90.

HIRSHMAN, MARC (MENACHEM), 'Rabbinic Universalism in the Second and Third Centuries', *Harvard Theological Review*, 93 (2000), 101–15.

—— *Torah for the Entire World: A Universalist Stream in Tannaitic Literature and Its Relation to Gentile Wisdom* [Torah lekhol ba'ei olam: zerem universali besifrut hatana'im veyaḥaso leḥokhmat he'amim] (Tel Aviv, 1999).

HORETZKY, ODED, 'Maimonides and Gersonides: A "Humanistic–Autonomous" Approach versus a "Theological–Heteronomous" Approach: Radicalism and Conservatism' (Heb.) (Ph.D. diss., University of Haifa, April 2018).

HOROWITZ, ELLIOT, 'From the Generation of Moses to the Generation of the Messiah: The Jews Confront "Amalek" and His Incarnations' (Heb.), *Zion*, 64 (1999), 425–54.

HYMAN, ARTHUR, 'Maimonides' Thirteen Principles', in Alexander Altmann (ed.), *Jewish Medieval and Renaissance Studies* (Cambridge, 1967), 119–44.

IDEL, MOSHE, 'Divine Attributes and Sefirot in Jewish Theology', in Sarah O. Heller-Wilensky and Moshe Idel (eds.), *Studies in Jewish Thought* [Meḥkarim behagut yehudit] (Jerusalem, 1989), 87–112.

—— *Kabbalah: New Perspectives* (New Haven, 1988).

—— '*Sitrei Arayot* in Maimonides' Thought', in Shlomo Pines and Yirmeyahu Yovel (eds.), *Maimonides and Philosophy* (Dordrecht, 1986), 79–91.

INBARI, MOTTI, *Jewish Fundamentalism and the Temple Mount* (Albany, NY, 2009).

—— *Messianic Religious Zionism Confronts Israeli Territorial Compromises* (Cambridge, 2012), 15–36.

ISH-SHALOM, BENJAMIN, *Rav Avraham Itzhak HaCohen Kook: Between Rationalism and Mysticism*, trans. Ora Wiskind-Elper (Albany, NY, 1993).

—— 'Tolerance and Its Theoretical Basis in the Teaching of Rabbi Kook' (Heb.), *Da'at*, 20 (1988), 151–68.

JACOBS, JONATHAN, *Law, Reason, and Morality in Medieval Jewish Philosophy: Sa'adia Gaon, Bahya ibn Pakuda, and Moses Maimonides* (Oxford, 2010).

JOSEPH, HOWARD, 'As Swords Thrust through the Body: The Neziv's Rejection of Separatism', *Edah Journal*, 1/1 (2000), 1–26.

JOSPE, RAPHAEL, 'Teaching Judah Halevi: Defining and Shattering Myths in Jewish Philosophy', in id., *Paradigms in Jewish Philosophy* (Madison, NJ, 1997), 112–28.

JUDAH HALEVI, *Kuzari*. Hebrew trans. Michael Schwarz (Be'er Sheva, 2017); English trans. Hartwig Hirschfeld (New York, 1964).

JUDAH LOWE BEN BEZALEL (MAHARAL OF PRAGUE), *see* Lowe, Judah (Maharal of Prague).

KAFIH, AMIT, 'Notes from Rabbi Joseph Kafih on his Commentary on the Mishnah' (Heb.), *Mesorah leyosef*, 4 (2005), 298–315.

KAFIH, JOSEPH, *The Bible in Maimonides* [Hamikra barambam] (Jerusalem, 1972).

KAMINETZKY, NATHAN, *The Making of a Godol* (New York, 2002).

KANARFOGEL, EPHRAIM, 'Compensation for the Study of Torah in Medieval Rabbinic Thought', in Ruth Link-Salinger (ed.), *Of Scholars, Savants, and Their Texts: Studies in Philosophy and Religious Thought—Essays in Honor of Arthur Hyman* (New York, 1989), 135–47.

KAPLAN, LAWRENCE J., 'The Love of God in Maimonides and Rav Kook', *Judaism*, 43/3 (1994), 227–39.

—— *Maimonides between Philosophy and Halakhah: Rabbi Joseph B. Soloveitchik's Lectures on the Guide of the Perplexed* (New York, 2016).

—— 'Rav Kook and the Philosophical Tradition', in Lawrence J. Kaplan and David Shatz (eds.), *Rabbi Abraham Isaac Kook and Jewish Spirituality* (New York, 1995), 41–77.

KASHER, HANNAH, 'Between the Idolater and the Believer in God's Corporeality' (Heb.), *Da'at*, 61 (2007), 73–82.

—— 'The Myth of the "Angry God" in the *Guide of the Perplexed*' (Heb.), *Eshel be'er sheva*, 4 (1996), 95–111.

—— 'Talmud Torah as a Means of Apprehending God in Maimonides' Teachings' (Heb.), *Jerusalem Studies in Jewish Thought* [Meḥkarei yerushalayim bemaḥshevet yisra'el], 5 (1986), 71–81.

KATS, HANAH, *Netsiv's Thought: Ideological and Pedagogical Approaches of Netsiv of Volozhin in Light of his Writings and Leadership* [Mishnat hanetsiv: shitato hara'ayonit vehaḥinukhit shel hanetsiv mivolozhin le'or ketavav vedarkhei hanhagato] (Jerusalem, 1990).

KELLNER, MENACHEM, 'Could Maimonides Get into Rambam's Heaven?', *Journal of Jewish Thought and Philosophy*, 8 (1999), 231–42.
—— 'Did the Torah Precede the Cosmos? A Maimonidean Study' (Heb.), *Da'at*, 61 (2007), 83–96.
—— *Dogma in Medieval Jewish Thought: From Maimonides to Abravanel* (Oxford, 1986).
—— 'Inadvertent Heresy in Medieval Jewish Thought: Maimonides and Abravanel versus Crescas and Duran?' (Heb.), *Jerusalem Studies in Jewish Thought* [Meḥkarei yerushalayim bemaḥshevet yisra'el], 3 (1983), 393–403.
—— 'The Literary Character of the *Mishneh Torah*: On the Art of Writing in Maimonides' Halakhic Works', in Ezra Fleisher, Gerald Blidstein, Carmi Horowitz, and Bernard Septimus (eds.), *Me'ah She'arim: Studies in Medieval Jewish Spiritual Life in Memory of Isadore Twersky* (Jerusalem, 2001), 29–45; repr. in Menachem Kellner, *Science in the Bet Midrash: Studies in Maimonides* (Boston, Mass., 2009), 45–61.
—— 'Maimonides' Commentary on *Mishnah Hagigah* II.1: Translation and Commentary', in Marc D. Angel (ed.), *From Strength to Strength: Lectures from Shearith Israel* (New York, 1998), 101–11.
—— *Maimonides' Confrontation with Mysticism* (Oxford, 2006).
—— 'Maimonides on the Decline of the Generations', in Yaakov Elman and Jeffrey S. Gurock (eds.), *Hazon Nahum: Studies in Jewish Law, Thought, and History Presented to Dr Norman Lamm on the Occasion of his Seventieth Birthday* (New York, 1997), 163–86.
—— *Maimonides on the 'Decline of the Generations' and the Nature of Rabbinic Authority* (Albany, NY, 1996).
—— *Maimonides on Human Perfection* (Atlanta, Ga., 1990).
—— *Maimonides on Judaism and the Jewish People* (Albany, NY, 1991).
—— 'Maimonides' Moses: Torah, History, and Cosmos' (Heb.), in Hannah Kasher (ed.), *Moses, Father of Prophets: His Image in [Jewish] Thought through the Generations* [Mosheh avi hanevi'im: demuto bire'i hehagut ledoroteiha] (Ramat Gan, 2010), 151–77.
—— 'Maimonides' "True Religion"—for Jews, or All Humanity?', *Me'orot* [= *Edah Journal*], 7/1 (2008); repr. in Kellner, *Science in the Bet Midrash: Studies in Maimonides* (Boston, Mass., 2009), 291–320.
—— '*Mishneh torah*: Why?' (Heb.), *Mesorah leyosef*, 4 (1985), 316–29.
—— 'Misogyny: Gersonides versus Maimonides', in id., *Torah in the Observatory: Gersonides, Maimonides, Song of Songs* (Boston, Mass., 2010), 283–304.
—— *Must a Jew Believe Anything?*, 2nd edn. (Oxford, 2010).
—— 'Philosophical Themes in Maimonides' *Sefer Ahavah*', in Idit Dobbs-Weinstein, Lenn Evan Goodman, and James Grady (eds.), *Maimonides and His Heritage* (Albany, NY, 2009), 13–35.

—— 'Rabbis in Politics: A Study in Medieval and Modern Jewish Political Theory' (Heb.), *Medinah veḥevrah*, 3 (2003), 673–98.

—— 'Rashi and Maimonides on Torah and the Cosmos', in Ephraim Kanarfogel and Moshe Sokolow (eds.), *From Rashi to Maimonides: Themes in Medieval Jewish Thought, Law and Interpretation* (New York, 2010), 23–58.

—— 'Religious Faith in the Middle Ages and Today' (Heb.), in Moshe Halbertal, David Kurzweil, and Avi Sagi (eds.), *On Faith: Studies on the Concept of Faith and Its History in Jewish Tradition* [Al ha'emunah: iyunim bemusag ha'emunah vetoledotav bimesoret hayahadut] (Jerusalem, 2005), 312–27.

—— 'Strauss's Maimonides' (Heb.), *Iyyun: The Jerusalem Philosophical Quarterly*, 50 (2001), 397–406.

—— *They Too Are Called Human: Gentiles in the Eyes of Maimonides* [Gam hem keruyim adam: hanokhri be'einei harambam] (Ramat Gan, 2016).

—— *Torah in the Observatory: Gersonides, Maimonides, Song of Songs* (Boston, Mass., 2010).

—— 'We Are Not Alone', in Michael J. Harris, Daniel Rynhold, and Tamra Wright (eds.), *Radical Responsibility: Celebrating the Thought of Chief Rabbi Lord Jonathan Sacks* (Jerusalem, 2012), 139–54; repr. in Hava Tirosh-Samuelson and Aaron Hughes (eds.), *Menachem Kellner: Jewish Universalism* (Leiden, 2015), 107–18.

—— and DAVID GILLIS, *Maimonides the Universalist: The Ethical Horizons of the Mishneh Torah* (forthcoming).

KLEIN-BRASLAVY, SARA, *King Solomon and Philosophical Esotericism in the Thought of Maimonides* [Shelomoh hamelekh veha'esoterism hafilosofi bemishnat harambam] (Jerusalem, 1996; repr. 2008).

—— *Maimonides' Interpretation of the Adam Stories in Genesis: A Study in Maimonides' Anthropology* [Perush harambam lasipurim al adam befarashat bereshit] (Jerusalem, 1986).

—— 'Maimonides' Interpretation of Jacob's Ladder' (Heb.), *Universitat bar ilan sefer hashanah lemada'ei hayahadut veharuaḥ*, 22–23 (1987), 329–49.

—— 'Solomon and Metaphysical Esotericism According to Maimonides', in ead., *Maimonides as Biblical Interpreter* (Boston, Mass., 2011), 163–94.

KLEINBERGER, AARON, *The Maharal's Educational Thought* [Hamaḥshavah hapedagogit shel hamaharal] (Jerusalem, 1962).

KRAEMER, JOEL, *Maimonides: The Life and World of One of Civilization's Greatest Minds* (New York, 2008).

—— 'Moses Maimonides: An Intellectual Portrait', in Kenneth Seeskin (ed.), *The Cambridge Companion to Maimonides* (New York, 2005), 11–57.

—— 'Naturalism and Universalism in Maimonides' Political and Religious Thought', in Ezra Fleisher, Gerald Blidstein, Carmi Horowitz, and Bernard Septimus (eds.), *Me'ah She'arim: Studies in Medieval Jewish Spiritual Life in Memory of*

Isadore Twersky [Me'ah she'arim: iyunim be'olamam haruḥani shel yisra'el bimei habeinayim lezekher yitsḥak tverski] (Jerusalem, 2001), 47–81.

KREISEL, HOWARD T., 'From Esotericism to Science: The Account of the Chariot in Maimonidean Philosophy till the End of the Thirteenth Century', in James T. Robinson (ed.), *The Cultures of Maimonideanism: New Approaches to the History of Jewish Thought* (Leiden, 2009), 21–56; repr. in Howard T. Kreisel, *Judaism as Philosophy: Studies in Maimonides and the Medieval Jewish Philosophers of Provence* (Boston, Mass., 2015), 209–69.

—— *Maimonides' Political Thought: Studies in Ethics, Law, and the Human Ideal* (Albany, NY, 1999).

KRINIS, EHUD, 'The Arabic Background of the Kuzari', *Journal of Jewish Thought and Philosophy*, 21 (2013), 1–56.

—— *God's Chosen People: Judah Halevi's 'Kuzari' and the Shi'i Imam Doctrine* (Turnhout, 2014).

LANDAU, BEZALEL, 'The Netsiv of Volozhin and the Campaign on Behalf of the Settlement of the Land of Israel in its Holiness' (Heb.), *Niv hamidrashiyah*, 11 (1974), 251–77.

LANGERMANN, Y. TZVI, '"Mori Yusuf": Rav Yosef Kafaḥ (Qafih) (1917–2000)', *Aleph: Historical Studies in Science and Judaism*, 1 (2001), 333–40.

—— 'Science and the Kuzari', *Science in Context*, 10 (1997), 495–522.

LASKER, DANIEL J., 'Original Sin and its Atonement According to Hasdai Crescas' (Heb.), *Da'at*, 20 (1988), 127–35.

—— 'Proselyte Judaism, Christianity, and Islam in the Thought of Judah Halevi', *Jewish Quarterly Review*, 81 (1990), 75–91.

—— 'Sub-Prophetic Inspiration in Judaeo-Arabic Philosophy' (Heb.), in Daniel Lasker and Haggai Ben-Shammai (eds.), *Alei Asor: Proceedings of the Tenth Conference of the Society for Judaeo-Arabic Studies* [Alei asor: divrei have'idah ha'asirit shel haḥevrah leḥeker hatarbut ha'aravit–hayehudit shel yemei habeinayim] (Be'er Sheva, 2008), 131–49.

LEAMAN, Oliver, *Evil and Suffering in Jewish Philosophy* (Cambridge, 1995).

LERNER, RALPH, 'Maimonides' Letter on Astrology', *History of Religions*, 8 (1968), 143–58.

LESTER, DAVID, *Suicide and the Holocaust* (New York, 2005).

LEVI BEN GERSHOM (GERSONIDES), *Commentary on Song of Songs by Rabbi Levi ben Gershom* (Heb.), ed. Menachem Kellner (Ramat Gan, 2001); trans. Menachem Kellner (New Haven, 1998).

LEVI, PRIMO, *The Drowned and the Saved*, trans. Raymond Rosenthal (New York, 1988).

LEVINAS, EMMANUEL, 'Useless Suffering', trans. Richard Cohen, in Robert Bernasconi and David Wood (eds.), *The Provocation of Levinas* (New York, 1988), 156–67.

LEWITTER, SIDNEY R., 'A School for Scholars—The Beth Medrash Govoha, the Rabbi Aaron Kotler Jewish Institute of Higher Learning in Lakewood, New Jersey: A Study of the Development and Theory of One Aspect of Jewish Higher Education in America' (Ed.D. diss., Rutgers University, 1981).

LIEBERMAN, SAUL, Hilkhot hayerushalmi (New York, 1947).

LIEBES, YEHUDA, The Sin of Elisha [Ḥeto shel elisha] (Jerusalem, 1990).

LOBEL, DIANA, Between Mysticism and Philosophy: Sufi Language of Religious Experience in Judah Ha-Levi's Kuzari (Albany, NY, 2000).

—— 'A Dwelling Place for the Shekhinah', Jewish Quarterly Review, 90 (1999), 103–25.

LOWE, JUDAH (MAHARAL OF PRAGUE), Netsaḥ yisra'el, vol. i, ed. Joshua Hartman (Jerusalem, 1997).

MCKENNY, GERALD, The Analogy of Grace: Karl Barth's Moral Theology (Oxford, 2010).

MAGID, SHAUL, Hasidism on the Margin: Reconciliation, Antinomianism, and Messianism in Izbica and Radzin Hasidism (Madison, Wis., 2003).

MALACHI, A. R., 'The Literary Work of Naftali Tsevi Yehudah Berlin' (Heb.), Jewish Book Annual, 25 (1967–8), 233–9.

MARK, ZVI, Mysticism and Madness: The Religious Thought of Rabbi Nachman of Bratslav (New York, 2009).

MARX, ALEXANDER (ed.), 'The Correspondence between the Rabbis of Southern France and Maimonides about Astrology', Hebrew Union College Annual, 3 (1926), 311–58.

MEIR, JONATHAN, 'Longing of Souls for the Shekhinah: Relations between Rabbi Kook, Zeitlin, and Brenner' (Heb.), in Yehoyada Amir (ed.), The Path of the Spirit: Eliezer Schweid Jubilee Volume [Derekh haruaḥ: sefer hayovel le'eli'ezer shveid], Jerusalem Studies in Jewish Thought [Meḥkarei yerushalayim behagut yehudit], vol. ii (Jerusalem, 2005), 771–818.

MEIR SIMHAH COHEN OF DVINSK, Meshekh ḥokhmah, ed. Yehuda Kupperman (Jerusalem, 1997).

MELAMED, ABRAHAM, Dat: From Law to Religion—A History of a Formative Term [Dat: meḥok le'emunah—korotav shel minuaḥ mekhonen] (Tel Aviv, 2014).

—— The Image of the Black in Jewish Culture: A History of the Other (London, 2003).

—— On the Shoulders of Giants: The Debate between Moderns and Ancients in Medieval and Renaissance Jewish Thought [Al kitfei anakim: toledot hapulmos bein aḥaronim lerishonim bahagut hayehudit bimei habeinayim uvereshit ha'et haḥadashah] (Ramat Gan, 2003).

MIRSKY, YEHUDAH, 'An Intellectual and Spiritual Biography of Rabbi Avraham Yitzḥaq Ha-Cohen Kook from 1865 to 1904' (Ph.D. diss., Harvard University, 2007).

MIRSKY, YEHUDAH, 'Rav Kook and Maimonides: A New Look' (Heb), in Baruch J. Schwartz, Abraham Melamed, and Aharon Shemesh (eds.), *Igud: Selected Essays in Jewish Studies* [Igud: mivḥar ma'amarim bemada'ei hayahadut], vol. i (Jerusalem, 2008), 397–405.

—— *Rav Kook: Mystic in a Time of Revolution* (New Haven, 2014).

NADLER, ALLAN, 'The "Rambam Revival" in Early Modern Jewish Thought: Maskilim, Mitnagdim, and Hasidim on Maimonides' *Guide of the Perplexed*', in Benny Kraut (ed.), *Moses Maimonides: Communal Impact, Historic Legacy* (New York, 2005), 36–61; repr. in Jay Michael Harris (ed.), *Maimonides After 800 Years: Essays on Maimonides and His Influence* (Cambridge, 2007).

NAHMAN OF BRATSLAV, *Likutei moharan* (Jerusalem, 1969).

NAHMANIDES, *Glosses on Maimonides' Sefer hamitsvot* [Sefer hamitsvot leharambam im hasagot haramban], ed. C. D. Chavel (Jerusalem, 1981).

NEUGROSCHEL, Z. A., *Netsiv's Thought: Investigations of Topics in Naftali Tsevi Yehudah Berlin's Thought* [Torat hanetsiv: berurei sugyot bemishnato shel rabi naftali tsevi yehudah berlin] (Jerusalem, 2002).

NOVAK, DAVID, *The Image of the Non-Jew in Judaism: An Historical and Constructive Study of the Noahide Laws* (New York, 1983); 2nd edn. (Oxford, 2011).

NURIEL, ABRAHAM, 'The Concept of Belief in Maimonides' (Heb.), *Da'at*, 2–3 (1978–9), 43–7; repr. in id., *Concealed and Revealed in Medieval Jewish Philosophy* [Galui vesamui bafilosofiyah hayehudit bimei habeinayim] (Jerusalem, 2000), 78–82.

—— 'On the Meaning of the Expression "Sharia of Moses" in Maimonides' (Heb.), in id., *Concealed and Revealed in Medieval Jewish Philosophy* [Galui vesamui bafilosofiyah hayehudit bimei habeinayim] (Jerusalem, 2000), 165–71.

PACHTER, MORDECHAI, 'The Kabbalistic Foundation of the Faith-Heresy Issue in Rav Kook's Thought' (Heb.), *Da'at*, 47 (2001), 69–100.

—— (ed.) *The Writings of R. Israel Salanter: Sermons, Articles, Letters* [Kitvei r. yisra'el salanter: derushim, ma'amarim, igerot] (Jerusalem, 1972).

PARENS, JOSHUA, *Maimonides and Spinoza: Their Conflicting Views of Human Nature* (Chicago, 2012).

PARKES, JAMES, *Whose Land? A History of the Peoples of Palestine* (London, 1971).

PARNES, YEHUDA, 'Torah u-Madda and Freedom of Inquiry', *Torah u-Madda Journal*, 1 (1989), 65–71.

PELEG, EREZ, 'A Critique of Jewish Rationalism in the Thought of R. Shem Tov b. Shem Tov' [Bikoret hasakhletanut hayehudit behaguto shel r. shem tov b. shem tov] (Ph.D. diss., University of Haifa, 2002).

PERL, GIL, 'No Two Minds Are Alike: Tolerance and Pluralism in the Work of Netsiv', *Torah u-Madda Journal*, 12 (2004), 74–98.

—— *The Pillar of Volozhin: Rabbi Naftali Zvi Yehuda Berlin and the World of Nineteenth Century Lithuanian Torah Scholarship* (Boston, Mass., 2012).

Perry, Edmund, 'The Meaning of "Emunah" in the Old Testament', *Journal of the American Academy of Religion*, 21/4 (1953), 252–6.

Pines, Shlomo, 'The Philosophical Purport of Maimonides' Halachic Works and the Purport of the *Guide of the Perplexed*', in Shlomo Pines and Yirmiyahu Yovel (eds.), *Maimonides and Philosophy* (Dordrecht, 1986), 1–14.

—— 'Shi'ite Terms and Conceptions in Judah Halevi's Kuzari', *Jerusalem Studies in Arabic and Islam*, 2 (1980), 165–219.

—— *Studies in the History of Jewish Philosophy: The Transmission of Texts and Ideas* [Bein maḥshevet yisra'el lemaḥshevet he'amim] (Jerusalem, 1977).

Polen, Nehemiah, *The Holy Fire: The Teachings of Rabbi Kalonymus Kalman Shapira, the Rebbe of the Warsaw Ghetto* (Lanham, Md., 2004).

Rabinovitch, Nachum L., *Yad peshutah* (Ma'aleh Adumim, 2007).

Raffel, Charles M., 'Providence as Consequent upon the Intellect: Maimonides' Theory of Providence', *AJS Review*, 12 (1987), 25–71.

Rapoport-Albert, Ada, 'Self-Deprecation ("qatnuth", "peshituth") and Disavowal of Knowledge ("eyni yode'a") in Nahman of Braslav', in Siegfried Stein and Raphael Loewe (eds.), *Studies in Jewish Religious and Intellectual History Presented to Alexander Altmann on the Occasion of his Seventieth Birthday* (Tuscaloosa, Ala., 1979), 7–33.

Ravitzky, Aviezer, *Messianism, Zionism, and Jewish Religious Radicalism* [Hakets hameguleh umedinat hayehudim: meshiḥiyut, tsiyonut veradikalism dati beyisra'el] (Tel Aviv, 1993); English trans. Michael Swirsky and Jonathan Chipman (Chicago, 1996).

—— 'The Question of Tolerance in the Jewish Religious Tradition', in Yaakov Elman and Jeffrey S. Gurock (eds.), *Hazon Nahum: Studies in Jewish Law, Thought, and History Presented to Dr Norman Lamm on the Occasion of his Seventieth Birthday* (New York, 1997), 378–85.

—— 'Rabbi J. B. Soloveitchik on Human Knowledge: Between Maimonidean and Neo-Kantian Philosophy', *Modern Judaism*, 6 (1986), 157–88.

—— 'Samuel Ibn Tibbon and the Esoteric Interpretation of the *Guide of the Perplexed*', *AJS Review*, 6 (1981), 87–123.

—— 'The Thought of R. Zerahiah b. Isaac b. She'altiel Hen and the Maimonidean–Tibbonian Philosophy of the 13th Century' [Mishnato shel r. zeraḥyah ben she'alti'el ben yitsḥak ḥen vehehagut hamaimonit–tibonit bame'ah hayodgimel] (Ph.D. diss., Hebrew University of Jerusalem, 1978).

—— '"To the Utmost of Human Capacity": Maimonides on the Days of the Messiah', in Joel Kraemer (ed.), *Perspectives on Maimonides: Philosophical and Historical Studies* (Oxford, 1991), 221–56.

Rosenak, Avinoam, *Rabbi A. I. Kook* [Harav avraham yitsḥak hakohen kuk] (Jerusalem, 2006).

—— 'Who's Afraid of Rav Kook's Hidden Treatises?' (Heb.), *Tarbiz*, 69/2 (2000), 257–91.

ROSENBERG, SHALOM, 'On Biblical Exegesis in the *Guide*' (Heb.), *Jerusalem Studies in Jewish Thought*, 1 (1981), 85–157.

—— 'Rav Kook and the Blind Serpent' (Heb.), in Hayim Hamiel (ed.), *In His Light: Studies in the Thought of Rabbi Abraham Isaac Hakohen Kook* [Be'oro: iyunim bemishnato shel harav avraham yitsḥak hakohen kuk zts"l vedarkhei hora'atah] (Jerusalem, 1986), 317–52.

ROSS, TAMAR, 'The Concept of God in the Thought of Rabbi Kook' (Heb.), *Da'at*, 9 (1983), 39–70.

—— 'Immortality, Natural Law, and the Role of Human Perception in the Writings of Rav Kook', in Lawrence J. Kaplan, and David Shatz (eds.), *Rabbi Abraham Isaac Kook and Jewish Spirituality* (New York, 1995), 237–53.

ROTH, LEON, 'Moralization and Demoralization in Jewish Ethics', *Judaism*, 11 (1962), 291–302; repr. in id., *Is There a Jewish Philosophy?* (London, 1999), 128–43.

RYNHOLD, DANIEL, *Two Models of Jewish Philosophy: Justifying One's Practices* (New York, 2005).

SA'ADYAH GAON, *The Book of Beliefs and Opinions*, trans. Samuel Rosenblatt (New Haven, 1948).

SAKS, JEFFREY, 'Rabbi Soloveitchik Meets Rav Kook', *Tradition*, 39/3 (2006), 90–6.

SALANTER, ISRAEL, *Or yisra'el* (Vilnius, 1900).

SCHACHTER, HERSHEL, 'Women Rabbis?', *Hakirah: The Flatbush Journal of Jewish Law and Thought*, 11 (2011), 19–23.

SCHACTER, JACOB, 'Haskalah, Secular Studies, and the Close of the Yeshiva in Volozhin in 1892', *Torah u-Madda Journal*, 2 (1990), 76–133.

—— 'Rabbi Jacob Emden's "Iggeret Purim"', in Isadore Twersky (ed.), *Studies in Medieval Jewish History and Literature*, vol. ii (Cambridge, 1984), 441–6.

SCHATZ [UFFENHEIMER], RIVKA, 'Utopia and Messianism in the Thought of Rabbi Kook' (Heb.), *Kivunim*, 1 (1979), 15–27.

SCHECHTERMAN, DEBORAH, 'The Doctrine of Original Sin and Commentaries on Maimonides in Jewish Philosophy of the Thirteenth and Fourteenth Centuries' (Heb.), *Da'at*, 20 (1988), 65–90.

SCHERMAN, NOSSON and MEIR ZLOTOWITZ (eds. and trans.), *Siddur Eitz Chaim: The Complete ArtScroll Siddur* (Brooklyn, NY, 1985).

SCHOLEM, GERSHOM, *Major Trends in Jewish Mysticism* (New York, 1974).

—— 'The Name of God and the Linguistic Theory of the Kabbala', *Diogenes*, 80 (1972), 164–94.

—— 'Sitra Ahra: Good and Evil in the Kabbalah', in id., *On the Mystical Shape of the Godhead*, ed. Jonathan Chipman, trans. Joachim Neugroschel (New York, 1991), 56–87.

Schwartz, Dov, *Central Problems of Medieval Jewish Philosophy* (Leiden, 2005).
—— *Challenge and Crisis in Rabbi Kook's Circle* [Etgar umashber beḥug harav kuk] (Tel Aviv, 2001).
—— *Faith and Reason* [Emunah utevunah] (Tel Aviv, 2001).
—— *Faith at the Crossroads: A Theological Profile of Religious Zionism*, trans. Batya Stein (Leiden, 2002).
—— 'Maimonides in Religious-Zionist Philosophy: Unity vs. Duality', in James T. Robinson (ed.), *The Cultures of Maimonideanism: New Approaches to the History of Jewish Thought* (Leiden, 2009), 385–408.
—— *The Philosophy of Rabbi Joseph B. Soloveitchik*, trans. Batya Stein, 2 vols. (Leiden, 2007–13).
—— 'R. Soloveitchik as a Maimonidean: The Unity of Cognization' (Heb.), in id. and Avraham Elqayam (eds.), *Maimonides and Mysticism: Presented to Moshe Hallamish on the Occasion of his Retirement* [Harambam benivkhei hasod] (= *Da'at*, 64–66) (Ramat Gan, 2009), 301–21.
Schwarzschild, Steven, 'Proselytism and Ethnicism in R. Yehudah Halevy', in Bernard Lewis and Friedrich Niewöhner (eds.), *Religionsgespräche im Mittelalter* (1992), 27–41.
Schweid, Eliezer, 'The Bush Is Aflame—But the Bush Was Not Consumed?' (Heb.), in id., *From Ruin to Salvation* [Bein ḥurban liyeshuah: teguvot shel hagut ḥaredit lasho'ah bizemanah] (Tel Aviv, 1994), 105–54.
—— *From Ruin to Salvation: Haredi Responses to the Holocaust in Its Time* [Bein ḥurban liyeshuah: teguvot shel hagut ḥaredit lasho'ah bizemanah] (Tel Aviv, 1994).
Seeman, Don, 'God's Honor, Violence, and the State', in Robert W. Jenson and Eugene Korn (eds.), *Plowshares into Swords? Reflections on Religion and Violence: Essays from the Institute for Theological Inquiry* (Kindle edn., 2014), 31 pages.
—— 'Ritual Efficacy, Hasidic Mysticism and "Useless Suffering" in the Warsaw Ghetto', *Harvard Theological Review*, 101 (2008), 465–505.
—— 'Violence, Ethics, and Divine Honor in Modern Jewish Thought', *Journal of the American Academy of Religion*, 73/4 (2004), 1015–48.
Seeskin, Kenneth, 'Judaism and the Linguistic Interpretation of Faith', in Norbert Max Samuelson (ed.), *Studies in Jewish Philosophy: Collected Essays of the Academy for Jewish Philosophy, 1980–1985* (Lanham, Md., 1987), 215–24.
—— *Maimonides: A Guide for Today's Perplexed* (New York, 1991).
—— 'Metaphysics and its Transcendence', in id. (ed.), *The Cambridge Companion to Maimonides* (New York, 2005), 82–104.
Sefer halakhot gedolot, ed. Ezriel Hildesheimer, vol. i (Jerusalem, 1972).
Shapiro, Marc B., 'Ani Ma'amin', *Encyclopaedia Judaica*, 2nd edn. (New York, 2007), 165.

SHAPIRO, MARC B., 'Of Books and Bans', *Edah Journal*, 3/2 (2003), 2–16.

—— *The Limits of Orthodox Theology: Maimonides' Thirteen Principles Reappraised* (Oxford, 2004).

SHEILAT, ISAAC, *Between the Kuzari and Maimonides* [Bein hakuzari larambam] (Jerusalem, 2011).

SHEM TOV IBN SHEM TOV, *Sefer ha'emunot* (Ferrara, 1556).

SHERMAN, MOSHE, *Orthodox Judaism in America: A Biographical Dictionary and Sourcebook* (Westport, Conn., 1996).

Shir hashirim rabah, ed. S. Dunsky (Jerusalem, 1980).

SHNEUR ZALMAN OF LYADY, *Tanya: likutei amarim* (New York, 1984).

SHOHAT, RAPHAEL, 'The Faith of our Father Abraham in the School of Hagra: Intellectual Faith versus Revealed Faith' (Heb.), in Moshe Hallamish, Hannah Kasher, and Yohanan Silman (eds.), *The Faith of Abraham in Light of Interpretation throughout the Ages* [Avraham avi hama'aminim: demuto bire'i hehagut ledoroteiha] (Ramat Gan, 2003), 193–204.

—— 'The Vilna Gaon and General Scholarship' (Heb.), *BDD: Journal of Torah and Scholarship*, 2 (1996), 89–106.

Siddur Eitz Chaim: The Complete ArtScroll Siddur (Brooklyn, NY, 1985).

Sifrei devarim, ed. Louis Finkelstein (New York, 2014).

SILMAN, YOHANAN, 'Commandments and Transgressions: Matters of Obedience or Intrinsic Quality' (Heb.), *Dine Israel*, 16 (1991–2), 183–201.

—— 'Halakhic Determinations of a Nominalistic and Realistic Nature: Legal and Philosophical Considerations' (Heb.), *Dine Israel*, 12 (1984–5), 249–66.

—— *Halakhic Instructions: As Guiding Principles or as Commands* [Bein 'lalekhet biderakhav' ve'lishmo'a bekolo'] (Gush Etzion, 2012).

—— 'Introduction to the Philosophical Analysis of the Normative–Ontological Tension in the Halakhah', *Da'at*, 31 (1993), pp. v–xx.

SILVER, DANIEL JEREMY, *Maimonidean Criticism and the Maimonidean Controversy: 1180–1240* (Leiden, 1965).

SINCLAIR, DANIEL, 'Legal Thinking in the Teachings of Maimonides and Nahmanides' (Heb.), in Ithamar Warhaftig (ed.), *Jubilee Volume: Minḥah Le'Ish, Presented to Ha-Rav Shimon A. Dolgin on the Occasion of his 75th Birthday* [Sefer yovel minḥah le'ish: kovets ma'amarim mukdash behokarah leharav avraham yeshayahu dolgin] (Jerusalem, 1991), 349–55.

SLIFKIN, NATAN, *Rationalist Judaism* [blog], <http://www.rationalistjudaism.com/>.

SOFER, MOSES, *Torat mosheh*, 3 vols. (Jerusalem, 2005).

SOLOVEITCHIK, HAYM, '*Mishneh Torah*: Polemic and Art', in Jay M. Harris (ed.), *Maimonides After 800 Years: Essays in Maimonides and His Influence* (Cambridge, Mass., 2007), 327–43.

SORASKY, AHARON, *Or elḥanan*, 2 vols. (Jerusalem, 1978). English adaptation: *Reb Elchonon: The Life and Ideals of Rabbi Elchonon Bunim Wasserman of Baranovich* (New York, 1982).

STADLER, NURIT, and EYAL BEN-ARI, 'Other-Worldly Soldiers? Ultra-Orthodox Views of Military Service in Contemporary Israel', *Israel Affairs*, 9 (2003), 17–48.

STAMPFER, SHAUL, *Lithuanian Yeshivas of the Nineteenth Century: Creating a Tradition of Learning*, trans. Lindsey Taylor-Guthartz (Oxford, 2012).

STRAUSS, LEO, 'How to Begin to Study the *Guide of the Perplexed*', in Maimonides, *Guide of the Perplexed*, trans. Shlomo Pines (Chicago, 1963), pp. xi–lvi.

STROUMSA, SARAH, 'Was Maimonides an Almohad Thinker?' (Heb.), in Daniel J. Lasker and Haggai Ben-Shammai (eds.), *Alei Asor: Proceedings of the Tenth Conference of the Society for Judaeo-Arabic Studies* [Alei asor: divrei have'idah ha'asirit shel haḥevrah leḥeker hatarbut ha'aravit–hayehudit shel yemei habeinayim] (Be'er Sheva, 2008), 151–71.

TOBI, Y., 'The Nature of Judaism in the Eyes of R. Joseph Kafiḥ' (Heb.), *Te'ima*, 8 (2004), 9–14.

—— 'Who Wrote *Sefer emunat hashem*?' (Heb.), *Da'at*, 49 (2002), 87–98.

TURKEL, ELI, 'Partial Bibliography of Works by and about Rabbi Joseph B. Soloveitchik Zt"l' <http://www.math.tau.ac.il/~turkel/engsol.html>.

TURNER, MASHA, 'The Patriarch Abraham in Maimonidean Thought' (Heb.), in Moshe Hallamish, Hannah Kasher, and Yohanan Silman (eds.), *The Faith of Abraham in Light of Interpretation throughout the Ages* [Avraham avi hama' aminim: demuto bire'i hehagut ledoroteiha] (Ramat Gan, 2003), 143–54.

TWERSKY, ISADORE, *Introduction to the Code of Maimonides (Mishneh Torah)* (New Haven, 1980).

—— 'Maimonides and Eretz Israel: Halakhic, Philosophic, and Historical Perspectives', in Joel Kraemer (ed.), *Perspectives on Maimonides* (Oxford, 1991), 257–90.

—— (ed.), *A Maimonides Reader* (New York, 1972).

—— 'On Maimonides: An Essay on His Unique Standing in Jewish History' (Heb.), *Asufot*, 10 (1997), 9–35.

—— *Rabad of Posquières: A Twelfth-Century Talmudist* (Philadelphia, 1980).

—— 'The *Shulḥan 'Aruk*: Enduring Code of Jewish Law', *Judaism*, 16 (1967), 141–58.

—— 'Some Non-Halakic Aspects of the *Mishneh Torah*', in Alexander Altmann (ed.), *Jewish Medieval and Renaissance Studies* (Cambridge, Mass., 1967), 95–118.

—— 'Some Reflections on the Historical Image of Maimonides: An Essay on his Unique Place in History', in Shalom Carmy and Yamin Levy (eds.), *The Legacy of Maimonides: Religion, Reason, and Community* (New York, 2006), 1–48.

URBACH, EPHRAIM E., *The Sages*, trans. Israel Abrahams (Jerusalem, 1975).

VINCENT, ALANA M., *Making Memory: Jewish and Christian Explorations in Monument, Narrative, and Liturgy* (Cambridge, 2014).

WAXMAN, CHAIM, 'Giyur in the Context of National Identity', in Adam Mintz and Marc D. Stern (eds.), *Conversion, Intermarriage, and Jewish Identity* (New York, 2015), 151–88.

WHITEHEAD, ALFRED NORTH, *Process and Reality* (New York, 1979).

WIJNHOVEN, JOCHANAN, 'The Zohar and the Proselyte', in Michael A. Fishbane and Paul R. Mendes-Flohr (eds.), *Texts and Responses: Studies Presented to Nahum N. Glatzer* (Leiden, 1975), 120–40.

WOLFSON, ELLIOT, *Abraham Abulafia, Kabbalist and Prophet: Hermeneutics, Theosophy, and Theurgy* (Los Angeles, 2000).

—— *Alef, Mem, Tau: Kabbalistic Musings on Time, Truth, and Death* (Berkeley, Calif., 2006).

—— 'Beneath the Wings of the Great Eagle: Maimonides and Thirteenth-Century Kabbalah', in Görge K. Hasselhoff and Otfried Fraisse (eds.), *Moses Maimonides (1138–1204): His Religious, Scientific, and Philosophical Wirkungsgeschichte in Different Cultural Contexts* (Würzburg, 2004), 209–37.

—— 'Jewish Mysticism: A Philosophical Overview', in Daniel Frank and Oliver Leaman (eds.), *History of Jewish Philosophy* (New York, 1997), 450–98.

—— *Luminal Darkness: Imaginal Gleanings from Zoharic Literature* (Oxford, 2007).

—— *Open Secret: Postmessianic Messianism and the Mystical Revision of Menaḥem Mendel Schneerson* (New York, 2009).

—— *Through a Speculum That Shines: Vision and Imagination in Medieval Jewish Mysticism* (Princeton, NJ, 1994).

—— *Venturing Beyond: Law and Morality in Kabbalistic Mysticism* (Oxford, 2006).

WOLFSON, HARRY AUSTRYN, 'The Classification of Sciences in Mediaeval Jewish Philosophy', in Isadore Twersky and George Williams (eds.), *Studies in the History and Philosophy of Religion*, vol. i (Cambridge, Mass., 1973), 493–545.

The Zohar: Pritzker Edition, vol. iii, trans. Daniel Matt, (Stanford, Calif., 2006).

ZUROFF, EFRAIM, *The Response of Orthodox Jewry in the United States to the Holocaust: The Activities of the Va'ad ha-Hatsalah Rescue Committee, 1939–1945* (Hoboken, NJ, 2000).

Index

A

Abrabanel, Isaac 50 n.34, 125 n.64, 129 n.81, 134 n.112, 154 n.20, 190 n.65
Abraham:
  in Kook 71–2
  in Maimonides 13, 70–4
  in Netsiv 19
  as philosopher or mystic 72–4
  in Soloveitchik 45–6, 56
Abraham ben David of Posquières, *see* Rabad
Abulafia, Abraham 80 n.95
action, attributes of 65–6
Adam and Eve:
  in Maimonides 34–5, 36, 83
  in Netsiv 34–5
Agudat Yisra'el 109 n.10, 110 n.13, 149 n.1
Akiva, Rabbi 71 n.58, 131–2, 134, 139, 144–5
Albo, Joseph, *Sefer ha'ikarim* 137 n.128, 150 n.2
Alfasi, Isaac 166
allegory, and Song of Songs 11–13, 30
Altschuler, Mor 1 n.4
Améry, Jean 89
Angel, Marc 5
angels:
  in Maimonides 30, 54–5, 118 n.45
  in Netsiv 31
anthropocentrism:
  and Holocaust 88
  in Netsiv 27–30
anthropomorphism:
  and Maimonides 77–8, 92, 145 n.175
  and Netsiv 29
Arba'ah turim, *see* Jacob ben Asher
Arendt, Hannah 91
Aristotle:
  and belief 130

and creation 122–3, 132 n.98
and God as thought thinking itself 94–5, 122, 197
and intellect 75 n.70, 111 n.16, 114, 118 n.45, 193
and Kook 63, 197
and Maimonides 63, 66, 75 n.70, 94–5, 111, 122–3, 146 n.177, 194, 201
and natural science 111, 114, 122
and teleology 27 n.77, 48 n.28
ArtScroll 12
astrology 103, 158–9
attributes, divine 65–6, 94
Aviner, Shlomo 7, 176–9, 195–6
  and Halevi 181–3, 184–9, 194, 200
  and Kafih 181–3, 194, 200
  and Zohar 183

B

Bar-Ilan, Meir 14
Baranowicze, Ohel Torah yeshiva 109–10
belief:
  and Aristotle 130
  degrees 143–5
  and Maimonides 128–9
  and Wasserman 128–38, 138–40, 141–3, 143–5
Ben-Gurion, David 180–1
Ben-Simon, Yisrael 134 n.111, 139–40 n.140, 185 n.47
Benor, Ehud 20 n.50
Berdyczewski, Mikhah Yosef 10, 37
Berlin, R. Naftali Tsevi Yehudah, *see* Netsiv
Bialik, Hayim Nahman 10, 37
Bleich, J. David 109 n.10
Blidstein, Gerald (Ya'akov) 56
Bloom, Harold 62 n.15
Blumenthal, David 64 n.20
Bokser, Ben Zion 69 n.50
Brill, Alan 19 n.39

C

chariot imagery, in Kook 68
Cherlow, Smadar 72 n.59
Chief Rabbinate 60
Cohen, David, *see* Nazir
Cohen, Hermann 45 n.16
Cohen, Meir Simhah 46 n.19
consciousness, divine 100–1
creation:
 and anthropocentrism 27–9
 hierarchy 19, 25, 27–9
 in Kook 68–9, 72–4, 81
 in Maimonides 17–18, 22–3, 25, 27, 74, 88, 108, 117–18, 120–3, 131 n.93, 137 n.129, 147, 192
 in Netsiv 26–9, 31
 in Shapira 91
 in Wasserman 131–5, 138–40
 see also ma'aseh bereshit
Crescas, *see* Hasdai ben Avraham Crescas

D

Dienstag, Jacob Israel 63 n.17
Dov Baer ben Avraham of Mezhirech 91

E

ein sof 65–6 n.30, 69–70, 74, 78
Elisha ben Avuya 113–14
elitism:
 in Halevi 193
 in Maimonides 68, 192–3
Emden, Jacob 3, 135 n.120
epistemology, *see* knowledge
Epstein, Moshe Mordekhai 10
Esh Kodesh, *see* Shapira, Kalonymus Kalman
esotericism:
 and Kook 68
 and Maimonides 79–80, 117, 152–3, 169–70, 201
 and Shapira 6
essentialism:
 in Aviner 178–9, 189 n.62, 194
 in Halevi 185, 194
 and Maimonides 193
 in Wasserman 162–3
eternity:
 and Aristotle 132 n.98, 135 n.113, 146 n.177

 and Kook 85
 and Maimonides 54, 68, 122–4
 and Soloveitchik 42–3, 46–7, 56 n.55
ethics:
 in Maimonides 13 n.17, 41 n.6
 in Netsiv 10–11, 15, 20 n.56, 36
 in Shapira 97–8
 in Wasserman 134 n.109
evil:
 as privation 87–8, 103
 in Shapiro 89–93, 103–4
 in Wasserman 136
exile:
 and divine hiddenness, in Soloveitchik 6
 of knowledge, in Shapira 91, 93–4, 98–9
existence of God:
 in Kook 71–2, 72–3
 in Maimonides 13, 28–9, 36, 52, 66 n.33, 117–18, 147, 155
 in Shapira 105
 in Soloveitchik 48–50
 in Wasserman 125 n.69, 129 n.85, 135 n.113, 137 n.128, 139–40 n.141
Eybeschütz, Jonathan 135 n.120

F

Fackenheim, Emil 89, 90–1, 101
faith:
 and belief 129, 134–5
 and knowledge 66–7, 102
 and suffering 101–3
fear of God 120–1, 142–3
 in Kook 74–6, 79–80, 82–3
 in Maimonides 74–80, 81
 in Netsiv 15–16
Feinstein, Elijah of Prushna 39, 125–6 n.69
Feldman, Aryeh 114 n.31, 116 n.33
Finkel, Nathan Tsevi 150 n.2
Fox, Marvin 48 n.26
Fraenkel, Carlos 44 n.13

G

Gellman, Jerome 25 n.69
Gemara 112–13, 124, 142–3, 161, 165, 168–72
 see also Talmud

Germany, and science and rationalism 97–8
glory, and thought 28
  see also Shekhinah
grace, and love of God 24–5, 26, 31, 71, 81
Greenberg, Gershon 109 n.9
Grimberg, Moshe 53 n.49
Grodzinski, Hayim Ozer 109
Guide of the Perplexed:
  and angels 54–5, 118 n.45
  audience 91–2
  and Aviner 184–5, 196
  canonical status 5, 37, 84–5
  and creation 122–3, 137 n.129, 139 n.141, 147, 192
  and divine knowledge 95
  and divine providence 41–3, 53–4, 89 n.4, 99, 157–8
  and halakhah and Torah 49–50, 152–4
  and heresy 138 n.137
  and intellect 193
  and Kook 63–4, 83–6
  and Kotler 159
  'Laws of Idolatry' 13 n.17
  and love of God 13
  and *Mishneh torah* 2–3, 63–4
  and nominalism 53–4
  opposition to 61, 135 n.113, 146–7
  and science 50, 111 n.16, 121–2
  seen as forgery 3

H
Habad-Lubavitch 4–5
Hafets Hayim (Yisra'el Me'ir Hakohen Kagan) 109–10
halakhah:
  and *keneset yisra'el* 54–6, 57
  and Kook 64, 81–2
  and Maimonides 24, 48, 51, 61–3, 79, 81, 135 n.116, 147, 167, 182
  and Netsiv 14, 16, 21
  and Soloveitchik 45–7, 51–2, 55
  and Wasserman 147
Halevi, Judah 7, 45–6, 190
  and Aviner 181–3, 184–9, 200
  and Jewish identity 53 n.49, 55, 125, 175, 182, 185–9, 191, 193–4
  Kuzari 45, 150 n.2, 177 n.8, 183–8, 196

  and Land of Israel 145–6
  and Maimonides 181–3, 183–4
  and Torah 181
Halkin, Abraham S. 11
Hanina ben Dosa 133 n.104, 142 n.161
Haredi Judaism:
  and Kotler 149–73, 198
  and Wasserman 109–10, 198
Harlap, Ya'akov Moshe 180 n.22
harmony:
  between Israel and God 98–9
  of opposition in Kook 85, 88
Harris, Jay M. 19 n.42
Harvey, Warren Zev 19 n.45, 27 n.77, 30 n.92, 112 n.19
Hasdai ben Avraham Crescas 116, 126, 129 n.81, 201
hasidism 4
  Habad 5, 77 n.80, 95
  and problem of suffering 94–5
  and Shapira 94
hester panim, see hiding of God's face
Hatam Sofer (Moses Sofer) 136
Heidegger, Martin 97, 193 n.80
Hellenism 60–1, 76, 83–6, 146
Heller, Chaim 50–1
heresy:
  and Maimonides 11, 138 n.137, 141
  and Wasserman 128–9, 131, 134, 139–40, 141–2
Herzman, Yosef 109 n.11
ḥesed, see grace
Hibat Tsiyon movement 15
hiding of God's face (*hester panim*):
  in Maimonides 33–4, 89
  in Netsiv 32–4
  and suffering 88–9
Hillel, Rabbi 113 n.25, 137 n.131, 142
Hoch, Liron 134 n.107
holiness of Israel 45–7, 57, 99–100
Holocaust, and suffering 87–9, 90–8, 100–1, 105, 108
holy spirit:
  in Kook 66
  in Maimonides 111, 114, 119, 121–2, 124
  in Netsiv 21, 25, 35–6
  in Wasserman 130

Hovevei Tsiyon movement 7
humility, in Maimonides 75, 76, 77
Hyman, Arthur 92 n.21

I
Ibn Ezra, Abraham 11
Ibn Pakuda, Bahya 129 n.80, 131, 138–9,
    150 n.2
Ibn Tibbon, Samuel 41 n.7, 111 n.16, 186
Idel, Moshe 65–6 n.301
identity, national:
    in Aviner 176–9, 184–9, 194
    in Halevi 53 n.49, 55, 125, 175, 182,
        185–9, 193–4
    and individual 52–5
    in Kafih 180–1, 194
    in Kook 60 n.6, 194
    and non-Jews 18, 175–94
    and Torah 16–18, 19, 31, 36, 176–8, 181,
        187–8, 194
idolatry:
    and Kook 72, 77–8
    and Maimonides 22, 77, 125, 129, 135,
        138 n.136, 141
    and Wasserman 128–9, 134, 138, 140,
        142
image of God:
    in Halevi 186
    in Kafih 180
    in Maimonides 191 n.72, 192, 194
immortality, in Soloveitchik 43–4
inadvertence, and heresy 110, 140, 141–2
incorporeality of God 92–3, 135 n.113, 138
    n.136, 141–2
innovation, and Torah 152–3, 172
intellect:
    in Aristotle 75 n.70, 111 n.16, 114,
        118 n.45, 193
    and arrogance 77–8
    in Kook 69, 75–9
    in Kotler 157
    in Maimonides 12–14, 15, 17–20, 21
        n.53, 23, 24–6, 34–7, 41–3, 53, 70–1,
        75–8, 81, 88–9, 99, 102, 111, 121, 191–2
    in Netsiv 18, 23, 25–7, 196
    and perfection 14, 21, 24–5, 36, 41–5, 48,
        78, 81–2, 83, 133 n.106, 134, 137 n.129,
        192

and providence 18, 41–5, 53, 81, 88–9,
    104
and science 111, 114–15, 118–21
in Shapira 91, 94–5, 96–8, 102
in Soloveitchik 42–3
and Torah study 151–7, 169, 171
in Wasserman 128
interpretation, and allegory 11–13
Ish-Shalom, Benjamin 60 n.4, 67 n.37,
    69 n.44
Israel:
    as chosen people 176–7, 185, 187
    harmony with God 98–9
    as holy 45–7, 57, 99–100
    and Netsiv 15
    unity 36, 56, 82, 98–9
Isserles, Moses, *see* Rema

J
Jacob ben Asher, *Arba'ah turim* 3
Jews and non-Jews 175–94
    and Aviner 176–9, 184–9, 194
    and Kotler 164
    and Maimonides 121, 122, 136–7 n.127,
        162, 182, 191–3
    and Netsiv 15, 18
    and Soloveitchik 41
    and Wasserman 111
    see also universalism
Judaism:
    conversion to 175, 178–9, 185, 187
    east European 5–7, 9–10, 150, 173
    Haredi 109–10, 149–73, 198
    Jews and *keneset yisra'el* 52–6, 57
    and science 2, 4, 18, 23, 24–5, 30,
        34–5, 37
    Thirteen Principles 1, 4, 49, 92–3,
        141 n.152, 193

K
kabbalah 3, 4, 26, 191 n.67
    and Halevi 182–3
    and knowledge 99–100
    and Kook 61–2, 68, 73, 76
    and philosophy 62 n.15, 68, 79–80
    and science 108, 112 n.20, 114
    and Shapira 94, 95, 97, 99–100, 103
    and Soloveitchik 149

Kadish, Seth 146 n.178
Kafih, Joseph 7, 52
  and Aviner 181–3, 194, 200
  and Maimonides 184, 189–94
Kafih, Yihye 183
Kaplan, Lawrence 61 n.8, 76 n.76, 81 n.99
Karo, Joseph, *Shulḥan arukh* 1, 3–4,
  111–12, 150 n.9
Kellner, Jolene 146
keneset yisra'el 52–6, 57
Kimhi, David, *see* Radak
kiss of death 26, 34
knowledge:
  and faith 66–7, 102
  hidden 6, 65, 67–8
  in Kook 60, 64–70, 80–2
  in Maimonides 13, 23 n.60, 24, 26, 34,
    75, 80–1, 99, 100
  in Netsiv 18, 27
  in Shapira 91–3, 93–4, 98–100, 104, 105
  in Soloveitchik 48–9, 96
  in Wasserman 128
kol ba'ei ha'olam 159 n.34, 160–1, 163, 164,
  178
Kook, Abraham Isaac Hakohen 4, 6,
  11–12, 59–86
  and Aviner 7, 176, 177 n.10, 181–3, 189,
    194
  defence of Maimonides 59–66, 84–6,
    196–7
  and fear of God 74–6, 79–80, 82–3
  and Hafets Hayim 110 n.13
  and harmony of opposition 85, 88
  and knowledge of God 60, 64–70, 80–2
  and messianism 84
  and mysticism 62–4, 71–4, 77–80, 84–5
  and problem of suffering 88
  theory of names 69–70, 73
  and Torah 85
  writings 60
Kook, Tsevi Yehudah 7, 177 n.10, 180 n.22,
  181, 189, 194
Kotler, Aharon 6, 149–73, 198, 199, 201
  and *kol ba'ei ha'olam* 163–4
  Mishnat rabi aharon 150–1, 159–60,
    173–4; 'On the Virtue of the Oral Law'
    168–71

  and Temple cult 159–61, 164, 167–8
  and Torah 150–4, 157, 159–64
  and universalism 161–3
Kreisel, Howard 74–5, 81 n.100

L

Landesman, Dovid 32 n.97
Langermann, Y. Tzvi 181
Lasker, Daniel J. 175 n.2
law:
  in Kook 82–3
  laws of nature 132
  in Maimonides 17, 36, 48, 59, 64–70
  in Netsiv 16–18, 19, 23, 37
  in Shapira 97–8
  and Torah 107
leadership, in Netsiv 13–15, 16
Leibowitz, Nehama 126
Leibowitz, Yeshayahu 5, 149
Lerner, Ralph 103 n.59
Levi, Primo 87 n.1, 89 nn.8, 9
Levinas, Emmanuel 105
Lifschitz, Yitzhak 125 n.68
love:
  sibling 34–5
  spousal 32, 34
love of God:
  exemplars 34–7
  in Kook 60, 70–1, 74, 82–3
  in Maimonides 13, 15–16, 17–18, 19–20,
    22–3, 24, 27–34, 70–1, 74–6, 81
  in Netsiv 11–16, 17–18, 19–21, 22–3,
    24–30, 31–4, 70
Lubavitcher Rebbe, *see* Schneerson,
  Menachem Mendel
Luzzatto, Moses Hayim 150 n.2

M

ma'aseh bereshit 110–27
  as concealed science 111, 114, 115,
    119–20
  as natural science 111, 114–22, 127, 152,
    155–6
ma'aseh merkavah:
  as divine science 117, 121, 125 n.68,
    155–6, 167
  as metaphysics 68, 108, 114, 116–24,
    152–3, 155

McKenny, Gerald 25 n.70
Maimonides, Moses:
  and attributes of action 65–6
  and belief in God 128–9
  Book of Divine Commandments 45 n.15, 50, 63, 66–7, 128–9, 171
  Book of Holiness 47
  canonical status 1–2, 4–5, 59, 84–5
  Commentary on the Mishnah 95 n.29, 117–18, 154–5, 161, 163–4 n.45, 165–7, 193
  and divine names 68–70
  in east European Judaism 5–7, 9–10, 150, 173
  Epistle to Yemen 144
  and Greek thought 60–1, 76, 83–6, 146
  Guide of the Perplexed, see separate entry
  and individual providence 18, 41–2, 53–4, 56–7, 81, 88–9, 104
  and Islam 67 n.37, 108
  in Israel 7
  and Jews and non-Jews 121, 122, 136–7 n.127, 162, 182, 191–3
  and knowledge of God 3 n.60, 13, 24, 26, 64–70, 75, 99, 100
  and law 17, 36, 48, 59, 64–70
  Letter on Astrology 103, 159 n.32
  Logical Terms 192–3
  and love of God 13, 15–16, 17–18, 19–20, 22–3, 24, 27–34, 70–1, 74–5, 81
  Medical Aphorisms 116 n.33
  Mishneh torah, see separate entry
  in New World 6–7
  as nominalist 53–4
  and numerology 161–2, 190
  as official physician 1
  opposition to 39–41, 61, 95, 112–14, 127, 157–8, 183–4, 196, 198–200
  as pantheist 96
  and problem of suffering 87–9, 90–9, 103
  as scholar 1
  and Song of Songs 13, 15, 25–6, 30–1, 37
  and teleology 27, 29–30, 48 n.28
  and Temple cult 16, 20, 22, 103, 160
  and tolerance 11
  and universalism 4, 15, 36, 48 n.26, 158–67, 172, 191–2
  see also under Aviner, Shlomo; Kafih, Joseph; Kook, Abraham Isaac Hakohen; Kotler, Aharon; Netsiv; Shapira, Kalonymus Kalman; Soloveitchik, Joseph B.; Wasserman, Elhanan Bunem
Mark, Zvi 67 n.35
Meimad movement 149, 180
Melchior, Michael 180
Meltzer, Isser Zalman 149 n.1, 173
messianism 4
  in Aviner 178
  in Kook 84
  in Maimonides 83, 100
  in Shapira 100–1
  in Wasserman 137
metaphysics:
  in Maimonides 108, 118–19, 122–4, 152–3, 155–6, 167, 170
  in Shapira 101
miracles, and Temple cult 22
Mirsky, Yehuda 64 n.23, 75 n.72
Mishnah:
  Avot 136 n.126, 164–5
  Ḥagigah 113, 117, 119, 124, 126, 152–4, 156
  Nedarim 164
  Rosh hashanah 163–4
Mishneh torah 1–2, 49, 135 n.116, 193
  as avocation 3
  Book of Agriculture 161
  Book of Knowledge 13, 50 n.34, 64
  canonical status 5
  glosses on 2
  and Kook 63–70, 82
  and Kotler 150–2, 157
  'Laws of Circumcision' 190
  'Laws Concerning the Recitation of the Shema' 51–2
  'Laws Concerning the Sanctification of the New Moon' 157
  'Laws of the Foundations of the Torah' 22, 23 n.60, 26, 42, 51, 54, 68 n.38, 95, 113 n.26, 114, 119–21, 150 n.2, 155–6, 172
  'Laws of Kings and Wars' 158–9 n.31
  'Laws of Repentance' 141 n.147

'Laws of the Sabbatical Year and Jubilee' 159–62, 164, 172
'Laws of Torah Study' 111–12, 164–5, 168–71, 190
'Laws of Trespass' 150–1
and love of God 24, 30–1
and *ma'aseh bereshit* 119
and *ma'aseh merkavah* 68, 154–6
and messianism 100
and non-Jews 177
and science 117–18, 154–6
and suffering 104
Moses hides his face before God 76
musar movement 150 n.2
mysticism, and Kook 62–4, 71–4, 77–80, 84–5

N
Nadler, Allan 64 n.22
Nahman of Bratslav 67 n.35, 95
Nahmanides, Moses (Ramban) 45–6, 55, 107 n.2, 124, 137 n.131, 143, 171–2, 173, 200–1
nakedness 34–5, 83
names of God:
  in Kook 73–4
  in Maimonides 68–70
naturalism:
  in Maimonides 25, 30, 67, 181 n.27
  in Netsiv 18, 21, 22, 31, 70
nature, in Netsiv 18
Nazir (David Cohen) 77 n.79
Netsiv (R. Naftali Tsevi Yehudah Berlin) 5–6, 7, 9–37, 195–7
  and anthropocentrism 27–30
  commentary on Song of Songs 10, 11–27, 31–3, 34–7, 70, 196
  and community ethics 36
  and community leadership 13–14
  and divine providence 18
  and halakhah 14, 16, 21
  and Jews and non-Jews 15, 18
  and knowledge of God 18, 27
  and law and national identity 16–18, 19, 31, 36
  and love of God 11–16, 17–18, 19–21, 22–3, 24–30, 31–4
  and modernity 199

students 9–10, 12, 37, 59, 70
and tolerance 10–11, 14
Nissim ben Reuven of Girona (Ran) 111, 114–17, 122, 124, 126
nominalism, and Maimonides 53–4
numerology 161–2, 190

O
Ohel Torah yeshiva (Baranowicze) 109–10
original sin 162 n.41, 191 n.67
orthodoxy:
  and Jewish identity 176–94
  and Kook 61
  and Kotler 149
  modern 4, 12
  and Netsiv 10–11

P
Pachter, Mordechai 78 n.87, 150 n.2
pantheism, and Maimonides 96
pardes (exegesis) 111–14, 119, 155, 169–71
Parnes, Yehuda 1 n.3, 27 n.77
Patriarchs, in Halevi 186–7
perfection:
  in Kook 81–2, 83
  in Maimonides 13–14, 17, 21, 24–5, 36, 41–5, 48, 78, 81–2, 133–4 n.106, 137 n.129
  in Netsiv 21
  in Soloveitchik 42–5
Perry, Edmund 108 n.3
philosophy:
  and kabbalah 62 n.15, 68, 79–80, 126
  and Kook 72–4, 77–8, 79–80
  and Maimonides 23, 35–7, 48, 50–1, 61–3, 71, 147, 195
  and mysticism 62, 72–4, 77–80, 85, 96
  and Netsiv 15–16, 195–6
  and Soloveitchik 48–52
  and Wasserman 133
  see also Aristotle
physics:
  and Kook 65, 79
  and Maimonides 19, 79, 111–24, 156, 170
  and Shapira 101
Pines, Shlomo 3 n.11, 62 n.12, 64 n.21, 80 n.92, 147

pluralism, and Kook 60–1
poetry, and Kook 62 n.15
prayer:
   in Maimonides 20
   in Netsiv 21
prophets and prophecy:
   in Halevi 125, 185–6, 188
   in Kook 61
   in Maimonides 13 n.17, 25, 49, 81, 111 n.16, 121–3, 130, 157
   in Netsiv 32, 35
   in Wasserman 136
providence:
   and intellect 18, 41–5, 53, 81, 88–9, 104
   in Kotler 157–8
   in Maimonides 41–3, 53–4, 89 n.4, 99, 157–8
   in Netsiv 18
   in Soloveitchik 41–5, 56–7

R
Rabad (Abraham ben David of Posquières) 2, 39–40, 62 n.15, 141, 142
Rabinovitch, Nachum L. 52 n.42
Radak (David Kimhi) 144–5
Rambam, *see* Maimonides, Moses
Ramban, *see* Nahmanides, Moses
Ran, *see* Nissim ben Reuven of Girona
Rashba (Shelomoh ben Aderet) 201
Rashi 107 n.2, 137 n.129, 142 n.159, 143
rationalism:
   and Kook 63, 75–6, 81, 86
   and Maimonides 2–4, 11, 23, 24, 33, 81, 89–90, 93, 103–4
   and Netsiv 16–18, 24
   and problem of suffering 89–93, 99, 101–4
   and Shapira 93–8, 98–100, 100–1, 102, 104
   and Wasserman 141–3
Ravitzky, Aviezer 3 n.11, 83 n.110, 180
reason, *see* rationalism
Rema (Moses Isserles) 112–14
Rivash (Yitshak ben Sheshet) 146–7
Rosenak, Avinoam 110 n.13
Rosenberg, Shalom 69 n.50
Ross, Tamar 65 n.27, 84 n.111

Rubinstein, Shmuel Tanhum 52 n.42
Rynhold, Daniel 45 n.16

S
Sa'adyah Gaon 107 n.2, 181 n.26
sabbath, in Shapira 99–100
sacrifice:
   in Maimonides 16, 20, 22, 125
   in Netsiv 21
Salanter, Israel 150 n.2, 168
Schneerson, Menachem Mendel 5, 63 n.18, 149
Scholem, Gershom 61 n.9, 77 n.80, 104, 135 n.120
Schwartz, Dov 63 n.19, 66 n.31
Schwarzschild, Steven 185–6 n.47, 191 n.69
Schweid, Eliezer 90 n.12
science:
   divine, *see ma'aseh merkavah*
   and Kook 68
   and Maimonides 1–2, 4, 23, 24–5, 30, 34, 37, 50, 111–22, 167
   and Netsiv 18, 23, 24, 35
   and Torah 2, 4, 18, 23, 24–5, 50, 111–14, 123–4, 172
   see also physics
Seeskin, Kenneth 17
sexuality, and love 31–2
Shapira, Kalonymus Kalman 6, 87–105
   Esh kodesh 89–90, 99 n.44, 100, 102–3
   and intellect 91, 94–5, 96–8, 102, 197
   and knowledge of God 91–3, 98–100, 100–1, 104, 105
   sermons 89–93
Shapiro, Marc B. 1 n.3
Sheilat, Isaac 191 n.72
shekhinah:
   in Kook 67
   in Maimonides 78
   in Netsiv 14
   in Wasserman 137
Shelomoh ben Aderet, *see* Rashba
Shem Tov ibn Shem Tov 50 n.33
Shkop, Simon 10
Shneur Zalman of Lyady 94
Shulḥan arukh 1, 3–4, 150 n.9
   and Wasserman 111–12

sickness:
  in Maimonides 30–2
  in Netsiv 31–2, 70
Silver, Daniel Jeremy 2
Sinai, revelation 35–6, 48
Slobodka yeshiva 10, 150 n.2
Sofer, Moses, *see* Hatam Sofer
Solomon, in Netsiv 13, 15–16, 20
Soloveitchik, Haym 6, 46, 141
Soloveitchik, Rabbi Hayim of Brisk 141
Soloveitchik, Joseph B. 5–6, 12, 39–57, 96, 197
  And from There You Shall Seek 39–40, 52 n.43
  'Community' 56
  The Emergence of Halakhic Man 43 n.12, 46–7, 48, 55
  and halakhah 45–7, 51–2, 55
  The Halakhic Mind 47
  and individual providence 41–5, 56–7
  and Jews and non-Jews 41
  and kabbalah 149
  and *keneset yisra'el* 52–6, 57
  and mysticism 96
  On Repentance 48–9, 55–6
  Worship of the Heart 52 n.43
Song of Songs:
  in Kook 71
  in Maimonides 13, 15, 25–6, 30–1, 37, 70
  in Netsiv 10, 11–22, 25–7, 31–3, 34–7, 196
Sorasky, Aharon 109 nn.8, 11
Steinsaltz, Adin Even-Yisrael 5
Strauss, Leo 147, 190
suffering:
  and the Holocaust 87–9, 90–8, 100–1, 105, 108
  and Kook 88
  and Maimonides 87–9, 90–9, 103
  and messianism 100–1
  senseless 101–2, 102–4, 105
  and Shapira 87–105, 197

T
Talmud 111–12, 165–6, 169–71
teleology:
  in Kook 65
  in Maimonides 27, 29–30, 48 n.28
  in Netsiv 29
Telz yeshiva 10
Temple cult:
  and Kotler 160–1, 164
  and Maimonides 16, 20, 22, 103, 160
  and Netsiv 21–2
theocentrism, in Maimonides 27–9
theology:
  negative 65–6, 87
  and suffering 87–9, 90–8, 100–1, 105, 197
Thirteen Principles of faith 1, 4, 49, 92–3, 141 n.152, 193
tolerance:
  and Kook 60
  and Netsiv 10–11, 14
Torah:
  as eternal 124–5, 137, 139
  and halakhah 48, 49–51, 79, 195
  and innovation 152–3, 172
  and Jewish identity 16–18, 19, 31, 36, 176–8, 181, 187–8, 194
  and love of God 15–16, 19–21, 23, 24–7, 31
  Oral 19, 63, 168–72
  and philosophy 9, 51–2, 63, 79, 195
  and problems of language 107–10, 126, 146
  and science 2, 4, 18, 23, 24–5, 50, 111–14, 123–4, 172
  secret 117, 152–3
Torah study, public support for 160–1, 164–7, 172, 190
transcendence, in Netsiv 18, 19, 24
Twersky, Isadore 41, 51, 52, 62 n.15, 124 n.57, 150 n.2, 189 n.62

U
Unetaneh tokef 163–4
unity of God:
  in Maimonides 22, 36, 51, 63, 73, 77, 96, 135 n.113, 167
  in Shapira 96, 98–9, 104
  in Soloveitchik 96
unity of Israel:
  in Kook 82
  in Netsiv 36

unity of Israel (*cont.*):
  in Shapira 98–9
  in Soloveitchik 56
universalism:
  and Kafih 191 n.71
  and Kotler 161–3
  and Maimonides 4, 15, 36, 48 n.26, 158–67, 172, 191–3
  and Torah 192
universals, in Maimonides 42–3, 53–5
Urbach, E. E. 194
utopia:
  in Kook 82, 84
  in Maimonides 34

V
Vilna Gaon (Eliyahu ben Shelomoh Zalman) 111, 112–14, 150 n.2, 184 n.42
Vincent, Alana 96 n.34
Volozhin, Ets Hayim yeshiva 5–6, 9, 11 n.9, 33, 37, 59, 195
Volozhiner, Hayim, *Nefesh haḥayim* 6, 150 n.2

W
Warsaw ghetto, and Shapiro 89–90, 92–3, 100, 101, 197
Wasserman, Elhanan Bunem 6, 107–47, 198–9, 201
  and corruption of concepts 141–3
  essay on belief: 'Contemplation, Wondrous and Simple' 138–40;
  examples of literal explanation 128–38
  Footsteps of the Messiah 110
  Kovets ma'amarim 79, 110, 127
  and *ma'aseh bereshit* 111, 114, 116–17, 122, 124
  and Torah 109, 110–11, 124–7, 146–7
Wasserman, Simha 109 n.108
wisdom:
  in Maimonides 167
  in Wasserman 128–30, 133
Wolfson, Eliot 3 n.13, 62–3 n.15, 80 n.95

Y
Yavetz, Zev 61
Yeshiva University (New York) 4
yeshivas:
  and military service 160 n.37
  and support for students 164–5
  see also individual yeshivas
Yeshivat Merkaz Harav Kook 176, 181

Z
Zionism:
  and nationalism 15, 59
  Orthodox 4, 6–7, 73 n.65, 136–7 n.127, 149, 176–9, 180, 181, 194
  and Wasserman 110
Zissel, Simha of Kelm 150 n.2
Zohar 4, 46 n.20, 94, 182–3
Zundel, Yosef of Salant 150 n.2

www.ingramcontent.com/pod-product-compliance
Lightning Source LLC
Chambersburg PA
CBHW061421300426
44114CB00015B/2023